# From Antarctica to Outer Space
Life in Isolation and Confinement

Albert A. Harrison
Yvonne A. Clearwater
Christopher P. McKay
Editors

# From Antarctica to Outer Space
## Life in Isolation and Confinement

Foreword by E. K. Eric Gunderson

With 26 illustrations

Springer-Verlag
New York  Berlin  Heidelberg  London
Paris  Tokyo  Hong Kong  Barcelona

ALBERT A. HARRISON, PH.D., Department of Psychology, University of California–Davis, Davis, CA 95616, USA

YVONNE A. CLEARWATER, PH.D., Aerospace Human Factors Research Division, NASA–Ames Research Center, Moffett Field, CA 94035, USA

CHRISTOPHER P. MCKAY, PH.D., Space Science Division, NASA–Ames Research Center, Moffett Field, CA 94035, USA

Library of Congress Cataloging-in-Publication Data
From Antarctica to outer space : life in isolation and confinement /
    Albert A. Harrison, Yvonne A. Clearwater, Christopher P. McKay,
    editors.
        p.   cm.
    Includes bibliographical references.
    Includes index.
    ISBN 0-387-97310-9 (alk. paper)
    1. Research — Psychological aspects.   2.  Space flight —
Psychological aspects.   3.  Antarctic regions — Psychological
aspects.   4.  Social isolation — Psychological aspects.   I. Harrison,
Albert A.   II. Clearwater, Yvonne A.   III. McKay, Christopher P.
Q180.55.P75F76   1990
155.9 — dc20                                                    90-36364

Printed on acid-free paper.

Typeset by Bytheway Typesetting Services, Norwich, NY, USA.
Printed and bound by Edwards Brothers, Inc., Ann Arbor, MI, USA.
Printed in the United States of America.

9  8  7  6  5  4  3  2  1

ISBN 0-387-97310-9 Springer-Verlag New York Berlin Heidelberg
ISBN 3-540-97310-9 Springer-Verlag Berlin Heidelberg New York

# Foreword

Human factors problems in spaceflight operations were first addressed by Dr. Robert Voas, who analyzed available laboratory and flight report data from the Mercury program. Bob and I were graduate students together at UCLA, and when I began studies of Antarctic communities in the early 1960s, we were eager to compare methods and approaches. In 1963, Bob, Dr. Paul Nelson, and I seriously discussed placing an experimental capsule in Antarctica to simulate some aspects of confined living in space, but at the time the idea did not receive much support. I also was greatly stimulated by the work of Dr. Ben Weybrew of the U.S. Navy; Drs. Jay Shurley, Chet Pierce, and Kirmach Natani of the University of Oklahoma; Drs. Roland Radloff and Robert Helmreich (SEALAB and TEKTITE); Dr. Otto Edholm of the British Antarctic Survey; Dr. Jean Rivolier of the French Polar Program; Dr. Tony Taylor of Victoria University, Wellington; and Dr. Desmond Lugg of the Australian Antarctic Program.

I was delighted to hear of the Sunnyvale Conference and to learn of this major effort to review and integrate Antarctic and related research for possible application to problems of long-duration spaceflight. The editors have succeeded in assembling a valuable and fascinating account of many critical issues that may affect success or failure in space missions and the safety, survival, productivity, and quality of life of crews and scientists.

The Antarctic experience has provided a useful model not only for difficult field behavioral research but also for international and multidisciplinary cooperation. Lessons learned in the Antarctic and other extreme settings should facilitate interplanetary exploration and establishment of permanent settlements in space.

E. K. ERIC GUNDERSON
Naval Health Research Center

# Acknowledgments

This volume is based on papers presented at *The Human Experience in Antarctica: Applications to Life in Space.* Both the conference and the preparation of this volume were supported by National Aeronautics and Space Administration Grant NCC-2-469 and National Science Foundation Grant DPP-87-00325. We are deeply appreciative of the encouragement and support of Arnauld Nicogossian, Mel Averner, Peter Willkness, Ted DeLaca, Polly Penhale, and many other people from both agencies. We are also grateful for the assistance of Barrett Caldwell, Philip Crabtree, Janet Lasick, Lisa Lockyear, Chuck Stovitz, and Nancy Struthers, who provided invaluable assistance at various points and who directly or indirectly helped to bring this manuscript to completion.

# Contents

# Contributors

HARRY H. ALMOND, JR.    National Defense University, Washington, D.C., USA

MARY A. ANDERSON    School of Hygiene and Public Health, The Johns Hopkins University, Baltimore, Maryland, USA

CLAUDE BACHELARD    Laboratoire de Psychologie Apliquee, Université de Reims, France

ARREED F. BARABASZ    Department of Counseling Psychology, Washington State University, Pullman, Washington, USA

MARIANNE BARABASZ    Department of Counseling Psychology, Washington State University, Pullman, Washington, USA

ROBERT B. BECHTEL    Department of Psychology, University of Arizona, Tucson, Arizona, USA

AMY BERNING    U.S. Department of Transportation, Washington, D.C., USA

SIDNEY M. BLAIR    Department of Psychiatry, Uniformed Services University of the Health Sciences, Bethesda, Maryland, USA

JOSEPH V. BRADY    School of Medicine, The Johns Hopkins University, Baltimore, Maryland, USA

BARRETT S. CALDWELL    Department of Industrial Engineering, University of Wisconsin, Madison, Wisconsin, USA

SYBIL CARRÈRE    Department of Psychology, University of Washington, Seattle, Washington, USA

GENEVIEVE CAZES    Laboratoire de Psychologie Apliquee, Université de Reims, France

YVONNE A. CLEARWATER    Aerospace Human Factors Research Division, NASA–Ames Research Center, Moffett Field, California, USA

MARY M. CONNORS    Aerospace Human Factors Research Division, NASA–Ames Research Center, Moffett Field, California, USA

PATRICK E. CORNELIUS    NASA–Lyndon B. Johnson Space Center, Houston, Texas, USA

RICHARD G. COSS    Department of Psychology, University of California–Davis, Davis, California, USA

WILLIAM K. DOUGLAS    Space Station Division, McDonnell–Douglas Space Systems Company, Huntington Beach, California, USA

GARY W. EVANS    Program in Social Ecology, University of California–Irvine, Irvine, California, USA

BEN FINNEY    Department of Anthropology, University of Hawaii, Honolulu, Hawaii, USA

RAINER GOLDSMITH    Department of Human Sciences, The University, Loughsborough, England, United Kingdom

RICHARD F. HAINES    Research Institute for Advanced Computer Studies, NASA–Ames Research Center, Moffett Field, California, USA

IAN F. G. HAMPTON    Department of Physiology, The University, Leeds, England, United Kingdom

PHILIP R. HARRIS    Harris International, LaJolla, California, USA; and Netrologic, Inc., San Diego, California, USA

ALBERT A. HARRISON    Department of Psychology, University of California–Davis, Davis, California, USA

PAUL N. KLAUS    Jamie Cannon Associates, Inc., St. Louis, Missouri, USA

MARC LEVESQUE    Graduate Program in Adult Education and Human Resource Development, University of Southern Maine, Portland, Maine, USA

ARLENE S. LEVINE    NASA–Langley Research Center, Hampton, Virginia, USA

DESMOND J. LUGG    Australian Antarctic Division, Kingston, Tasmania, Australia

IAN MCCORMICK    Department of Psychology, Victoria University of Wellington, Wellington, New Zealand

CHRISTOPHER P. MCKAY    Space Science Division, NASA–Ames Research Center, Moffett Field, California, USA

JAMES GRIER MILLER    Department of Psychiatry, University of California–Los Angeles, Los Angeles, California, USA; and Department of Psychiatry, University of California–San Diego, La Jolla, California, USA

KIRMACH NATANI    McDonnell Douglas Missile Systems Company, Saint Louis, Missouri, USA

DONNA C. OLIVER    United States International University, San Diego, California, USA

LAWRENCE A. PALINKAS    Department of Community and Family Medicine, University of California–San Diego, La Jolla, California, USA

CHESTER M. PIERCE    Faculties of Medicine and Public Health, Harvard University, Cambridge, Massachusetts, USA

WOLFGANG F. E. PREISER    College of Design, Architecture, Art and Planning, University of Cincinnati, Cincinnati, Ohio, USA

DOUGLAS RAYBECK    Department of Anthropology, Hamilton College, Clinton, New York, USA

JEAN RIVOLIER    Departmente de Psychologie Appliquee, Université de Reims, France

F. KENNETH SCHWETJE    Compliance, Testing and Space Division, Joint Chiefs of Staff, Washington, D.C., USA

DONALD M. SCOTT    Wider Focus NASA Projects, San Francisco, California, USA

DANIEL STOKOLS    Program in Social Ecology, University of California–Irvine, Irvine, California, USA

PETER SUEDFELD    Department of Psychology and Faculty of Graduate Studies, University of British Columbia, Vancouver, British Columbia, Canada

A. J. W. TAYLOR    Department of Psychology, Victoria University of Wellington, Wellington, New Zealand

ROBERT J. VALEN    National Park Service, Guadalupe Mountains National Park, Texas, USA

BENJAMIN B. WEYBREW    Department of Psychology, University of New Haven, New Haven, Connecticut, USA

# Introduction

ALBERT A. HARRISON, YVONNE A. CLEARWATER, AND
CHRISTOPHER P. MCKAY

Antarctic communities are important in their own right and because studies conducted within them yield results that are of general interest and applicability in communities throughout the world. As laboratories for human behavior, Earth's southernmost settlements are relatively uncomplicated and self-contained, and found within them are naturally occurring conditions that are not easily created elsewhere because of practical or ethical considerations. Also, because they vary widely in terms of size, living conditions, group composition, support needs, historical trends, and projected developmental changes, Antarctic communities provide, in the aggregate, excellent opportunities for cross-sectional and longitudinal research. The lessons learned in Antarctica are instructive not only for many other communities on Earth but also for extraterrestrial human communities.

Plans for the phased exploration of space by the United States call for the Space Station *Freedom* joining the ongoing Soviet Space Station *Mir* in the mid-1990s, followed within a few decades by the development of a permanent lunar base and the establishment of an initial camp on Mars (National Commission on Space, 1986). The success of these missions will depend, in part, on human abilities to maintain high levels of motivation and mental health and to work cooperatively with a diverse group of fellow crewmembers and support personnel under exceptionally trying conditions. Because behavioral research can answer essential questions about the relationships among individuals, groups, and environments, it can provide crucial underpinnings for tomorrow's space missions.

Among the arenas available for conducting such research are spaceflight-analogous, or "analogue," environments, that is, terrestrial settings that capture some of the conditions associated with life in space itself. Since tomorrow's space missions will take many forms, no single location on Earth provides the "best" analogue for all future space expeditions. However, Antarctic communities provide good analogues for a wide range of intended space missions—and truly excellent analogues for those that will involve landing on lunar or planetary surfaces. Similarities between Antarctic and space settlements include harsh, potentially lethal natural environments; an absence of indigenous populations; habitats whose size, design, and provisioning have been severely limited by engineering and economic considerations; preselected, work-oriented inhabitants who have been brought in from the "outside" to conduct research in geoscience, atmospheric sciences, and life sciences; and, for the inhabitants, prolonged social isolation from the home community, forced confinement with a limited number of other people, and accountability to authorities who are far removed from the actual work site. Because of the variability of Antarctic communities, one can find in Antarctica today communities that approximate many different types of camps, bases, and settlements expected in space tomorrow.

During the late 1950s and the 1960s, increasing human presence in Antarctica, under the seas, and in outer space prompted numerous studies of human adaptation to isolation and confinement, including Mullin's classic research on states of consciousness (Mullin, 1960), the work of Gunderson and Nelson and their colleagues on adaptation to Antarctica (Gunderson, 1973, 1974), and laboratory studies of group dynamics undertaken by Altman and Haythorn and their associates (Altman, 1973; Haythorn, 1973). Much of this research, which peaked in the late 1960s, has been summarized in Edholm and Gunderson (1973), Rasmussen (1973), and Vinograd (1974) and, more recently, by Connors, Harrison, and Akins (1985, 1986), Harrison and Connors (1984), Stuster (1986), Taylor (1987), and Arreed Barabasz (chapter 3, this volume).

There have been many developments since this earlier research was completed, including changes in psychological theories and methods; changes in polar and spaceflight habitats; changes in the numbers and kinds of people who occupy these environments; changes in the conditions and duration of occupancy; changes in technology; and a growing significance of civilian as well as military applications. In recognition of such developments, over the past decade there have been repeated calls for improving our understanding of life in isolation and confinement (Brady, 1983; Cheston & Winters, 1980; Cheston, Chafer, & Chafer, 1984; Christensen & Talbot, 1986; Clearwater, 1985; Connors et al., 1985, 1986; Finney & Jones, 1985; Harris, 1986, 1989; Harrison & Connors, 1984; Harrison, Clearwater, & McKay, 1989; Helmreich, 1983; Kanas, 1985; Nicholas, 1987).

A primary conclusion of a Polar Research Board (1982) study of biomedical and sociocultural issues was that, in polar regions, sociocultural factors, as compared to strictly medical factors, were responsible for a disproportionate number of human problems. The Board assigned the highest priority in the social sciences to research dealing with those factors that are likely to contribute to a positive "quality of life" in polar regions. More recently, the Committee on the National Science Foundation's (NSF's) Role in Polar Regions noted that Antarctica "provides a natural laboratory for studying the impact of extreme conditions on individual and collective behavior," that such understanding will promote "safety, productivity, and quality of life in polar and analogous environments," and that "the NSF has an opportunity, as . . . manager of the U.S. Antarctic Program, to foster greater awareness and increased efforts in social and behavioral sciences research" (National Science Board, 1987, pp. 40-41). Concurrently, the Committee on Space Biology and Medicine of the Space Science Board noted that

Although the evidence is fragmentary, it seems likely that behavioral and social problems have already occurred during long-term missions and that such problems will become exacerbated as missions become more complex, as mission duration is increased, and as the composition of crews becomes more heterogeneous. An understanding of the problems and their amelioration is essential if man desires to occupy space for extended periods of time. Even more important from a scientific perspective, it seems likely that significant advances in our basic knowledge of human interaction and group processes will emerge from the research needed to ensure effective performance and adjustment in space. (Space Science Board, 1987, p.169)

The Space Science Board acknowledged the value of ground-based models based on research conducted in laboratories and such "fully operational situations as underseas habitats, submarines, and polar stations" (Space Science Board, 1987, p.169). Increased interest in the goal of promoting a positive quality of life may also reflect the transition from a period of initial exploration to a period of firm commitment to polar regions and to outer space:

Whenever people enter environments that are extreme for them, the principal objective of medical science is to ensure human survival. . . . However, when what was once experienced by but a few is experienced by many . . . the emphasis is on conditions that will facilitate human adjustment, that is, on providing a situation in which a person can expect to be healthy, happy, and effective in family life, work, and community relationships, without crippling emotional symptoms, such as fear, anger, loneliness, envy, or greed. We believe that U.S. development in the high latitudes in the next decades demands this [latter] biomedical research strategy. (Polar Research Board, 1982, p. 36)

In August 1987, the Division of Polar Programs of the National Science Foundation and the National Aeronautics and Space Administration co-sponsored a 3-day conference entitled *The Human Experience in Antarctica: Applications to Life in Space* (the Sunnyvale Conference). The primary goal was to revitalize and encourage behavioral research in spaceflight, polar, and comparable settings. Subsumed under this goal were three objectives: (1) to assemble managers, operational personnel, and social and behavioral researchers to mutually explore research interests, priorities, and strategies; (2) to explore the application of contemporary theories and methods to human behavior in isolation and confinement; and (3) to encourage support for behavioral research and the application of findings. Underlying the Sunnyvale Conference was the conviction that because people in different isolated and confined environments are subjected to roughly comparable conditions and respond in roughly comparable ways, students of different isolated and confined environments — polar, undersea, and outer space — can benefit from one another's ideas and accomplishments. The current volume presents chapters that evolved from papers presented at the Sunnyvale Conference.

*From Antarctica to Outer Space: Life in Isolation and Confinement* is divided into four parts. Part 1, Settings, provides, through firsthand accounts and research reviews, an introduction to the human side of isolated and confined environments, including Antarctica, outer space, submarines, and remote national parks. Part 2, Orientations and Perspectives, discusses some of the theoretical issues underlying research on isolated and confined people and shows the applicability of certain general theories of behavior. Part 3, Isolation and Confinement Effects, focuses on basic psychological and social responses to isolation and confinement. Part 4, Interventions and Outcomes, describes studies whose primary purpose is to explore the effects of selection, training, and environmental design on human behavior and mission outcomes. Finally, in the Conclusion, we, the editors, present recommendations based on the Sunnyvale Conference and on other developments.

## References

Altman, I. (1973). An ecological approach to the functioning of isolated and confined groups. In J. Rasmussen (Ed.), *Man in Isolation and Confinement* (pp. 241–270). Chicago: Aldine.

Brady, J. V. (1983). *Human behavior in space environments: A research agenda*. Baltimore: The Johns Hopkins School of Medicine.

Cheston, T. S., & Winters, D. L. (1980). *The human factors in outer space production*. Boulder, CO: Westview Press.

Cheston, T. S., Chafer, C. M., & Chafer, S. B. (Eds.). (1984). *Social sciences and space exploration* (EP-192). Washington, DC: National Aeronautics and Space Administration.

Christensen, J. M., & Talbot, J. M. (1986). A review of the psychological aspects of spaceflight. *Aviation, Space, and Environmental Medicine, 57*, 203–212.

Clearwater, Y. A. (1985, July). A human place in outer space. *Psychology Today*, 5ff.

Connors, M. M., Harrison, A. A., & Akins, F. R. (1985). *Living aloft: Human requirements for extended spaceflight* (NASA SP-483). Washington, DC: National Aeronautics and Space Administration.

Connors, M. M., Harrison, A. A., & Akins, F. R. (1986). Psychology and the resurgent space program. *American Psychologist, 41*, 906–913.

Edholm, O. G., & Gunderson, E. K. E. (Eds.). (1973). *Polar human biology: Pro-*

*ceedings of the SCAR/IUPS/IUBS symposium on human biology and medicine in the Antarctic*. London: William Heinemann Medical Books, Ltd.

Finney, B. R., & Jones, E. M. (Eds.). (1985). *Interstellar migration and the human experience*. Berkeley: University of California Press.

Gunderson, E. K. E. (1973). Individual behavior in confined or isolated groups. In J. E. Rasmussen (Ed.), *Man in isolation and confinement* (pp.145–164). Chicago: Aldine.

Gunderson, E. K. E. (1974). Psychological studies in Antarctica. In E. K. E. Gunderson (Ed.), *Human adaptability to Antarctic conditions* (pp. 115–131). Washington, DC: American Geophysical Union.

Harris, P. R. (1986). The influence of culture on space development. *Behavioral Science, 31*(1), 29–41.

Harris, P. R. (1989). Behavioral science space contributions. *Behavioral Science, 34*, 207–236.

Harrison, A. A., & Connors, M. M. (1984). Groups in exotic environments. In L. Berkowitz (Ed.), *Advances in experimental social psychology*, (Vol. 18, pp. 49–87). New York: Academic Press.

Harrison, A. A., Clearwater, Y. A., & McKay, C. P. (1989). The human experience in Antarctica: Applications to life in space. *Behavioral Science, 34*, 253–271.

Haythorn, W. W. (1973). The miniworld of isolation: Laboratory studies. In J. E. Rasmussen (Ed.), *Man in isolation and confinement* (pp. 219–241). Chicago: Aldine.

Helmreich, R. L. (1983). Applying psychology in outer space: Unfulfilled promises revisited. *American Psychologist, 38*, 445–450.

Kanas, N. (1985). Psychological factors affecting simulated and actual space missions. *Aviation, Space, and Environmental Medicine, 56*, 806–811.

Mullin, C. S. (1960). Some psychological aspects of isolated Antarctic living. *American Journal of Psychiatry, 117*, 323–325.

National Commission on Space. (1986). *Pioneering the space frontier*. New York: Bantam Books.

National Science Board. (1987). *The role of the National Science Foundation in polar regions* (NSB-87-128). Washington, DC: National Academy of Sciences.

Nicholas, J. M. (1987). Small groups in orbit: Group interaction and crew performance on Space Station. *Aviation, Space, and Environmental Medicine, 58*, 1009–1013.

Polar Research Board, National Research Council. (1982). *Polar biomedical research: An assessment*. Washington, DC: National Academy Press.

Rasmussen, J. E. (Ed.). (1973). *Man in isolation and confinement*. Chicago: Aldine.

Space Science Board. (1987). *A strategy for space biology and medical science*. Washington, DC: National Academy Press.

Stuster, J. W. (1986). *Space station habitability recommendations based on a systematic comparative analysis of analogous conditions*. Santa Barbara, CA: Anacapa Sciences.

Taylor, A. J. W. (1987). *Antarctic psychology*. (DSIR Bulletin No. 244). Wellington, NZ: Science Information Publishing.

# Part I  Settings

## Introduction

Since the completion of the seminal research programs of two decades ago, polar, underseas, outer space, and laboratory settings have remained popular but not exclusive locations for studying life in isolated and confined environments (ICEs). The chapters in this part provide an introduction to some of these settings and the kinds of research that are conducted within them.

The first two chapters, by Patrick Cornelius and Marc Levesque, provide first-hand descriptions of life in Antarctica. These authors identify behavioral issues that are of particular interest to operational personnel and discuss practices that can either build or destroy a researcher's rapport with his or her potential research subjects. Next, Arreed Barabasz reviews Antarctic behavioral research, ranging from early studies on psychiatric screening through more recent studies of selection, group performance, and mental states. Desmond Lugg describes the Scientific Committee for Antarctic Research (SCAR) and discusses some of the international research programs undertaken in Antarctica, including that of the Australian National Antarctic Research Expeditions. Then, A. J. W. Taylor presents the first of several chapters in the volume describing the International Biomedical Expedition to Antarctica (IBEA). This constituted a major international effort to understand biological, psychological, and social adaptation to a difficult Antarctic trek. Of particular interest are the intensive and extensive research procedures and the use of a pretest–posttest design with control subjects. The introduction to Antarctica concludes with Sidney Blair's highly pragmatic discussion. Blair brings home the fact that larger Antarctic bases more closely resemble industrial communities than the more colorful, harsh, and primitive camps established by the earliest explorers.

The next two chapters focus on spaceflight. Philip Harris notes that preparing for tomorrow's missions will require space personnel deployment systems for the orderly exchange of people to and from Earth and the space frontier. He analyzes space missions as sequences of events: attraction and selection, training, on-site support, and reentry—and reminds us that crews must be viewed within larger social and cultural contexts. William Douglas, one of the astronauts' physicians, provides a context for reviewing the psychological and sociological aspects of manned spaceflight. He notes that in their thirst for information, many otherwise careful researchers have accepted as fact disputable anecdotal accounts of life in space.

Antarctica and outer space are but two of the locales where groups of people live in isolation and confinement. These characteristics are also associated with surface ships, especially the sailing ships of yesteryear, which undertook long voyages and lacked radio links with other ships and people ashore. Anthropologist Ben Finney notes that we can expect many space missions to involve crews consisting of a flight crew combined with a group of scientists or others who have specialized functions. He discusses approximately 300 years of attempts to combine naval and scientific personnel for voyages of discovery and identifies cultural, sociological, and psychological variables that have resulted in mixed successes for many of these missions.

Submarines and subaquatic research vessels have long been considered analogous to spacecraft. A 30-year veteran of submarine research, Ben Weybrew presents the results of a long-term, far-reaching Navy research program, a program whose results have only recently been declassified. The thrusts of this research include psychiatric screening, crew training and development, crew composition and adjustment, human factors, and stress.

To conclude this section, Robert Valen and Barrett Caldwell propose that isolated national parks are useful sites for studying human behavior. Although national parks may not be "high-fidelity" analogues for Antarctica or outer space, many are located substantial distances from full-amenity communities and are effectively cut off from the outside during the winter. Rangers are similar to astronauts in that they are physically and mentally healthy individuals who have a long-term career commitment. Additionally, because it is possible to find parks of almost any size in urban, suburban, and rural settings, it is relatively easy to make controlled comparisons of isolated and non-isolated groups.

# 1

# Life in Antarctica

PATRICK E. CORNELIUS

Antarctica covers the Earth's south pole and represents 10% of the world's landmass. That is larger than the United States and Europe combined, but there is no indigenous human presence. The area surrounding the actual South Pole (90° South) contains no life because of the extremely harsh conditions. Antarctica is the coldest and least accessible of all the Earth's continents. Antarctica is covered by an ice sheet that can be up to 3 km thick and surrounded by an annual ice pack. Surprisingly, the ice sheet represents 97% of the Earth's ice and 70% of its fresh water. The mountains and ice sheet that cover 98% of Antarctica make it the highest continent on Earth. As you can see, one tends to use superlatives in describing Antarctica. The high altitude, lack of humidity, and extreme cold make the conditions very harsh. The largest indigenous land animal is a mite that is the size of a pea and lives in the relatively warm Palmer Peninsula. The Antarctic plateau is a desert but, ironically, experiences almost constant blizzards. The humidity is extremely low, and the temperature ranges from $-25°$ C to $-80°$ C. There is no sunlight at the pole for almost 6 months a year. No country owns the continent. A 30-year-old treaty sets aside the continent for science and peaceful purposes. The Antarctic Treaty is about to expire and must be ratified again, soon.

Since the International Geophysical Year (IGY) in 1957, there has been a continuous human presence in Antarctica. Only two of the signatory nations have inland bases on a year-round schedule (the United States and the USSR), but many of the signatory nations have coastal bases throughout the year. This is due to the relatively high costs of logistics for inland stations. Most activity occurs during the short Antarctic summer (from November to early February). The pack ice that surrounds the continent breaks apart partially and allows resupply by icebreaker and large cargo airplane. The crews are replaced at the beginning of the Antarctic summer (around late October or early November). The summer weather is relatively more pleasant for flying. Summer storms, "white outs," temperatures as low as −60° C, and other hazards can still occur, but the conditions are much better than during the winter period. During the winter, travel is almost impossible and, practically speaking, is not attempted. The summer crewmembers usually leave around February, and the stations close to outside travel. Summer resupply has been accomplished, and the long period of isolation begins for the crew.

The "winter-over" varies from station to station. The isolation period for Palmer Station on the coast is about 7 months, and the South Pole Station winter-over is about 9 months. The isolation is almost complete: no mail, no visitors, no leaving, and no fresh supplies. Outside contact is primarily by the high-frequency radio and sometimes a satellite link. The first-ever midwinter airdrop at South Pole was accomplished with a C-141B (refuelable version) in June of 1981 and has been done almost every year since. The airdrop brings some mail, fresh fruit and vegetables ("freshies"), movies, "care packages from home," and so forth. This erodes the completeness of the isolation somewhat. The ham radio, radioteletype, and voice transmissions are sometimes unavailable due to solar storms.

The crewmembers must adjust to many stressors, which include things that people in a normal environment take for granted. For example, absent are windows, privacy, living green things and animals, the sun, thick moist air to breathe, freedom to travel, or freedom to leave a rumor-infested, isolated human outpost. The "rumor mill" can be quite potent. Cliques can develop and be quite cruel and stressful to an individual with a different background than the rest of the crew. Cliques can also be quite insensitive to their own kind. Lack of acoustic privacy in the small "private" rooms can also lead to stress. Privacy becomes a cherished commodity. Time away from the group alone is very important for "charging one's batteries." Lack of a partner of the opposite sex can also lead to stress. Married couples who have wintered tend to handle the isolation much better. Constant low light levels can cause stress, too. It was observed that much higher light levels inside the dome at South Pole Station during the isolation period seemed to increase the morale of the crew. The higher light levels tend to decrease stress.

The crew at McMurdo and Palmer (two of the four winter-over U.S. bases) usually consists of four major groups of people. South Pole and Siple stations have no winter–over military. The National Science Foundation (NSF) sends grantees to the bases. They are usually well-educated scientists or graduate students. The support contractor provides personnel to manage the station, see to medical needs, keep the power plant operating, cook, run communications equipment, and maintain and repair the station. In addition, scientists from other countries sometimes winter-over. Military support is quite large at McMurdo, and there is only one Navy corpsman at Palmer.

The winter-over support jobs include station manager, physician, facilities engineer, communications engineer, power plant operator/mechanic, materialsman, chef, meteorology technician, sometimes a craftsman such as an electrician or a carpenter, and sometimes a general field assistant. The winter-over science activity can vary but usually includes atmospheric chemistry (National Oceanic and Atmospheric Administration), geological monitoring (U.S. Geological Survey), biology experiments (mostly coastal stations), cosmic ray experiments, Earth tide experiments, aurora monitoring, and very-low-frequency-radiation experiments. Various universities are given grants by NSF. The station science leader coordinates the rest of the scientists' needs and requests support directly from the station manager.

Daily activities vary for the individual crewmember. Some crewmembers are on a schedule that is fixed. For example, an upper atmosphere radiosonde balloon must be launched at a specific time every day, or certain seismic data or a satellite pass must be recorded at a specific time. Other crewmembers are on a schedule that allows more freedom. It has been observed that these individuals usually "free cycle" forward about an hour per day. In about a month they will have moved their schedule completely around the clock. There are individual exceptions, of course. On occasion, some crewmembers "power sleep" for periods of about 14 to 15 hours, and others stay up for periods of over 24 hours. Usually, this does not last long and seems to be an escape from boredom or the routine after several months of the same old schedule.

## Amundsen–Scott South Pole Station
## (90° South Latitude, 1,350 km South of McMurdo)

South Pole Station was established during the IGY 1957, and the new Amundsen–Scott South Pole Station was completed in 1975 and built closer to 90° South (about 100 m away; the ice sheet actually moves about 3 m per year, which brings the station closer to the pole each year). The plateau (ice sheet) is flat and almost featureless. It extends over most of the continent. It is more than 3,000 m thick at the pole and is covering a landmass of about 150 m mean sea level; therefore, the surface altitude at the South Pole Station is about 3,150 m. In addition, there is an intense low-pressure system that makes the effective physiological altitude vary between 3,300 m and a high of 4,000 m. Breathing can be quite difficult for the first few days, but most people can acclimatize fully within a month. The humidity is extremely low and causes drying of the eyes, nose, mouth, and skin. This can complicate sunburns caused by the lack of water vapor in the air and the harsh sunlight during the 6-month day. The temperature usually rises to about −25° C on the warmest day of the summer and drops to about −80° C during the winter. The station is built of aluminum in the form of a geodesic dome (50 m in diameter and 15.8 m high) and has an archway connecting the fuel bladders and the power plant. The power plant furnishes the life support for the station, including the electricity, water, and heat. Three diesel electric generator sets (one is always on; two as backup) provide 275 kW of electricity. An ethylene glycol heat exchanger system takes waste heat from the generators and pumps it into the three 2-story buildings inside the unheated dome. Another waste heat loop melts ice in an outside unit that provides water for the station.

The isolation period at South Pole Station contrasts sharply with the hectic summer period. After closing, the isolation is almost welcome to those winter–overers who have "psyched" themselves to stay. The sun circles slowly down and sets; finally the sun is gone and the flow of daily activities is established. The circadian rhythms have already been disrupted during the summer, but after the sun is gone, some people are even more affected. The body cues and light cycles, or perhaps even the changes in magnetic fields (on their daily sweep), may contribute to the effect, as do the intense social dynamics. The human social interaction in an isolated and confined environment depends on differences in background, maturity levels, tolerance levels, cliques, sex, compatibility, level of education, rumors, interests, and many other factors. The authority structure is quite an important factor. The station manager usually maintains a modified authoritarian (almost military) style for governing the station. Sometimes authority is derived by expertise. Perhaps a scientist or one of the technicians who is well trained and informed in a particular area will make decisions that affect the whole group.

Showers are quite a luxury because of the time and energy necessary to make water from ice. It is recommended that people who winter-over take no more than one 3-minute shower every other day or perhaps two per week. To understand why this is so, one must understand how water is made. Water preparation begins by starting the front-end loader (bulldozer) everyday in the garage. Hopefully, a storm has not blocked the garage door. Then several loads of ice and snow must be hauled in the dark from the upwind area. The bulldozers do not work well at −60° or −70° C. They continually break, and maintenance takes many times longer than during the summer because of the bulky clothing and awkward use of tools. Sometimes a hot air unit must be hooked to the oil pan, and another hot air unit inflates a parachute around the bulldozer to facilitate maintenance. Several crewmembers may be involved, fetching tools and items whose need was unanticipated. A small electric generator may have to be set up to provide lighting. The tools and small air and electricity units may themselves break during the process. The ice melter has been the subject of many studies for improvement and automation, but all attempts have failed. The crew usually acts as the back-up mechanism when all else fails.

Friction occurs when a "prima donna" scientist takes a "Hollywood shower." The "uncultured support people" (mostly the diesel mechanic and facilities engineer) become very irritated because the water level is lower than it could be, especially when they themselves have not taken a shower for a week. Some crews have avoided this potential source of friction by cross-training as many of the crew as possible to use the bulldozer to fill the ice melter. The scientist is usually interested in learning to drive the bulldozer and learning the operation of the heat exchanger and water system. After a few times out in the cold, the scientist achieves an appreciation for the shower water. The same principle can be applied to the support personnel. Many of them may be interested in some of the scientific experiments, and the scientists can teach them to help in the collection of data, thereby benefiting the science effort. This cross-training increases the crew solidarity and cohesiveness and at the same time adds welcome redundancy to the work system.

Off-duty activities depend on the individual but include conversation, watching movies and videos, listening to music, short excursions outside; looking out of the only set of windows in the station; finding an excuse for a party (sunset, midwinter, birthdays, holidays); and group projects (for example, one crew built a jacuzzi).

Some customs at South Pole Station may appear strange to the uninitiated observer. For example, the custom of the 300 Degree Club may appear foolhardy. During the winter, usually just past midwinter in September, the outside temperature drops below −100° F. At this time, all of the crew proceeds to the sauna, which is set to 200° F (a dry heat, but tolerable). They dress in only their tennis shoes. After a heat-soak period of about 10 to 15 minutes, their bodies are sweating profusely. The liberal amount of sweat is quite important. Then the crew madly dashes out of the dome to the pole (about 100 m) and poses for a quick picture and dashes back into the dome. One must be extremely careful not to fall down, because the snow is very cold and would quickly cause burns like dry ice. The whole gloriously mad custom is possible because of the quick freezing of the sweat on the bodies of the candidate club members, just like the orange buds are protected in Florida during cold weather with a mist of water, which, when it freezes, protects them.

One group recreational area at South Pole Station (the bar) has a large mural of a birch tree forest. This decoration was much appreciated by the winter-over crew. Sometimes, tiny cutout figures were put on the mural. This amused the crew and was probably a method of stress relief during the long isolation period. Many nature scenes and posters of the opposite sex decorated the small private quarters.

## Palmer Station (About 64° South and 64° West)

Palmer Station is located on Anvers Island, near the coast of the Palmer Peninsula, in a polar maritime environment. The conditions are quite different from the plateau. All of the indigenous plants and animals in Antarctica are located near the coastal areas. The lichens and mosses furnish shelter for the land mites, and the rich, cold ocean furnishes an oxygen-rich environment for diatoms and plankton. The krill (a shrimp-like creature) eat the rich plankton, which blooms in the austral summer. Most of the mammals eat the krill, which are at the base of the pyramidal food chain. Many whales, seals, and penguins visit the Antarctic coast during the summer. Many ships, also, stop to visit. These include tourist ships and research ships from various countries. The station is situated on bare rock, which is quite rare in Antarctica. A glacier field thrusts up behind the station, and on either side, huge icebergs calve off the glacier and fall into the sea with a thundering crash, creating great waves.

There are several differences in the isolation period at Palmer Station as compared to the high-plateau base at South Pole. The period of time is less (about 7 months), and the conditions are less harsh, except for the sea spray. The station also is designed quite differently. There are many windows as compared to South Pole's single pair. Windows are a great stress reliever. In spite of the greater number of windows, Palmer Station is of a much poorer design than South Pole Station. The private quarters at Palmer Station have windows, which is a significant plus, but the acoustic privacy leaves much to be desired. Problems and additional stress result from this poor design. One can hear the crewmember in the next room breathing, making love, or listening to *his* music.

Relative to South Pole, the outside area around Palmer is more accessible, and more trips outside are attempted by the winter-over crew. If the ocean is not frozen, the zodiac boats can be used to go to nearby islands to observe wildlife. Almost total darkness occurs only a few days of the year due to the latitude. Most days during the winter have at least a few hours of sunlight or skyglow. The desalinator must be used to make fresh water, and if the unit is properly maintained, there is sufficient fresh water for a daily shower by the 10 or so crewmembers. One can even have a barbeque on the front veranda of the station near the large picture windows if the winter weather permits. Even with all these differences, however, the isolation at Palmer is much the same as at the South Pole Station.

# 2

# An Experiential Perspective on Conducting Social and Behavioral Research at Antarctic Research Stations

MARC LEVESQUE

During the year that I spent at South Pole Station in Antarctica, I often felt that it was the closest Earthbound people could come to living on another planet. Our station's wintering crew was a small, confined group of 18. We were isolated from outside contact, with the exception of radio, for nearly 9 months. Winter temperatures hovered at −80° to −90° F for weeks and often dropped below −100° F. Total darkness lasted nearly 5 months. Given these conditions, among the harshest known on Earth, it has been suggested that Antarctica's small research stations might serve as an excellent operational analogue for human factor space research (Bluth, 1985). Indeed, during the 1960s, South Pole Station was used as the site for extensive social and behavioral research. A review of these studies found

. . . South Pole Station to be an ideal site for a broad range of fundamental research in human adaptation, man-machine interactions, and small group dynamics. The station is small in size, offers a protracted period of physical and social isolation, maintains excellent radio communications, has minimal environmental pollution, and imposes upon its personnel multiple stresses and significant, measurable, psychosocial and physiologic alterations. (National Research Council, 1971, p. 4)

As this early research and personal experience have shown, people who have wintered-over at the South Pole during the past 30 years have much to share with those who will be spending long periods of time in space. One of the most important insights is that living and working for extended periods in hostile, isolated, and physically confined environments requires adaptation at many levels. Physically, people at the South Pole or in space must adapt to a totally new set of environmental conditions: extreme temperatures, long periods of darkness, and alien landscapes. On one occasion at

South Pole, I spent 2 hours working outdoors in total darkness at $-117°$ F, wearing every piece of cold-weather clothing possible. This awkward, yet intense, experience shares many similarities with a space walk. With this extremely hostile physical environment posing a constant threat to life, wintering crewmembers must adopt a continuous survival situation mentality. While an Antarctic research station does provide a relatively safe shelter, its integrity can be only a few minutes of fate away from failure. As we witnessed during our winter, five more minutes of a fuel bladder fire might have meant the loss of our station, forcing us to evacuate to our adequate, but somewhat suspect, emergency shelter. A similar situation on a space station would have even more dire consequences.

Perhaps the most difficult adaptations to life in a confined, isolated setting are psychological, social, and cultural. Psychological adaptation to an environment characterized by severely reduced sensory input is difficult. With few changes in the physical setting or routine over the course of months, the mind becomes understimulated and must seek new inputs. For many, this meant voracious reading; for others, extended movie watching. Socially, instead of a world of familiar and supportive family and friends, our crewmembers at South Pole had to develop, at the very least, working relations with some people whom we may not have preferred to be around but whom we could not escape. Without the ability to physically remove oneself from others, mentally plotting the exact time, place, and method for a fellow crewmember's demise became one of the few options available for coping. (Fortunately, this "imaginative involvement" remained in the mind.) Other, less drastic techniques, such as scheduling one's arrival at dinner so as to avoid a particular individual who ate early and another who dined later, were only relatively successful. Finally, without the accustomed multitude of cultural options for recreation, social activities, and intellectual gratifications, running on a treadmill day after day became the metaphor for one's existence.

Why are physical, psychological, social, and cultural adaptations to hostile, confined, and isolated conditions important? How people adjust and adapt to these conditions can affect not only their mental health and social cohesion but also their performance of assigned duties. For example, the inability or unwillingness of certain crewmembers during our winter to maintain healthy life-styles and attitudes toward their work had a significant impact on group morale and crew performance. With continued station operation and scientific data collection essential to the well-being of station personnel and expensive ongoing scientific research, adjustment to on-site conditions is an important factor to consider. With the planning of long-duration missions in space, this will become all the more crucial:

We are now at the point of development of spaceflight where the range of psychological and social requirements of the human participant must be given full consideration. . . . [I]t seems clear that tomorrow's manned spaceflights will involve large numbers of people living and working together under close confines and in "unnatural" environments for long periods of time. Adjustment to such conditions has important implications for mental health, for social organization, and ultimately for mission success. (Connors, Harrison, & Akins, 1985, p.1)

With renewed interest in social and behavioral research in Antarctica and its applicability to life in space, my first recommendation is that such research should concentrate on the practical: How can we help people adapt to the extreme conditions they will face? Antarctic wintering crews and space crews move from a familiar, normal set of physical, psychological, social, and cultural conditions to radically different ones that require a change in thinking and behavior. Seen in human-development terms, what research can we undertake that will help individuals learn how to deal with these changes so they can create and maintain a new perspective for a healthy and productive existence?

One of the most pressing areas in need of further practical research is crew selection. All candidates for wintering Antarctic crews must undergo psychological examinations prior to being selected. These evaluations attempt to determine who might be able to cope with the confined and isolated conditions. Despite such screenings, wintering crewmembers have reported a variety of symptoms, such as insomnia, depression, irritability, and impaired cognition (Gunderson, 1971). From our experience at South Pole, we also saw that some individuals can become a threat to the emotional and physical well-being of others, suggesting that certain personalities may be more adaptable than others to existence in extreme environments. With improved instrumentation and new social and personality theories, cannot better predictors be identified? A related suggestion is to examine the effectiveness of a group-selection process, rather than just focusing on individuals. This seems particularly pertinent, since social disruptions within our wintering crew were as significant as individual maladjustment. Also, with increasing (and much welcomed) participation of women in wintering crews, a group-selection process may be even more desirable.

Second, while various influences on behavior have been suggested in earlier social and behavioral research in Antarctica, techniques for facilitating individual adaptation to extreme environments have yet to be tested. Such research in other remote locations, as reported by Gunderson (1971, p. 127), has indicated that

. . . experimental work on sensory deprivation studies . . . thus far indicate[s] that the absence of stimulation makes the individual less efficient and induces strong affective states associated with marked changes in motivation. Varied environmental stimulation, then, seems to be vital in maintaining the efficiency and stability of behavior.

Measuring the effect of the use of personal computers for intellectual and psychological stimulation is but one possibility in this area.

A third suggestion for practical research is to determine effective techniques for group leadership and training. The role of the station manager can be central to group health and performance, especially in isolated settings. Gunderson (1973) has suggested an important link between leadership styles and crew morale and performance. It has also been stated that crew training programs can be helpful in promoting group morale and performance: " . . . negative reactions to isolation . . . can effectively be prevented with proper psychological preparation, training, self-discipline, and definite regulation of daily activities . . . " (Natani & Shurley, 1974, p. 93). Providing people with techniques that can be used in dealing with the inevitable social conflicts that will occur should be one important component of such training.

While my first recommendation relates to focusing social and behavioral research in Antarctica on the practical, my second recommendation concerns the human subjects of such research. There are many reasons why people choose to spend a year at a place like South Pole. One of the more common ones is a sense of adventure. To experience a winter at South Pole, something that fewer than 600 people in the world have ever done, was, without question, the greatest adventure of my life. It may also be likewise for many others. This quest for adventure is also true of scientists conducting research. Is not the search for new knowledge also characterized by a situation where the outcome is unknown and where conditions are frequently adverse?

In addition to a strong interest in exploring new personal horizons, people who winter-over at Antarctic research stations are also, not unexpectedly, often fascinated by science. Given these two factors, they can make cooperative subjects for study, but only under certain conditions. Participating in research and adult learning processes have much in common. Adults learn best when they feel that there is a need, when they can be involved in their own learning process, and when they can see practical results for their efforts. The same is true when participating in research. During our year at South Pole, most of the crew participated in human biological research. As long as we understood the need for that sharp, pricking needle drawing blood from our arms each month, were aware of what would happen to the samples, and could comprehend the practical benefits of participating in the research — how it would help us and others — then we were more likely to honestly and enthusiastically cooperate. Involving the human subjects with the research projects, which, in essence, are learning experiences for researcher and subject, is something that should be stressed.

In this vein, three other thoughts bear consideration when scientists study people who live in isolated, confined places like South Pole. One is that the confined setting tends to force people away from each other. Personal privacy becomes one of the few opportunities wintering crewmembers have to escape the monotony of their daily existence. This must always be respected. This is also true when wintering crews are asked to participate in a study. They should be informed at the point of hire that they will be asked to do so.

To decide to conduct a winter study only a month before closing for the winter, as was once done at an Antarctic station, can place people in a very difficult and awkward situation. Second, and most crucial, is that all data collected in research studies must be held in the strictest confidence. While this is something that should not have to be stated, past experiences in Antarctica unfortunately dictate otherwise. Finally, there should be no surreptitious research.

In summary, there is much to gain from conducting space-related social and behavioral research in Antarctica. Building upon what was previously learned from such research in the 1960s and early 1970s, researchers might find new insights into how humans react to isolation. Since the time that this earlier research was conducted at the South Pole, there have been changes in crew composition (military/civilian, male/female) and communications (ham radio to satellite telephone calls) and refinements in social and behavioral research theories and techniques. What social engineering concepts will work to enhance the productivity of humans living and working in these environments and what practical techniques can be applied to promote individual and group adaptation are but two of many new and old areas for investigation. Previous social science research in Antarctica has been successful in exploring the human reaction to exotic environments and in contributing to the development of the space program. Future research can undoubtedly do the same. Also, with the U.S. space program behind schedule and access to the actual conditions of a space station even further away, a long-term, ongoing program of this kind could contribute much towards solving human factors problems. This effort could be beneficial as a joint study supported by the National Science Foundation, Division of Polar Programs, and the National Aeronautics and Space Administration.

Palinkas (1986) has suggested that people are capable of adapting to a variety of extreme, isolated environments for long periods of time. Despite such well-founded optimism, much more practical research needs to be conducted to further facilitate human adaptation to extreme environments. From an experiential perspective, the topics of highest priority for future research should include (1) better predictors of personality traits most adaptable to isolated and confined environments; (2) a group-selection process; (3) techniques for increasing intellectual and other forms of psychological stimulation; and (4) useful techniques for group leadership and training.

In order to gain the best results of such research, however, it is necessary to involve the human subjects as much as possible. This includes not only their participation in the research as subjects but also, possibly, their participation with research design and scope. Those who live the experience of isolated and confined environments can provide researchers with much valuable practical information, often much more than can be learned in a laboratory. Their full and enthusiastic cooperation can, therefore, be most helpful. Requesting this involvement, however, requires that the subjects' privacy be respected and protected. As social researchers in Antarctica have found, trust, once lost, is difficult to regain.

By focusing on practical social and behavioral research and by involving the research subjects in the research process, we give space–related research its proper perspective: consideration of the human element. It is long past the time that we began seriously considering human factors in Antarctic and space living. While our technology allows us to live and work in such extreme environments, it is what people do there and how they live there that are truly most important.

## References

Bluth, B. J. (1985). *Space station/Antarctic analogs* (Contractor Reports NAG 2-255 and NAGW-659). Washington, DC: National Aeronautics and Space Administration.

Connors, M. M., Harrison, A. A., & Akins, F. R. (1985). *Living aloft: Human requirements for extended spaceflight* (NASA SP-483). Washington, DC: National Aeronautics and Space Administration.

Gunderson, E. K. E. (1971). *Psychological studies in Antarctica* (Report 71-4). San Diego: Naval Health Research Center.

Gunderson, E. K. E. (1973). Individual behavior in confined or isolated groups. In J. E. Rasmussen (Ed.), *Man in isolation and confinement* (pp. 145–164). Chicago: Aldine.

Natani, K., & Shurley, J. T. (1974). Sociopsychological aspects of a winter vigil at South Pole Station. In E. K. E. Gunderson (Ed.), *Human adaptability to Antarctic conditions. Antarctic research series, Vol. 22* (p. 89–114). Washington, DC: American Geophysical Union.

National Research Council. (1971). *Biomedical and behavioral science research in Antarctica*. Oklahoma City: Oklahoma Medical Research Foundation.

Palinkas, L. A. (1986). *Long-term effects of environment on health and performance of Antarctic winter-over personnel* (Report 85-48). San Diego: Naval Health Research Center.

# 3

# A Review of Antarctic Behavioral Research

ARREED F. BARABASZ

Twenty-five years ago, Sladen (1965) described the history of physiological and psychological studies at U.S. stations in Antarctica as "brief, sporadic, and extremely limited in scope" (p. 103). Except for the Oklahoma Sleep Project conducted in the 1960s by Shurley, Pierce, and Natani and their colleagues (Shurley, 1974; Shurley, Pierce, Natani, & Brooks, 1970), Sladen's characterization of Antarctic behavioral research seems as true today as it was in 1965. Behavioral research by U.S. scientists published during the past decade has been largely dependent upon data obtained in cooperation with Antarctic treaty nations with ongoing psychological research programs, such as New Zealand, or the willingness of U.S. scientists, supported by the National Science Foundation in other fields, to assist in data collection using their own research teams as subjects.

Despite the myriad of limitations faced by Antarctic behavioral scientists, a number of discoveries by pioneer researchers such as Mullin and his psychologist colleagues Connery and Wouters during the International Geophysical Year (IGY) 1957 have recently been supported theoretically and empirically with clear implications for applications to life in space (A. F. Barabasz, 1980a, 1982, 1984; A. F. Barabasz & M. Barabasz, 1989; A. F. Barabasz & Gregson, 1979; M. Barabasz, A. F. Barabasz, & Mullin, 1983).

A review of the major studies reveals a remarkable trend toward progress in methodology and focus. Beginning with the earliest incidental anecdotal logs, methodology has progressed through the use of psychological screening tests such as the Minnesota Multiphasic Personality Inventory (MMPI), a measure that is most appropriate for the identification of pathological personalities, to the most recent systematic interview procedures and use of standardized psychological tests specific to Antarctic adaptive responses.

Instruments employed in the most recent research are, for example, sensitive to alterations in consciousness and vigilance.

## Early Studies

The earliest anecdotal information highlights awareness of behavioral issues. In describing why he felt it was unwise to staff bases in the Antarctic with only two men, Admiral Byrd (1938, p. 107) raised a number of important points in his report:

. . . it doesn't take two men long to find each other out. And, inevitably, this is what they do whether they will it or not, if only because once the simple tasks of the day are finished there is little else to do but take each other's measure. Not deliberately, not maliciously. But the time comes when one has nothing left to reveal to the other; when even his unformed thoughts can be anticipated, his pet ideas become a meaningless drool, and the way he blows out a pressure lamp or drops his boots on the floor or eats his food becomes a rasp and an annoyance. And this could happen between the best of friends.

Even at Little America, I knew of bunk mates who quit speaking because each suspected the other of inching his gear into the other's allotted space; and I knew of one who could not eat unless he could find a place in the mess hall out of sight of the Fletcherist who solemnly chewed twenty-eight times before swallowing. In a polar camp, little things like that have the power to drive even disciplined men to the edge of insanity. During my first winter at Little America, I walked for hours with a man who was on the verge of murder or suicide over imaginary persecutions by another man who had been his devoted friend. For there is no escape anywhere. You are hemmed in on every side by your own inadequacies and the crowding measures of your associates. The ones who survive with a measure of happiness are those who can live profoundly off of their intellectual resources. . . .[1]

Boredom constituted another major theme of the early anecdotal reports. Gunderson (1973) cited the first party to endure a winter in the Antarctic. The group of men included the crew of the *Belgica*, a Belgian scientific party, and Roald Amundsen. A detailed account of the party's struggle for survival in the 13 months locked in the ice was kept by the ship's physician, Frederick Cook. It was noted that though the men suffered from scurvy and exhaustion, they suffered even more so from "mental disturbances and boredom."

Research in long-term-confinement experiences has confirmed the boredom issue. Levine (1965) summarized Antarctic studies and commented that boredom is so often felt in spite of the fact that numerous facilities are available to alleviate such a condition. Similar findings come from aerospace studies. David (1963) summarized a number of experiments by Cra-

---

[1]From *Alone* by R. E. Byrd, 1938, p. 107. Copyright 1984 by Island Press. Reprinted by permission.

mer and Flinn (1963) involving confinement of pairs during simulated spaceflight. The chief problem noted during these experiments, lasting 17 to 30 days, was monotony. In another study, by Alluisi, Chiles, Hall, and Hawkes (1963), three groups, described as highly motivated, endured confinement in a simulated space system crew compartment. All subjects reported suffering from boredom. Boredom was exacerbated after programs had been learned well enough to become completely routine. Smith's (1966) findings, as an investigator participant in a group of seven men working in Antarctica, are entirely consistent with the early anecdotal reports. The group's reactions to monotony included widespread daydreaming and intense desire for change even though the change wasn't in the best interests of the mission.

## Systematic Studies

The first systematic psychological studies of Antarctic personnel were conducted during the IGY. These early studies by Mullin, Connery, and Wouters (Mullin, 1960; Mullin & Connery, 1959; Mullin, Connery, & Wouters, 1958) focused on the effects of wintering–over. The subjects consisted of a total of 85 men who were nearing the end of the wintering-over period at a number of stations. Station groups were all volunteers for Antarctic service with widely varying interests and backgrounds. As Mullin (1960, p. 324) noted, scientists, officers, and enlisted personnel were "thrown together in personal association isolated from all society for the largest part of the year." There was no communication with the outside world except by radio and, for several months, 24 hours of darkness per day. "During this time the physical milieu, the routine of life, and the small exclusive society was, of course, characterized by an inevitable sameness and monotony" (Mullin, 1960, p. 324).

Data were obtained from interviews and, to a lesser extent, from paper-and-pencil instruments. Interviews lasting from one to several hours were conducted in Antarctica and during the trip back to the United States by two psychologists and a psychiatrist. All 85 men agreed to be interviewed and tape-recorded. Interviews were characterized by a "high order of cooperation with the study team and much good will and frankness" (Mullin, 1960, p. 325).

Consistent with early studies of restricted environmental stimulation (Bexton, Heron, & Scott, 1954; Lilly, 1956), the findings revealed "an intense desire for stimuli, action, and increases in group suggestibility" (Mullin, 1960). Mullin found that nearly 30 of the 85 subjects studied indicated that they experienced "absent mindedness and wandering of attention" (p. 326). Usually this response was noted only after several months on the ice. Mullin concluded that the "change in alertness or awareness was a rather striking phenomenon and requires more study" (p. 326). In a few cases, the reaction was fairly extreme and took the form of "mild fugue states" (p. 326). The individual would recall leaving his quarters, but nothing thereafter until he "came to" moments later in some other part of the camp wondering how he got to that area and why he was there. Mullin's (1960) discovery of the occurrence of fugue-like, or dissociative, states of consciousness is entirely consistent with absorption and imaginative involvement demonstrated in hypnosis. These phenomena are explained by E. R. Hilgard's (1977, 1979) neodissociation theory. Mullin's observations, combined with this strong theoretical base, have been elucidated by several recent studies (A. F. Barabasz, 1980b, 1982, 1984; M. Barabasz, et al., 1983; E. R. Hilgard, 1979; J. R. Hilgard, 1974). The Mullin studies also generated the recommendation for consistent attention to screening for Antarctic service in the report to the United States Navy. Data from the Mullin studies and screening suggestions provided the impetus for the next generation of inquiry, which emphasized the selection of personnel for Antarctic duty.

## Screening Studies

Psychological studies were begun at U.S. stations by the United States Navy Bureau of Medicine and Surgery and the Office of Naval Research. McGuire and Tolchin (1961) analyzed test responses, diary observations, and medical records of the South Pole group wintering in 1959 and evaluated individual and group adjustment at this station. Nardini, Hermann, and Rasmussen (1962) created a psychological assessment program for selection of U.S. personnel after the IGY and concluded that it had been relatively successful in predicting Antarctic performance as measured by supervisors' ratings. Palmai (1963) studied a group of 14 men who wintered at Macquarie Island. The Palmai study noted a decline in morale, increases in group conflict, and, confirming the Mullin (1960) data, an increase in psychosomatic complaints.

Following these studies, a new program of psychological research was sponsored by the Bureau of Medicine and Surgery and instituted at the Navy Medical Neuropsychiatric Research Unit in 1961. The studies were coordinated under the direction of Erik Gunderson. At the beginning of the program, Gunderson reviewed the test data collected during the IGY and immediately thereafter developed a psychological framework for a planned series of investigations. The major studies involved wintering-over groups during 1963 through 1969 at six U.S. stations, including the South Pole Station, Byrd, Eights, Hallett, Palmer, and Plateau. Screening information was based on three major areas, including (1) clinical evaluations by psychologists and psychiatrists; (2) biographical information; and (3) attitude and personality tests. Interrater reliabilities were established between psychologists' and psychiatrists' evaluations on a sample of 719 Navy volunteers for Antarctic service ($r = .47$). Biographical information emphasized life history and occupational-experience data. Standardized attitude and personality tests were employed (Gunderson, 1963, 1965, 1973).

The screening data were evaluated in a series of studies using supervisor ratings and peer nominations as performance criteria. These resulted in a general concept of effective individual performance that included three essential behavioral components: emotional stability, task motivation, and social compatibility. The contributions of the various sources of screening information to the prediction of individual and group adjustment during the Antarctic winter were determined, and a high degree of specificity in the relevance of screening predictors for the various behavioral criteria in occupational subgroups was found. Navy men showed significant deterioration in morale or satisfaction during the winter months, whereas civilians showed little or no change. It was concluded that occupational role was a major determinant of job satisfaction during long-term isolation and confinement in Antarctica (Gunderson, 1966).

Owens (1966, 1967, 1968) studied wintering–over parties of the Australian National Antarctic Research Expedition at four stations involving groups ranging from 7 to 32 men. Owens was the first to view two distinct environmental situations in Antarctica: (1) living at a permanent base [relative safety and comfort with low stimulus variation] and (2) participating in field parties [high hazard and high stimulation]. Owens found married men received poorer performance ratings than single men. Since age did not account for the difference, it appeared that marriage might have affected the subjects' emotional adjustment during prolonged separation from home. Performance evaluations of the married men were even less favorable on the field trip criterion than on the overall criterion. Previous Antarctic experience was not related to overall performance but was positively related to the field trip criterion.

Psychological studies at New Zealand stations stressed standardized general personality tests of the paper-and-pencil type as well as interviews by a clinical psychologist. Taylor (1978) summarized the results of several years' work in his paper entitled "Antarctica Psychometrika Unspectacular." Taylor concluded that while many of the men gave subjective reports of slowing down and complained of poor memory and feelings of apprehension before returning home, no significant differences were found on the personality measures following Antarctic exposure. Gregson (1978) tested the "slowing down" and memory impairment observations using objective tests of recall and time estimation at Scott Base. Gregson found no significant change following pre- and post-winter-over measures on any test. The International Biomedical Expedition to the Antarctic emphasized field party rather than base party data. Again, standardized paper-and-pencil personality tests and clinical observations were employed. Again, no significant differences were found in contrast to baseline data.

The comprehensive, five-year Oklahoma project was largely biomedical in nature and, therefore, beyond the scope of the current review of behavioral studies (Shurley, 1974). The psychophysiological study of sleep at the South Pole Station did, however, reveal chronic hypobaric hypoxia, which might significantly influence human behavior in this environment (Brooks, Natani, Shurley, Pierce, & Joern, 1973). The pressure altitude at the South Pole is approximately 3,350 m (11,000 ft), whereas New Zealand's Scott Base is at sea level. The difference in physiological stress appears to have shown some interesting psychological correlates. In a comparison of positive personality changes in men at New Zealand's sea level Scott Base with those at the South Pole, Taylor and Shurley (1971) found greater changes on the Cattell 16 Personality Factor test at the South Pole. In contrast to this finding, Natani and Blackburn used the MMPI at South Pole and Plateau stations on two occasions in the late 1960s, early winter and late winter. Natani (Natani & Shurley, 1974) found no significant changes in profiles of individual men or between occupational subgroups, while Blackburn's (Blackburn, Shurley, & Natani, 1973) data indicated a significant reduction in verbally expressed anxiety and some minor differences in occupational subgroup responses. The Natani and Blackburn studies suggested that a relatively high level of psychological and/or physiological stress is required to induce personality changes, either positive or negative, and that standardized personality tests emphasizing psychopathology are not sensitive to the effects of intermediate levels of stress in men who volunteer for Antarctic duty and who typically show initial MMPI profiles suggestive of health and strength.

The ineffectiveness of sophisticated standardized measures of personality function to shed light on adaptive responses to the Antarctic environment convinced some researchers to reexamine many of the original findings of the early pioneers. The Mullin, Connery, and Wouters (1958) discovery of fugue states, inattentiveness, and loss of vigilance remained unexplained in light of Gregson's (1978) demonstration of no significant changes in time estimation or memory performance and the lack of significant information from the years of paper-and-pencil personality measures. If Antarctic behavioral research was to advance, new approaches had to be explored.

## Recent Studies

Mullin and co-workers (1958) findings of absentmindedness, wandering of attention, and fugue states were viewed as "a striking phenomenon" (p. 18) requiring further study. Individuals recalled leaving their quarters, but nothing thereafter until they "came to" later in some other part of the station wondering how they got there and why they were there. It occurred to the current investigator that the occurrence of fugue-like, or dissociative, trance states under conditions of restricted environmental stimulation (or REST) (Suedfeld, 1980) could be explained by E. R. Hilgard's (1977, 1979) neo-dissociation theory of hypnotic phenomena. It seemed appropriate to explore the possibility of increases in hypnotic susceptibility as a consequence of Antarctic living. Intriguingly, alterations in consciousness have also been revealed in spaceflight (Connors, Harrison, & Akins, 1986; Oberg & Oberg, 1986).

Hypnosis may be conceptualized as a specialized form of imagination or concentration. Electroencephalogram (EEG) studies have shown that the hypnotic state can be represented as an attentional shift (A. F. Barabasz & Lonsdale, 1983; Crawford, Kitner-Triolo, & Clarke, 1988; Spiegel, Cutcomb, Ren, & Pribrim, 1985). Recent preliminary investigations in Antarctica have shown increases in both absorption and imaginative involvement following exposure to brief and long-term Antarctic isolation (A. F. Barabasz, 1980b, 1984; M. Barabasz, et al., 1983). Perceptual changes in the ability to identify inverted figures have also been demonstrated in subjects exposed to both brief and winter-over Antarctic living. After Antarctic isolation, abstract figures were identified by the same conformity process used by children (A. F. Barabasz & M. Barabasz, 1986).

These exciting findings lend credence to an initial pilot study discovery suggesting increases in hypnotizability following wintering-over at Scott Base (A. F. Barabasz, 1978, 1980a). Although this study was supported indirectly by EEG evoked potential responses to suggestion (A. F. Barabasz & Gregson, 1979), this fascinating discovery remains to be verified. A standardized hypnotic scale was not employed, follow-up testing was not possible, and no measure of generalizability beyond test scores was possible. A pilot investigation of brief summer Antarctic isolation (M. Barabasz et al., 1983) used short, standardized measures of hypnotizability and absorption, but in this case, the unfunded status of the study meant logistics prevented immediate post-isolation testing. The investigators were excited to find that a 3-month follow-up still showed dramatic increases in absorption as measured by a standardized scale (Tellegen & Atkinson, 1974).

In summary, it appears that exposure to Antarctic isolation may produce alterations in consciousness. Increases in hypnotizability bring increased capacity and probability of experiencing a variety of phenomena. Consistent with Smith's (1966) findings of widespread daydreaming, these include deep imaginative involvement (A. F. Barabasz, 1980b, 1984; J. R. Hilgard, 1974, 1979) and absorption (M. Barabasz et al., 1983). Changes in susceptibility to hypnosis may also result in increases or decreases in vigilance performance (A. F. Barabasz, 1980b); dissociative, or fugue, states (Mullin, 1960); positive or negative hallucinations (E. R. Hilgard, 1975; Weitzenhoffer & E. R. Hilgard, 1962); and changes in perception of odors (A. F. Barabasz & Gregson, 1979; Weitzenhoffer & E. R. Hilgard, 1962). These phenomena have the potential to facilitate, degrade, or endanger adaptation to Antarctic living, and, by analogy, to life in space. The instances of "bizarre imagery" occurring in space travelers (Bluth, 1979), for example, might be understood through controlled studies of hypnotizability, individual adaptation, and absorption in Antarctica. The findings would, most likely, have direct implications for environmental design and personnel selection for both space and Antarctica (A. F. Barabasz, 1988). The potential for clinical applications in normal Earth environments might also be far-reaching.

## References

Alluisi, E. A., Chiles, W. D., Hall, T. J., & Hawkes, G. R. (1963). *Human group performance during confinement* (Tech. Rep. No. AMRL-TDR-63-87). 6570th Aerospace Medical Research Laboratory, Wright-Patterson AFB, Ohio–Lockheed Aircraft Corporation.

Barabasz, A. F. (1978). Electroencephalography, isolation, and hypnotic capability at Scott Base. *New Zealand Antarctic Record, 1*, 35–42.

Barabasz, A. F. (1980a). EEG alpha, skin conductance and hypnotizability in Antarctica. *International Journal of Clinical and Experimental Hypnosis, 28*, 63–74.

Barabasz, A. F. (1980b, August). *Imaginative involvement and hypnotizability in Antarctica*. Paper presented at the 10th Annual Congress of the Australian Society for Clinical and Experimental Hypnosis, Hobart, Tasmania.

Barabasz, A. F. (1982). Restricted environmental stimulation and the enhancement of hypnotizability: Pain, EEG alpha, skin conductance, and temperature responses. *International Journal of Clinical and Experimental Hypnosis, 30*, 147–166.

Barabasz, A. F. (1984). Antarctic isolation and imaginative involvement: Preliminary findings. *International Journal of Clinical and Experimental Hypnosis, 32*, 296–300.

Barabasz, A. F. (1988, August). *Flotation restricted environmental stimulation produces spontaneous hypnosis*. Paper presented at the International Congress of Hypnosis and Psychosomatic Medicine, The Hague.

Barabasz, A. F., & Barabasz, M. (1986). Antarctic isolation and inversion perception: Regression phenomena. *Environment and Behavior, 18*, 285–292.

Barabasz, A. F., & Barabasz, M. (1989). Effects of restricted environmental stimulation: Enhancement of hynotizability for experimental and chronic pain control. *International Journal of Clinical and Experimental Hypnosis, 37*, 217–231.

Barabasz, A. F., & Gregson, R. A. M. (1979). Antarctic wintering-over, suggestion and transient olfactory stimulation: EEG evoked potential and electrodermal responses. *Biological Psychology, 9*, 285–295.

Barabasz, A. F., & Lonsdale, C. (1983). Effects of hypnosis on P300 olfactory-evoked potential amplitudes. *Journal of Abnormal Psychology, 92*, 520–526.

Barabasz, M., Barabasz, A. F., & Mullin, C. S. (1983). Effects of brief Antarctic isolation on absorption and hypnotic susceptibility: Preliminary results and recommendations. *International Journal of Clinical and Experimental Hypnosis, 31*, 235–238.

Bexton, W., Heron, W., & Scott, T. (1954). Effects of decreased variation in the sensory environment. *Canadian Journal of Psychology, 8*, 70–76.

Blackburn, A. B., Shurley, J. T., & Natani, K. (1973). Psychological adjustment at a small Antarctic station: An MMPI study. In O. G. Edholm & E. K. E. Gunderson (Eds.), *Polar human biology*: Proceedings of the SCAR/IUPS/IUBS symposium on human biology and medicine in the Antarctic (pp. 369–383). London: Heinemann.

Bluth, B. J. (1979). Consciousness alterations in space. In *Space Manufacturing 3: Proceedings of the 4th Princeton/AIAA Conference* (pp. 525–532). New York: American Institute of Aeronautics and Astronautics.

Brooks, R. E., Natani, K., Shurley, J. T., Pierce, C. M., & Joern, A. T. (1973). An Antarctic sleep and dream laboratory. In O. G. Edholm & E. K. E. Gunderson (Eds.), *Polar human biology* (pp. 322–341). London: Heinemann.

Byrd, R. E. (1938). *Alone.* New York: Putnam. (Reissued by Island Press, Covelo, CA, 1984.)

Connors, M. M., Harrison, A. A., & Akins, F. R. (1986). Psychology and the resurgent space program. *American Psychologist, 41*, 906–913.

Cramer, E. H., & Flinn, D. E. (1963). *Psychiatric aspects of the SAM two man space cabin simulator* (Tech. Rep. No. SAM-TDR-63-27-USAF). Brooks AFB, Texas: School of Aerospace Medicine.

Crawford, H. J., Kitner-Triolo, M., & Clarke, S. (1988, November). *EEG activation patterns accompanying induced happy and sad moods: Moderating effects of hypnosis and hypnotic responsiveness level.* Paper presented at the Annual Scientific Meeting of the Society for Clinical and Experimental Hypnosis, Ashville, NC.

David, H. M. (1963). Prolonged space flight poses monotony problem. *Missiles and Rockets*, 31–32.

Gregson, R. A. M. (1978). Monitoring cognitive performance in Antarctica. *New Zealand Antarctic Record, 1*, 24–32.

Gunderson, E. K. E. (1963). Emotional symptoms in extremely isolated groups. *Archives of General Psychiatry, 9*, 362–368.

Gunderson, E. K. E. (1965). The reliability of personality ratings under varied assessment conditions. *Journal of Clinical Psychology, 21*, 161–164.

Gunderson, E. K. E. (1966). Personality differences among Navy occupational groups. *Personnel and Guidance Journal*, 956–961.

Gunderson, E. K. E. (1973). Psychological studies in Antarctica: A review. In O. G. Edholm & E. K. E. Gunderson (Eds.), *Polar human biology*: Proceedings of the SCAR/IUPS/IUBS Symposium on human biology and medicine in the Antarctic (pp. 352–361). London: Heinemann.

Harrison, A. A. (1986). On resistance to the involvement of personality, social, and organizational psychologists in the U.S. space program. *Journal of Social Behavior and Personality, 1*, 315–324.

Hilgard, E. R. (1975). The alleviation of pain by hypnosis. *Pain, 1*, 213–231.

Hilgard, E. R. (1977). *Divided consciousness: Multiple controls in human thought and action.* New York: Wiley.

Hilgard, E. R. (1979). Consciousness and control: Lessons from hypnosis. *Australian Journal of Clinical and Experimental Hypnosis, 7*, 103–116.

Hilgard, J. R. (1974). Imaginative involvement: Some characteristics of the highly hypnotizable and non-hypnotizable. *International Journal of Clinical and Experimental Hypnosis, 22*, 138–156.

Hilgard, J. R. (1979). Imaginative and sensory-affective involvements in everyday life and in hypnosis. In E. Fromm & R. E. Shor (Eds.), *Hypnosis: developments in research and new perspectives* (2nd ed.) (pp. 483–517). New York: Aldine.

Levine, A. S. (1965). Prolonged isolation and confinement: A problem for naval medical research. *Navy Magazine*, 26–28, 44–45.

Lilly, J. (1956). Mental effects on reduction of ordinary levels of physical stimuli on intact, healthy persons. *Psychiatric Research Reports, 5*, 1–9.

McGuire, F., & Tolchin, S. (1961). Group adjustment at the South Pole. *Journal of Mental Science, 107,* 954–960.

Mullin, C. S. (1960). Some psychological aspects of isolated Antarctic living. *American Journal of Psychiatry, 117,* 323–326.

Mullin, C. S., & Connery, H. (1959). Psychological study of an Antarctic IGY station. *Armed Forces Medical Journal, 10,* 290–296.

Mullin, C. S., Connery, H., & Wouters, F. (1958). *A psychological-psychiatric study of an IGY station in Antarctica* (project report). United States Navy, Bureau of Medicine and Surgery, Neuropsychiatric Division.

Nardini, J. E., Hermann, R. S., & Rasmussen, J. E. (1962). Navy psychiatric assessment program in the Antarctic. *American Journal of Psychiatry, 119,* 97–105.

Natani, K., & Shurley, J. T. (1974). Sociopsychological aspects of a winter vigil at South Pole Station. In E. K. E. Gunderson (Ed.), *Human adaptability to Antarctic conditions* (pp. 89–114). Washington: American Geophysical Union.

Oberg, J. E., & Oberg, A. R. (1986). *Living on the next frontier: Pioneering space.* New York: McGraw-Hill.

Owens, A. G. (1966). *The assessment of individual performance in small Antarctic groups, 1, OIC's Rating Scales* (research report). Melbourne: Psychological Research Unit of the Australian Military Forces.

Owens, A. G. (1967). *The assessment of individual performance in small Antarctic groups, 2, ratings on the Leary Interpersonal Checklist* (research report). Melbourne: Psychological Research Unit of the Australian Military Forces.

Owens, A. G. (1968). *Some biographical correlates of assessed performance in small Antarctic groups* (research report). Melbourne: Psychological Research Unit of the Australian Military Forces.

Palmai, G. (1963). Psychological observations on an isolated group in Antarctica. *British Journal of Psychiatry, 109,* 364–370.

Shurley, J. T. (1974). Physiological Research at U.S. stations in Antarctica. In E. K. E. Gunderson (Ed.), *Human adaptability to Antarctic conditions.* (pp. 71–87). Washington: American Geophysical Union.

Shurley, J. T., Pierce, C. M., Natani, K., & Brooks, R. E. (1970). Sleep and activity patterns at South Pole Station. *Archives of General Psychiatry, 22,* 385–389.

Sladen, W. J. L. (1965). Staphylococci in noses and streptococci in throats of isolated and semi-isolated Antarctic communities. *Journal of Hygiene, 63,* 103–116.

Smith, W. M. (1966). Observations over the lifetime of a small isolated group: Structure, danger, boredom and vision. *Psychological Reports, 19,* 475–514.

Spiegel, D., Cutcomb, S., Ren, C., & Pribrim, K. (1985). Hypnotic hallucination alters evoked potentials. *Journal of Abnormal Psychology, 94,* 249–255.

Suedfeld, P. (1980). *Restricted environmental stimulation.* New York: Wiley-Interscience.

Taylor, A. J. W. (1978). Antarctica psychometrika unspectacular. *New Zealand Antarctic Record, 6,* 36–45.

Taylor, A. J. W., & Shurley, J. T. (1971). Some Antarctic troglodytes. *International Review of Applied Psychology, 9,* 367–376.

Tellegen, A., & Atkinson, G. (1974). Openness to absorbing and self-altering experiences ("absorption"), a trait related to hypnotic susceptibility. *Journal of Abnormal Psychology, 83,* 268–277.

Weitzenhoffer, A., & Hilgard, E. R. (1962). *The Stanford Hypnotic Susceptibility Scale: Form C.* Palo Alto, CA: Consulting Psychologists Press.

# 4

# Current International Human Factors Research in Antarctica

DESMOND J. LUGG

Polar Privation
Antarctic Life Proves Hard Even for Those Who Love Their Work
Boredom and Isolation Lead to Alcohol, Drugs
An Ideal Space Simulator
Seeing "Cat Ballou" 87 Times

Thus wrote Burrough (1985), a staff reporter of *The Wall Street Journal*, as a leader to the second of two articles on life in Antarctica. Another report, by Reinhold in the *New York Times* in 1982, titled "Strife and Despair at South Pole Illuminate Psychology of Isolation," details a night of violence at South Pole Station. However, the writer qualifies his story:

Though an extreme example, that night of violence underscores the powerful mental effects of protracted isolation. And many psychologists believe the unusual nature of Antarctic isolation — in which a small group of scientists and support personnel is confined to a tiny life-sustaining cocoon surrounded by an impenetrable hostile environment that permits no quick escape — may hold lessons for an approaching age of prolonged space travel and space colonization.

As the above articles illustrate, the aftermath of an Antarctic winter is always great copy for the press. Similarly, a review of pictures taken over 40 years of the Australian National Antarctic Research Expeditions (ANARE) identifies behavioral, social, and psychological aspects of wintering in Antarctica in graphic detail. These pictures capture the feelings of isolation and show how people look after themselves and their work places, how they relax, and especially the "culture" of the small, totally isolated groups. This latter subject varies from group to group and shows customs such as shaving heads, wearing crew cuts or long hair with bands and bows, ceremonials such as mating husky dogs or a mock wedding, theatrical productions that include "female" characters organized to the very last detail, and the staging of a crucifixion at Easter.

In addition to the pictorial record, there are factual descriptions of other Australian Antarctic experiences. These include a chef who went on strike, a leader who was hanged in effigy as a spectacle for the incoming expedition, people who refused to speak for weeks, people who threatened to do an "Oates" (commit suicide) on the sea ice, people who would not use toilets or wash or change clothes, groups who lisped or used "quaint" language, the standoff of a chef with a meat cleaver and a diesel mechanic with a fire axe, the dogs that assumed human status, and other myths and folklore.

Due to the abundance of anecdotal reports, it has been assumed that environmental stresses encountered in Antarctica adversely affect physical and mental health. What is the truth of these reports? Does current international human factors research in Antarctica help to answer some of the questions?

Human studies were carried out on early Antarctic expeditions, but the research was ad hoc and had little continuity or coordination. Examples of these studies are the work of Klovstad (Borchgrevink, 1901) and McLean (1919). Although behavioral research per se was not performed and published, we do have a legacy today in the form of considerable writings from these expeditions. On a number of early expeditions, psychiatric problems were experienced, but only vague reference was made to them. An example of such a case and the attitude of the doctor treating it occurs in the records of the Australasian Antarctic Expedition 1911–1914. McLean (1915) wrote:

Adelie Land can only be regarded as an intolerable country in which to live, owing to the never-ceasing winds. Usage and necessity helped one to regard the weather in the best possible light; for the sake of a few hours of calm which might be expected to occasionally intervene between the long spells of the blizzards. It is, therefore, with regret and some diffidence that I speak of the illness of Mr. S. N. Jeffryes, who took up so conscientiously the duties of wireless operator during the second year (1913); but upon whom the monotony of a troglodytic winter life made itself felt. It is my hope that he is fast recovering his former vigour and enthusiasm. (pp. 309–310)

A footnote to McLean's 1915 report has been added by Sir Douglas Mawson:

With the advent of summer, Jeffryes became normal, but unfortunately suffered a temporary relapse upon his return to Australia. (p. 310)

Priestley (1921), who was a member of both Shackleton's *Nimrod* expedition 1907–1909 and Scott's *Terra Nova* expedition 1910–1913, was one of the first to write on the psychology of polar exploration. He concluded his article with the following:

Before closing the subject, short reference should be made to that very real danger to the polar expedition, the peculiar mental trouble which might perhaps best be called *polar* madness. It is a well-established fact that men mentally unsuited for polar exploration are liable to suffer from temporary mental aberration either during or immediately after an expedition. Cases have occurred in nearly all recent expeditions where real hardships have been incurred. The most extraordinary hallucinations afflict the patient and for the time being he is quite irresponsible. It is a merciful fact that this aberration is apparently temporary only, though in extreme cases it may last for months and even years. One factor worth mentioning is that it appears to be most inelastic temperaments and minds that succumb. The higher strung and more sensitive the organisation, the better it will withstand extraordinary strain. (p. 9)

Evans (1937) also reinforces what Priestley said. Writing some years after his involvement in polar exploration, he said:

Psychology plays an important part in Polar exploration as well as in war, and during the winter darkness one has to be constantly watching one's subordinates. Many men have gone mad after their return to civilization. Few go mad during the expedition, when the tension is not relaxed.

Of course, the reason why so few men go mad on these expeditions is, according to some authorities, that we were all mad before we started on such a hare-brained enterprise! Looking back, I calculate that 13 per cent of Scott's men were mentally deranged after the expedition. I will not give their names. Four are dead, and the others are sane enough to sue me for libel! (p. 24)

The establishment of the Scientific Committee on Antarctic Research (SCAR) in 1958 and the intensive planning for the International Biological Programme, which was conceived as a logical sequel to the International Geophysical Year 1957–58, brought together a group of interested medical workers including psychologists and those interested in behavior on polar expeditions. They recommended a variety of standardized techniques and measurements to be made on Antarctic personnel and attempted to coordinate Antarctic studies of human biology.

The first international gathering specifically on the special needs of humans in polar regions was held in 1962. This was the Conference on Medicine and Public Health in the Arctic and Antarctic, organized by the World Health Organization in Geneva (WHO) (World Health Organization, 1963).

By the middle 1960s, most nations involved in Antarctica had national programs in human biology, but there was minimal collaboration. The substantial research that had been carried out up to 1972 was shown, in Cambridge, England, by the presentations at a Symposium on Human Biology and Medicine in the Antarctic. These were later published in a volume edited by Edholm and Gunderson (1973), *Polar Human Biology*. No longer was the research a collection of simple ad hoc observations, but well-planned systematic studies. At the 1972 Symposium, the future of human studies in Antarctica was discussed, and this resulted in the establishment by SCAR of the Working Group on Human Biology and Medicine (WG HB&M). The interim secretary was Dr. O. G. Edholm, and at the first meeting of WG HB&M at XIII SCAR in 1974, Dr. J. Rivolier was elected secretary, a post he held until 1984.

At the 1972 Symposium, there was strong support and enthusiasm for genuine international collaboration in Antarctic biomedical studies. The establishment of the WG HB&M furthered this interest, and organization of the International Biomedical Expedition to the Antarctic (IBEA) commenced. At the XV meeting of SCAR, in 1978, the permanent delegates to SCAR endorsed the IBEA proposal and encouraged the group to proceed with its plan under appropriate national sponsorship. France agreed to the principal sponsorship with other SCAR nations assisting. The logistic support for IBEA changed several times, but the expedition was successfully carried out in the austral summer of 1980–1981. Figure 4.1 shows the location and route of the IBEA. The importance of logistics support in transferring research concepts to reality and the inherent difficulties in mounting international Antarctic research expeditions is described by Rivolier, Goldsmith, Lugg, and Taylor (1988).

Figure 4.2 shows the current international network for Antarctic and polar human studies. The interaction of SCAR, the International Council of Scientific Unions, and the newly created International Union for Circumpolar Health and space agencies is clearly shown. At present, 21 countries actively engaged in Antarctic research are members of SCAR, and 17 have members on the WG HB&M. Three additional members represent the International Union of Physiological Science (IUPS), International Union of

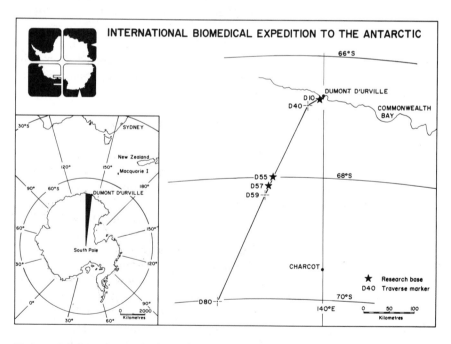

FIGURE 4.1. Location and route of the International Biomedical Expedition to the Antarctic. From J. Rivolier, R. Goldsmith, D. L. Lugg, and A. J. W. Taylor (Eds.), 1988, *Man in the Antarctic*. London: Taylor and Francis. Copyright 1988 Taylor and Francis. Reprinted by permission.

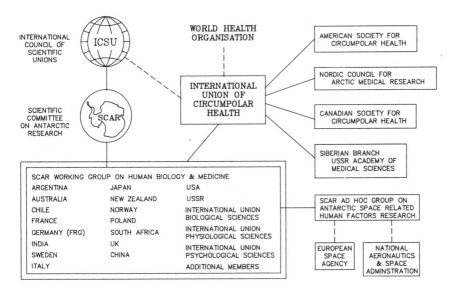

FIGURE 4.2. Antarctic human factors research international network.

Psychological Science (IUPSYS), and International Union of Biological Science (IUBS), while a fourth, from Canada, has been co-opted in his own right.

Past research in Antarctica in human biology has included biochemistry and hormone studies, biorhythms, biometeorology, cold acclimatization, epidemiology, immunology, microbiology, virology, sleep, and the pathophysiology of cold injury. Studies on nutrition, clothing, buildings, and ergonomics have resulted in better living and working conditions. Research on the psychology and behavioral adaptation of wintering groups has assisted in the selection of personnel. Specific research papers have not been cited here in order to keep this chapter to a manageable size.

Current research continues a multidisciplinary approach on the interaction of man with the Antarctic environment. Table 4.1 summarizes national programs as taken from the 1985–1987 reports to SCAR of the various nations operating in Antarctica. Recent research places particular emphasis on studies that facilitate living in Antarctica. Increases in visitors and in private and national expeditions mean increasing populations. Large numbers of scientists are now visiting Antarctica each summer. The advent of families and increasing numbers of women have changed the traditional all-male groups. Many countries are now replacing primitive, small stations with large, modern ones. These changes will require continuing studies, many of which will be applied research.

Reviewing one national program gives a better idea of the current research being performed in Antarctica. As coordinator and program manager of

TABLE 4.1. Antarctic human factors research national programs: 1985–1987.

| | |
|---|---|
| Argentina | Human behavior |
| | Microbiology |
| Brazil | Reactions to cold with emphasis on stomach functions |
| Chile | Acclimatization studies |
| | Blood lipids |
| | Evaluation hypothalamic–hypophyseal axis in adults of both sexes. Comparison studies Antarctica and "normal" environment |
| France | Psychological and psychophysiological studies |
| | Validation of predeparture psychological examinations and development of specific polar tests |
| | Responses to stress – longer term studies |
| | Endocrinology and metabolic studies |
| | Epidemiology – alcohol and tobacco studies |
| Japan | Adaptation studies |
| | Hormonal and circadian rhythms |
| | Microbiology of human pollution |
| | Clothing assessment |
| New Zealand | Psychological studies and counseling of base wintering personnel |
| United Kingdom | Human performance, particularly psychological, in association with physical stressors – cold, dehydration, increased atmospheric pressure, fatigue |
| | Acclimatization to cold in divers – thermal stress and protection |
| | Attempt eradication of coagulase-positive staphylococci |
| | Effect of ethanol on thermogenic mechanisms – hypoglycemia, melatonin, hypothalamic and pituitary gland function |
| | Environmental health |
| | Proteinuria in polar travelers |
| | Comparisons of isometric and dynamic training |
| | Melatonin, mood, and performance |
| USA | Respiratory virus transmission |
| | Psychological, sociological, and endocrinological studies |
| USSR | Influence of psychological factors on Antarctic explorers' health |
| | Cardiovascular studies |
| | Anthropology |
| | Selection of staff |
| | Assessment and management of somatic disorders |

Australian human studies, it is relevant for me to describe them. Figure 4.3 shows the Australian program in detail. The research is supported by research groups in Australia, including Polar Medicine Branch, Antarctic Division; Baker Medical Research Institute; Department of Defence; Army Psych Research; Fairfield Hospital; Flinders Medical Centre; Garvan Institute of Medical Research; Monash University; Royal Hobart Hospital; and University of Tasmania. Experiments are designed in Australia and performed in Antarctica, and the provisional generalizations of man's interaction with the Antarctic environment are continually modified to fit new facts.

# Human interaction with the Antarctic environment

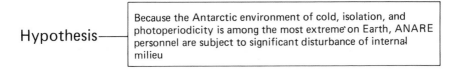

Hypothesis —— Because the Antarctic environment of cold, isolation, and photoperiodicity is among the most extreme on Earth, ANARE personnel are subject to significant disturbance of internal milieu

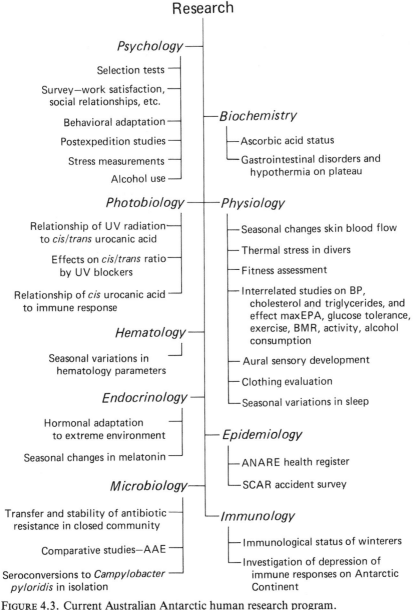

FIGURE 4.3. Current Australian Antarctic human research program.

The constraints on research in Antarctica are considerable, as can be seen in Table 4.2. The "A" Factor, as we call it, is a combination of the isolated environment, the subjects, the researcher, his skills and the laboratory provided, and the ability of the supervisors remote from the researcher. It is a tribute to man's ingenuity, patience, and application that so much excellent research has resulted from Antarctic studies.

In the period 1947 through 1990, 3,087 wintering positions have been occupied on ANARE, 64 of these being occupied by women from 1976 through 1990. The number of winters per person has ranged from 1 to 11. This is a substantial group to have studied, and by looking at the occurrence of mental health disorders (according to the WHO's, International Classification of Diseases, ICD-9, 1977), one is able to assess morbidity associated with psychological and psychiatric problems. Law (1960) gives an excellent review of the selection and adaptation of the men on the early years of ANARE. Over the past 25 years, adaptability screening has been carried out for ANARE. Post-expedition review is also most important, and the "retribalization" of ANARE personnel is a well-observed phenomenon.

Studies on ANARE by Lugg (1973), Dick (1985), and Williams (1986) show a low occurrence of mental disorders as a percentage of total morbidity. For recent groups ($n = 87$), around 4 to 5% of the total morbidity is in the category of mental disorders. The 25-year survey (Lugg, 1977) gives a figure about half of that for the later wintering groups, but with half the 25-year study group of 2,000 being summer expedition staff, it is considered that the larger survey is not at variance with the result of 4 to 5%. Cases and

TABLE 4.2. Constraints on Antarctic human research: The "A" factor.

| | |
|---|---|
| Subjects | Attitude |
| | Compliance |
| | Small number — statistical problems |
| | Dislocation of groups |
| | Illness |
| | Occupation, other tasks, availability |
| Environment | Isolation |
| | Group confinement |
| | Cold |
| | Photoperiodicity |
| Researcher | Experience and expertise |
| | Professional isolation |
| | No laboratory staff |
| | Fluctuations in morale |
| Laboratory | Relatively primitive |
| | Lack of backup |
| | Logistical problems — frozen chemicals, nondelivery |
| | Apparatus malfunction |
| Supervising laboratory | Lack of knowledge of Antarctic conditions |
| | Communications |

numbers seen in the three studies done during the 1980s include anxiety states: 2; hysteria: 1; depression: 1; alcohol dependence syndrome: 1; non-dependent abuse of drugs: 2; anorexia nervosa:1; insomnia: 7; psychalgia (tension headache): 5; acute stress reaction: 1; adjustment reaction: 6.

Many nations and Antarctic operators deny the existence of psychiatric and psychological problems. Some nations do vast batteries of preselection tests; others do nothing. In private discussions with doctors and researchers from a number of nations currently working in Antarctica, the figures given here that 4 to 5 % of the total morbidity is related to mental health probably represent the average finding for groups in Antarctica. With insomnia and other conditions being included in the classification, it is obvious that severe psychotic and neurotic illness occurs at a frequency much lower than 4%.

Gunderson (1968) drew attention to mental health problems in Antarctica in the 1960s, but very few actual figures have been published since that time. King (1986) has pointed out the merits of doing epidemiological work in Antarctica, and further research is needed. Recently established health registers (King, 1987) will help to quantify mental health problems in isolated Antarctica as well as to further the study of long-term effects of the Antarctic winter on personnel (Palinkas, 1985a,b; Palinkas, Stern, & Holbrook, 1986; Rivolier, 1979).

What is the future of international research? The isolation of Antarctica is an ideal situation for the study of viral, immunological, bacteriological, and psychological research. In this age of space exploration and the current evaluation of man's impact on the world and of the world on himself, human studies in Antarctica are most appropriate.

International scientific collaboration will maintain the research at a level of high quality, while also giving great opportunity for cross–cultural studies. With a strong SCAR Working Group encouraging groups to work together (Lugg, 1987), research subjects may be organized by different nations doing studies in the same discipline. Work on IBEA has shown that physiological, microbiological and immunological research can be greatly helped by parallel psychological studies (Rivolier et al., 1988). Similarly, psychological and social data from small, isolated Antarctic groups indicate a need for more sophisticated research in this area to include biological factors. One recent study (Godwin, 1984) highlighted the perception by the wintering staff that the operating agency was itself one of the greatest sources of stress to those in Antarctica.

The benefits of collaborative and continuing research are illustrated by the initial small immunology project of IBEA (Roberts-Thomson, Lugg, Vallverdu, & Bradley, 1985). Follow-up immunological studies on the wintering Australian Antarctic expeditions, assessing cell-mediated immunity, indicate decreased cutaneous responses with significant anergy and hypoergy (Williams, Climie, Muller, & Lugg, 1986). This may reflect altered immune activity induced by environmental and stress factors. Although no correlations were found with psychological or endocrine measurements made on the same expeditioners, the interaction of brain, endocrinological functions, and immunological status in Antarctica remains of great importance. The vulnerability of totally isolated, Antarctic wintering groups, whose ability to resist infections may be influenced by anxiety, depression, or other environmental stresses, is of great concern to those responsible for health maintenance in Antarctica.

Further studies, including analysis of lymphocyte subclasses and skin blood flow, are in progress, and these should give a more refined view of the immunological mechanisms and their relationship to psychological, behavioral, and endocrinological processes.

Suggestions have been made that Antarctic medical studies would be more appropriately done in the Arctic, where indigenous Inuit people have lived in family communities for millennia. In recent times, groups from temperate zones live in military and in oil- and mineral-exploration establishments in the Arctic. These are not totally isolated, with staff having opportunities to travel to regional centers. In the Arctic, there is chronic and endemic disease, as well as the indigenous and nonnative groups with their differing cultures. For these reasons, much of the research done in the Antarctic cannot be done in the Arctic.

How does the international Antarctic research described above fit in with life in space? One can conclude that

- Antarctica as the most isolated continent on Earth is an excellent analogue for space.
- Current Antarctic human factors research is a satisfactory base and the international network a strong foundation for future studies that could be used for benefiting life in space.

These conclusions can be borne out in a practical way when one reviews reports to the National Aeronautics and Space Administration (NASA) (Stuster, 1986) and sees the application of Antarctic work to future NASA projects.

At present, human studies in Antarctica continue in accordance with SCAR objectives, so that scientists in all other disciplines, who are acquiring scientific knowledge necessary for the judicious management of the environment and the resources of the region, can carry out their research safely and efficiently in this hostile area. These studies can readily be utilized for the benefit of future travelers in space.

## References

Borchgrevink, C. E. (1901). *First on the Antarctic continent being an account of the British Antarctic Expedition 1898-1900*. London: George Newnes.

Burrough, B. (1985, December 10). *Polar privation. The Wall Street Journal*, Vol. CXIII, No. 114.

Dick, A. F. (1985). *Work, health and applied physiology of an expedition in Antarctica*. Master's thesis, University of Sydney.

Edholm, O. G., & Gunderson, E. K. E. (Eds.). (1973). *Polar human biology: The proceedings of the SCAR/IUPS/IUBS symposium on human biology and medicine in the Antarctic*. London: Heinemann.

Evans, E. R. G. R. (1937). How a sailor looks at the surgeon and the medical aspect of polar exploration from a sailor-explorer's viewpoint. *Journal of the Royal Navy Medical Service, 23*, 14–30.

Godwin, J. (1984). *A preliminary investigation into stress in Australian Antarctic expeditions*. Master's Thesis, University of Melbourne.

Gunderson, E. K. E. (1968). Mental health problems in Antarctica. *Archives of Environmental Health, 17*, 558–564.

King, H. (1986). Epidemiology in Antarctica? *Journal of Epidemiology and Community Health, 40*, 351–356.

King, H. (1987). A new health register for Australian National Antarctic Research Expeditions. *Polar Record, 23*, 719–720.

Law, P. G. (1960). Personality problems in Antarctica. *Medical Journal of Australia, 1*, 273–282.

Lugg, D. J. (1973). *Anatomy of a group in Antarctica*. Medical doctoral thesis, University of Adelaide.

Lugg, D. J. (1977). *Physiological adaptation and health of an expedition in Antarctica with comment on behavioral adaptation*. ANARE Scientific Reports, No. 126. Canberra: Australian Government Publishing Service.

Lugg, D. J. (1987). International co-ordination of Antarctic medical research and medicine. *Arctic Medical Research, 46*, 29–34.

McLean, A. L. (1915). Medical report, main base (Adelie Land). In D. Mawson (Ed.), *The home of the blizzard: Being the story of the Australasian Antarctic Expedition, 1911–1914*. London: Heinemann.

McLean, A. L. (1919). Bacteriological and other researches. *Australasian Antarctic Expedition, 1911–1914*. (Scientific Reports Series, C, Vol. VII, Part 4). Sydney: Government Printer.

Palinkas, L. A. (1985a). *Health and performance of Antarctic winter-over personnel: A follow-up study* (Report No. 85-18). San Diego: Naval Health Research Center.

Palinkas, L. A. (1985b). *Long-term effects of environment on health and performance of Antarctic winter-over personnel* (Report No. 85-48). San Diego: Naval Health Research Center.

Palinkas, L. A., Stern, M. J., & Holbrook, T. L. (1986). *A longitudinal study of personality and disease incidence among Antarctic winter-over volunteers* (Report No. 86-25). San Diego: Naval Health Research Center.

Priestley, R. E. (1921). The psychology of exploration. Unpublished manuscript, p. 9.

Reinhold, R. (1982). Strife and despair at South Pole illuminate psychology of isolation. New York *Times*, January 12.

Rivolier, J. (1979). *Groupes isoles en environments inhabituels et hostiles — Approche psychoecologique*. These de Doctorat es Lettres et Sciences humaines, Sorbonne: Paris.

Rivolier, J., Goldsmith, R., Lugg, D. J., & Taylor, A. J. W. (1988). *Man in the*

*Antarctic — The scientific work of the International Biomedical Expedition to the Antarctic (IBEA)*. London: Taylor and Francis.

Roberts-Thomson, P., Lugg, D. J., Vallverdu, R., & Bradley, J. (1985). Assessment of immunological responsiveness in members of the International Biomedical Expedition to the Antarctic, 1980/81. *Journal of Clinical and Laboratory Immunology, 17*, 115–118.

Stuster, J. W. (1986). *Space station habitability recommendations based on a systematic comparative analysis of analogous conditions* (NASA Contractor Report 3943). Santa Barbara: Anacapa Sciences, Inc.

Williams, D. L. (1986). *Health, hormonal and stress-related studies in isolated Antarctic and sub-Antarctic communities*. Medical doctoral thesis, University of New South Wales, Sydney.

Williams, D. L., Climie, A., Muller, H. K., & Lugg, D. J. (1986). Cell mediated immunity in healthy adults in Antarctica and the sub-Antarctic. *Journal of Clinical and Laboratory Immunology, 20*, 43–49.

World Health Organization. (1963). *Conference on medicine and public health in the Arctic and Antarctic* (Technical Report No. 253). Geneva: World Health Organization.

# 5

# The Research Program of the International Biomedical Expedition to the Antarctic (IBEA) and its Implications for Research in Outer Space

A. J. W. TAYLOR

Antarctica is a vast continent that is about 13.5 million km², and much the same size as the United States and Mexico combined. It is the coldest place on Earth, with the lowest temperature recorded at Vostock of −121° C. Unlike the Arctic, it is a landmass with an average ice thickness of 2 km rather than a central ocean with an average ice thickness of 3.35 m (Couper, 1983, pp. 62–63). It holds more than 90% of the world's ice, and were it to begin to thaw, some of the major capitols of the world would be flooded (Browne, 1984, pp. 45–48).

The continent captured the imagination of the 1892 Geographical Conference in London about the time that exploration in the Arctic was losing its appeal. Many explorations from European and Scandinavian countries and from Japan followed in a race to establish the territorial claims and to be the first to reach the South Pole. This heroic era of exploration gave way to the technological era and then to the modern scientific era. Pioneers Richard Byrd, Vivian Fuchs, and Paul-Emile Victor used machinery and sophisticated equipment to build a corpus of knowledge about the "white continent." Their focus was primarily on the natural sciences, but from their introspective accounts it is clear that they were concerned also with matters of the social sciences. The political desire to establish peaceful safeguards after World War II led to U.S. Operation High-Jump in the Antarctic in 1947–1948, and to U.S. Operation Deep Freeze there in 1958–1959 to coincide with the International Geophysical Year. These moves led to the construction of many permanent bases, the formulation of systematic research programs, the introduction of a cooperative international venture, and the suspension of squabbles over territorial ownership.

Behavioral science in Antarctica was established quickly as an equal partner with other sciences in the post-World War II years, thanks to the tireless work of Gunderson (1974), Owens (1975), and Rivolier (1975). Before that time, studies relied mainly on the recorded observations of medical officers and the introspective reports of expeditioners to touch upon matters of selection, performance, and follow-up of personnel (Taylor, 1987, Ch. 1).

The purpose of the present chapter is to focus upon the latest and the most comprehensive biomedical study that has ever been conducted in Antarctica (Rivolier, Goldsmith, Lugg, & Taylor, 1989). This study, the International Biomedical Expedition to Antarctica (IBEA), was organized in 1977 on the initiative of Dr. Jean Rivolier, at that time Chairman of the Working Group on Human Biology and Medicine of the Scientific Committee on Antarctic Research (SCAR). It was to be a complex and multidisciplinary research project to investigate human behavior during an expedition in the Antarctic. There had been few comprehensive studies done before of such behavior, and it was undertaken because of the growing interest both in the specifics of polar research and in the generalities of environmental stress.

## The IBEA

The general aims of the study were (1) to determine the nature and extent of human physiological adjustment to the cold; (2) to measure the effects of cold and isolation on physical and mental performance; and (3) to study the various individual and group psychological responses to stressful conditions. One specific aim of the study was to discover any preacclimatization effects from exposure to a series of cold baths.

The research had three separate phases. The first consisted of a 31-day period of nonstop laboratory examinations, experiments, and discussions at the Commonwealth Health Institute of the University of Sydney in Australia. The second consisted of a 72-day traverse on the polar plateau in French Antarctic territory. The third consisted of 13 days of follow-up laboratory studies and debriefing sessions back in Sydney.

## Subjects

The subjects were 12, mostly self-selected, biomedical scientists, all but two of whom had previous Antarctic experience. Eight of them were physicians with a range of specialties from physiology to high-altitude medicine, and the others were a biochemist, a physicist, a cameraman, and a technician. They had all to be biomedical scientists, because they were obliged to conduct their own experiments, as well as being subjects for each other. The participant–experimenter arrangement obviated the logistical problems that would otherwise have arisen had there been the conventional two groups of experimenters and subjects. It also promised to minimize the friction that sometimes arises between those groups (Connors, Harrison, & Akins, 1985).

The subjects were all male, since there was no pool of experienced female biomedical Antarctic researchers available at the time. But even had they been available, they would probably not have been selected — for experimental, logistic, and pragmatic reasons. Experimentally, the reduction of the number of subjects from one group of 12 males to two smaller groups of males and of females would have made for difficulty when trying to establish the statistical significance of the results. Logistically, the total number of subjects could not be increased with people of both sexes, because of the limits on life support systems that were available. Pragmatically, males were taken as subjects because they were still more likely than females to undertake hazardous fieldwork in Antarctica. Even though modern technology has made such fieldwork less hazardous today, and women now go to Antarctica to do the same range of work as men, the majority of field expeditioners are still men. Therefore, data gathered about men under field conditions retains high relevance.

The number of subjects was too small to allow a conventional randomization into experimental and control groups, but a "quasi-control" was arranged from a matched pool of 12 men from a collected pool of 114 university and medical school scientists and clinical psychologists from the Department of Justice and the hospital staff in Wellington (McCormick, 1983, pp. 66–81). These controls were matched on a 26–item biographical and occupational questionnaire. No baseline differences were found between experimental and control individuals in clinical tests of stress and arousal, symptom checklists, reaction times, and series completion tasks. The controls stayed at home with their families and continued at their usual occupations throughout the studies.

## Research Expectations

The expectations were that the entire group of 12 Antarctic subjects would show more indicators of stress than the controls when in the Antarctic than either before or after, and that those who were assigned to preacclimatizing cold baths would show less stress than those who were not. Stress was defined as the substantial imbalance between the demands made on individuals and their ability to cope (cf. McGrath, 1970, p. 17). It was conceptualized as the complex interaction of physical, physiological, psychophysiological, and psychological variables together with those of climate, clothing, environmental hazards, food, and shelter.

# Stress Parameters

Stress was measured by several biochemical, electronic, electrophysiological, mechanical, thermal, and paper-and-pencil tests. In turn, those tests were based on clinical, developmental, experimental, introspective, observational, and psychometric methods. Strange as it may seem to the uninitiated,

> . . . there is no method that gives us a royal road to the truth; no rule, technique, or set of principles that will ensure that we shall not fall into error. The most we can hope for are informal maxims, habits of mind, attitudes, and so forth, that constitute what we call objectivity, honesty, open–mindedness, etc., and which govern our practice in such a way that we fall into error less often and less readily. (Williams, 1983)

If multiple methods of measurement are used, the chances of error can be further reduced (Nay, 1979, p. 283). With the IBEA, the physical studies involved measures of weight change, detailed intake of basic food rations and supplements, sickness calls, and hematological and immunological reactions. The physiological measures consisted of blood flow and temperature reactions to thermal chambers, cold air, and cold water; functional respiratory gas values; sleep studies; reactions to noradrenalin; and cardiac and body temperature recordings. There were also studies of heat transfer through layers of clothing, and daily recordings of rest and activity.

The psychophysiological studies were designed to measure perception, attention, memory, reaction time, and problem solving. It was thought that these cognitive attributes might deteriorate when the subjects were under stress and affect the efficiency and accuracy of their behavioral performance. The studies used the Necker Cube test of perceptual ambiguity, the modified Stroop Test of color and word conflict, an estimate of 60-second time duration, the Vigil HP97 digit memory and string of digits comparison tests, push button reaction time to a light stimulus, and speed and accuracy of information processing with mental paper-folding and series completion paper-and-pencil tests.

The psychological measures were based upon conventional clinical, psychometric, and observational methods. The first consisted of intake interviews with subjects individually, and videotaped discussions with the group collectively. The interviews were conducted by psychologists in Paris and Sydney as dictated by language, and were based upon information from certain biographical medical, motivational, life change, and family questionnaires that subjects had completed in advance. These different sources of information were included to reveal any stress reactions from those quarters that might have compounded any stress from Antarctica. The videotaped group discussions took place in Sydney and Antarctica: The former, with the entire group, was conducted by an independent "examining" psychologist, and the latter by the psychologist IBEA member.

## Maintenance of Objectivity

In gathering their data and in making any interpretations, judgments, and opinions for the record from their individual and group encounters, the psychologists were obliged to refer to specific test items, incidents, and observations and to circumstances of group complexity. They were not permitted to rely upon their unsubstantiated clinical judgment because of the difficulty others might have in confirming their conclusions. Accordingly, they selected numerous tests and rating scales that were known to have been among the most reliable, valid, relevant, and appropriate for use in both consulting rooms and the field, and they introduced a few innovative tests on a trial basis.

The psychologists who interviewed the participants in Phase I were required to write confidential reports about the subjects individually and collectively and to make predictions about their ability to cope with forthcoming stress in Antarctica. They were not concerned with selection, because such matters had been left to the attention of the nominating committees, but they had to be satisfied that no subject would cause physical harm to himself or the others either from depression or aggression when in Antarctica. Although the examining psychologist in Sydney was so satisfied, he did find it necessary to depart from his given role to satisfy himself that the group had sufficient cohesion with which to face any interpersonal difficulties that might arise when in Antarctica.

In Phase III, when the group returned from Antarctica, the examining psychologist interviewed each of the subjects, conducted a follow-up group discussion, administered certain personality tests, and again prepared a confidential report.

## The Field Phase: Phase II

The major component of the research was the experience of a traverse in random pairs for 14-day periods, involving traveling on open skidoos and living in tents. These conditions promised a greater variety of critical stressors such as intense cold, high winds, geographic hazards, monotonous food, uncomfortable camping facilities, and greater isolation with more environmental contact than would be experienced at a base camp. Many of those important stressors might have been compromised had the biomedical studies been a subsidiary of any other research program.

However, there was substantial technical support in the form of a French Glaciological Expedition on hand. The function of that support was not to modify the physical, psychological, and social constraints of the research design but to provide transportation of food and petrol, to support a heated laboratory trailer, to maintain the transport, to monitor radio communications with the outside world, and to provide such emergency services as might be required. The personnel of such a support group were not involved as subjects in the research, nor did they have experimental limitations placed upon their food and comfort.

Some of the activity, blood, body weight, and sleep studies were continued during specified camping stops on the traverse. They were augmented with studies of heat transfer through layers of clothing and the monitoring of wind speed and temperature readings of the outside climate, as well as microclimatic readings of temperature inside tents, sleeping bags, and clothing.

Psychological observations in the field focused upon the attitudes, behavior, and work performance of each individual and on the formation of any subgroups of individuals. From time to time, the psychologist also completed standardized questionnaires on the adaptability of the individual subjects to the situation in which they currently were placed. At less frequent intervals, the other participants themselves completed exactly the same ratings as the psychologist about themselves and about their colleagues. They also provided carbon copies of their daily diary entries and of their periodic assessments of the project as it proceeded.

## Data Analysis and Presentation

Each experimenter was personally responsible for collecting, preserving, processing, interpreting, and sharing his data. This proved to be a formidable task within each of the four major participating disciplines long before the integration of data for each phase, and then for the entire research program, could be undertaken. The task was not made easier by the wide geographical dispersion of the international group of scientists during the data processing stage. The plan called for the separate sponsoring research organizations to process the data from experiments for which they were responsible and to forward them to the Chairman in Paris for distribution to any participant who requested them — with the exception of some of the more emotionally sensitive psychological data, about which it was agreed that confidentiality should be maintained. Any researcher who required data from another discipline that might have some bearing upon his own research was then able to make the appropriate requests for such data through the Paris "clearinghouse."

In each case, the data were prepared to examine different questions. The data analysis of the entire group was followed by analysis for the experimental cold bath group as compared to its controls, then for each of the subjects separately, and finally for any comparative groups such as the good and the poor performers who emerged at the end of the study. The latter were those who were judged from the records by independent psychologists not to have acquitted themselves as well, personally and interpersonally in Phases I, II, and III, as might have been expected.

To ensure a high degree of critical independence in the evaluation of psychological matters, no single researcher had immediate access to the full range of psychological data. Even when psychologists were given access to raw data, as with the Rorschach and Rozensweig's Picture–Frustration tests, they were encouraged to get them analyzed independently by other specialists. Conclusions based upon material from different areas of psychological inquiry were thus available for triangulation and comparison.

## Results

The data for separate experiments were processed by the researchers as arranged and then related within the series of studies within the disciplines. Some 80% of the experiments were brought to a satisfactory conclusion, and the remainder suffered the usual vicissitudes of being conducted in unstable field conditions. In general, the outcome of the extensive matrix of physical, physiological, psychophysiological, and psychological hypothesis tests was virtually negative.

1. The Antarctic phase of the expedition was neither more nor less stressful than the laboratory phase of the expedition.
2. The cold bath artificial acclimatization was only of initial benefit in enhancing the ability to withstand stress.
3. Higher or lower levels of stress did not appear to be related to adaptability as judged by the examining psychologists.
4. The stress levels reported by IBEA subjects were no higher than those reported by the scientists that remained at home.

The psychological studies of individual differences showed that (a) of the biographical items, past polar experience and age were the best predictors of self-reported minimal stress and high arousal; (b) of the standard clinical predictors, those used by the examining psychologist with the benefit of personal interviews were able to predict stress and adaptability more accurately than those used separately by other psychologists from test data alone; (c) of the psychometric predictors, the initial stress scores predicted later stress and arousal; the initial arousal scores predicted later stress and self-adaptation ratings; (d) the interpersonal distance scale predicted observer ratings and peer ratings; and (e) although the subjects were inclined towards the denial pole of the repression/sensitivity continuum when completing questionnaires about themselves, they were less defensive in completing questionnaires about others and in writing or speaking of them (Taylor, Robinson, & McCormick, 1986).

The psychological studies of group behavior showed that the group rejected one particular individual in the laboratory phase and a different individual in the field phase. Subdivisions that occurred between members of different national groups and within national groups in the field also carried over to the follow-up laboratory phase.

The individual and group conflicts and tensions were also clear to the psychologist examiner and to the psychologist observer. The examiner even found it necessary to modify his role and to intervene with group dynamics to halt disruption when he found some of the scientists threatening to disrupt particular experiments, to provide misleading responses, and to withdraw in protest from certain experiments altogether (as three of them actually did). One subject withdrew from the entire project as a matter of emergency, but for personal rather than interpersonal reasons. He had been selected for his occupational ability and social compatibility, but not for his environmental adaptability to Antarctic field conditions.

The subjects themselves wrote of their personal and interpersonal tensions in daily diaries, and featured them in reports they wrote at the end of each phase of the study. Their mutual animosity was such that, some five years after the event, one of the subjects reported to a medical conference that "serious tensions between erstwhile colleagues still exist" (Goldsmith, 1986). Some of that tension might have spilled over to family relationships, because no fewer than three of the subjects were known to have had disruptive relationships with their partners at home within a 16-month period afterwards (Taylor & McCormick, 1987).

Although stress is known to have behavioral, cognitive, health, physiological, organizational, and subjective effects (Bloom, 1985; Bradley & Cox, 1978), in the present study, the cognitive, physiological, and psychophysiological effects were not evident. Before some misguided researchers would be inclined therefore to dismiss the results that were demonstrated as being subjective and unimportant, they should be reminded that

. . . what the mechanist disparagingly calls "the subjective" is not that of which we are least, but rather of which we are *most* certain. . . . Undoubtedly there are good reasons for distinguishing the "Objective" from the "Subjective" phenomena when our purpose is to study the first. But there is no justification for calling only the one real (Krutch, 1956, pp. 122–123).

The most likely explanation for the lack of objective data — about subjective experience, other than the evacuation of 1 of the 12 subjects, the withdrawal of 3 others from experiments, and the evidence of bad feelings recorded on audio- and videotape and in free written form — is consistent with the Rahe and Arthur theory (1978). According to that theory, life situations present a series of stressors, only the most persistent of which filter through perceptual and psychological defenses to the psychophysiological and physiological domains. It follows that anyone inclined to dismiss the precursors as insignificant would be taking an unnecessarily limited approach to the study of human behavior and to the nature of potential disasters.

There is also the point that laboratory techniques and technologies do not always apply to everyday life (Hockey, 1983, p. 372). But even more important is that human beings have the capacity to exert short-term, and sometimes even long-term, cognitive control over potential stressors to prevent them from causing harm (Mandler, 1984). However, the more control they feel obliged to exert, and the longer they feel obliged to exert it, the less emotional energy they have available for attending to their everyday aspects of life.

Overall, there was the usual variability between individuals in responding, and the usual problem with small group data, but at this point it is helpful to recall Binder's advice to

. . . face our problems realistically and not retreat to the land of fashionable sterility, [to] learn to sweat over our data with an admixture of judgment and intuitive rumination, and accept the usefulness of particular data even when the level of analysis available for them is markedly below that available for other data in the empirical area (quoted by Gunderson, 1973, p. 190).

In following such advice, it is necessary to look for evidence of stress reducers that were used by the IBEA participants. According to Rice (1987), the personality variables of control, commitment, and challenge affect the particular methods that individuals adopt for coping with stress. Those able to control the situation, who are committed to the outcome and regard it positively as a challenge, together with those who are somewhat defensive in denying the significance of stress, are more likely to show fewer effects than others.

The IBEA subjects were mostly authoritative, responsible, self-selected volunteer scientists with a capacity for exercising situational control. They were very committed professionally to the outcome, and they valued the unique opportunity for participation in the enterprise. They were also defensive in not reporting their own reactions to stress while reporting them for others. In fact, there was a high positive correlation between sensitization and reported stress and high arousal, on the one hand, and repression, unreported stress, and low arousal on the other. In the judgment of the field psychologist, and of their teammates, the sensitizers judged themselves harshly, but the repressors did not judge themselves harshly enough.

Evidently, the cost of the sensitivity and repression were the prolonged, unsatisfactory relationships that developed between members, even affecting the good relationships that some of them had previously established with each other and with their families. In these circumstances, it is difficult not to accept Pozner's (1965) conclusion that "the critical, mental stresses of exploration are not so much those implicit in the impact on the human being of climate geography or disease as in the complexity of . . . relationships."

These findings point to problems that can arise from overdemanding researchers and overdemanding research schedules. They point to the specific need for the proper selection of personnel with sufficient ability, stability, and compatibility to provide group cohesion and mutual support that will offset stress rather than cause it. The assessment of stress should be related to levels of repression and sensitization, and use a variety of simple scales by which interpersonal measures of adaptability and performance could be obtained.

The training of the personnel should include some experience in group dynamics that might be used when appropriate to reduce conflict and tension. Research programs should be so arranged as to give opportunities for regular periods of rest and relaxation. Any procedures that involve invasive techniques should be explained carefully to the personnel in advance and the procedures be conducted with sufficient skill as to cause no physical or psychological harm (Taylor & McCormick, 1985). Projects involving interdisciplinary and international participants should allow sufficient lead time for them to reach a firm understanding of the common research concepts and methods that they will be expected to use—and for them to become bilingual.

During the conduct of the research, contact between subjects and their partners at home should be maintained rather than discouraged, both to reduce emotional uncertainty and to utilize a possible source of emotional support when needed. Obviously, there is much to be gained from including families as respondents in isolation research.

Finally, on their return the expeditioners should all receive equal shares of any public acclaim, recognition, and reward. They should also have regular debriefing sessions and continuing supportive attention as needed to help them resettle.

Although the IBEA was organized and conducted by part-time researchers with very limited budgets, it might provide some pointers for the more extensive and substantial National Aeronautics and Space Administration (NASA) program. For example, it is paramount for people in spacecraft, in space stations, and eventually in space colonies to remember that they are people, and for scientists conducting experiments to remember it, too. Evidence is hard to come by, except anecdotally, but there was a familiar if ominous ring about the report from a Dutch scientist aboard U.S. Challenger on November 2, 1985, who refused to comply with instructions to rest and said, "Thank you for your concern . . . but I am over 18 and I'm getting 5 or 6 hours of sleep and that's enough." There was also the admission in a news broadcast from the West German director of the project involving 76 experiments in seven days that "we may have been too ambitious in planning the experiments for this mission . . . our colleagues in space are overworked and overburdened . . . they and the experimenters need time to think."

Subject–ground control tension is also suspected to have induced the crew of Skylab 4 to cut off all communication for 24 hours, but there is no evidence that the phenomenon was a dependent variable in a specific study of stress. As a matter of fact, the entire Skylab medical program seems to have included no psychological or psychophysiological studies of stress. No relevant key word appears in the index of the bound, 491-page report of the Skylab program (Johnston & Dietlein, 1977), although a flight surgeon, Hordinsky (1977, p. 133), did report that "new experiments, stowage confusion, on board equipment malfunctioning and the sheer length of the mission were all contributing factors to produce psychological stresses which were slowly resolved over the first half of the mission."

The onset and resolution of stress among people in space are too important to be treated lightly. The failure of NASA to give behavioral science an equal footing with biological and natural sciences in space research is an omission that needs to be rectified, and until that has been done, few of the pointers from the IBEA research will be construed as sufficiently relevant to be transferred to that sphere of operations.

To a behavioral scientist, the signs of potential stress among people in space are not exceptional, but the passing reference to its resolution — and the absence of specific studies to discover the precise variables — are. This is especially so when it was claimed that the Skylab experiments "gave great confidence that man can perform effectively for long periods of time in space if his health is properly maintained and his bodily needs satisfied" (Kraft, 1977, p. v), and provided the general conclusion that "man adapts well to, and functions effectively in, the space environment for time periods approaching 3 months" (Dietlein, 1977, p. 416).

It must freely be acknowledged that the Skylab experiments did detail the physiological consequences of weightlessness, but they ignored the psychological and psychophysiological parameters that the IBEA found necessary to monitor. It is difficult to think that the Russians have ignored those factors (Aldasheva, 1984). Certainly, there have been plaintive appeals for NASA to remedy the omissions from such well-recognized U.S. researchers as Rasmussen (1973), Helmreich (1983), Santy (1983), Connors, Harrison, and Akins (1985), and Harrison (1986). Why, then, have they not succeeded? And why has NASA not adopted the interdisciplinary policies of the United States Army, Navy, and Air Force that have generated so much worthwhile applied research? And finally, if that is the case, what chance is there of NASA's learning from the small group of part-time biomedical researchers known collectively as the IBEA?

The answer must involve the conceptual model of human behavior that NASA adopted — and that organization could make up for lost time and surge ahead if it were to reconsider its stance. To do this it would need to adopt the mainstream General Systems Model of knowledge, in which contributions from different disciplines were given mutual respect, evaluated, and integrated (Sundberg, Taplin, & Tyler, 1983; Warheit, 1979). The reconsideration is a difficult matter, because "methodological chauvinists" (Williams, 1983) do not appreciate the value of "soft data" and the subsequent sharing of prestigious research areas. There is no reason why they should be spared the difficulty — an alternative is for them to give way to more flexible researchers who will not hold up scientific progress. Having changed their research paradigm, NASA researchers will know what lessons they themselves might draw from the IBEA, and I look forward to reading about them.

## References

Aldasheva, A. A. (1984). Strategy of psychological adaptation to Antarctic conditions. *Human Physiology, 10*(1), 12–18.

Bloom, B. L. (1985). *Stressful life event theory and research: Implications for primary care*. Rockville, MD: National Institute of Mental Health.

Bradley, C., & Cox, T. (1978). Stress and health. In T. Cox (Ed.), *Stress* (Ch. 4). London: Macmillan.

Browne, T. (Ed.). (1984). *The mind alive encyclopedia: The earth*. London: Marshall Cavendish.

Connors, M. M., Harrison, A. A., & Akins, F. R. (1985). *Living aloft: Human requirements for extended spaceflight* (NASA SP-483). Washington, DC: National Aeronautics and Space Administration.

Couper, A. (Ed.). (1983). *The Times atlas of the oceans*. London: Times Books.

Dietlein, L. F. (1977). Skylab: A beginning. In R. S. Johnston & L. F. Dietlein (Eds.), *Biomedical results from Skylab*. (Ch. 40). Washington, DC: National Aeronautics and Space Administration.

Goldsmith, R. (1986, November). *Isolation in the cold of 12 men in the cold*. Annual conference abstract. London: British Medical Association.

Gunderson, E. K. E. (1973). Individual behavior in confined or isolated groups. In J. E. Rasmussen (Ed.), *Man in isolation and confinement* (Ch. 5). Chicago: Aldine.

Gunderson, E. K. E. (1974). Psychological studies in Antarctica. In E. K. E. Gunderson (Ed.), *Human adaptation to Antarctic conditions* (pp. 115–131). Boston: Heffernan Press.

Harrison, A. A. (1986). On resistance to the involvement of personality, social, and organizational psychologists in the U.S. space program. *Journal of Social Behavior and Personality, 1*, 315–324.

Helmreich, R. L. (1983). Applying psychology to outer space: Unfulfilled promises revisited. *American Psychologist, 38*, 445–450.

Hockey, R. (1983). *Stress and fatigue in human performance*. New York: Wiley.

Hordinsky, J. R. (1977). Skylab crew health—Crew surgeon's reports. In R. S. Johnston & L. F. Dietlein (Eds.), *Biomedical results from Skylab* (Ch. 5). Washington, DC: National Aeronautics and Space Administration.

Johnston, R. S., & Dietlein, L. F. (Eds.). (1977). *Biomedical results from Skylab*. Washington, DC: National Aeronautics and Space Administration.

Kraft, C. C. (1977). Foreword. In R. S. Johnston & L. F. Dietlein (Eds.), *Biomedical results from Skylab*. Washington, DC: National Aeronautics and Space Administration.

Krutch, J. W. (1956). *The measure of man: On freedom, human values, survival and modern temper*. London: Alvin Redman.

Mandler, G. (1984). *Minds and body: Psychology of emotions and stress*. New York: Norton.

McCormick, I. A. (1983). *Psychological aspects of stress in the Antarctic*. Doctoral thesis, Victoria University of Wellington.

McGrath, J. E. (Ed.). (1970). *Social and psychological factors in stress*. New York: Holt Rinehart & Winston.

Nay, W. R. (1979). *Multimethod clinical assessment*. New York: Gardner.

Owens, A. G. (1975). *The performance and selection of men in small Antarctic groups* (Report 4/47). Melbourne: Australian Military Forces, Psychological Research Unit.

Pozner, H. (1965). Mental fitness. In O. G. Edholm & A. L. Bacharach (Eds.), *A practical guide for those going on expeditions* (pp. 77–97). Bristol: Wright.

Rahe, R. H., & Arthur, R. J. (1978). Life change and illness studies: Past history and future directions. *Journal of Human Stress*, March, 3–15.

Rasmussen, J. E. (Ed.). (1973). *Man in isolation and confinement*. Chicago: Aldine.

Rice, P. L. (1987). *Stress and health: Principles and practice for coping and wellness*. Belmont, CA: Brooks/Cole.

Rivolier, J. (1975). *Selection et adaptation psychologiques des sujects vivant en groups isoles en vivernage dans l'Antarctique*. Paris: Comite Nationale Francais Reserche Antarctique.

Rivolier, J., Goldsmith, R., Lugg, D., & Taylor, A. J. W. (Eds.). (1989). *Man in the Antarctic: The scientific work of the International Biomedical Expedition to the Antarctic*. London: Taylor and Francis.

Santy, P. (1983). The journey out and in: Psychiatry and space exploration. *American Journal of Psychiatry, 140*, 519–527.

Sundberg, N. D., Taplin, J. R., & Tyler, L. E. (1983). *Introduction to clinical psychology: Perspectives and contributions to human services*. Englewood Cliffs, NJ: Prentice-Hall.

Taylor, A. J. W. (1987). *Antarctic psychology*. Wellington: Department of Scientific and Industrial Research.

Taylor, A. J. W., & McCormick, I. A. (1985). Human experimentation during the International Biomedical Expedition to the Antarctic (IBEA). *Journal of Human Stress, 11(4)*, 161–164.

Taylor, A. J. W., & McCormick, I. A. (1987). The reactions of family partners to Antarctic expeditioners. *Polar Record, 23*, 691–700.

Taylor, A. J. W., Robinson, R., & McCormick, I. A. (1986). Written personal narratives as research documents: The case for their restoration. *International Review of Applied Psychology, 35*, 197–208.

Warheit, G. (1979). Life events, coping, stress and depressive symptomatology. *American Journal of Psychiatry, 136*, 502–507.

Williams, G. (1983). Methodological chauvinism in the philosophy of science. *British Journal of Medical Psychology, 56*, 293–297.

# 6

# The Antarctic Experience

SIDNEY M. BLAIR

Contained environments such as space vehicles and Antarctic winter-over stations share characteristics that cause similar human problems for their inhabitants. All contained environments are stressful. Three important factors that influence the type and severity of stressors in a contained environment are the kind of hostile environment from which the contained environment protects its inhabitants, the mission of the contained environment, and communications between the contained environment and the outside friendly environment. The threat of the hostile environment forces physical constraints on design and use of the contained environment. The mission of the contained environment configures community organization for the inhabitants. Communications determine the locus of control inside or outside the contained environment. After differing physical constraints, differing community organization, and differing patterns of communication are carefully analyzed and evaluated, knowledge about one contained environment can be applied to plans for another contained environment.

In this chapter, we will be concerned with identifying types of human dysfunctions occurring in contained environments, with finding and suggesting reasons why these dysfunctions occur, and with examining ways in which dysfunctions can be prevented or corrected. When the United States Air Force began to design contained environments for the protection of medical personnel and casualties during chemical warfare, we reviewed experience with existing contained environments and, particularly, the well-documented experience with winter-over in the isolation, cold, and dark of Antarctica. That review with its list of references and detailed recommendations for the Air Force's contained environment, the Survivable Chemical Protection Shelter-Medical (SCPS-M), will be published elsewhere, but it will be useful here to describe some features of the Antarctic experience that are also of relevance to the design and use of a space station.

## Life in Contained Environments

It is intuitive that life in a contained environment is an adverse experience and may lead to human dysfunction: We put people in confinement as a punishment and talk colloquially about the dysfunctional states of having "cabin fever" or being "stir crazy." Some of the stressors of a contained environment are obvious: danger from a surrounding hostile environment, limitation of available life support, cramped living spaces and enforced intimacy with individuals not of our choosing, lack of usual social and family supports, reduced recreational and social activities, artificial light or artificially purified air, and inability to move out of the contained environment without the aid or permission of some outside authority. Some of the stressors are less immediately obvious: Inhabitants of a contained environment lack the variety of sensory input and diversity of motor activity that are important for maintaining optimal thinking, feeling, and behavior in the human.

### *Human Dysfunction in Antarctica*

Review of Antarctic experience indicates that unwanted changes in thinking, feeling, and behavior were common since the earliest explorations. The success of an Antarctic station depends on the absence of these unwanted changes or, to view things in an operational and positive manner, by work performance in service of the mission of the Antarctic station. If we limit our examination to modern Antarctic stations, where the hostility of the cold, dark environment is well defended against and the contained environment itself becomes more the focus of attention, we may examine some of the unwanted changes in detail.

Disturbances in vegetative functions such as appetite and sleep are common during winter-over. Food is very important in Antarctica, and the reasons are not hard to understand: Food is one of the few gratifications available, and the mess hall is a communal area that becomes an important social center. Increased food intake coupled with decreased activity leads to a weight gain in most winter-over personnel. Because food is important, the persons who are responsible for providing food become correspondingly important, and their adequate performance is crucial to maintaining morale.

Sleep disturbances are so frequent in Antarctica as to be an expected part of the discomforts of winter-over and have been variously attributed to decreased activity and to loss of normal light–dark and ambient temperature cycles. Poor sleep is rarely severely distressing to the insomniac, but insomniacs who choose to be active at odd hours can be painfully disruptive to others who want to sleep. Those who can arrange their work schedules so that they can sleep at any time they wish are sometimes much resented by those who must adhere to regular shifts.

Disorders of mood, such as anxiety and depression, are also so common in Antarctica that they are not considered by the winter-over group to be particularly pathological, and when symptoms are evaluated by standard rating scales, they seldom are scored as "severe." When depression manifests itself by social withdrawal, hostility, irritability, and decrease in motivation and work performance, the depression may then become a significant disruption for the community, even when the subjective distress of the depressed individual is not great.

Disorders of thinking and cognitive disturbances, when tested objectively, tend to be mild. Nevertheless, personnel often complain of preoccupation, poor memory, poor concentration, and impaired attention. Judgments are increasingly based on emotional considerations rather than on objective facts. One cognitive disturbance that may have an impact beyond its apparent severity is disturbance of sense of time. The origin of this dysfunction is not clear, and it may in part be simply a habit pattern resulting from having much time available. Some individuals describe a conscious attempt to ration their activities so that available activities will fill the days and weeks of winter-over. Many who winter-over act as if the time available to them for a task were unlimited and do not adhere to schedules. They feel as if they were moving at a normal pace, but to outside observers, they seem to be moving very slowly indeed. This change in sense of time may occasion conflict with outside authorities who are concerned with productivity. The winter-over personnel feel they are working very hard and not being recognized for their good work; the outsiders see only poor productivity.

Psychosomatic disorders can be severe, especially when personnel attempt work that is beyond their competence. When these severe psychosomatic disorders impair work performance, they have a significant impact on the community. Other types of severe psychological disorders, such as overt psychosis, are essentially unknown since personnel screening procedures were instituted, and these disorders usually occur in younger men and within 8 weeks after their arrival in Antarctica.

Substance abuse in Antarctica is both a moral and a practical problem. Because individual human performance may be a life-and-death matter for the community as a whole, the presence of mind-altering drugs is a threat, but community norms of solidarity and tolerance may prevent effective response by either community or leader in the face of the threat. When intoxicants such as alcohol are legally present, they are rationalized as an aid to relaxation and recreation. However, intoxicated behavior is tolerated poorly in the contained environment, and this rationalization is not supported by any verifiable improvement in morale or work efficiency. When illegal intoxicants are present, the authority of the leadership is compromised by a situation that is realistically very difficult to control.

It is not only during the winter-over period that experience in Antarctica may have a psychological impact. There have been far too few studies of long-term psychological changes after winter-over, but every gathering of Old Antarctic Explorers (known as OAEs) has at least a few stories of personnel who have suffered prolonged insomnia, depression, alcoholism, or failure to re-adapt to the conditions of ordinary life. That there may well be long-term ill effects from stressful life experience is now well recognized; what remain to be studied are whether the Antarctic experience has a specific impact and how this impact can be identified and ameliorated.

## How Dysfunction in Antarctica Is Controlled

Dysfunction can be managed by prevention, by treatment, and by measures that decrease long-term disability.

Major emphasis has been given to prevention of psychopathology during winter-over. During the International Geophysical Year 1957–1958, an overt psychosis in one of the winter-over personnel was very disruptive, and in subsequent years, winter-over candidates were subjected to a psychiatric screening procedure with the initial intention of preventing further occurrence of severe illness during winter-over. This initial goal was reached, and over the next 30 years, the screening program gradually moved toward an attempt to select optimal personnel for winter-over. At the end of each winter-over period, a psychiatrist or psychologist was sent to each station to debrief the personnel, so that screening procedures were constantly validated and improved.

All candidates for winter-over are preselected by the requirement that they have already acquired fairly high-level job skills. All candidates are self-selected in that they are seeking to work under climatic, vocational, and social conditions that are generally recognized as unusual and stressful. The actual psychiatric screening procedure has varied in detail over the years, particularly in that various paper-and-pencil psychological tests have been favored. Two screening procedures are now considered to be of proven worth: One is a pair of interviews, one by a psychiatrist and one by a psychologist; and the other is a questionnaire concerning biographical data and avocational preferences. The total examination looks for the favorable elements of task motivation, social compatibility, and emotional composure and the unfavorable elements of rigidity of personality, excess enthusiasm, and substance abuse. The good candidate likes his work and is interested mainly in doing that. He is comfortable in conventional social situations but has neither a great need nor a dislike for socializing. He can tolerate change but does not try to change others. Those who do best during winter-over are often not very interesting people—they do their work and, afterwards, drink a few beers and "shoot the breeze" or watch movies with their buddies. In modern Antarctica, there is little room for people who are testing limits of their own endurance, of social situations, or of their professions. Antarctica is a very task-oriented place, and the tasks are decided long before winter-over begins.

Selection of leaders for winter-over is a special problem. Long lists of desirable characteristics have been made, but the sum of it all seems to be that the best leaders let their crews do their work with minimal interference but recognize when group activity needs to be organized and organize that activity.

The psychiatric screening for winter-over in the Antarctic has an effect that goes beyond improved personnel selection. The examinations are part of the winter-over culture, they discourage some candidates who might otherwise apply, and they remind everyone that winter-over is a special situation with special requirements. The candidates discuss among themselves their ideas of what is expected by the examiners and, in this way, reach some awareness of the stressors they will face and of what may be expected of them in coping with these stressors.

There is little doubt that the selection process has been a success, but careful review of the available literature concerning the Antarctic winter-over makes it clear that many types of dysfunctional thinking, feeling, and behavior are still prevalent. It may be that a wish to emphasize the success of personnel screening has led to a failure to critically evaluate mild to moderately severe degrees of dysfunction and the ways in which the winter-over community copes with this dysfunction.

When one looks around an Antarctic winter-over station and tries to identify the measures that have consciously been taken to prevent or ameliorate the psychological impact of winter-over, one sees little in evidence. Nevertheless, important things have evolved over time and are embedded in the customs and traditions of the station. It is probably important that any contained environment be given an opportunity to evolve its own set of customs and traditions and gain its own specific adaptive equilibrium.

Group identity is a stabilizing factor in any community. In Antarctica, the first determinant of group identity is the differentiation of those who will winter-over from those who will not. During the summer, the winter-over group identifies itself and begins to make tentative contacts under conditions that are much less confined and stressful than those of winter. Substitutes who come in at the last moment for winter-over are viewed as outsiders, and if they adjust favorably during winter-over, this is deemed worthy of comment.

Once winter begins, the predominating organizing force is work. The winter-over society should be viewed as a constellation of subgroups, and those who work together have a natural community of interest and usually have a geographic center for their activity. They often acquire a group personality with which an individual can identify — or against which he can rebel. Educational and ethnic background, berthing arrangements, and especially preference for various types of music are also important organizing principles. Subgroups tend to be stable once formed and, for the most part, are a positive influence in the lives of individuals, for whom the subgroups are often family surrogates with identifiable parental figures and a hierarchy of siblings.

The importance of work in Antarctica is paramount. The personnel are selected to be work oriented, and the work ethic is pervasive in the community. Individuals must accomplish their own work (which may have practical importance to the maintenance or survival of the station) and must also do their part in communal work. Communal projects are self–generating; to outside observers they may appear wasteful of valuable resources, but to those involved they provide a necessary means of gaining visible community involvement and recognition.

Within the community, privacy is hard to obtain and is highly valued. Those who work in isolated locations, and especially those who are able to organize their own cooking facilities in these locations, are viewed as particularly fortunate. The workplace often becomes the most private place available to an individual and will become de facto home for that person.

In Antarctica, relationships with the outside friendly environment are ambivalent, with some weighting on the side of hostility. Those who go to winter-over usually do not do so with the intention of maintaining close contact with the rest of the world. Except for those who are in the business of communications, such as leaders and radio operators, winter-over personnel narrow their interest in the outside world. There is a pervasive feeling that nothing can be done about outside events, and with this comes a reluctance to hear bad news from the outside. Contacts with the outside world, such as the midwinter air drop, may be eagerly awaited but are always disappointing in the event and are usually followed by feelings of depression. The ease of communication afforded by modern technology is a mixed blessing. Good communication makes the locus of control ambiguous, and both outside authority and the winter–over group may feel that only they are adequate judges of a problem situation. Conflict is almost inevitable, because locus of control for contained environments is a problem for which adequate rules have not been worked out.

The community usually manages human dysfunction with nonmedical resources. The available medical personnel rarely have special training that would prepare them to help, and they are rarely consulted unless the disorder has some physiological component that would seem to make medical intervention appropriate. For the most part, the dysfunctions are viewed by the community as being expected reactions to life stressors such as isolation. The way in which the community manages dysfunction has had little specific study and remains a rich and important area for investigation. The major maneuvers involve social isolation of dysfunctional individuals, with specific but not explicit assignment of caretakers who provide for the well-being and safety of the individual and the community. Because work performance is seen to be essential to survival of the community, the individual is usually removed from the workplace, his work is taken over by others, and some substitute but nonessential role is given to him. All these things are accomplished in a parsimonious manner and with minimum impairment of individual status and dignity. Everything may be done without notification or involvement of the designated station leaders, but the leaders are rarely unaware that something is amiss.

## Application of the Antarctic Experience to the Design of Other Contained Microenvironments

The first lesson to be learned from the Antarctic experience is that it is worthwhile to try and avoid human dysfunction in contained environments. The major means used to avoid dysfunction in Antarctica has been selection of personnel, with positive selection for those who are job oriented, conventionally social, and minimally emotional and negative selection for those who are overly enthusiastic, rigid, or substance abusers. Even though the community organization is not purposefully manipulated in Antarctica, experience has shown that identifiable aspects of community organization function to stabilize the community and help to manage dysfunction that is manifest. Minor degrees of dysfunction are common in the contained environment of Antarctica, are managed adequately by the community, and do not seriously impair the mission of the winter-over group.

As these lessons are applied to new contained environments such as the SCPS-M unit and the space station, there will be some significant factors to consider. The SCPS-M unit will have to accept occupants who are not selected — at best the population can be given some appropriate training for life in a contained environment. For the space station, the pool of individuals trained to do a particular job may be so small that essentially no selection is possible. All new contained environments lack the core of custom and tradition that stabilizes the Antarctic community from the first moments of its formation and provides that community with an expectation for success and techniques for coping with dysfunctional members. Even the most realistic exercises of new contained environments usually fail to permit the community to organize itself, partly because it is difficult to mimic realistically the kinds of communication that will exist between the contained environment and the outside world. Once the physical constraints of a new confined environment, the organization of the community, and the locus of control are observed and understood, then one can make concrete recommendations concerning manipulations of living conditions, possible within the constraints of the contained environment, that will contribute to optimal function of individuals in that environment. These recommendations will concern criteria for selection of personnel, design of living and work spaces, scheduling of activities, balance of activity and rest, recreation, stimulus level, and internal and external communications. The points always to be emphasized are that the mission of the contained environment, that is, the work to be done, is the major organizing factor for the community and that many important recommendations will depend on the organization the community adopts in doing its work.

# 7

# Personnel Deployment Systems: Managing People in Polar and Outer Space Settings

PHILIP R. HARRIS

A recent issue of *Canada Today* contains a vivid illustration of life in polar settings (Kelly, 1986):

Miners on Little Cornwallis Islands — Since 1981 these Canadians work at the Polaris lead and zinc mines, some 875 miles below the North Pole — one of the northernmost and richest mines in the world. The $150 million investment is expensive because the 200 workers must be protected from loneliness and isolation, as well as the elements. Despite temperatures of 50 below, winds at 70 mph, mining work at 500 feet below the surface, and severe outside travel, there are waiting lists of hundreds to apply for positions from cooks and miners to metallurgists and geologists. This is due, in part, to the very high pay, two week vacation flights every ten weeks on assignment, and luxurious living conditions and food in the residence building which includes basketball courts, pool, saunas, lounges, and jogging tracks.

Within decades, we may be reading comparable stories about scientists at a lunar outpost or workers at an asteroid mine. The survival and adjustment of such space pioneers could be enhanced if contemporary scholars could learn more about how people get deployed to polar regions such as described, how they perform when there, and how they readjust after they return home. We are all aware of the high value of the behavioral literature on spaceflight, polar, and submarine environments. However, there is another important literature: that which addresses the foreign deployment of executives, technicians, scholars, and volunteers (Harris & Moran, 1991; Johnson, 1970; Moran & Harris, 1982; Torbiorn, 1982; Ward, 1984). To illustrate the relevance of such studies, we can consider the research on expatriates conducted by Dr. Rosalie L. Tung (1982, 1988). Professor Tung studied 80 U.S. multinational corporations and discovered that more than half had high failure rates on expatriate assignments. Seven percent of the corporations reported as high as a 30% recall rate, and more than half reported a 10 to 20% recall rate. The American managers who were unable to perform effectively abroad had several different kinds of problems: (1) inability of the manager or spouse to adjust to a different physical or cultural environment; (2) family-related difficulties; (3) personality problems or emotional immaturity; (4) inability to cope with managerial responsibilities abroad and lack of motivation to work there; and (5) lack of technical competence (Tung, 1987).

Tung's findings are consistent with similar relocation studies, which attribute such maladjustment and high premature return rate on foreign postings to (1) poor selection and training for the overseas assignment; (2) overemphasis on technical competence to the disregard of other qualities that ensure effective cross-cultural performance; and (3) short duration of such assignments and overconcern with repatriation.

Tung then compared her American results with results of comparable surveys of 29 West German and 35 Japanese transnational firms. The former reported an average expatriate failure rate ranging from under 5% to 10%, while most of the latter reported failure rates of under 5%, and the maximum reported failure rate was under 20%. She identified several reasons for the lower failure rates among European and Japanese relative to American expatriate managers: (1) longer term orientation regarding overall planning and performance assessment; (2) more rigorous training programs to prepare candidates for overseas assignments; (3) provision of a comprehensive expatriate support system; (4) overall better qualification of candidates for overseas work, including foreign language capability; and (5) emotional and social support from both the family and the sponsoring organization.

Tung's findings confirm my own foreign deployment research (Harris & Moran, 1991; Moran & Harris, 1982). Premature return of expatriates is a critical managerial issue that has serious implications for polar and outer space assignments. Depending on place and circumstances, researchers estimate that it costs governmental agencies and private corporations between $50,000 and $200,000 per employee or family to bring such persons back home ahead of schedule — and this is from normal, or foreign, locations.

There are ways to reduce such costs. Yet, I suspect that there has been little "technology transfer" of such research to those agencies that currently send people to polar, underseas, and outer space regions. From the perspective of deploying people to polar or space sites, the sponsors have much to gain by examining the foreign deployment, or expatriate, literature (Furnham & Bochner 1986; Holmes, 1978; Johnson, 1970; Russell, 1978; Tung, 1982, 1988).

The movement of large masses of people around this planet has spurred increasing interest and investment by international corporations and associations in the phenomenon of culture/reentry shock. When people are rapidly transported from their home culture to strange and alien environments abroad, they may experience severe disorientation, confusion, and anxiety (Furnham & Bochner, 1986). Very little appears to have been done in the area of Antarctic or space "shock" (Nicogassian, Huntoon, & Pool, 1989; White, 1987). Another area of terrestrial investigation that has implications for space living is that which addresses the return from expatriate living (Austin, 1987). Ample reports exist from the Peace Corps, the military, and transnational organizations that some personnel experience reentry shock when reassigned from a host to a home culture. It is reasonable, then, to project that readaptation to Earth after long-duration spaceflights will necessitate innovative programs to cope with the physical and psychological effects of living aloft (Harris, 1986b).

Perhaps the basic deployment issue is how to reduce stress on a person when he or she leaves or returns to a home base, whether on this planet or another. The traveler's sense of identity is threatened when he or she is removed from the comfortable and familiar and thrust into the unknown and uncertain. Such expatriates, especially when away for many months or years, usually go through a transitional experience that includes phases of growing awareness of differences, rage, introspection, and, eventually, integration or disintegration. As a result, many multinational businesses and foundations have developed relocation services to facilitate acculturation of their personnel to new cultural changes and challenges.

Although it is unlikely, for the moment, that spacefarers will have to deal with extraterrestrial "foreigners," they will have to increasingly cope with and adapt to the unique cultural environment of space such as outlined in Figure 7.1 (Harris, 1986a), which utilizes the Moon as a background. Strategies, policies, and programs can be devised that facilitate extraterrestrial deployment and limit the psychological shock of isolation, loneliness, and strangeness of prolonged living on the high frontier. Whether in remote terrestrial or extraterrestrial environments, planners should be studying ways to reduce social and health problems (both mental and physical) while optimizing performance in isolated and confined circumstances. Research should be directed, especially, to sensory deprivation in isolated, confined environments.

## Antarctica as a Laboratory

Currently, Antarctica may be the best deployment laboratory for behavioral research analogous to the challenges inherent in space habitation. However, the scope of human behavior studies in the South Pole regions needs to be expanded and to become more systematized and comparative. For example, within the various institutions sending Americans to Antarctica, are there synergistic planning and analysis of deployment issues among the sponsoring agencies? How much sharing and cooperation on recruitment and

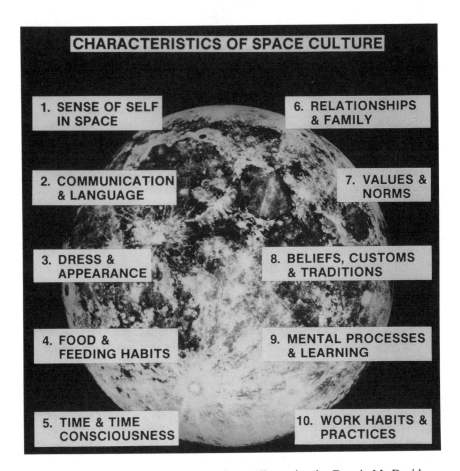

FIGURE 7.1. Characteristics of space culture. Illustration by Dennis M. Davidson, aerospace illustrator.

selection, for example, exists between ITT Corporation (ITT), a National Science Foundation (NSF) contractor, and the United States Navy? ITT Antarctic Services advertises in the press for those with engineering and mechanical backgrounds who can manage plant facilities in remote, self-sustaining research stations; who can exercise organizational and leadership skills consistent with the requirements of a small, closed community; who have the education and academic interest to interface successfully with diverse scientific investigators; who have the flexibility to react and manage effectively the fast-paced, changing, and unusual site operations on a 7-day-per-week basis. This advertisement for a year's Antarctic assignment is not unlike that which may appear someday in the media for technical personnel to go to a space station or a base on the Moon or Mars (Harris, 1987a).

The issue I raise for consideration now is what does ITT do in its assessment process to ensure that qualified people are indeed hired? What does it do to ensure the effectiveness of that new hire on site, and how does it help that employee upon return to normal civilian life? Is there a *system* to this process, and is it applicable not only to space but also to other organizations who send personnel to the Antarctic? Are the various agencies engaged in such deployment sharing information and insight and comparing their experience with the experience of other national groups serving at the North or South Pole? How much ongoing human factor data gathering is occurring at polar research installations? Are sponsoring entities even aware of the cross-cultural literature on relocation? Is there utilization of the Canadian International Development Agency's predeparture program? This is intended to instill seven skills: (1) to communicate respect; (2) to be nonjudgmental; (3) to personalize knowledge and perceptions; (4) to convey empathy; (5) to practice role flexibility; (6) to demonstrate reciprocal concern; and (7) to tolerate ambiguity.

## Implications for Space Living

Within the human family today, only a select group of people have actually flown into space and lived there (Baker, 1985). Whether called astronauts or cosmonauts, our extraterrestrial experience is very limited — about 100 Russians and 100 Americans, most of whom have been there only for a short time. Currently, the Soviets possess the long-duration record for manned flights by staying at their *Mir* space hotel, or station, for 5 to 12 months. If human presence is to be expanded and extended, then behavioral science research on deployment and acculturation should be increased now. In preparation for the multitudes that will begin to go into space during the 21st century, consideration should be given to people relocation efforts that go beyond the astronaut corps. If the National Aeronautics and Space Administration (NASA) is to maintain a leadership position in controlling or guiding the human access to space, then it must move beyond its narrow human factors research (Pitts, 1985) and studies of the human role in space (S. E. Hall, 1985). Policies, practices, and programs that have been suitable in the past for astronauts will not necessarily be suitable in the future for scientists, contractors, and other civilians who may gain entry to space. Antarctica is a good place to begin.

Before mass migration aloft, the Space Station *Freedom*, to be erected in the late 1990s, could become another orbiting laboratory for studying deployment issues, as well as for designing and creating a human habitation amenable to long-duration stays beyond the Earth's atmosphere (Harris, 1987c). What is learned in this prototype environment would be useful for later bases to be established on the Moon and Mars, as well as for future planetary settlements. NASA envisions an international space station with inhabitants who may live there for 6 months or more, though there is a probability of rotation on the average of every 90 days. Current plans call for visitors from Earth coming and going 4 to 6 times a year. Apart from the astronauts, a variety of mission specialists, "technauts," and "VIPs" may be anticipated. Who will or should go aloft for this purpose? How will the station inhabitants be supported – physically, psychologically, socially, and financially? What guidance and assistance is to be provided to family dependents while spacefarers are aloft for longer and longer time periods? What preparation and counsel is to be provided to these space travelers and their families not only prior to launch but also prior to reentry at the space station and later back on Earth? What are the implications of this deployment process for larger, more permanent space communities that will emerge? The beginning studies are under way on crew factors at McDonnell Douglas Aerospace in Huntington Beach, California, as well as at "manned" systems in Boeing Aerospace, Huntsville, Alabama.

Impending unprecedented human experiences of isolation and confinement require that positive programs be in place to ensure the safety and quality of life in space, while counteracting impairment of mental/emotional performance. Apart from the American and Soviet short-duration flight experience in space, Antarctica offers the best terrestrial analogue. Why not create now in the South Pole deployment systems demonstration models that are marked by collaboration among all the diverse entities involved, so as to enhance human space life in the future? Possibly, the following model can first be tested and adapted as an Antarctic Personnel Deployment System.

## Space Personnel Deployment Strategies

A *space personnel deployment system* (SPDS) may be defined as a planned and orderly means for the exchange of people to and from Earth and the space frontier. The essential components for this would consist of four phases as illustrated in Figure 7.2: assessment, orientation, on-site support, and reentry.

### *Assessment*

Assessment involves initially selecting the most suitable people and screening out potential misfits who would jeopardize their own or another's well-being. Space developments in the decades ahead will find a variety of organizations, in addition to national space agencies, sending people aloft. In time, we can expect sponsors to range from aerospace contractors and commercial enterprises to various public agencies, media networks, and even

Personnel Flow To and From Orbit

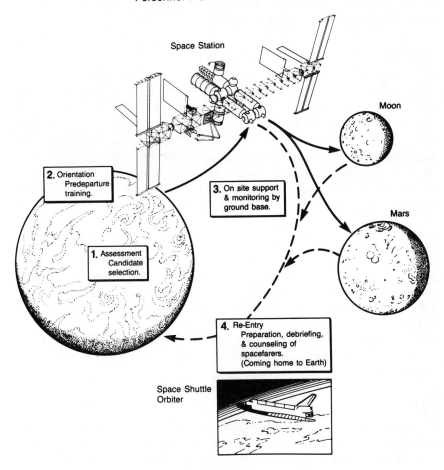

FIGURE 7.2. A space personnel deployment system. Illustration by Dennis M. David-son, astronautical artist, Hayden Planetarium, New York, New York. Printed by permission.

tourist firms. Whatever the institution that sends a human into space, it should exercise a measure of responsibility in the spacefarer's selection, preparation, and well-being, particularly with reference to that person's impact on the space community. Predeparture evaluation of candidates de-limits care and rehabilitation aloft. By next century, the selection and train-ing issues may be beyond the competency of individual sponsoring organiza-tions, and some world entity may have to be established, such as a global space agency, to control and monitor space assessment and access, as well as to resolve other multinational space issues. In the attempt to evaluate personnel for long-term missions, the following guidelines may first be tested in Antarctica or aboard the space station.

## Who

Screening requirements of space travelers and settlers would apply to all who utilize tax-supported shuttle or spaceplane transportation, whether NASA personnel, contract workers, visiting professionals, public servants, media representatives, members of the armed forces or Congress, foreign dignitaries, and eventually tourists. When the time arrives that family members accompany personnel into space, they, too, should be included in the assessment process. For the 21st century, at least, the principle proposed here is selectivity, and the time for experimentation with such a process is in the immediate decades ahead, perhaps in Antarctica.

## What

The aim of the evaluation should be to determine the suitability and adaptability of space candidates to deal effectively with the new environment and the situation aloft; both physiological and psychological evaluations should determine the individual's capability to deal with differences and difficulties in long space travel, to live in outer space under constrained conditions, and to cope with its stressors. Essentially, the process seeks to identify proneness to space culture shock, as well as areas for special training so as to improve coping and human relations skills.

## How

Assessment might be conducted through a specialized center that would utilize a variety of disciplines and means for evaluation purposes, such as psychological interviews and group meetings, instrumentation and testing, and simulations (both live gaming and computer based). In the beginning, the objective might be to choose those with competencies that ensure survival and mission accomplishment, but eventually, the aim may be to group spacefarers by personalities and interests that share values, goals, and concerns for a specific type of settlement.

## Why

Recruitment and selection should not only seek suitable candidates for space but should also determine special counseling and training needs of those chosen, particularly with reference to the family that is left behind on Earth. Obviously, the first concern is to exclude from space communities those who would be unsatisfactory for such an assignment, subject to premature return symptoms, or likely to become a disruptive influence.

Initially, the sheer cost of transporting people to and from space should justify a careful assessment policy and program. Certainly, the costs associated with premature extraterrestrial return would warrant investment in a deployment system. Outside of space agency personnel, the mission specialists are the prototype of other civilian space workers to come. Preferences may, for example, be given to those with special qualifications, such as having already benefited from some type of astronaut training, proven commitment to long-term space living and willingness to assume inherent risks, and healthy, well-balanced married couples with dual competencies. Although much is to be gained by the NASA assessment experience with elite astronauts, the space program proposed here must move beyond the practices of one agency (Atkinson & Shafritz, 1985).

## *Orientation*

Orientation involves self–learning and training for living beyond this planet. The spacefarer's curriculum and its scope would vary depending on the intended orbit, length of stay, particular mission, and previous spaceflight experience.

### Who

A short-term visitor, for example, might not be required to undergo as extensive an indoctrination as one who is expected to stay months or years aloft. A novice spacefarer, on the other hand, might undertake a longer training course than one who is a veteran in spaceflight. Families of the space voyagers should be involved, and their program would vary, depending on whether they will remain on the ground or go aloft. Those who are to become space settlers on the Moon or Mars, for instance, might be exposed to the most rigorous and lengthy preparation.

### What

The predeparture training should focus upon the challenges in extraterrestrial living, from survival and safety to cultural and interpersonal. One area of learning has to do with achievement of mission objectives, including the technical and operational aspects of transport, equipment, ecosystems, and coping in a zero-gravity or low-gravity environment. Another would be in the area of the behavioral sciences so that crewmembers and future settlers function effectively as a space community. The latter preparation might include human behavior issues and skills related to motivation, communication, conflict management, negotiation, leadership, and team and family relations. Consideration needs to be given to appropriate mission instruction in subjects such as (a) space sciences, such as astronomy, and Earth resource assessment; (b) space technologies, such as automation and robotics, communications and computers, and orbital construction and mining; (c) space migration, such as wellness and creative use of leisure aloft and, eventually, community development; and (d) foreign language/cultural understanding for multicultural crews and missions, such as basic flight Russian, Japanese, or Chinese. The experience of the International Space University (636 Beacon Street, Boston, MA 02215) may be insightful in this regard.

How

Innovation in predeparture orientation of spacefarers must extend from the design of self-learning and intensive group learning to new educational methodology and technology. The instructional possibilities for conveying the above subject content might include interactive video, video case studies, simulations (live and through computerized graphics), programmed learning, instrumentation and tests, and a variety of group processes. Partnerships should be formed among government, corporations, and institutions of higher education not only to produce human resource development instructional programs and materials for the deployment of spacefarers but also, perhaps, to plan for the establishment of space academies and universities.

Why

The costs, complexities, and risks currently inherent in long-duration space missions demand that, initially, access be limited to the competent, educated, and multiskilled, as well as those who are well-balanced "copers" and "can doers." In a space-based culture, knowledge and information ensure survival and success. As E. T. Hall and S. E. Hall (1987) remind us, any culture is primarily a system for creating, sending, storing, and processing information, with communication underlying everything, whether in words, behavior, or material things.

## In-Space Services

In-space services refers to the on-site support and monitoring, both physical and psychological, that is necessary for survival and mission accomplishment.

Who

Those who depart from the Earth to live and work aloft deserve support from their sponsoring organizations until such time as a space settlement or colony can function somewhat independently. In addition to the families of space voyagers, a host of professional personnel on the ground will be necessary to provide in-space services. Once at a space station or base, some specialists there should be designated responsible for the distribution and maintenance of such services. One proposal, for example, calls for contract corporation employees at NASA's planned space station to render separate services ranging from hotel accommodations and food to heat and fuel (both for the station and the spacecraft).

## What

The support services aloft are usually of three types. The first is operational — ensuring the technical or mechanical aspects of a station or base so that it remains in orbit or is functional. Another dimension involves physical and biological support to maintain a group of people in outer space (S. E. Hall, 1985). Obviously, this involves transport, habitat, communication, nourishment, equipment, and supplies to accomplish the mission. More specifically, it involves provision of "biospheres" for a total Earth-like environment: a closed ecological system for recycled air, water, food, and waste management. Support also includes training in activities in a gravity-free or gravity-reduced environment. The final dimension of in-space services is psychosocial, helping to limit space culture shock on long-term flights. Throughout the spaceflight, there have to be mechanisms and procedures in place for those on the ground and in orbit to evaluate human need, progress, and performance.

## How

In-space services begin before lift-off, with the planning of propulsion, habitat, and life-support systems. Upon reaching a space station or base, life-support systems are explained and utilized. Perhaps the new arrival might be paired off with an experienced "buddy" and participate in some form of indoctrination briefings. Communication procedures are established to link the individual not just with "mission control" but with families and friends on the home planet, as well. Medical and mental health services are made available, particularly to cope with stressors related to gravity-free living and space sickness, circadian rhythms and sleep patterns, lack of privacy, and anxieties. The work schedule, as well as social and recreational opportunities afforded spacefarers, are important for enhancing the quality of space life. Education and training aloft can be continued by means of team development or technology-assisted learning.

A group of scientists providing input to the National Commission on Space report observed

The experimental and demanding nature of human settlements in space will require constant, nonintrusive monitoring of experience, as well as analysis of the social forces in an isolated environment that is without precedent. Progress will depend heavily on learning from this process of feedback. (Jones, 1985, p. 13)

The Living Systems project proposed at the California Space Institute envisions a computer/sensor technology for such nonintrusive monitoring of inhabitants of a space station or base (Harris, 1989b). Besides improved management and safety that could result from such procedures, a continuing learning cycle could be established for the benefit of future spacefarers. Behavioral scientists are likely to make unique contributions to the ground support team to serve the needs of space pioneers on long-duration missions (Harris, 1989b).

### Why

Until space settlements become self–sufficient, well into the next century, space voyagers will be dependent upon the home planet. Robinson and White (1986) suggest that two mutually dependent types of people and societies are emerging: Earthkind and Spacekind. In the synergistic relations created between these two kinds, the former provide support and service to those who live and work in space, so that its resources may be utilized to the benefit of all. The situation is somewhat analogous to that of the 17th and 18th century colonists to the New World who depended upon Old World institutions until they could eventually function on their own and contribute much more back to Europe than they initially received.

As the third element in a deployment system, in-space services require the building of an infrastructure on Earth to support space-based activities. This would necessitate more than the construction of space vehicles and the providing of life support. It would include on this planet, for instance, regional bases, spaceports, space training centers, tracking systems, and so forth. Similarly, other infrastructures have to be financed and erected in space so that humans can live and work there, as well as explore and settle the solar system.

## Reentry

Reentry policies and programs are required to deal with spacefarers' relocation back to Earth and reacculturation problems.

### Who

Just as with predeparture orientation, the space voyager's family should be involved, whether the family members accompany that individual into space or remain back on Earth. The off-terrestrial experience, especially one that may involve many months or years aloft, affects the spacefarer's family and organizational relations. Even in the next century, when space settlers volunteer permanently for the new orbiting colonies, reentry counsel and procedures will be necessary for their possible visits to this planet. Perhaps astronauts and cosmonauts who have been in space are the best persons to act as consultants in this and other aspects of the deployment system.

How

Policies need to be established on pragmatic matters as to (1) when sabbatical leaves may be taken from space assignments, such as the space station or lunar base, and how long these may be before any return to orbit is feasible; (2) when, where, and how the reconditioning is to take place; (3) the length and process of debriefing; (4) data gathering and follow-up procedures to be undertaken upon return to Earth; and (5) rights, benefits, and assignments the spacefarers may expect upon return to the sponsoring organization, and so forth. Before any rotation back to this planet from long-duration missions, the reentry program should likely be inaugurated while still in orbit.

What

To close the deployment loop, the reentry process must deal with physical, psychological, social, and organizational aspects of return to gravity living. Research in this area will have to deal with programs that recondition the body, foster reacculturation to home conditions and societies, and guide further career development or retirement.

Why

Spaceflight for most people will involve a "transitional experience" (Harris, 1985a; Harris & Moran, 1991). Upon return, some may complain of severe adjustment problems, or reentry shock. Oberg (1985) reported on this "homegoing" phenomenon among astronauts, brought on by the fiery reentry, adulation by well wishers, sense of gratitude for safe return, and even letdown. Constructs and perceptions may be so altered as to require psychological counseling so as to lead a normal Earth-like life again.

# Deployment Information Systems

Ideally, under NASA's leadership, a data, or knowledge, bank should be developed with a pattern recognition and retrieval system relative to broad human role, performance, and problems in space. In addition to storing findings of terrestrial analogues, as described earlier, this information system would be a comprehensive storehouse on the on-going human experience aloft. Perhaps the living systems template, which Dr. James Grier Miller describes in another chapter of this book, would serve as a framework for this cross-disciplinary analysis. Expert systems and artificial intelligence will contribute much to improve space deployment.

Although NASA has been forthright about medical and biological insights gained from previous spaceflights (Pitts, 1985), the agency has been hesitant on studying or releasing information on the psychosocial experience of its personnel in space. Generally, NASA has limited the access to astronauts by social science researchers, even by its own psychiatrists and psychologists; the agency has failed to capitalize on the data it has collected that could improve spaceflight and living for others to follow. For example, there are indications that transcripts of crew communications going back as far as the Mercury flights have not been analyzed from a behavioral science perspective so as to obtain clues to improve future missions and avoid tragedies.

There do not appear to have been any systematic data gathering surveys of past and present astronauts who have actually flown in space. This expert group could provide valuable input to better human performance in space if behavioral scientists were given the opportunity to construct an appropriate questionnaire and analyze the results. Douglas (1984) did attempt an interview from the perspective of a flight surgeon but with a limited sample of astronauts (10) and imperfect methodology.

There is evidence of some Soviet–American exchange on the human experience in spaceflight, but certainly such cross-cultural communication should be encouraged and expanded (Bluth & Helppie, 1986; Newkirk, 1989). All international interchanges of this type, including United States–USSR polar living, can improve human survivability, habitats, and life style. The range of data exchanged, whether about living in polar regions or in space, should be multidimensional (e.g., the requirements for food and shelter, health and wellness, group dynamics and interpersonal skills, transport and ecosystems, as well as play, performance, and productivity). Coping successfully with exotic environments contributes to self-discovery and the actualization of human potential (Harris, 1989c). Our concern should be to ensure high performance under such circumstances (Harris, 1989a).

## Conclusions and Recommendations

If space habitation is to advance rapidly, then a more comprehensive systems approach to personnel deployment would seem to be appropriate. The model described in this chapter offers components that could be utilized in this decade for the analysis of wintering-over experience in Antarctica, both previously and for planning future habitation. For example, organizations sponsoring expeditions to the South Pole might jointly adopt a personnel deployment strategy. Comprehensive findings from such a system would provide insight for expanded habitation in polar regions and would also be transferable to space.

Antarctica is an ideal, ground-based location to experiment with deployment issues, with establishing new cultural outposts for humanity, and with the macromanagement of such large-scale enterprises (Harris, 1987b). That knowledge can then be applied in space voyaging and settlement. During the next 50 years, the initial stations and bases aloft are the "laboratories" for improving later interstellar migration of our species. The next thousand space "expatriates" could make a remarkable contribution to a fund of knowledge organized around life in zero or low gravity.

## References

Atkinson, J. D., & Shafritz, J. M. (1985). *The real stuff: History of NASA's astronauts selection program.* New York: Praeger.

Austin, C. N. (Ed.). (1987). *Cross cultural re-entry: A book of readings.* Yarmouth, ME: Intercultural Press.

Baker, D. (1985). *The history of manned spaceflight.* New York: Crown Publishers.

Bluth, B. J., & Helppie, M. (1986). *Soviet space stations as analogs.* Washington, D.C.: NASA.

Douglas, W. K. (1984). *Human performance issues arising from manned space station missions.* Huntington Beach, CA.: McDonnell Douglas Astronautics Company.

Furnham, A., & Bochner, S. (1986). *Culture shock: Psychological reactions to unfamiliar environments.* New York: Methuen.

Hall, E. T., & Hall, M. E. (1987). *Hidden differences.* Garden City, NJ: Anchor Press/Doubleday.

Hall, S. E. (Ed.). (1985). *The human role in space: Technology, economics, and optimization.* Park Ridge, NJ: Noyes Publications.

Harris, P. R. (1985a). *Management in transition.* San Francisco: Jossey Bass.

Harris, P. R. (1985b, April). Space deployment systems. *Space World,* 2.

Harris, P. R. (1986a). The influence of culture on space developments. *Behavioral Science, 31*(1), 12–28.

Harris, P. R. (1986b, October). Space systems deployment. *Space Frontier,* 17.

Harris, P. R. (1987b). Innovations in space management – Macromanagement in the NASA heritage. *Journal of the British Interplanetary Society, 40,* 109–116.

Harris, P. R. (1987c). Human futures on the high frontier. *Futures Research Quarterly, 3*(2), 53–81.

Harris, P. R. (1989a). *High performance leadership: Strategies for maximizing career productivity.* Glenview, IL: Scott, Foresman.

Harris, P. R. (1989b). Behavioral science space contributions. *Behavioral Science, 34,* 207–236.

Harris, P. R. (1989c, May). Human dimensions in space development. *Space Policy, 5,* 147–154.

Harris, P. R. (in preparation). *Human enterprise in space: Behavioral science insights on living and working in the high frontier.*

Harris, P. R., & Moran, R. T. (1991). *Managing cultural differences: High performance strategies for today's global managers,* 3rd ed. Houston: Gulf Publishing Co.

Harris, P. R. et al. (1987a, April). Space activities 1985–2010: NASA summer study executive summary. *Space Frontier,* 21–25.

Holmes, B. (1978). *An experimental study of intercultural contacts of Americans in other cultures.* Doctoral dissertation, University of Colorado, Boulder.

Johnson, M. B. (1978). Training needs of American workers overseas as perceived by Americans who have worked in Asia. (Unpublished Ph.D. thesis, University of Colorado). Ann Arbor, MI: University Films.

Jones, E. M. (Ed.). (1985). *The space settlement papers* (Paper LA-UR-85-3874). Los Alamos: Los Alamos National Laboratory.

Kelly, T. (1986). Frozen assets. *Canada Today/d'Aujourd'hui.*

Moran, R. T., & Harris, P. R. (1982). *Managing cultural synergy.* Houston: Gulf Publishing Co.

Newkirk, K. D. (1989). *Almanac of soviet manned spaceflight.* Houston: Gulf Publishing Co.

Nicogossian, A. E., Huntoon, C. E., & Pool, S. H. (Eds.). (1989). *Space physiology and medicine.* Philadelphia: Lea & Febiger.

Oberg, A. R. (1985). *Spacefarers of the 80's and 90's: The next thousand people in space.* New York: Columbia University Press.

Pitts, J. A. (1985). *The human factors: Biomedicine in the manned space program to 1980* (NASA SP-4213). Washington, DC: National Aeronautics and Space Administration.

Robinson, G. S., & White, H. M. (1986). *Envoys of Mankind.* Washington, D.C.: Smithsonian Institution Press.

Russell, P. W. (1978). *Dimensions of overseas success in industry.* Doctoral dissertation, Colorado State University, Fort Collins.

Torbiorn, I. (1982). *Living abroad: Personal adjustments and personnel policies in overseas settings.* New York: Wiley.

Tung, R. L. (1982). Selection and training of U.S., European, and Japanese multinationals. *California Management Review, 25,* 57–71.

Tung, R. L. (1987). Expatriate assignments: Enhancing success and minimizing failure. *Academy of Management Executive, 1,* 117–126.

Tung, R. L. (1988). *The new expatriates: Managing human resources in an international context.* Cambridge, MA: Ballinger.

Ward, T. (1984). *Living overseas: A book of preparations.* New York: The Free Press/Macmillan.

White, F. (1987). *The overview effect: Space exploration and human evolution.* New York: Houghton-Mifflin.

# 8

# Psychological and Sociological Aspects of Manned Spaceflight

WILLIAM K. DOUGLAS

If none but the true and useful things were recorded, our immense historical libraries would be reduced to a very narrow compass, but we should know more and know it better

— Voltaire

When one reads *Mutiny on the Bounty* (Nordhoff & Hall,1932), one develops the concept that Captain Bligh was a sadistic tyrant and that Fletcher Christian was a noble defender of the rights of the downtrodden English seaman. Henry Cooper's *A House in Space* (Cooper, 1978) would lead the reader to believe that the crew of Skylab 4 was a mutinous lot and that this unastronaut-like behavior was, in some ways, a result of living in the mysterious environment of outer space. The fictional representation of life aboard the *Bounty* has been reinforced so strongly by several cinematic versions of this exciting bit of history that fiction has gradually replaced fact. Tom Wolfe's *The Right Stuff* (Wolfe, 1979) and the motion picture version have also implanted a totally erroneous, but widely believed concept of test pilots and of astronauts in the public mind, and, I am sad to say, in the minds of many professionals. Almost forgotten is the detailed account of the *Bounty*'s voyage that Bligh wrote upon his return to England (Bligh, 1961). More overlooked than forgotten are the objective reports of many astronauts that tell their own versions of their experiences.

Captain Bligh was cast adrift with 18 other men in the *Bounty*'s launch. He navigated this small, overcrowded, underprovisioned, and ill-equipped boat to the island of Timor in the East Indies, a voyage of some 3,600 miles, with the loss of only one man, and he at the hands of savages on the island of Tofoa.

The *Bounty* was a small, 90-foot vessel of only 215 tons. She carried a crew of 46 men. On the outward voyage from England, the *Bounty* arrived at the Cape of Good Hope 5 months after her departure from Spithead. It is noteworthy that not a single man on board was ill with scurvy.

When we consider life aboard the space station, we ponder the kind and the amount of exercise that might be prescribed for the crew. Captain Bligh had a similar concern for his crew, but his solution was somewhat different than ours. Rather than reason with them, he simply punished any man who did not dance to the fiddle for 2 hours every night.

One might legitimately point out that *The Mutiny on Board HMS* Bounty was a somewhat self-serving account, but it must be recognized that then-Lieutenant Bligh was exonerated by an exhaustive investigation of the incident. He continued to serve in the Royal Navy and was chosen to lead a second expedition to Tahiti, in 1791, to collect breadfruit trees for propagation in the West Indies. In 1801, he was elected a Fellow in the Royal Society. During the battle of Copenhagen, his ship was in direct support of Nelson, and after the battle, Vice Admiral Lord Nelson gave him a special commendation for his action. Bligh died in 1817 after having attained the rank of Vice Admiral (*Encyclopaedia Britannica*, 1984).

From the viewpoint of the psychologist, the mutiny was almost inevitable, regardless of who was in command. In those days, crew selection was frequently accomplished with a blackjack in some back alley or by press gangs in a waterfront tavern. No reasonable manager today would even suggest that a crew be launched for an extended voyage into space on Christmas Eve, yet the *Bounty* left port on December 23, 1787. Captain Bligh wrote, "At night the wind increased to a strong gale, with a heavy sea. It moderated, however, on the 25th, and allowed us to keep our Christmas with cheerfullness . . . " (p. 25). Because of the inability to round Cape Horn, the voyage was extended, and rations had to be curtailed on the leg to the Cape of Good Hope. Finally, for 6 months the crew remained in Tahiti, a truly tropical paradise, collecting breadfruit seedlings. They made lasting attachments to the young ladies of the island and were understandably reluctant to depart. Taking into full account the crew selection processes of the time, the harsh disciplinary measures accepted by the Royal Navy, the crowded conditions on the *Bounty*, and the amorous attachments of the men to the maidens, I doubt that any commander of today, if transported back to 1789, could have done any better.

Nordhoff and Hall's book *Mutiny on the* Bounty, if taken as history, is quite comparable to *A House in Space*. There are the happy-go-lucky crew members of Skylab 2, and the dedicated scientists of Skylab 3. And then there are the so-called "mutineers" of Skylab 4, who participated in the first "Revolt in Space." If one examines the reference section of the papers published on the psychological aspects of spaceflight, one will find *A House in Space* listed in many of them. Use of such a source as confirmatory evidence of what really happened in the Skylab is comparable to using Nordhoff and

Hall's books as a source document when reporting on the psychological factors at play in the mutiny of the *Bounty* crew.

Nearly every article addressing the psychological aspects of manned spaceflight speaks of the paucity of factual information emanating from the U.S. space program. As a result, the publications frequently rely on anecdotal evidence of emotional problems in both U.S. and Soviet spaceflights. Frequent references are made to the popular press, but rarely do the authors refer to the statements of astronauts published in the scientific literature. It is true that many astronauts have written books, but these, too, are meant to sell as well as to inform. Two astronauts, James Lovell (1979) and Frank Borman (1982) have addressed the annual scientific meetings of the Aerospace Medical Association. Mr. Borman discussed the sometimes-adversarial relationship between flight surgeons and pilots, but he also applauded the work of several flight surgeons with whom he had direct contact.

It is often alleged that pilots look with great disfavor on physicians and psychologists. *The Right Stuff* is frequently cited to confirm this allegation. This attitude is said to result from the threat that these professionals pose to the career of the flyer. There is undoubtedly an underlying concern on the part of the flyer that his next encounter with the medical man may result in the loss of his job, but there is something more basic than that at work. The pilot has had years of training and experience. He, too, is a professional. When he associates with other professionals, be they pilots, psychologists, or flight surgeons, he evaluates them and makes a judgment. In some cases he finds them wanting in professional competence. In other cases he stamps them with his seal of approval. He respects good physicians and good psychologists, but he abhors poor physicians and poor psychologists the same way he abhors poor pilots and poor engineers. Mr. Borman made that quite clear in his Bauer lecture of 1982. Mr. Lovell made the same point when he gave the Bauer lecture in 1978. Both gentlemen spoke of this relationship with humor and affection.

Mr. Lovell gives an excellent example of how we fail:

I can recall vividly one day working as a backup for the four-day Gemini IV mission—having just been selected for the 14–day Gemini VII flight—when one of the medical personnel in our crew system division approached me and said "Don't worry about training for that flight. These fellows won't even last four days." (Lovell, 1979)

Here is the perfect example of our hubris. We tend to express opinion as fact even when the opinion is not based on fact. Whoever made that statement had not the slightest shred of evidence that the crew of the Gemini 4 mission could not last 4 days. In fact, the existing evidence was quite to the contrary. We medical people continue to write review articles about the human experience in space, but Mr. James Lovell's lecture, "A Reflective Review of Man's Venture into Space," says it all—and with wit as well as with insight.

We perceive that we have a problem obtaining hard, factual data about the experiences of astronauts in space and forget the possibility that nothing alarming has happened. If we want the truth about what really happened in space, and I am not for a moment suggesting that we have not been told the truth, we must gain the confidence and acceptance of the pilot. This has been accomplished by some flight surgeons and some behavioral scientists. Mr. Borman speaks of physicians who have gained his respect, and I would like to mention people like Dr. George Ruff, Dr. Terry McGuire, and Dr. Robert Voas. All three gained the respect and confidence of astronauts. It can be done.

I have spoken about individuals, and individuals are frequently put to the test, but the real problem is that the profession as a whole has been put to the test and found wanting. When we make predictions based on intuition and not on fact, we fail the test. The person who predicted that the Gemini 4 crew would not last 4 days is an example—he failed Jim Lovell's test. When we, collectively, rely on the popular press in the absence of hard data, we also fail the test.

A short time ago, a document (Collins, 1985) was published by a well-known government agency, in which the author wrote, "The psychological effects of space flight have included aberrant behaviors and impaired judgment. For example, astronaut Carpenter wasted valuable control fuel, during a Mercury space flight, to obtain unauthorized photographs of scenic sunsets." The author gave *A House in Space* as the source of his information. He then wrote: "Why an experienced test pilot, turned astronaut, would exhibit such irrational behavior remains unknown."

Carpenter did not use up precious fuel to satisfy some artistic urge to take unauthorized pictures of sunsets. In fact, he was exercising one of the attributes for which we send humans into space—he was making an observation that explained a phenomenon reported by Colonel John Glenn on his orbital flight. Colonel Glenn had reported seeing sparkling particles outside the window of his spacecraft. Commander Carpenter noted that when he knocked on the walls of his cabin, he saw these same particles outside his window. Water vapor from the environmental control system had condensed and frozen on the spacecraft exterior. When Commander Carpenter knocked on the cabin wall, these "snow flakes" came off in showers. Commander Carpenter was not engaging in "irrational behavior." He was using his intellect, and we send humans into space because they can use their intellects.

Another example from the aforementioned publication (Collins, 1985) is the author's statement that "the psychological incompatibility among members of the crew caused the Apollo 13 mission to now be infamously referred to as 'the flight that failed.'" Here the author refers to another popular book, *13: The Flight That Failed* (Cooper, 1973), as his source. The truth is that an oxygen bottle had exploded in the service module 2 days into the mission. Had it not been for the close cooperative interactions among the Apollo 13 crewmembers and between them and the ground, Apollo 13 would have been not just a "flight that failed"—it would have been a tragic disaster.

One more example of how we fail is the continued references in the literature to the so-called revolt of the third Skylab crew. Again, a commonly used reference is *A House in Space*. If this entertaining book is read with the thought in mind of analyzing the author's writing skills rather than his historical accuracy, the reader will see how our profession has been set up. Beginning on page 10 of the book, the crewmembers are described as "reluctant," "lethargic," "negative," "irritable," "complaining," "bitching," "grumbling,"—and all of this in just 19 lines of print. On page 11, the denigration continues: Gibson complains that he doesn't like brown clothing and is characterized as being the "contrariest, bitchingest astronaut that ever departed vertically from Cape Kennedy." Two of the crewmembers grew "revolutionary-looking beards" and used "blistering language." This sets the stage for the rest of the book, throughout which they "blow up," "fume," "bitch," "fulminate," "gripe," "explode," "mutter," "shout," exhibit "bursts of anger," and even "grouse," until finally, on page 128, "—Carr, the commander, told the flight controllers, in a memorable bitch, that he had had enough." The first mutiny in space had occurred. When we take this literary diatribe as fact, we fail again.

What really happened? It was an 84-day mission, and Sundays were to occur every 10 days instead of every 7. They worked on their first three Sundays to keep up with the burdensome schedule. On the fourth Sunday, Mission Control suggested that they had some tasks for the astronauts to perform. Colonel Carr (1986) has written that when he received that suggestion from the ground, he said, "We better not work today. We better do our own thing and get some rest."

The fact that they took their Sunday off for the first time in four straight 10-day weeks was considered by some to have been a mutiny. When things didn't improve after the mutiny, Colonel Carr told the flight director that perhaps they should have a discussion of where things stood. Two days later, they had what Carr has described as the "first sensitivity session" in space. As a result of this session, Mission Control came up with a new plan. All things that were not time or orbit critical, such as Earth or astronomical observations, would be taken off the schedule and given to the crew as a shopping list. This list was posted on the wall of the Skylab, and as the crewmembers found free time, they would choose a task from the list and work on it. Using this method, they not only completed all of the formerly scheduled tasks but also managed to develop some of their own. Even the author of *A House in Space* wrote that "Carr, Gibson and Pogue would go on to be one of the most productive and interesting crews to go into space . . . " (p. 14).

Our intuition tells us that surely life in space must be so different from life on Earth that unearthly things must happen to astronauts. We know that there are physiological changes in the human organism and believe that there must be some comparable psychological changes. We believe this with so much fervor that we accept the anecdotal information that comes to us as fact. We search for analogues of the space environment and see in those analogues only the examples of human frailty. We do not see the far more prevalent examples of human greatness. We read that the incidence of psychiatric cases in the Fleet Ballistic Missile submarines is 4/1,000, but overlook the fact that the rate of reported psychiatric illness is lower in the submarines than it is in the surface Navy (Weybrew and Noddin, 1979). We exhibit the same attitude towards the magnificent accomplishments of those dedicated people who winter-over in Antarctica.

History provides us with many examples of how people have performed admirably in stressful circumstances. Captain Cook's third voyage lasted 4 years. His crew visited such great cultural centers as Tasmania, New Zealand, Tahiti, and Hawaii, where their captain was beaten to death by natives (*Encyclopaedia Britannica*, 1984). That expedition was a far more arduous experience than a mission to Mars, yet we forget that those 18th century explorers brought back volumes of scientific information. The crew of Nansen's *Fram* left home on June 24, 1893, and did not return for over 3 years. More than 2 years of that absence were spent frozen in the polar ice with no outside contact (*Encyclopaedia Britannica*, 1984). Here, again, these men returned with a wealth of valuable information.

I have no idea how Cook's men or the *Fram*'s crew coped with their psychosocial problems—and I am confident that they had them. Perhaps conflict is an essential part of the human social makeup. Perhaps it is important. Perhaps when all is sweetness and light the human intellect stagnates. We must accept the fact that there will be differences of opinion, personality, and preferences on long-duration space missions, but we must not assume that they will be any more disastrous than similar problems that arise whenever humans of goodwill and common purpose are confined together in small groups. There are many examples of cultures that strive to live lives of great peace and tranquility. Admittedly, their scale of values is different from ours, but when they are measured by our yardstick, they come up short. Here is an area where the cultural anthropologists can be of help. Perhaps they can tell us how tranquil and how conflict-free our space culture should be. Finally, let me remind you of the good things we have done. We have learned much in the quarter century since man first orbited the Earth. These lessons have already been incorporated into the design of space station *Freedom*, and I am sure they will be applied to the design of a Mars mission. There will be a floor and a ceiling. The color scheme will be considered in designing a pleasant and productive decor. There will be individual private quarters. There will be the ability to talk, in private, to friends and loved ones at home.

I have only one serious concern: I am not convinced that those who develop the schedule of tasks to be performed each day are fully aware of the need to provide enough free time for the crew to gaze out of the windows at the magnificence of the Earth and the heavens. We can only pray that the lesson has been learned.

## References

Bligh, W. (1961). *The mutiny on board HMS* Bounty. Reprint. New York: The New American Library of World Literature, Signet Classics.

Borman, F. (1982). (the 27th annual Louis H. Bauer lecture to the Aerospace Medical Association, May 1982). *Aviation, Space, and Environmental Medicine, 53,* 1030–1033.

Carr, G. P. (1986). Behavioral issues associated with isolation and confinement. In J. Stuster (Ed.), *Tenth psychology in the DoD symposium.* Santa Barbara, CA: Anacapa Sciences.

Collins, D. L. (1985). *Psychological issues relevant to astronaut selection for long-duration space flight: A review of the literature* (Research Report AFHRL-TP-41). Brooks AFB, Texas: Air Force Human Resources Laboratory.

Cooper, H. S. F. (1973). *13: The flight that failed.* New York: Dial Press.

Cooper, H. S. F. (1978). *A house in space.* New York: Bantam Books.

Encyclopaedia Britannica, Inc. (1984). *Encyclopaedia Britannica.* (15th ed). Chicago: Author.

Lovell, J. A. (1979). A reflective review of man's venture into space (The 24th annual Louis H. Bauer lecture to the Aerospace Medical Association, May 1978). *Aviation, Space, and Environmental Medicine, 50*(1), 63–67.

Nordhoff, C., & Hall, J. N. (1932). *Mutiny on the* Bounty. Boston: Little, Brown.

Wolfe, T. (1979). *The right stuff.* New York: Farrar, Straus, Giroux.

Weybrew, B. B., & Noddin, E. M. (1979). Psychiatric aspects of adaptation to long submarine missions. *Aviation, Space and Environmental Medicine, 50,* 575–580.

# 9

# Scientists and Seamen

BEN FINNEY

Scientists and seamen and how they relate to one another on long research voyages form the focus of this chapter. But, though my immediate perspective is oceanic, my gaze is really directed over the horizon, outward toward space and the evolving relationships between, on the one hand, those who command and operate spacecraft and space stations and, eventually, the first planetary bases and, on the other hand, those whose primary responsibility is to conduct research in or from those facilities.

My experience undertaking experimental voyages with a reconstructed Polynesian sailing canoe has made me acutely aware that scientific values and ideals are not widely shared throughout society and that during long sea voyages the "cultural" differences between scientists and seamen can lead to conflict. In addition, the literature on oceanic exploration has shown me that the issue of how scientists and seamen should relate to each other is neither new nor passing. This issue surfaced on the very first voyages to have scientific goals and to include scientists and remains a concern for those scientists and seamen who go to sea together today. In this chapter, I offer a cursory analysis of evolving relationships between scientists and seamen over 2 centuries of maritime exploration, in the hope that this oceanic perspective might help us think about how astronauts/cosmonauts, scientists, and others can work and live together more congenially and productively in space.

## The Second Age of Exploration

The first great European age of exploration has little to do with scientific discovery. The goal of Prince Henry, da Gama, Columbus, Magellan, and other early maritime explorers of the 15th and 16th centuries may have been discovery, but of new sea routes opening direct access to the wealth of Asia, not of new lands or species or of unique geophysical and astronomical findings. Scientific discovery did not become a major goal of oceanic exploration until the late 18th century, when a second, scientific age of exploration dawned among European maritime powers (Goetzmann, 1986).

In terms of the mobilization of government resources and the expenditures of large sums for scientific ends and in terms of intense national competition between exploring nations, this age foreshadows the space race of the 1960s (Dunmore, 1969). The maritime powers of the day sent their ships on great, globe-girdling voyages in which, not unlike later space ventures, the goals of scientific discovery, of national aggrandizement, and of commercial and military advantage were intertwined. The focus of this competition was on the Pacific, a huge and largely uncharted expanse at first thought to hold rich islands and the fabled *Terra Australis*, the Southern Continent then considered by geographers as necessary to balance the great landmass of the Northern Hemisphere. The competition began in earnest during the late 1700s with Britain and France sending expedition after expedition into the Pacific and then around the world on exploring missions that lasted up to 3 years and, sometimes, longer. Spain, already in decline as a maritime power, halfheartedly joined in by sending a few expeditions. The Russians entered the field in the early 1800s with a series of well-carried-out voyages, while the United States, the last great power to join the competition, did not send out an expedition until the late 1830s.

## The British

The most famous scientific voyage of the era was virtually the first one to set sail. In 1768, Britain sent the bark *Endeavour* to the newly discovered South Sea island of Tahiti. The primary goal of the voyage was astronomical: to observe from Tahiti the transit of Venus across the face of the Sun and thereby provide data needed to calculate the distance between Earth and Sun. This project, which was part of an international scientific effort to measure exactly the distance between the Earth and the Sun so that it could be used as the basic unit of astronomical measure, was promoted by the Royal Society, funded by the Crown, and assigned to the Royal Navy for execution.

Who should command such an expedition—a scientist or a seaman—was an immediate issue. Seventy years earlier, in 1698, the great Edmond Halley, the astronomer who had first proposed using the transit of Venus for measuring the Earth–Sun distance, had in fact been commissioned by the Admiralty to command an expedition that has been called "the first sea journey undertaken for a purely scientific object" (Thrower, 1981, p. 16). Halley's assignment, which he himself had promoted and for which he had secured Royal Society backing, was to study magnetic variation throughout the Atlantic. Scientifically, the voyage was a success. Halley's chart of magnetic variation was immediately acclaimed and became the standard for years to come (although his goal of using magnetic variation to determine longitude proved unattainable). However, Halley had to cut the voyage short and return to England earlier than planned because of insubordination among his officers resentful at having a landsman in command. Halley complained that one officer in particular, a lieutenant in the Royal Navy, had a habit of countermanding his orders when his back was turned. The officer was reprimanded, and Halley was sent out on two more, shorter expeditions. But evidently, the idea of having a landsman command a naval vessel, even one so skilled in the theory and practice of navigation as Halley, did not sit well with the Lords of the Admiralty. When it came time to choose a commander for the *Endeavour*, they would not entertain the idea that a civilian scientist might command.

The Astronomer Royal, Nevil Maskelyn, was asked for his recommendation as to who should command the expedition to observe the transit of Venus. He proposed Alexander Dalrymple, a passionate advocate of oceanic exploration who was later to become the first hydrographer to the Royal Navy. The Royal Society seconded Dalrymple's nomination and forwarded his name to the Admiralty as their choice to lead the expedition. Dalrymple, however, was not a professional seaman and had not served in the Royal Navy. Whatever experience at sea he might have had, the Lords of the Admiralty were not about to appoint him to command a vessel. Such an appointment, they wrote to the Royal Society, would be "totally repugnant to the rules of the Navy." The First Lord of the Admiralty amplified this stand, vowing that "he would suffer his right hand to be cut off rather than sign such another commission as had gone to Halley in the *Paramour Pink* in 1698—a civilian in command of a naval vessel on a scientific voyage, whose difficulties with his officers had been painful" (Beaglehole, 1974, p. 125).

There could be no question. A professional seaman, an officer in the Royal Navy, must command—not a scientist. But who? The Admiralty made an inspired choice: a young officer named James Cook, who had risen from able seaman to master of his own vessel. Cook, who was already renowned for his navigating and surveying skills, was promoted to lieutenant and given command of the *Endeavour*. A complement of scientists and their assistants sailed with him: astronomer Charles Green, who earlier had served as assistant to the Astronomer Royal; Joseph Banks, a young and wealthy botanist who financed his own way and that of his assistants, including Daniel Solander, a pupil of Linnaeus considered to be the ablest botanist in Britain; and two artists assigned to draw islands, geological formations, scenes, and plants and animals discovered.

Cook's task was to sail the *Endeavour* to Tahiti, so that the transit of Venus could be observed, and then to reconnoiter the Pacific for other islands and to search for the hypothesized Southern Continent and, in general, to facilitate the observations and collecting of the scientific staff.

The job of the scientists and their assistants, civilians all, was to make the astronomical observations and to describe and illustrate the plants and animals they found, as well as the island societies encountered. This division of labor between seaman and scientist was seen as the obvious, rational formula to be followed.

It worked well during that first voyage of Cook. Cook sailed the *Endeavour* to Tahiti without incident. The transit of Venus was observed, and the data were later delivered to the astronomical community in England. A search westward across the South Pacific latitudes revealed no Southern Continent between 30° and 40° South latitude, though it brought the *Endeavour* to New Zealand, which the English were then able to reconnoiter. Next they explored the east coast of Australia, then sailed through the Torres Straits for Batavia and from there to England via Capetown (Beaglehole, 1968).

During this magnificent circumnavigation, which took 3 years to complete, Cook "very efficiently brought the scientists to their material" (Beaglehole, 1974, p. 699). As a result, in addition to the making of major astronomical and geographical observations, a wealth of specimens, drawings, and experience with the South Sea islanders was gained. Furthermore, except for an ill-fated stay in pestilential Batavia, the voyage was a healthy and happy one. The scientists and seamen apparently worked well together, particularly Cook and Banks—who had emerged as the chief scientist aboard. For example, in addition to carrying out his botanical duties, the linguistically talented and culturally sensitive Banks was most useful in developing good relations with their Tahitian hosts—so essential if the English were to be allowed to conduct their astronomical observations unmolested. The formula of having seamen command and scientists do the research seemed to have worked well.

But this synergistic partnership between Cook and Banks unraveled once they reached England. The seeds of discord were, if not initially sown, well fertilized when the press proclaimed the voyage to be a triumph of Banks, not Cook. So lionized by press, public, and royalty was Banks that it was immediately assumed that he would lead a second expedition to the South Seas to extend his researches. The attention received led Banks to recruit an oversized scientific entourage and to require that an extra deck be added to the expedition's ship, the *Resolution*, to house his people and their scientific gear. Cook, who had been chosen to lead this second expedition, at first acquiesced. But, when during sea trials the *Resolution* proved impossibly top heavy, he ordered the extra deck cut off. Banks objected, but the Admiralty backed their man. Banks quit the expedition in disgust. Although later Banks, in his capacity of President of the Royal Society, was to be an influential voice in planning British scientific voyages, he was never again to sail on one of them.

The departure of Banks did not, however, spell an immediate end to the formula of having naval officers command scientific expeditions and civilian scientists carry out the scientific work. The second Cook expedition, which had as its primary purpose to search the high latitudes of the South Pacific for the Southern Continent, sailed with a number of scientists: two professional astronomers and, as a replacement for Banks, the naturalist Johann Reinhold Forster and his son Georg Forster. During the voyage, Cook was able to lay to rest forever the idea of a continent in the temperate latitudes of the South Pacific (though he correctly guessed that a landmass was to be found at higher latitudes), and, also, to survey many islands, and—thanks to one of the first practical chronometers and the aid of the astronomers on board—to fix their exact positions. In addition, during the voyage, the Forsters were able to continue the botanical work started by Banks and to undertake other natural historical and anthropological research. However, the relationship between Cook and Johann Forster was not, apparently, a happy one. We do not know exactly what happened. Cook's biographer considers the "dogmatic, humourless, suspicious, censorius, contentious, demanding" naturalist made life extremely difficult for Cook and others during the voyage (Beaglehole, 1974, p. 302). Forster, for his part, gives vent in his journal to his own frustrations as to what he considered unwarranted interference by Cook and others in his scientific projects (Hoare, 1982, 1, pp. 74–75, 80; 2, p. 551).

Once back in England, Cook was promoted and pensioned off with half pay. He was soon tempted back to sea again, however, when command of a third grand expedition to the Pacific was offered. This time the central object was the search for a sea passage between the North Pacific and the North Atlantic, with the charge of making scientific observations along the way. On this voyage, however, the division of labor between science and seamanship that had prevailed on the previous two voyages was drastically modified. Only three civilians sailed with Cook: an artist, an astronomical observer sent by the Board of Longitude, and a botanical collector. They were technicans, not independent scientists. Conspicuously absent were any prominent scientists of the stature of Banks or the elder Forster. Instead, Cook was to utilize the services of his officers to carry out many of the scientific functions of the voyage: Lieutenant James King, who because of his study of astronomy at Oxford and Paris, could make precise astronomical observations; a young William Bligh, who was an expert draftsman and surveyor; and three surgeons, who had talents in natural history, writing, and drawing.

We really do not know whether Cook, the Admiralty, or both were behind this virtual exclusion of civilian scientists and their substitution by naval officers. However, when Lieutenant King called on Captain Cook before the voyage to pay his respects and to express his regret that no scientific person was going on the voyage as before, King was answered with a tirade from Cook that reportedly included the words "Curse all the scientists and all science into the bargain!" (Beaglehole, 1974, p. 502).

After his experience with the exhilarating, but overly ambitious Banks and then the cantankerous Forster, Cook apparently wanted nothing more to do with prominent scientists. He had a job to do, to search for the northwest passage, and he apparently wanted no one on board who would question his methods or carp at him to go here and there for purposes of making scientific observations or of collecting unique specimens. If there was anything scientific to be done, he would rely on his officers and the malleable technicians on board. For the English naval establishment, the honeymoon between scientists and seamen was over, and a separation, if not a divorce, was in order.

## The French

The French followed a similar progression as their British rivals. They, too, started sending civilian scientists out with their Pacific expeditions, and they, too, ended up virtually banning civilians and having naval officers with scientific training and inclination make the scientific observations and do the scientific collecting.

The first French voyage with scientific pretensions sailed for the Pacific in 1766 under the command of Bougainville. Bougainville's expedition was less serious in a strict scientific sense, however, than Cook's near-contemporaneous first voyage. Although Bougainville did bring along the distinguished naturalist Commerson, who had been nominated for the post by Buffon, the motivation for the voyage was more geopolitical than scientific, and the voyage had little impact other than to fuel French ambitions in the Pacific and to reinforce romantic ideas of natural man and accompanying critiques of the *ancien regime* — largely based on an inaccurate protrayal of Tahitian society penned by an enraptured but uncritical Commerson.

With subsequent voyages, French scientific exploration came to the fore, large complements of scientists were carried, and an effort was made to dovetail the work of scientific and naval personnel. But French naval enthusiasm for science was not to last. Friction between scientists and seamen grew as the complement of scientists expanded. When Baudin sailed in 1800 to survey the largely unknown Australian continent, he carried no less than 22 scientists and their assistants on board. The voyage was most difficult. Baudin was incapacitated from consumption, which finally killed him on the way back to France; food ran short; and scientists and seamen kept getting in each other's way. The sailors were especially resentful of the mass of scientific gear carried, the amount of food consumed by the "useless" scientists, and above all, the time "wasted" in collecting natural history specimens ashore. When, for example, a young French officer met the English navigator Matthew Flinders, who had beat the French to the south Australian coast, he is reported to have said to Flinders: "Captain, if we had not been delayed so long picking up shells and collecting butterflies in Van Dieman's Land [Tasmania] you would not have discovered the South Coast before us" (Dunmore, 1969, p. 29).

Thereafter, no French expedition was to be so burdened by scientists. In fact, in 1817, Louis de Freycinet sailed for the Pacific with not a single civilian scientist on board. Instead, he had his young lieutenants handle the telescopes and make oceanographic and geophysical measurements and had the two surgeons and the pharmacist double as botanists and zoologists. Freycinet had learned from personal experience on the Baudin expedition that "a group of scientists is likely to be a source of trouble, and he preferred to have scientific work carried out by naval officers, whom he could easily control" (Dunmore, 1969, p. 63).

The French naval officers, like their British rivals, were apparently glad to be rid of civilian scientists cluttering their decks. For scientific tasks, the employment of "naval officers with some scientific training, including a knowledge of natural history, became the rule." These naval men were considered "far more valuable [than civilian scientists] because they would obey orders in a way no passenger, no guest, however bound by agreements or a sense of duty, ever would" (Dunmore, 1969, p. 389).

## The Russians

The Russians did not begin their grand exploratory voyages into the Pacific until 1803, when Krusenstern sailed from the Baltic port of Kronstadt for the North Pacific. Over the next three decades, some 30 ships were to sail from there to the Pacific, many making the circumnavigation after completing their tasks. Although most of the Russian voyages were linked in one way or another with the needs of Russian outposts on both sides of the Bering Strait, scientific goals were proclaimed for many of their voyages, and the ships commonly carried a scientist or two and often an artist, as well. I do not know the literature well enough to say whether the trend of starting out with grand scientific projects and then later downgrading science and scientists was operative in the Russian case. However, from the journal of the naturalist Chamisso on the Kotzebue expedition (1815–1818), it is apparent that the Russian seamen and scientists were not immune from conflict. Like Forster, Chamisso (1856) complains of the restraints placed upon him by a captain who, he says, did not understand the needs of science.

## The Americans

Although the Americans may have been late on the scene, once aroused their scientific ambitions were anything but modest. Americans did not start thinking seriously about sending a major exploring expedition into the Pacific until more than a half century after those first voyages by Bougainville and Cook. Coming so late upon the scene, they apparently wanted to play catch-up with a vengeance.

Through a grand scientific voyage, the United States, said expedition promoter Jeremiah Reynolds before the House of Representatives on April 3, 1836, could "wipe out, at one glorious effort, the taunting imputation so long cast upon the American character" that we are but unlettered receivers of knowledge from Europe, and "throw back on Europe, with interest and gratitude, the rays of light that we have received from her" (Stanton, 1975, p. 32). Reynolds then told the assembled congressmen that the object of the expedition would be to

> . . . collect, preserve, and arrange every thing valuable in the whole range of natural history . . . and accurately to describe that which cannot be preserved; to secure whatever may be hoped for in natural philosophy; to examine vegetation, from the hundred mosses of the rocks, throughout all classes of shrub, flower, and tree, up to the monarch of the forest; to study man in his physical and mental powers, in his manners, habits, and disposition, and social and political relations; and above all, in the philosophy of his language; to examine the phenomena of winds and tides, of heat and cold, of light and darkness. . . ." (Stanton, 1975, p. 32)

To those amazed listeners who were asking themselves how all this might be done, Reynolds calmly offered the formula already discredited in British and French naval circles: "By an enlightened body of naval officers, joining harmoniously with a corps of scientific men, imbued with the love of science." Chosen wisely, the officers and the "lights of science" would, "like stars in the milky way, shed a lustre on each other, and all on their country" (Stanton, 1975, p. 32).

Many influential people drank this in. Congress voted funds for a naval expedition carrying civilian scientists. Members of the budding American scientific establishment lined up for the promised positions as botanists, geologists, astronomers, philologers, and zoologists, in what Reynolds had promised would be a "scientific faculty, complete in all departments" (Stanton, 1975, p. 41). But when, after much wrangling and many delays, Charles Wilkes, a young naval officer with scientific ambitions, was chosen to command the expedition, he decimated the ranks of the scientists. Wilkes may have been acquainted with the history of British and French scientific expeditions, or perhaps it was just his seaman's reasoning that made him follow the European model. Whatever the case, he decided that all work pertaining to astronomy, surveying, hydrology, geology, geodesy, magnetism, meteorology, and physics in general would be handled exclusively by his naval officers, and he also tried to cut down the size of the scientific complement (Stanton, 1975, p. 63).

Wilkes did not totally get his way. James Dwight Dana, a young civilian geologist who was to make outstanding contributions to the knowledge about volcanism from the study of Pacific islands, was allowed to remain on the crew, and Horatio Hale, the young Harvard graduate whose linguistic and anthropological researches conducted on the expedition were to bring him worldwide fame, escaped the axe only through political intervention.

The expedition, known as the United States Exploring Expedition, sailed from Norfolk in 1838 and returned in triumph to New York 4 years later. On board the three main ships were 12 civilians: naturalists and their assistants, plus the geologist and linguist mentioned above. Wilkes proved to be a stern disciplinarian and, after the voyage, was court-martialed and reprimanded for his treatment of the crew. Although no official charges were lodged by the scientists, many complained privately that Wilkes had hindered their scientific work, in particular by severely limiting their time ashore. For example, during the voyage the geologist Dana had written from Valparaiso to the Harvard botanist Asa Gray to congratulate him and other scientists left behind for their "narrow escape from Naval servitude" (Stanton, 1975, p. 137).

The Wilkes expedition was the last experiment for many years to come in joining large numbers of civilian scientists with naval personnel on a grand voyage of exploration. After its return, and especially given the rancorous disputes that followed between the Navy and various other government agencies and the scientific establishment over the care and housing of the enormous scientific collections brought back and the publication of the research results, there was no attempt to follow so difficult a model. Like their British and French counterparts, American naval vessels might carry a naturalist or two when sent on an exploring mission, but mostly what science was done at sea was carried out by naval officers.

## Too Much Too Soon?

The ideal model of having groups of civilian scientists and naval personnel work cooperatively at doing science and exploration at sea was, judging from the experience reviewed, prematurely applied.

Of course, if we take the scientists' point of view, it is easy to sympathize with, for example, Forster, who, when frustrated by restrictions placed upon his research work ashore, rails against "people who know nothing of Sciences & hate them, never care whether they are enlarged & knowledge increases or not" (Hoare, 1982, 3, p. 551), or with Commerson, his French colleague on the Bougainville expedition, when he describes his ship as "that hellish den where hatred, insubordination, bad faith, brigandage, cruelty, and all sorts of disorder reign" (Dunmore, 1965, p. 76). After all, if voyages were really for science, it would seem logical that every effort should have been made to facilitate research in every way.

However, I think a better case can be made that the naval officers charged with sailing their ships halfway around the world to explore the globe's largest ocean, and then with getting back safely home, had good reasons for restricting science and scientists. In an era when ocean voyaging was so hazardous, when a sudden storm or unseen reef could wreck a ship, leaving absolutely no prospect for rescue, and when scurvy and other illnesses regularly took their toll, these seamen had their hands full just keeping their ships intact and their crews alive. To carry out the minimal geographical explorations required by their orders was a big enough job in itself. All the rest, the collecting, the sketching, the inquiring into native customs, was frosting on the cake — to be done only if these activities did not compromise the safety and schedule of the expedition.

In the end, some scientists realized this. For example, however frustrated he may have felt while at sea on the U.S. Exploring Expedition, the geologist Dana had to admit that Wilkes respected science and that all the scientists were brought home safely and with loads of botanical and zoological specimens, drawings, rock samples, vocabularies and descriptions of Indian tribes and island societies, and the like. Furthermore, Dana admitted that he doubted that with any other commander would the scientists "have fared better or lived together more harmoniously" (Stanton, 1975, p. 363).

But, to ban civilian scientists altogether from the voyages was certainly too drastic a solution to this problem. Some naval officers, most notably Cook, may have been able to make important scientific observations, but their activities were necessarily limited by their training, or lack thereof, and their all-important shipboard duties. An argument can even be made that learned natural scientists could actually enhance the safety of a voyage through their judicious advice to naval officers on how to relate to islanders along the way.

The great Cook did not live to see England again after leaving on the third voyage. After finishing his survey of the Northwest Coast and finding no passage to the Atlantic, Cook returned to Hawaii, an archipelago he had discovered on his way north. While anchored at Kealakekua Bay, a ship's boat was stolen. An enraged Cook went ashore to take the high chief hostage to ensure the return of the craft. An angry crowd gathered, and when Cook tried to take the chief back to the ship, the Hawaiians killed the navigator. Forster wrote later that the absence of an "educated, scientific gentleman" on the third voyage had contributed to the tragedy. In Forster's opinion, Banks and Solander on the first voyage, and then Forster himself and his son on the second voyage, had been civilizing influences on Cook: Their presence had prevented Cook from acting too rashly with the islanders. But, as there were no "educated, scientific gentlemen" on the third voyage, there was no one to restrain the great navigator from making that fatal error of judgment (Beaglehole, 1961, pp. xlvi–xlvii; Hoare, 1976, 237).

## Oceanographic Research

Once oceanic voyaging became less hazardous and more routine, once steam displaced or at least supplemented sail, once accurate charts and navigation instruments made it possible to navigate with precision, and once preserved foods and the ability to easily obtain provisions from ports along the way banished hunger and scurvy, then naval officers could afford to relax a little. The idea of taking groups of scientists on extended cruises once again surfaced, for the learned gentlemen could now be accommodated much more easily than before. For example, in 1872, a hundred years after Cook, the Royal Navy's *Challenger*, a three-masted, square-rigged, wooden vessel with a steam engine, sailed on a round-the-world oceanographic cruise that marked a new era of "doing science" at sea. This modern and well-equipped vessel carried six marine scientists — complete with their dredging and sampling gear, and laboratories as well. The ship, her officers, and her crew were totally dedicated to making this research possible on this pioneering oceanographic voyage (Linklater, 1972).

Given the subsequent growth of oceanographic research, wherein specially designed ships carry oceanographers and other scientists on research cruises throughout our planet's oceans, it is tempting to assume that there should be no more problems between scientists and seamen. However, casual inquiries among my oceanographic colleagues, and a study of the relations between scientists and crewmen carried out by anthropologist H. Russel Bernard, indicate that even routine oceanographic cruises are far from being problem-free.

Currently, oceanographic research is primarily conducted — in the United States, at least — by universities and oceanographic institutes that send research vessels on extended cruises that may last for several months. The research vessels are essentially floating laboratories for the conduct of research in physics, chemistry, geology, and biology at sea. Although the officers and crew are civilians, most have served in the Navy, and all are professional seamen. The scientific party, which is usually equal in number to the officers and crew, is made up of a chief scientist, typically the principal investigator whose grant funds the cruise or a major portion thereof, plus other scientists, graduate students, and technicians.

While resident at the Scripps Institute of Oceanography during 1973, Bernard was able to go to sea on a research cruise to observe behavior at sea firsthand and to interview both scientists and seamen at sea and ashore. He concludes from his research that tension between the two groups is inevitable because they essentially form two separate subcultures with different values and goals (Bernard & Killworth, 1973, 1974). For example, the scientists, who typically only join the vessel for short periods of time, are totally interested in gathering data in relation to highly focused research projects, while the seamen, for whom the vessel is a home for many months at a time, are primarily interested in the smooth operation of the vessel and in maximizing their time ashore. Class differences between highly educated scientists and, in particular, those ordinary seamen with a high school education only, further demarcate these two subcultures.

Bernard cites numerous examples of conflict between, on the one hand, data-hungry scientists who cannot understand why crewmen won't do everything, including giving up time in port, to help them wring every last bit of information out of the sea and, on the other hand, seamen who do not want to be disturbed in their routine by outsiders who insist on the priority of their research. While in a dispute, aggrieved scientists may rightly argue that the whole purpose of a cruise is to undertake research, but if they press their case too hard, their projects may be sabotaged. Bernard cites the case of a dispute over a refrigerator, originally designated to house biological specimens, in which the crew had been storing their liquid refreshments. When their supplies were evicted and the refrigerator was locked, the crewmen countered by breaking open the refrigerator and dumping all the biological specimens into the sea, thereby ruining weeks of costly work.

## Discussion

From the perspective of the history of the grand voyages of exploration of the 18th and 19th centuries, what has occurred during the first stages of manned spaceflight begins to look more natural, if not inevitable. During the first decade of American manned spaceflight, pilot astronauts were overwhelmingly dominant; only one scientist astronaut, for example, ever reached the Moon. During the shuttle era, there appears to have been a conscious effort to fuse pilot astronauts and mission specialist astronauts (i.e., scientist astronauts) into a tightly knit team. However successful that effort has been, in the process of building this pilot–scientist team, the role of the outsider, with accompanying misunderstandings and antagonisms, seems to have been transferred to the payload specialists, who are, in effect, visiting scientists/technicians who receive less training and do not belong to the elite astronaut corps. These developments would seem to parallel the evolving relationship between seamen and scientists during the earlier, maritime era of scientific voyaging.

The development of modern oceanographic research provides a model of how large groups of visiting researchers who, for reasons of time and other constraints, would not be able to undertake lengthy astronaut training might one day be accommodated in space facilities. However, the contemporary oceanographic situation indicates that if space research were to be made routine to the extent that ocean research now is, subcultural differences, and hence tensions, between scientists and those pilots, stationkeepers, and others whose job it will be to enable researchers to carry out their tasks in space may become critical considerations. If so, space analogues of the mechanisms that have evolved to accommodate differences between scientists and seamen aboard oceanographic ships may have to be developed. However, it should be noted that Bernard (Bernard & Killworth, 1974, p. 12) proposes that the main mechanisms for controlling conflict between scientists and seamen is the maintenance of "subcultural privacy" wherein the seamen attempt to shut out the scientists from their own world aboard ship. Difficulties in assuring subcultural privacy in already cramped space facilities would indicate that conflict reduction efforts through cross-training and other sensitizing methods will be needed for future space ventures, particularly those involving large numbers of scientists.

## References

Beaglehole, J. C. (1961). *The voyage of the* Resolution *and* Adventure *1772-1775*. Cambridge, England: Cambridge University Press.

Beaglehole, J. C. (1968). *The voyage of the* Endeavour *1768-1771*. Cambridge, England: Cambridge University Press.

Beaglehole, J. C. (1974). *The life of Captain James Cook*. London: Hayklyut Society.

Bernard, H. R., & Killworth, P. (1973). On the social structure of an ocean–going research vessel. *Social Science Research, 2*, 145–184.

Bernard, H. R., & Killworth, P. (1974). *Scientists at sea: A case study in communications at sea* (Report BK-103-74, Code 452, Contract N00014-73-4-0417-0001). Prepared for the Office of Naval Research. Springfield, VA: National Technical Information Service.

Chamisso, A. von (1856). *Reise um die Welt mit der Romanoffischen Entdeckungs Expedition in den Jahren 1815-1818*. Berlin: Weidmann.

Dunmore, J. (1965). *French explorers of the Pacific*, Vol. 1. Oxford: Clarendon Press.

Dunmore, J. (1969). *French explorers of the Pacific*, Vol. 2. Oxford: Clarendon Press.

Goetzmann, W. H. (1986). *New lands, new men*. New York: Viking.

Hoare, M. E. (1976). *The tactless philosopher*. Melbourne: Hawthorn.

Hoare, M. E. (1982). *The* Resolution *journal of Johann Reinhold Forster 1772-1775*. *Vols. 1-4*. London: Haykluyt Society.

Linklater, E. (1972). *The voyage of the* Challenger. London: John Murray.

Stanton, W. (1975). *The great United States exploring expedition of 1838-1842*. Berkeley, CA: University of California Press.

Thrower, N. J. W. (1981). *The three voyages of Edmond Halley in the* Paramore *1698-1701*. London: Haykluyt Society.

# 10

# Three Decades of Nuclear Submarine Research: Implications for Space and Antarctic Research

Benjamin B. Weybrew

Launched in 1954, the *Nautilus*, the first nuclear submarine, ushered in a new era in the history of submersible vehicles. Since oxygen is not necessary for the nuclear propulsion system, the submerged duration of the more than 40 nuclear-powered, ballistic missile submarines (SSBNs) and the more than 100 nuclear attack submarines (SSNs) now operational is limited only by the amount of food, oxygen, and vital essentials that the "sub" is able to transport, synthesize, or manufacture. Thus, in contrast to maximum submerged periods of 72 hr possible with World War II diesel subs, modern nuclear submarines such as the *Nautilus* and *Triton* have remained submerged for 60 to 90 days while transiting beneath the Arctic ice cap and circumnavigating the globe. Moreover, "nukes," as they are called, have a classified crush depth of at least 800 ft. Tending to improvise on this point was a bumper sticker frequently seen around New London, Connecticut, in the 1960s: "Nuke submariners do it deeper." With the size of the nuke subs increasing from 300 ft in length and 3,200 displacement tons for World War II diesel subs to the length of 560 ft and 18,000 tons for the *Trident* came the requirement for an increase in crew size from 9 officers and 64 enlisted men to 16 and 148, respectively, for the *Trident*, the most recent sub to join the fleet.

The environment of the nuclear submariner, sometimes called *inner* space, as compared to the *outer* space of the astronaut, has some similarities

The author was a member of the research staff of the Naval Submarine Medical Research Laboratory for three decades prior to retirement in 1979. The views and opinions expressed in this chapter are those of the author and should not be construed as the official views of the United States Navy.

and some differences. Surrounded by a thick, steel, pressure hull, the sub's atmosphere is sustained at 1 atm pressure. Thus, fear of pressurization, called *bathophobia*, with the submarine at, for example, 1,000 ft depth (31 atm absolute, or about 32 t/ft², pressure), is very real. Evidence for this preoccupation with accidental pressurization may be inferred from the submariners' readiness to transform the standard units of pressure, pounds per square inch, (PSI) to units of other measurement systems, such as Newtons per square meter (Nm⁻²), Pascals (Pls), or Toricellis (torr). In contrast, the astronaut, in the rare atmosphere of outer space, is concerned with depressurization and not pressurization. Loss of power at great depths results in the inability of the sub to "blow ballast" (water) sufficient to allow the Archimedes buoyancy principle to effect a surfacing. Similarly, loss of thruster power in the space vehicle removes the capacity to decelerate sufficiently to allow the Earth's gravity to effect reentry and a terrestrial landing. On the other hand, the related problems of atmospheric revitalization and decontamination, radiation effects, and space restrictions are common to the two habitats.

Apart from a few papers in the area of vision and audition, there were relatively few research papers published in the field of submarine psychology prior to keel laying of the *Nautilus* in 1952. While an attempt was made to summarize this prenuclear research (Committee on Undersea Warfare, 1949; Weybrew, 1963, 1979), the program in personnel psychology at the Naval Submarine Medical Research Laboratory (NSMRL) became focused at that time on five main areas: (1) psychiatric screening; (2) training and development; (3) crew composition and adjustment; (4) human factors; and (5) stress.

The theoretical framework for the program was Kurt Lewin's 50-year-old equation:

$$B = f(P \times E) \tag{1}$$

where

P = personality

and

E = environment.

Starting with the "E" in the equation and working backward, our approach was two-pronged: (1) to learn all that we could about the environment of the deeply submerged nuclear sub in order to find operationally definable adjustment criteria; then, (2) to identify reliably measured traits or characteristics that predict individual differences in the submariner's capacity to adapt to the unique conditions existing during long submerged missions.

# Psychiatric Screening

All recruits for the submarine service are volunteers. Thus, with the annual input population of 5,000 to 6,000 enlisted men and 400 to 500 officers and depending upon many determinants such as the job market, public image of the service, turnover, and so forth, the selection ratio (SER) has of necessity varied from 50% in the late 1950s to 95% in the late 1970s. When SER was high, the selection/screening strategy was to minimize false positives, and when SER was low, to minimize false negatives.

## *Derivation of Validation Criteria*

The three major methods of obtaining criterion dimensions were (1) to use all available proximal criteria such as grades and pass/fail in sub school, qualify/fail to qualify for the dolphins, the prestigious symbol of the submariner, and reenlist/fail to reenlist at the end of a tour of duty; (2) to use scores from rating scales based on observations made by staff psychologists and section chief petty officers during the training phase and, later, on ratings from senior crewmembers during submerged missions; and (3) to identify specific criterion dimensions from factor analysis of data collected by means of Flanagan's Critical Incident Technique.

## *Psychological Screening Variables*

There were six major kinds of data obtained from each nuclear submariner candidate: biographical inventory data including medical history; aptitude test scores; measures of emotional stability; appropriateness and intensity of motivation for, and attitudes towards, sub duty; evidence of psychopathological trends; and stress coping capacity (SCC) (Weybrew, 1971).

## *Research Findings*

### Aptitude Tests

The Basic Test Battery (BTB), consisting of Verbal, Mechanical, and Arithmetical subtests, yielded a positive multiple correlation coefficient in the .50s with performance in basic submarine school. However, the nonlinear correlations with the more distal criterion, did/did not reenlist, was low and generally negative.

### Biodata

Criterion-keyed items of biodata, such as educational achievement level, socioeconomic background, interests, preferred subjects in high school, and so forth, have significant validity with training criteria but not with the more distal retention criteria mentioned above.

Emotional Stability

A brief, self-report inventory, the Personal Inventory Barometer (PIB), with high convergent validity with the Depression and Psychaesthenia scales of the Minnesota Multiphasic Personality Inventory (or MMPI), has significant validity for identifying those submariners prone to have anxiety attacks, the most frequently occurring psychopathology observed during long submerged missions. Absence of any signs of panic in a pressure chamber at 4 Atm absolute pressure screens for claustrophobia; however, behavior in the pressure test has no relationship to performance at sea. It has been shown experimentally that the resiliency of a candidate's autonomic nervous system as measured by skin conductance change during and recovery following exposure to a contrived stress situation tends to identify those submariners with the highest SCC.

Motivation and Attitudes

The Self-Report Motivation Questionnaire (SMQ) consists of 50 items related to reasons for volunteering, to goals and modes-to-goals supporting the decision to join the services, and expectancies (subjective probabilities) of satisfying high-valent (i.e., essential) needs in this branch of the military. Of those candidates with low-average aptitude test scores, only those with above-average SMQ scores were considered qualified as recruits for the sub service. Another test, the Submarine Attitude Questionnaire (or SAQ), served to demonstrate the kinds of attitudes that become negative during long missions. A multiple cutoff accept/reject decision strategy involving the BTB, PIB, and SMQ has been identified that would result in a 95% success ratio (or SUR) — but only if the SER could be 35% or less.

Psychopathological Trends

Information pertaining to a history of delinquency, treatment for mental disorder, or unstable job history is scrutinized closely. If decompensatory trends seem probable, additional psychodiagnostic data are obtained before the accept/reject decision is finally made. In this context, a factor analysis of Rorschach inkblot test results suggested that the scores derived from responses to the chromatic cards may be correlated with broad adjustment criteria. (Weybrew and Molish, 1986).

Stress Coping Capacity

Based upon certain biodata and observations made during escape tank and pressure chamber training coupled with selected response patterns to critical items on the PIB and SMQ, a judgment was made regarding the SCC of a given submariner candidate.

## *Generalizations from the Research Findings*

1. Factor analysis of paired-comparison rating scales derived by means of Flanagan's Critical Incident Technique has been shown to be an effective approach to criterion development for submariner selection research.
2. Aptitude test scores have significant predictive validity with proximal training criteria but not with distal criteria, such as qualification and end-of-tour reenlistment.
3. Distal criteria are predicted from measures of motivation, emotional stability, and attitudes.
4. The results of from 8 to 10 experiments suggested that the concept "autonomic nervous system (ANS) resiliency," operationally defined as the degree of recovery of peripheral indices of ANS change (blood pressure, skin resistance, and so forth) resulting from exposure to contrived stress situations, may be significantly predictive of adequate SCC during long submerged missions.
5. Objective, inventory-type personality tests tend to have higher validity with psychopathological trend criteria than do projective-type test data.

## Training and Development

Three components of the training and development program were considered relevant: (1) training needs assessment, (2) training methodology, and (3) training outcomes evaluation. Most of the research associated with these three components is conducted by the Naval Bureau of Personnel; however, certain observations during training served as corroborative information for the selection/screening data collected earlier in the submariner candidate orientation program.

## *Generalizations from the Research Findings*

1. For officers, performance on the attack, fire control, and mooring/docking simulators yielded low but nonchance correlations with under way criteria. While the empirical validity of simulator performance was not highly significant, the following basic assumption was not contraverted: If the submariner candidate cannot perform adequately in the simulated situation under relatively bland stress conditions, it is highly unlikely he will be able to perform effectively in the high-stress environment of the deeply submerged submarine.
2. Although grades in enlisted sub school correlate with performance ratings at sea, this relationship disappears at the qualification and reenlistment decision level.
3. Programmed instruction and computer-assisted instruction have been

successfully used in advanced electronic, sonar, and missileman schools.
4. Still being validated is the computer-assisted-diagnosis procedure, a program designed to aid the nuclear submarine medical technician (NSMT) in the diagnosis of both organic and functional disorders while at sea.

## Crew Composition and Adjustment

### Intracrew Small Groups

Quite circumscribed barriers define intracrew subgroups demarcated by the eight skill specialties (electronics, ordnance, medical, clerical, and so forth) making up the submarine crew. Communication channels are described as double-inverted Y networks involving the commanding officer, the executive officer, and the chief of the Boat.

### Generalizations from Research Findings

1. Data from both diesel and nuclear sub crews show that the greater the role congruency, that is, the degree to which a crewmember's enacted role is consistent with his expected role, the more adequate his adjustment.
2. The same data showed that rigid authoritarian/task-oriented leadership style is the most effective in emergencies but that the participative/supportive style is the most effective in routine, day in and day out situations and, furthermore, tended to enhance the cohesiveness of the submarine crew at the same time.
3. As submerged missions of 30 to 80 days progress, submariners' attitudes regarding possibly untoward effects of atmospheric contaminants become more negative, that is, change in the direction of greater perceived risk. However, these attitudes tend to moderate in intensity during the shore-based rest and rehabilitation periods.
4. The major social psychological characteristics differentiating effective from ineffective sub crews are open communication and feedback channels, group-accepted formal and informal norms, and clearly defined contingencies for achieving important individual and group goals.

## Human Factors (HF)

The focus of human factors (HF) research in the mid-1950s may be capsulized by the Double Fit Principle: Find the best "fit" of the submariner candidate to the machine and build the machine to "fit" that person. Accordingly, during the early missions of the *Nautilus* in the late 1950s, copious amounts of data dealing with reported tensions, sleep problems, appetite changes, interpersonal relations, and perceived "annoyances" of all kinds were collected by means of the Daily Health Diary, a confidential, self-report, symptom or annoyance instrument. These data yielded a number of insights concerning the submariners' man/machine interactions during protracted missions. Some of these environmental aspects, to be labeled "stressors" in the next section of this chapter, were, in descending order of frequency, possible harm from gaseous, particulate, and radiation contaminants in the ambient atmosphere; spatial limitations, crowding and sense of constriction; diurnal flattening; and boring and fatiguing work/rest schedules.

## Generalizations from Research Findings

1. Confidential diaries provide a useful source of data from which problems associated with man/machine interfaces may be identified and, in some cases, alleviated.
2. Training sessions presenting factual data pertaining to the type and level of radiation exposure, and to the concentration of the some 200 gaseous and particulate atmospheric contaminants identified at the time, were shown to be effective in reducing crewmember anxiety.
3. The so-called red/green "Christmas tree" display showing the open/closed condition of the submarine hatches was made bimodal, that is, both shape and color-coded indicators were incorporated into the display systems in order to reduce error.
4. Psychologists specializing in vision demonstrated in the late 1940s that the close viewing distance in subs caused the lateral phorias to become esophoric. In response to this finding, it was recommended that landscapes and seascapes with deep depth cues be installed on the bulkheads of selected compartments.
5. Dark-adaptation procedures were established to enhance periscopic viewing under low illumination levels.
6. Ear defenders were prescribed for men whose duty stations were located in compartments with high-intensity, mixed-frequency noise levels occasionally in excess of 70 db.
7. The perceptual basis for dubbing the submarine a "seagoing sewer pipe or pigboat" is the well-documented fact that the absolute level of olfactory stimulation becomes very high soon after submergence. As a result, the Weber fraction, $\Delta s/s$, the ratio of a perceptible difference to the absolute level of stimulation, increases remarkably. It seems plausible, therefore, that since olfaction, gustation, appetite, and food preferences are intrinsically interrelated, this atmospheric attribute may pose a significant health problem during long patrols.
8. As the pace at which nuclear submarines were being built in the 1960s increased, the HF specialists at NSMRL began to establish closer consultative relationships with the design engineers while the sub was still in its

blueprint stage. This new relationship served to bring to bear a wide range of facts related to the psychological capabilities and limitations of the typical submariner during the time when the preconstruction design decisions were being made.

# Stress

## *Concepts Used in Submarine Stress Research*

Assuming in the mid-1950s that stress-related research should receive high priority, the staff of NSMRL formulated the program around the following discursive equation (Weybrew & Jex, 1988):

$$POSR_j = f(Mods)[IED_j/AR_j] \qquad (2)$$

where

$POSR_j$ = patterns of stress reactivity for person j;

Mods = moderator variables;

$IED_j$ = intensity of environmental demands for person j;

and

$AR_j$ = adaptive resources for the same person.

Stated simply, equation (2) becomes "the intensity and perhaps the nature of the POSR are directly proportionate to the IED imposed and inversely proportionate to the AR of person j, the relationship being moderated by the Mods." A useful definition of the term *stress* becomes, "the total organismic response to an environmental situation or circumstance in which the IED significantly exceeds the AR of the person." For example, stress would likely occur when the carbon dioxide concentration of the sub atmosphere, normally at .03% on the surface with the hatches open, reaches 1.2% or higher while submerged. IED may be expressed as:

$$IED = SEP_{Stressor\ I} + SEP_{Stressor\ II} + \ldots SEP_{Stressor\ K} \qquad (3)$$

where

$SEP_{Stressor\ I}$ = stress evocation potential of stressor I (in standard score units)

and

$SEP_{Stressor\ II} + \ldots SEP_{Stressor\ K}$ = the SEP of the Kth stressor.

AR may be defined as a complex function of the abilities, personality trait patterns, and experiences in high-SEP situations.

Taken together, the component processes making up POSR closely resemble emotional reactions such as anxiety, fear, and panic. There are six main classes of processes included in POSR: (1) skeletal muscular activity (screams, agitation, tremor, etc.); (2) perceptual/cognitive processes (meanings of stimuli); (3) affective or subjective components (sad, fearful, etc.); (4) autonomic nervous system reactivity (blood pressure, pupil diameter, etc.); (5) endocrine/neurohormonal changes (catecholamines, adrenocorticoids, etc.); and (6) unique to the sub environment, the reduction in the efficiency of the oxygen transport system as indicated by increases in carboxyhemoglobin, carbohemoglobin, and methemoglobin levels.

Finally, SCC is defined as the reciprocal of equation (2) presented above, i.e., SCC = (Mods)(AR/IED) with the terms defined as used in that equation.

In those days, we saw our research task as fourfold: (1) Conduct a psychological analysis of the sub environment in order to identify and rank order the major stressors in terms of their SEP. This technique, involving Q-sorting these stressors, was called stressor identification and rank ordering (SIRO). (2) Define and rank order, in terms of severity, the major classes of processes constituting the POSR. (3) Determine which Mods significantly affect the POSR/IED relationship. (4) Delineate some reliable and valid measures of AR or SCC.

## Generalizations from the Research Findings

1. Application of the SIRO procedure in the 1950s and 1960s as a means of operationalizing IED in the basic equation (2), above, yielded a list of major stressors characterizing the environment of the nuclear submarine. In descending order of SEP, these were found to be: perceived danger of radiation and gaseous atmospheric contaminants including possibly pathogenic flora and fauna (for example, oral *Escherichia coli* from the back pressure from blowing sanitary tanks); concern about seawater pressurization, space restriction, and family and shore–base separation; effects of absence of circadian cues upon sleep; noise level, work overload and underload, and environmental conditions tending to produce boredom and fatigue.

2. The major variables tending to moderate the relationship between POSR and IED were length of time in the sub service, age, educational achievement level, and amount of experience in high-SEP situations.

3. The incidence of acute or chronic psychopathology occurring during long missions is incredibly low, between 1 and 4%. The classes of disorders are, in descending order of frequency, reactive anxiety and depression, antisocial or characterological problems, and psychophysiological reactions.

4. During the 84-day submerged circumnavigation of the world by *Triton* in 1960, the affective tone of the crew, measured daily by self-rating scales, improved significantly following "periscope liberty," a period of time during which interested crewmembers were allowed to take a quick look at the outside world, for example, Tierra del Fuego, South America, on

the starboard side and an iceberg floating on the port side as the sub rounded the rough waters of Cape Horn. The beneficial effect of periscope liberty was interpreted as evidence of "cognitive anchoring," a concept similar to the old Gestalt concept "need for cognitive structure" appearing in the perceptual literature of the 1930s.

5. As the duration of the submerged mission progresses, errors in time perception tend to occur in the direction of overestimation of time intervals. An example of the submariners' preoccupation with the passage of time may be inferred from the notation found on the combat center plotting board of the *Triton* during the global circumnavigation: "Time remaining on the mission, 10,200 minutes, 171 hours, 7.3 days, 0.23 months, 0.195 years, and 0.000195 centuries." Constants to be used to reduce each equivalent unit of time for every 5 min of clock time were also provided.

6. The ambient atmosphere of the nuclear submarine apparently supports pockets of high concentrations of free ions, both negative and positive. During the *Triton* circumnavigation, mood and other affective indicators tended to fluctuate or covary with hydrogen ion concentrations, suggesting that airborne ions may be related to certain emotional states.

Following the replacement of submarine medical officers (that is, M.D.s) by enlisted NSMTs on operating subs in the mid-1960s, an attempt was made to include in the extensive, year-long training course for NSMTs an instructional segment dealing with the causes and management of stress reactions (i.e., POSR) at sea. As part of this segment, a series of suggested techniques, actually embellishments upon modern behavioral modification principles, were presented to the NSMTs as a means of maximizing the SCC of the crewmembers. These suggestions were (a) identify the most important needs of the crewmembers, needs that, when satisfied, tend to sustain appropriate motivation and attitudes during long missions; (b) by means of SIRO or some similar approach, localize those aspects of the sub environment, i.e., stressors, that tend to be tension-producing for the majority of the crew; (c) attempt to maximize the crewmembers' expectancy (subjective probability) that their day-to-day activities (contingencies) will result in favorable outcomes (reinforcement) for them; (d) clearly indicate which contingencies will and will not most likely lead to high-valent outcomes (reinforcers), which, in turn, tend to satisfy highly compelling needs for the submariner.

At the time of these instructional sessions, a discursive representation of these principles was presented:

Maximum SCC = f(Mods)
- Expectancy of RF ± /PU ±
- Clarity of PRCs and ARCs
- Relative presence of (+) valent outcomes and absence of (−) and (0) valent outcomes

where

SCC = stress coping capacity;

RF ± /PU ± = the outcome ratio (OR), or the ratio of (+) and (−) reinforcement (RF) to (+) and (−) punishment (PU);

PRCs and ARCs = perceived and anticipated reinforcement contingencies respectively;

Mods = moderator variables;

and

Expectancy = subjective probability that PRCs and ARCs will tend to maximize OR.

With the exception of a few favorable comments from a small sample of experienced NSMTs who had been exposed to this stress management approach during training, substantial empirical evidence for the efficacy of this or similar approaches to this important training problem has failed to materialize.

## Methodological Observations Regarding Submarine Research

Emerging from these research findings across five areas are two major methodological observations: (1) Multivariate methods such as R-, Q-, and P-technique, as well as Incremental R-technique of factor analysis, are to be recommended. (2) In stress research in particular, the "time" dimension is critical — for example, stress reactions *over time* and adaptive trends *over time*.

In 1972, this author was privileged to have been the discussion leader for the subpanel on submarine research, part of the U.S. delegation to the six-nation North Atlantic Treaty Organization (or NATO) Defense Research Group 14-day exercises in Coblenz, West Germany. In addition to the submarine group, subpanels on helicopters, fixed-wing high-performance aircraft, and tanks and troop carriers spent 12 hours daily for 14 days attempting to reach a consensus prioritization for research projects investigating the medical and psychological problems of nuclear submarines as well as of the other branches of the military. In decreasing order of relevance, this prioritization for subs was as follows: identification and control of potentially harmful atmospheric contaminants; psychiatric screening of submariner candidates; and development and validation of training and other approaches to maximizing submarine crew effectiveness during long submerged missions. Consistent with the objectives of this text, *From Antarctica to Outer Space: Life in Isolation and Confinement*, the research areas identified for nuclear submarines may be justifiably extended to encompass important aspects of spaceflight and space and Antarctic habitation as well. Accordingly, in order of decreasing relevance for the nuclear submarine program, the Antarctic program, and the space program, the salient research issues appear to be (Weybrew, Helmreich, & Howard, 1986):

1. Atmospheric revitalization and contaminant control.
2. Development and validation of procedures for the medical and psychological screening of recruits.
3. Identification of techniques for initiating and sustaining individual motivation and group morale.
4. Stressor identification, assessment of the severity of POSR, and development of effective stress coping strategies.

In conclusion, the kinds of research findings required for an understanding of the adaptation processes of space vehicle inhabitants and Antarctic wintering-over personnel are most likely to emerge from studies employing multivariate, time–series research designs. The classes of variables to be included (and excluded) in studies of this kind pose a challenging dilemma. Hopefully, this cursory overview of three decades of nuclear submariner research has provided some useful hints as to the most promising variables to be included in future spaceflight and Antarctic research.

## References

Committee on Undersea Warfare. (1949). *A survey report on human factors in undersea warfare*. Washington, DC: National Research Council.

Weybrew, B. B. (1963). Psychological problems of prolonged periods of marine submergence. In N. Burns, R. F. Chambers, & E. Hendler (Eds.), *Unusual environments and human behavior* (pp. 87–125). Glencoe, IL: Free Press.

Weybrew, B. B. (1967). Patterns of psychophysiological responses to military stress. In M. H. Appley & R. Trumbull (Eds.), *Psychological stress: Issues in research* (pp. 324–362). New York: Appleton-Century-Crofts.

Weybrew, B. B. (1971). *Submarine crew effectiveness during submerged missions of 60 or more days duration* (Report No. 686). New London: United States Naval Submarine Medical Research Laboratory.

Weybrew, B. B. (1979). *History of military psychology at the U. S. Navy Submarine Medical Research Laboratory* (Report No. 917). New London: United States Naval Submarine Medical Research Laboratory.

Weybrew, B. B., & Jex, S. (1988). Stress in a seminar on stress: A methodological study. *Psychological Reports, 63*, 367–380.

Weybrew, B. B., & Molish, H. B. (1986). *Prediction of nuclear submariner adaptability from autonomic indices and Rorschach inkblot responses*. (Report No. 1080). New London, CT: United States Naval Submarine Medical Research Laboratory.

Weybrew, B. B., Helmreich, R. L., & Howard, N. (1986). *Psychobiological and psychosocial issues in space station planning and design: Inferences from analogous environments and conditions*. Unpublished report prepared for the National Aeronautics and Space Administration.

# 11

# National Park Service Areas as Analogues for Antarctic and Space Environments

ROBERT J. VALEN AND BARRETT S. CALDWELL

In her Master of Science degree thesis, "Social Isolation Among National Park Service Rangers," Donna Bessken (1985) states in the abstract, " . . . the data suggest recommending self-motivated, independent, socially compatible and professionally competent individuals for assignments at socially isolated duty stations." National Park Service (NPS) managers administering socially isolated areas of the NPS have, intuitively and in most cases, assigned to isolated areas ranger personnel who possess qualities mentioned by Bessken. Yet, the assignment process benefits from the fact that many rangers elect to live and work with a positive attitude in an array of physically, socially, and culturally isolated park areas. These qualities are positive driving forces that have created an esprit de corps among park ranger personnel. This spirit is comparable to that found in other small groups of highly specialized professionals, such as astronauts.

It is suggested by the authors that groups of park ranger personnel assigned to socially isolated NPS areas represent an untapped research potential. The infrastructure has been in place for nearly a century and yet remains untouched. Research conducted among these groups should add more depth to the behavioral and social science fields. Research findings in NPS areas should further enhance criteria used for the selection of personnel involved in future space missions. The everyday living and working environments of future spacecraft and space stations might also reflect research findings derived from studies conducted in NPS areas.

As an example of socially isolated assignments in the NPS, the following is taken from a Vacancy Announcement dated July 15, 1987, for a position at Channel Islands National Park, California, on San Miguel Island. The island is 56 miles offshore of Ventura, California. Addressing the area information, the announcement stated:

The occupancy of government housing on San Miguel Island is required of the position during the specific tour of duty—a ten day tour of duty including travel time. The quarters available are on a shared occupancy basis of a temporary facility which is a converted cargo container or Conex Box (10' x 20') that also serves as the ranger station for the island. Fresh water is shipped to the island on an annual basis and shower facilities are limited. Electricity is by solar panels (12 volt) and often is inadequate during long cloudy periods during the winter. No clothes washing facilities are provided on the island. Transportation to and from the island is by boat, military or charter helicopters and fixed-wing aircraft. Quarters may be used by relief ranger when incumbent is on lieu days. There is very little storage for other than items necessary for surviving on the island. The rental rate for the box is $2.20 per day. (National Park Service, Western Region Office, 1987)

The announcement continues by stressing the physical and mental hardship that one will encounter in this position. This position is an example of extreme isolated conditions in the NPS. There are many other isolated positions in the NPS, and each has a unique set of determinants defining isolation.

Of the more than 350 units administered by the NPS, a measurable number are or could be considered isolated. The obvious determinant is physical. Other definitions are cultural, occupational, and limited contact and access beyond immediate surroundings (Bessken, 1985). Currently, the NPS identifies areas it administers as being in one of three categories: Urban (and subdefinitions of Suburban and Outlying), Rural, and Remote. These definitions are based solely on relative location to a Metropolitan Statistical Area, and in the case of Remote, special travel arrangements are needed to reach these areas. Under the official NPS title of Rural, there are 156 units, while the title Remote has 27 units.

## Establishment of the National Park Service

The concept of protecting and preserving geographical areas for their ecological or historical values is rooted in the histories of the earliest civilizations. The rulers of India proclaimed some forests protected from woodcutting and wood gathering due to their natural qualities long before the birth of Christ. Our history shows that the preservation concept at the federal government level spans nearly 200 years. One such history is that of the Hot Springs Reservation, Arkansas Territory (today, Hot Springs National Park), which was set aside in 1832. Though Hot Springs does not occupy major chapters in the history of the NPS, it was one of the first areas to be protected by federal action because of the "medicinal properties" of the springs. Some early events that indirectly brought about the eventual establishment of the NPS were the Folsom–Cook Expedition (1869) and the Washburn–Langford–Doane Expedition (1870). These expeditions explored the Yellowstone Region of the Wyoming Territory and resulted in the establishment of Yellowstone National Park in 1872, the world's first national park.

Certainly, in the early histories of our oldest national parks, travel arrangements and the time needed to travel to the parks were very important factors to park visitors a century ago. These areas were truly physically isolated. Those working in the parks, mainly United States Army personnel, who functioned as the early caretakers of these parks (the Army administered Yellowstone from 1886 to 1918), perceived the duty like the traveler perceived the visit: an experience in isolation. There were 32 national parks and monuments in the United States, primarily in the West, prior to the establishment of the NPS as a bureau in the U.S. Department of the Interior on August 25, 1916.

In 1880, Harry Yount, government gamekeeper, remained all winter long in Yellowstone National Park to prevent poachers from entering the territory. Mr. Yount is considered to be the first park ranger by many and one of the first men to experience a winter in Yellowstone—"wintering-over." Mr. Yount saw the hopelessness of his duties and stated in a report that it was impossible for one man to patrol the park and urged the formation of a ranger force (Albright, 1929).

## Modern-Day Park Service Isolation

Conditions associated with physical and environmental isolation have not changed much from the 1880 wintering-over of Mr. Yount in Yellowstone. In a February 1985 Associated Press news article, "Crater Lake Workers Find Ways to Deal With Winter," appeared the following comments:

. . . one of the toughest places to live in the park system (NPS), with a winter nine months long and an average annual snowfall of 600 inches. . . . Living in a place that is still snow-covered while spring can be found just a short drive down the mountain creates unique psychological problems. . . . When Benjamin started to talk, one of the first words was "plow." It's really quite understandable. Snowplows are such a big part of his life. (p. 18A)

In his book *The National Park Service*, William Everhart (1972) addresses the social isolation that is typically found in many of the rural and remote areas of the NPS:

Family life in a park community to some degree reverses accustomed life styles. Most citizens have all the necessities of life at hand. Their problem is to get away. For park families, even the normal conveniences of civilization can be a problem.

Shopping, which may involve a 200-mile round trip or more, may be made the occasion of a social spree much as earlier pioneers used their infrequent opportunities to get into town. Some park families rely on the latest edition of "Merck's Manual" (The *Merck Manual of Diagnosis and Therapy*, first published in 1899). (pp. 157–158)

The hardship of both social and cultural isolation has been experienced by NPS rangers and their families, as well. There are many areas of the NPS that are located near or in culturally isolated regions. About one half of Badlands National Park, South Dakota, is on the Oglala Sioux Pine Ridge Indian Reservation, and all of Canyon de Chelly National Monument, Arizona, is located on the Navajo Indian Reservation. For the majority of ranger personnel, working and living in an area that contrasts with one's cultural experience must tax one's independent and social compatibility skills to the fullest. The same form of cultural isolation has been experienced by rangers stationed at NPS areas on the Hawaiian and Virgin islands. NPS rangers stationed in the state of Alaska experience a form of cultural isolation—the "Alaskan culture."

NPS personnel living and working in a multidisciplinary environment with the same group of people in isolated park units for 3 to 5 years witness unique problems found only in a few groups of professionals. Topics that might be addressed in long-term research projects are the social interaction in the work and park community; work and nonwork conflict resolution; behavioral and psychological issues involved in emergencies such as law enforcement, search and rescue, and medical actions; and the relatively positive behavioral response to the physically, socially, and culturally isolated environment.

## National Parks as Analogous Environments

Despite the physical and social isolation seen in some NPS areas, national parks are not often considered in studies of isolation. The two major works classifying analogous isolation experiences (Sells, 1973; Stuster, 1986) do not mention national parks at all. One obvious reason for this might be the NPS's association with highly visible (and visited) parks such as Yellowstone or Grand Canyon. However, areas under NPS direction have an enormous variety of task requirements and ecological facets. Less visited, more remote NPS areas obviously provide greater validity as potentials for analogue research.

Stuster's (1986) classification and rating system shows that analogous environments differ in similarity to the proposed space station. This similarity can vary within the same environment because of the diversity of rating categories. One advantage of the rating system is that it becomes possible to specify similarity requirements for classes of research settings. It then becomes easier to enumerate possible analogues that have not been previously considered. Any group meeting the similarity requirements can be considered, limited only by the type of research or specific disqualifying characteristics. Suedfeld (this volume) also points out that research in isolated environments should focus on the environment as perceived by its inhabitants. Thus, qualities of isolation exist in those places where rangers experience isolation in ways similar to inhabitants of other types of environments.

The mission sense and enthusiasm of NPS employees (Everhart, 1972; Foresta, 1984) make them good candidates for analogues to space or Antarctic personnel. Selection of preferred group size provides an easy method for choosing among more than 350 NPS areas. Risk, environmental hostility, and habitat concerns, however, quickly reduce the pool of appropriate sites. Requiring psychological and physical isolation from large numbers of visitors further reduces the number of appropriate parks.

A number of remote NPS areas still provide opportunities for high-fidelity analogues, despite these restrictions. The official NPS classification of a remote park is one where public transportation or paved road is not available to the park or where special travel arrangements are required (Bessken, 1985). Several parks fitting this description exist in the lower 48 states. One of them requires a 20-mile drive from the nearest paved road, while several others are on islands. The addition of the Alaska Park Lands to the NPS in 1980 provides even more desirable candidates. Some park sites are so remote, even central administrative offices overseeing the park can be in locations considered isolated. Employees working in the same park may be 100 or more miles apart (Belous, 1989, personal communication).

Of course, not all research on isolation needs high-analogue fidelity on all dimensions. Conceptual questions of group organization, leadership style, or interpersonal processes can be studied in a variety of locations. Many issues in these or other topics do not require strict adherence to more extreme considerations of isolation and physical danger. Studies that compare groups according to relative location on given dimensions may also be completed in NPS areas. The diversity of physical and social environments provides a wide range within a consistent framework of general agency organization, mission, and employee characteristics.

## Directions for Future Research

The authors wish to emphasize the great and basically unused potential for analogue research utilizing the NPS. On the other hand, such research should be of high quality and not rely on excessive demands of NPS employees. Past unprofessional and unclear research efforts have often overloaded and discouraged otherwise enthusiastic employees. Conversely, systematic research with clear and broad utility for the NPS can elicit cooperation and constructive input by employees. Thus, we would like to propose the following three research initiatives.

1. A widespread study can be developed to provide a fine-grained description of the extent and type of isolation experienced at various NPS areas. This description would provide NPS management with information regarding important organizational aspects relevant to those areas. Selection, training, and employee satisfaction issues can also be specified and reinforced with increased knowledge of the stresses of isolated and remote areas.
2. More in-depth research should be undertaken to determine the location of high-fidelity isolation analogue research sites. Alaska is a prime potential resource for such sites, due to its low population, vast area, and often extreme weather conditions.

   Such research could be undertaken as part of a National Aeronautics and Space Administration/NPS cooperative agreement, at a fraction of the cost and interagency bureaucracy common with Antarctic research sites.
3. Conceptual issues of small-group interaction, organizational management, and responses to isolation can be addressed in a variety of park areas. These issues should not be ignored as a fundamental foundation for inquiries in applied environmental, organizational, and social psychology. Participant observation fieldwork is a rewarding methodology for these studies. It provides opportunities for the researcher to gather subtle and "insider" information about the group being observed. Enhanced ecological validity and employee cooperation result when compared to detached researchers using only generalized self-report measures.

These initiatives can provide great benefits to the study of isolation and analogous environments. The mission of the NPS as the custodian of vast, untamed areas for future generations makes it an ideal candidate for research into the interactions of humans with the isolated and wild environment.

## References

Albright, H. M. (1929). *Oh, ranger! A book about the national parks*. Palo Alto, CA: Stanford University Press.

Belous, R. (1989). Personal communication.

Bessken, D. (1985). *Social isolation among Park Service rangers*. Unpublished master's thesis, Slippery Rock State University, Slippery Rock, PA.

The El Paso Times/Associated Press. (1985, February 17). Crater lake workers find ways to deal with winter (p. 18A).

Everhart, W. C. (1972). *The National Park Service*. New York: Praeger.

Foresta, R. A. (1984). *America's national parks and their keepers*. Washington, DC: Resources For The Future, Inc.

National Park Service. (1987, July). Vacancy announcement. San Francisco, CA: Western Region Office.

Sells, S. B. (1973). A taxonomy of man in enclosed space. In J. E. Rasmussen (Ed.), *Man in isolation and confinement* (pp. 281–303). Chicago: Aldine.

Stuster, J. W. (1986). *Space station habitability recommendations based on a systematic comparative analysis of analogous conditions*. Santa Barbara, CA: Anacapa Sciences.

# Part II  Orientations and Perspectives

## Introduction

Within contemporary psychology, much research lacks strong theoretical underpinnings. Although atheoretical research can be valuable, conceptual frameworks and theories serve to integrate and explain results and guide further efforts. The chapters presented in this section have strong conceptual or theoretical components.

In the lead chapter, Chester Pierce offers a useful organizational framework for addressing the analogies between spaceflight and Antarctic environments, including time lines and research opportunities as well as environmental and behavioral similarities. Pierce introduces the concept of "microaggressions," small acts that are almost innocuous in and of themselves but that, in the aggregate, can undermine self-esteem and destroy interpersonal relationships. Next, Peter Suedfeld reminds us that responses to environments, including isolated and confined environments, reflect an interaction between the environment and the person. He offers five principles to help guide inferential thinking and research, and he identifies specific personality variables that are likely to moderate a person's experience of isolation and confinement. Suedfeld's organizing principles are that researchers should think in terms of experiences within environments rather than of environmental characteristics; researchers should study differences and similarities between experiences, which are not the same as those between environments; analogies should be based on similarities of experience, not necessarily of environments; research should look at systematic links between personality factors and experience; and experience is continuous and integrated rather than discontinuous and fragmented.

If people are to spend lengthy periods of time in isolation and confinement, as will be the case on a lunar or Mars mission, they will require high-quality spacecraft and habitats. Wolfgang Preiser applies cybernetics—the "science of effective organization"—to the design of settlements in outer space. From the cyberneticist's point of view, environmental design is an iterative process involving sequential planning, programming, design, construction, and evaluation. Preiser draws on Maslow's hierarchy of needs and explores numerous design parameters for extraterrestrial facilities.

This section concludes with brief presentations of two general theories of behavior that may be suitable for application to Antarctica and outer space. First, Joseph V. Brady and Mary A. Anderson argue that systematic, carefully controlled experimental studies provide the most promising methods for managing the performance and welfare of isolated and confined groups. The roots of this technology are to be found in "programmed environments" that allow the application of behavior modification principles to enhance productivity, morale, and social compatibility. The authors review their 15-year program of experimental, programmed environment research.

Finally, James Grier Miller proposes an application of living systems theory (LST) to life in space. An extension of open systems theory, living systems theory provides a framework for the description and analysis of biological and social systems. According to this theory, there are certain important similarities and parallels among systems at all levels, including, but not limited to, the individual, group, organizational, community, and societal levels. Over the past 30 years, LST has been applied successfully in a wide range of situations and contexts, and it is here applied to the analysis and improvement of outer space habitats.

# 12

# Theoretical Approaches to Adaptation to Antarctica and Space

CHESTER M. PIERCE

The many general similarities in the factors governing life science research in the Antarctic and space suggest that each environment might serve the other as an analogue. Both environments seem destined in the near and intermediate future for increased exploration. This destiny is generated by strategic considerations of commerce, science, defense, and politics. To accomplish such strategies, each environment must be tamed, so that humans see them as increasingly friendly, inviting, and commonplace rather than unruly, foreboding, and alien.

Yet, well into the more remote future, both environments probably will be classified as exotic. Relatively few people will venture into them and remain there, and they will be obliged to live under stressful conditions of prolonged isolation, confinement, uncertainty, and hazard.

In both situations, it is known, some people at some time during their stay will manifest sleep disturbances, anxiety, increased territoriality behavior, decreased performance, reduced motivation, impaired mental efficiency, withdrawal, and perhaps augmented suggestibility and biological dysrhythms. Likewise in both environments, emotional and material support, given generously, are critical for diluting depression and apathy.

Some important differences should be observed. At present, there are no polar-peculiar illnesses or derangements. On the other hand, space motion sickness or even jet lag derangement seem to demand very rapid passage, over time, through space. In addition, it remains to be discovered whether long-duration flights of several years or multiply repeated passages of short-duration flights will produce maladies now alien to medical knowledge. Such maladies might arise as a result of microgravity, radiation, chronodesynchrony, motion, and space-dependent psychological alterations.

So far, humans, usually highly selected and trained, have been able to function admirably in short-duration flights in space, as well as for longer periods of time in the Antarctic. The Antarctic, compared to space, has demonstrated with more certainty and over a greater number of years that heterogeneous groups of people can accomplish their missions under conditions of prolonged isolation. These groups have included persons from diverse trades and professions with different sex, racial, national, linguistic, cultural, educational, and social backgrounds. In the Antarctic there has accumulated considerable experience with the heterogenous groups that are expected in future spaceflight.

The theoretical contribution of life science research to adaptation in Antarctica or space may be approached in different ways. Among these approaches are analogies based on symptom development, on the basis of problems that occur at predictable points along the mission's time line, and on the basis of scientific research opportunities. This chapter will address briefly some of these analogies. Organization is on the basis of psychobiosocial studies in the Antarctic.

## Analogy from Symptoms

Little is known from previous work in the field about differentiating cold-sensitive and cold-resistant persons. Similarly, we have made little progress predicting any person's ability to withstand or resist space motion sickness when on a space expedition. Whether or not common protective mechanisms for cold resistance and space motion resistance would be found, mutually useful approaches and methods could be sought. At minimum, investigators will continue to search for space-specific and polar-specific illness as well as to inquire into possible symptom development from relationships between immune competence and group dynamics.

Inhabitants in both places are subject to important psychosocial stresses that affect the success of the expedition. These include lack of privacy, boredom, inability to escape, forced socialization, anxiety, and nostalgia. While operating under these burdens, each individual must comply with a welter of regulations, formal and informal. Some of these are imposed by outside authorities, some by the person's culture, and others by developing traditions within the group. Sensitivity to obligations and regulations is compounded in stressful environments because of the heightened importance of vigilance and leader–follower relations. Constantly, the individual must assess and evaluate each crewmember's entitlements.

Under these conditions, orders from the outside world, differences in lifestyles, differing preferences for such things as music, and conflicts over the use of an exercise facility can develop compliance frictions. This psychosocial travail can yield offending slights, or microaggressions, rather than full-blown explosions or social turbulence.

Microaggressions are subtle, stunning, usually automatic trivialization and depreciation of another person. The victim's code of honor is damaged by these annoyances, but the events themselves are so minimal and so obscured and innocuous that it would seem extraordinary to pursue reparative action with the offender. Often, too, microaggressions are unrecognized by one or both interactants. Yet they are part of the structure and function of a group's etiquette, which helps define members' behavior as acceptable or unacceptable.

Perhaps most microaggressions are nonverbal or a blend of verbal and nonverbal elements. As one American reported an insulting, annoying conversation, "From the *way* he talked, not what he said, I knew he thought I was lousy at my job." The relationship between the men dissolved irrevocably from that point.

When microaggressions are noticed, they may be registered and nursed as grievances until the aggravation becomes exquisite. The cumulative weight of persisting, new, or expanding small indignities sustains smouldering anger and resentment. This interpersonal dynamic enters into the appraisal of each interactant and can result in perceptions and behavior characterized by prejudice, distorted communication, and counterhostility. Individual and group dynamics may be adversely affected in small, crippling ways, diminishing mission efficiency and satisfaction. Periodically, the dynamics of these offensive and counteroffensive behaviors will erupt into obvious, important frictions. Yet the rage from microaggressions can be maintained and influential in group interaction for very protracted periods of time, as commonly witnessed in everyday cross-social, cross-national, cross-cultural, cross-racial misunderstandings.

The elucidation and cataloging of compliance conflicts producing microaggressions would benefit from study in each environment. A continuing study of microaggressions could lead to diagnostic, prognostic, and preventive management of group psychosocial symptomatology, which contributes to performance slippage, depression, and somatic complaints. In theory, microaggressions can be operationalized and quantified by the analysis of space, time, energy, and mobility.

## Analogy from a Mission's Time Line

For convenience, the time line for a journey to space or Antarctica can be described in terms of preembarkation, mission, and reentry. The spacefarer or Antarctic expeditioner may confront overall problems throughout the time line, relating to warding off depression, complying with regulations, engaging a hostile surrounding, and adapting to changing life-styles. Further, these concerns may serve as a cause and/or effect in promoting turmoil for administrative and debarkation site personnel, as well as family and close associates of the travelers.

In the preembarkation phase in both environments, life scientists have made their most appreciated and perhaps their most significant contributions. The specific contribution is in the selection of participants and their orientation to the mission.

Historically, much of the selection for the U.S. Antarctic program evolved from the experience of the Naval Medical Corps. In the case of the U.S. space program, much of the selection and training contributions evolved from the experience and inquiries of the Air Force Medical Corps. In both instances, the missions have been exceedingly well served. However, the evolutionary thrust suggests continuing usefulness in deliberate exploration of how to synthesize and integrate the selection process. Such exploration would have to contemplate proactive, nonmilitary influences and their potential contribution and role in the nation's anticipated expansion of polar and space programs.

Once selected, even in the preembarkation phase, each expeditioner to Antarctica or space must be observed carefully for subtle changes of withdrawal, augmented impulsivity, and despondency. These minor but real alterations also could affect family, friends, and working colleagues. Still another consideration in this phase is that satisfactory mission adaptation places immense importance on exactly what job the individual will be required to do and his or her skill in doing that job. Vocational adaptability in a group setting, especially in increasingly heterogeneous crews, may become of more concern than specific personality features.

The second, or mission, phase speaks to time at the base for the Antarctican but includes flight and possible base time for the spacefarer. Specifically, the journey itself to the Antarctic is fairly routine and can be accomplished in a relatively short period.

Common for both environments, once the person is in the habitat of an Antarctic station or a spacecraft, is the overwhelming importance of demonstrated support/interest and contact maintenance with those at home. Means and methods of providing support and contact will pose taxing problems in long-duration flights. More experimental research about ensuring sufficient evidence of support, interest, and contact may have to be done on short-duration flights and in analogue situations such as Antarctic bases prior to very long-duration flights.

Several other analogues during the mission can be emphasized. The first is the need to focus on what the traveler does with disposable time. Compliance to schedules for habitat maintenance, vocational duties, exercise regimens, training rehearsals, and some social conventions, such as conforming to eating hours, can be difficult to sustain. How, when, where, and for how long a person controls time and what resources and persons are available when one spends free time may be of utmost value in diminishing the microaggressive nidus, which is prefatory to conflict and symptomatology. Therefore, leisure-time use in the conditions of forced and clustered socialization and meager and limited facilities becomes a paramount focus for study. Protective components of the use of disposable space, time, energy, and mobility may include complex interactions with such diverse factors as leadership style, integrity of the sleep cycle and other biological rhythms, job satisfaction and progress, and clique formation.

Mention of clique formation implies possible volitional, relatively exclusive, smooth, collaborative, cooperative endeavor by some members of the unit. Should such a clique have a sexual component, there is the foundation for possible lament, chagrin, and disruption of the overall group dynamic. Of all sorts of desired and probable heterogeneity, in space voyages and Antarctic undertakings, the sagacious and considered integration of more females may be the most likely to promote a climate congenial for mission success.

In fact, heterogeneity of status, occupation, national origins, language, and race have been commonplace in the Antarctic for many years. Much of such heterogeneity has been researched in the practical service of improving group performance (Gunderson, 1973). This corpus of data and the methods used to accumulate it should be helpful to space research, particularly since severe limitations of sample size and access to participants in space voyages may exist for some time. An international protocol with input from many countries could be designed to maximize a compilation of data about male–female experiences under conditions of isolation, confinement, and hazard. This would be an ideal cooperative protocol for the Scientific Committee on Antarctic Research or for National Aeronautics and Space Administration-sponsored research. Insights into issues of selection, training, and group dynamics would be underlined. Of particular concern, medically, would be to anticipate management of successful or unsuccessful pregnancies and their complications, as well as the care of healthy or unhealthy infants, whose childhood would be in an isolated, confined environment. The particular and general medical concerns eventually will find expression in on-going selection, training, and task performance in the relevant environment.

One final analogue to be mentioned during the embarkation stage is the development of depression. Depression may be precipitated in these environments by a multitude of causes. A partial listing of causes acting alone or in conjunction includes injuries, accidents, illnesses, bad or no news from home, unrelenting danger, death of a crewmember, eroding job satisfaction, sleep disturbance complications, and possible natural or induced cycles of relative despondency. One approach would be to refine the search in each environment for protectors against depression, in addition to enhancing ways for the expeditioners to help themselves and others to anticipate and dilute melancholy, hopelessness, and despair. The successful model of anticipatory guidance in Peace Corps volunteers demonstrates the value of such activity.

Pertinent to the discussion of depression is the probability that in the case of the return voyage from space the expeditioners may be more at risk to succumb to depression than during any other point in the time line. This has occurred on polar traverses and in many military, commercial, diplomatic, and research tenures. The orientation and preparation for reentry must be part of the preembarkation and embarkation phases. On a return space journey, the balance between time spent on structured obligations and on free use of time will take on added significance in terms of keeping an ample amount of time for reentry preparation.

Antarctica and space can inform each other by giving over more focus to reentry preparation. The reentry phase must be inaugurated at the time of selection for the mission. Twenty-five years ago, some Navy relatives were told not to expect their returning loved one to "be himself" for at least a year following the wintering experience in Antarctica. Forewarning and ongoing longitudinal, supportive, preventive, and concurrent outreach programs may be required for long-duration space voyagers, their families, and colleagues. It would seem to be a cautious prediction that reentry from long-duration space travel will be accompanied by fairly gross, definite physical changes and definite, even if barely observable, psychological changes. Likewise, the family of the voyager, as do families of submariners on short-duration cruises, will perforce make many adjustments that will have to be modified to accommodate reunion with the expeditioner. Reentry and reunion studies and demonstrations done in either environment should aid both environments.

Recent data from a longitudinal study of Navy personnel indicate the crucial importance of securing baseline information for long-term follow-up (Palinkas, 1986). Besides acute reentry and reunion focus, both environments should engage in and compare long-term follow-up and prospective predictions of expeditioners, as contrasted to controls.

## Analogy from Research Opportunities

For a variety of reasons, behavioral science research has had relatively slender support in both environments. Many of these reasons are both necessary and understandable. In each environment, there are also substantial and insubstantial reasons for the paucity and relative insignificance of psychological contributions.

What may be germane is to consider some of the mechanisms that are linked with acceptance of the behavioral science branch of life sciences by other scientists and engineers, who correctly must dominate and guide the research and development of any extreme environment. True acceptance, not mere tolerance, can come only when behavioral scientists are able as a matter of routine to be consistently involved and invested participant observers in each environment. Secondary investigations may be very rich in terms of science but do not greatly reduce the skepticism of other scientists or engineers. Nor do they provide the degree of acceptance of shared danger and responsibilities. Many simulation experiments that risk death would have enormous resistance getting approval from human experiment committees.

Pre- and postmission data collections, with or without collections done during the mission by nonspecialists, are highly suspect, because there could be misleading or inaccurate reporting. Unobtrusive monitoring summons outrage concerning violation of privacy and confidentiality. Therefore, a major analogy is that both investigators in space and the Antarctic must discover and ensure ways for behavioral science researchers to have more and sustained on-site presence.

The second analogy is related intrinsically to the first. It may be that from the vantage point of other scientists and engineers, behavioral science enterprise seems to dwell more on what it can do to help the expeditioners than on what the expeditioners and expedition can do to help the advancement of social science knowledge and its widespread application.

A major studied effort is required by the organized behavioral science community to be certain that other scientific colleagues appreciate that behavioral scientists are both modest in their claims and intellectually anxious to use these environments to bring broad benefits to humankind. This appreciation by others also would facilitate the certainty in their minds that such goals are attainable. Of course, behavioral scientists would then have to produce effectively and progressively to earn acceptance.

In essence, behavioral science in both environments will suffer from abbreviation and indifference by the total science community unless (1) behavioral scientists are fully engaged in the field and (2) behavioral scientists are perceived more as seekers after truth than self-stated providers of solutions. Even though these two conditions are in many ways not due to the wishes, desires, intentions, or expectations of behavioral scientists, their negotiation may require serious dedication and coordination by all organized behavioral science. The organized effort should help promote unqualified and full partnership by behavioral scientists in enterprises of big and little research in both environments.

## Conclusion

There are many possible next steps. All these illustrative possibilities can be incorporated into published recommendations that have been made in the recent past for each of the two environments (Brady, 1983; Committee on Space Biology and Medicine, 1987; Polar Research Board, 1982). This means it should be possible to elaborate studies that are mutually useful and compatible with previously recommended aims for both the nation's space and Antarctic biomedical research.

Both sets of aims, for instance, would be congruent with placing high priority on learning more about male–female interactions; reentry and reunion problems for traveler, family members, and support personnel; emphasis on delivering support from and keeping contact with the outside world; and discovering more about the possible relationship of thermoregulation, immunocompetence, and group dynamics. In addition, over a number of years, committees from both the space and the Antarctic biomedical research communities have urged more study about chronodesynchrony, including the sleep cycle; how to minimize the depression, somatic ills, and emotional tensions that may be associated with living under prolonged and stressful isolation and confinement; and how to augment effective multidisciplinary and interdisciplinary international research. In addition, these same community spokespersons call for extracting as much use as possible from the literature on analogous situations.

Perhaps Antarctic research provides an older distillate about all of these issues. Space research, however, probably is more commanding and in greater depth for many of the issues. The next step is to actualize experiments whereby one environment would aid and abet the other. These inquiries can be done in laboratories, in analogous situations, in library searches, and in various types of simulators. The most crucial experiments must be done in the designated field itself. Perhaps the most important nonfield studies would be generated from data registry of inhabitants of either environment. Medical studies from molecular biology of animals and humans to behavioral pharmacology and biometeorology can be done in both environments. From the more narrow aspect of emotional and behavioral concerns as opposed to more comprehensive biomedical problems, one study that could be most easily conducted for quick and long-lasting advantage in both environments would be to obtain a sharper delineation of male–female interactions in both situations. Already in both environments, male–female interactions have been well observed in programs in more than one country.

Another set of "big science" projects that could be done in both environments to their mutual advantage is designing and implementing psychological self-assessment and psychological self-help programs. Such programs should be multifaceted to include coping, stress management, peer counseling, biofeedback, cross-cultural analysis, environmental manipulation, and crisis management techniques.

There are numerous "little science" projects to be pursued in both environments. Some to consider immediately include demonstrations about reduction of conflict and the provision of support.

Happily, no matter where we begin, *The Human Experience in Antarctica* conference served the useful purpose of stimulating scientific dialogue. It should catalyze proposals from extragalactic to submolecular science about how to help people live better and live longer, whether in the highest latitudes of the Earth, the outer reaches of space, or anywhere else where humans live or wish to live.

# References

Ad Hoc Committee on Polar Research, Polar Research Board, National Research Council. (1982). *Polar biomedical research: An assessment*. Washington, DC: National Academy Press.

Brady, J. V. (1983). *Human behavior in space environments: A research agenda*. Baltimore: Johns Hopkins University School of Medicine.

Committee on Space Biology and Medicine, Space Science Board, National Research Council. (1987). *A strategy for space biology and medical science*. Washington, DC: National Academy Press.

Gunderson, E. K. E. (1973). Individual behavior in confined or isolated groups. In J. E. Rasmussen (Ed.), *Man in isolation and confinement* (pp. 144–154). Chicago: Aldine.

Palinkas, L. A. (1986). Health and performance of Antarctic winter-over personnel: A follow-up study. *Aviation, Space and Environmental Medicine, 57*, 954–959.

# 13

# Groups in Isolation and Confinement: Environments and Experiences

Peter Suedfeld

One of the most fascinating aspects of "space psychology" may be the fact that from the beginning it has drawn heavily upon research on environments whose significant features were in some way considered to be analogous, similar, or equivalent to space vehicles. Obviously, there was no way to avoid this: after all, planning for all of the aspects of spaceflight had to occur before anyone had any actual experience in space. I remember, for instance, participating in North Atlantic Treaty Organization and National Aeronautics and Space Administration (NASA) symposia on long-duration missions back in the mid-1960s (e.g., Suedfeld, 1968).

The reason why I was invited to participate in those meetings was my research on what was then called sensory deprivation, a laboratory technique that was one then-popular analogue of spaceflight. In sensory deprivation, there is isolation from other people; a reduction in the level and variability of physical stimulation; and very restricted mobility (Zubek, 1969). These were thought to be characteristics that would also be encountered by astronauts on long missions, and data from sensory deprivation experiments were considered to be relevant to what we could expect among space voyagers (cf. Flaherty, 1961).

It seemed strange to me then, and it still does, to expect such parallels in the human response to the two situations. Sensory deprivation subjects typically spent one, or a few, days lying in bed in a dark, soundproof room, doing nothing. Most of them were university students who participated in the experiment for a modest payment (Bexton, Heron, & Scott, 1954; Solomon, Kubzansky, Leiderman, Mendelson, Trumbull, & Wexler, 1961; Suedfeld, 1980; Zubek, 1969).

By contrast, space crews would be made up of highly qualified, competitively chosen individuals, for whom participation would be a unique adventure, a significant career step, and a source of prestige and fame. They would be involved in a major national and international effort. They would be called upon to perform sometimes-complicated tasks during the flight and would have to be prepared to deal with life-threatening emergencies. Their trip would take weeks, months, or even years. True, they might be alone or in a small group, but socially isolated otherwise; true, the level and variety of physical stimulation would be lower than in normal urban society; true, movement would be limited. But the psychological meaning of the two environments, or of what was expected within them, was so strikingly different that only a philosophy of extreme environmental determinism could justify equating them (Suedfeld, 1980).

The same problem arises with other examples of analogical thinking about space, such as the pioneering work of Haythorn and Altman in Bethesda, Maryland (reviewed in Altman, 1973). Confining two naval recruits for several days and giving them various tasks to perform is, on the face of it, closer to the actual conditions of space cabins than the sensory deprivation chamber could ever be; but it, too, fails to capture the psychological Gestalt.

Other analogues — submarines, polar stations, prolonged sailing voyages, expeditions, prison cells — all share the same difficulties. They are superficially similar in some of their physical, and perhaps even some psychological, dimensions. But whether these similarities are enough to enable us to predict the behavior of astronauts is by no means obvious. Environmental psychology has long puzzled over the issue of ecological validity (Brunswik, 1956; Streufert & Swezey, 1985; Winkel, 1985), and the problem appears to be especially acute in space psychology.

No one can object to investigating and comparing environments with similar physical parameters. But the results of such studies must be extrapolated very cautiously. Extreme environmental determinism is a solid and simple foundation for hypotheses and, sometimes, may even be an adequate one (although, I would guess, only rarely); but it ignores much of what we know about factors that affect human behavior (cf. Brownstein & Moos, 1976).

I should enter two warnings here. One is that the use of these laboratory analogies should not be viewed too severely; after all, given that research could not be performed on real space crews during real missions, the analogue environment was as close as we could come. In fact, for truly long-duration missions (i.e., those measured in years), we still have to rely on analogy and extrapolation.

Second, the analogies were neither completely invalid nor completely useless. For example, those early conferences came up with suggestions such as the desirability of designing spacecraft living quarters with a variation of colors, patterns, and materials; providing food that was tasty and diversified, as well as nutritious; allowing for privacy as well as communality within the cabin; satisfying the needs for territoriality, control over one's personal space and spare-time activities, markers to denote one's boundaries, and so on. These principles still seem valid. Apparently, psychological input is appreciated in the Soviet space program (Chaikin, 1985; Connors, Harrison, & Akins, 1986), and the principles described above have been followed in the design of Soviet space stations (Bluth & Helppie, 1986) — ironically, since it appears that after the initial burst of interest, NASA itself has tended to de-emphasize the relevance of the human sciences (Harrison, 1986; Helmreich, 1983).

NASA's lack of interest has been explained on the grounds that early concerns about astronaut adaptation have been unfounded. No space mission has yet been jeopardized because of negative effects of sensory deprivation, confinement, interpersonal disharmony, and so forth (Connors et al., 1986) — although some disruption due to sociopsychological causes clearly has been noted. I would guess that, in addition, the immensity of the scientific and technical problems of spaceflight, coupled with the technical background of many NASA personnel and the "can do" attitude of the astronauts themselves, militates against giving much scope to psychology outside the boundaries of human factors engineering.

Connors et al. (1986), among others, have called for psychologists to demonstrate their ability to contribute to the exploration of space. While any evidence that such contributions would be possible within the rubric of actual flight is of course important, it seems clear to me that, realistically, we still expect to rely on analogue research. It is therefore crucial that our analogues be appropriately chosen and well understood.

Recently, while writing the chapter on extreme and unusual environments for Stokols and Altman's monumental *Handbook of Environmental Psychology* (Suedfeld, 1987), I faced the problem of thinking about how to define and categorize environments. As we all know, some outstanding colleagues have devoted much time to developing useful taxonomies and identifying relevant variables. But even taking all of these into consideration, I bogged down on such dilemmas as whether, for example, military recruit training represents an extreme and/or unusual environment. Although I eventually dealt with this and similar problems, the difficulty of doing so led me to hypothesize that perhaps the emphasis on environmental variables was somewhat misleading and that we should refocus on a more complex set of factors: the environment as experienced by the person or group. Below, I propose a few guidelines for the use of such inferential thinking and research; let us see where they lead us.

## Principle 1: Researchers Should Think in Terms of Experiences Within Environments Rather than of Environmental Characteristics

The relations between environmental features and behavior must be studied in terms of interaction, not main, effects. As several investigators have pointed out, the environment has no direct impact on human beings. Rather, it is filtered through their psychological and physiological information-processing systems. In consequence, the crucial determinant of the response is not an environment, but an experience, this being defined as the environment *and* its meaning to the individual.

Researchers should, therefore, adopt some new ways to gain an understanding of environmental impact on people. The most obvious one is to measure not only how individuals behave in the environment but also how they perceive it. Such questions as the perceived meaning of the environment, the individual's feeling of control, and how the person views his or her own handling of the situation are all crucial (S. E. Taylor, 1983). Strangely enough, even the researchers who in their theoretical writings emphasize such points seldom follow them up in their empirical work.

A situation that may clearly appear stressful to the investigator may not to the subject, or vice versa. For example, a recent study of stress among crews and passengers on two ships proceeding towards the Antarctic fortuitously included one vessel that suffered a potentially extremely hazardous engine failure. Much to the surprise of the researcher—and, I suspect, of most psychologists—little if any change in subjective stress was evidenced during this episode (Mocellin, 1987). This example has many counterparts among highly trained professionals who, when faced with an emergency, concentrate on problem solving to the exclusion of at least conscious fear or disruption.

Adopting some new concepts, such as the measurement of daily hassles and uplifts, as well as new approaches to coping (Lazarus & Folkman, 1984) could add much to our understanding of how people experience their environments. For example, widespread criticism of solitary confinement in prisons has been based on analogies from experimental sensory deprivation and social isolation literature (e.g., Grassian & Friedman, 1986). But actual convicts in solitary confinement frequently indicate that they find the time out from the constant dangers and demands of the normal prison routine to be pleasant; and when they do complain about being put into solitary, the complaints center on such issues as food being cold by the time it reaches a remote solitary unit or guards being especially hostile, rather than on any inadequacy of stimulation (Suedfeld, Ramirez, Deaton, & Baker-Brown, 1982).

# Principle 2: Researchers Should Study Differences and Similarities Between Experiences, Which Are Not the Same as Those Between Environments

It follows from Principle 1 that (a) the same environment may lead to different experiences for different people; (b) an environment can figure in different experiences for the same person at different times; and, conversely, (c) physically very different environments may figure in very similar experiences.

Again, the derivations from the principle are obvious. In discussing the effects of "extreme and unusual environments," for example, we quickly realize the difficulty of defining in any general way what such environments are. The frozen ice fields of the Arctic are customary and satisfying to the Inuk hunter; the rush of loud and quickly moving stimuli is normal for the psychologist. We view the Arctic as extreme and unusual, but we are really characterizing our view — that is, our experience — of the Arctic, not the environment itself.

Another, and to me fascinating, example is that of the people whom A. J. W. Taylor and Shurley called "Antarctic troglodytes" (1971). Psychologists have seldom differentiated between the novice and the veteran in unusual environments, although it seems clear that the meaning of the situation is very different for the two groups. On a recent trip to the High Arctic, I was struck by the divergences in adaptive mode between young weather technicians, usually in their first 2-year tour, and supervisory and maintenance people who have spent many years in the North. The former spent much of their spare time in large groups, reminiscing about life "back in Canada," engaging in loud horseplay, and drinking; some of the remainder of the time was spent in watching television or other passive pursuits. The latter socialized in small groups of two or three close friends; they devoted some time and effort to personalizing their living quarters; and they all seemed to have consuming hobbies, many having to do with the Arctic, such as geology or archaeology, that they pursued avidly.

It was clear to me that the Arctic experience was very different for these two groups in the same environment. We also found that the novices had high scores on the Sensation Seeking Scale (Zuckerman, 1979), a measure on which the veterans scored low. I do not believe that the age difference explains the finding; or, rather, I think it contributes to an interaction that explains it. The veterans are indeed older than the newcomers, almost by definition. But they are also self-selected from the large number of workers in the North, most of whom do not choose to stay or return there. Perhaps the difference is between those who can make much out of what an outside observer would call little stimulation and those who cannot and who, therefore, must generate a higher level for themselves. I am not sure I would call the veterans augmenters or sharpeners (see, for example, Petrie, 1979); I would be more comfortable calling them *deepeners*, a construct for which no measure yet exists but that evokes their ability to look for, find, and examine complex aspects of a superficially monotonous setting.

One more example. A content analysis of materials written by Antarctic explorers of the Heroic Age (Mocellin & Suedfeld, 1987) found that one of the common themes of their dreams and fantasies was food. They spent much of their imagination on remembering meals that they had had and planning those they would have upon their return. Content analysis of materials written by Antarctic base personnel in the late 1980s, on the other hand, showed practically no food imagery. Instead, dreams focused on family life back home, with frequent images of rejection and abandonment. Clearly, the contemporary polar crewmembers had little reason to be concerned about whether they would have enough to eat; perhaps the explorers of the 19th and early 20th centuries had little reason to fear that their wives would be estranged from them upon their return. Equally clearly, we could not adequately understand the experience of either group without these data, which—I may point out—draw upon a type of information that is seldom collected. This example also shows the tremendous influence of sociocultural factors on how an environment is actually experienced.

## Principle 3: Analogies Should Be Based on Similarities of Experience, not Necessarily of Environment

It follows from Principle 1 that while analogies between environments may be an acceptable first step in predicting human behavior in a particular environment, finding analogous experiences would be more useful. Further, Principle 2(c) implies an increase in latitude for researchers, since a close approximation of physical and environmental characteristics is not required.

Principle 2 and Principle 4, below, suggest some approaches to identifying appropriate analogies. If we do not need to worry about whether there is in fact a comparable level of, let us say, stimulus reduction across the sensory deprivation laboratory, the solitary confinement cell, the one-man sailboat, and the space capsule, we can, rather, try to identify similarities and differences in how these situations are experienced (cf. Suedfeld, 1980). Since the experience will be shaped not only by physical and social parameters but also by personality, previous experiences, and the like, we must use these factors as quasi-independent variables.

Such a procedure is in some ways more difficult, since it requires data collection before the analogy is accepted rather than an a priori decision to use two environments as analogous; but it is also easier, since it opens up a wider range of possibly acceptable situations.

It also may save us from embarrassing mistakes. Let me refer to one such problem, emanating from sensory deprivation research. You may recall that the original methodology, invented by Donald O. Hebb and labeled as perceptual isolation, had the subject lying on a bed with a moderate but constant level of homogeneous light and sound fed into the chamber (Bexton et al., 1954). Later versions used drastically lowered levels of stimulation, achieved by putting the subject into a situation of darkness and silence either in a chamber (Vernon, 1963) or in a tank of water (Lilly, 1956, 1977).

For a long time, researchers assumed that the homogeneously stimulating and the stimulus-reduced environments were analogous—in fact, equivalent. Reviews showed some differences between their effects, but these did not seem to be very consistent nor very important (Zubek, 1973).

Recent research shows that, when such confounds as expectancy are controlled for, the two techniques have drastically different effects. "Perceptual isolation" is experienced as unpleasant and seems to have no beneficial consequences. Stimulus reduction, by contrast, has facilitating effects on memory, imagery, and creativity; it is a powerful therapeutic tool in habit modification, such as smoking cessation, and in its flotation version, results in both psychological and psychophysiological signs of deep relaxation and tension reduction (Suedfeld, 1980; Suedfeld & Kristeller, 1982).

Closer to our current concerns is the issue of intragroup hostility among small parties—more specifically, hostility between group members and the leader—and even more specifically, between one or more key subordinates and the leader. We know that such frictions arise in Antarctic groups and in teams of explorers and mountain climbers (Suedfeld, 1987). Such groups are isolated together for long periods of time, confined in their movements, deprived of privacy, and faced with complex, demanding, and sometimes dangerous tasks. The loss of cohesiveness and the exacerbation of rivalry may be outgrowths of these salient environmental factors; is a similar deterioration, therefore, unavoidable in long-duration space missions?

Obviously, we cannot answer that question directly. But one clue is to look at nonobvious differences between spaceflight and the endeavors mentioned above. For example, a spacecraft is in constant communication with a base. As has already happened, the crew may redirect aggressiveness and resentment towards base personnel, thus avoiding potentially disastrous deteriorations in their own relationships. A clever leader may in fact facilitate this process, and an astute control team at home may play along. Thus, one particular feature of the environment, which is not present in otherwise analogous situations, may make a critical difference.

The previous examples illustrate the perils of "false positive" analogies. There are also "false negatives," where the physical dissimilarity between environments may lead researchers to overlook common, and interesting, reaction patterns. For example, living in a rural environment seems quite different from being in a space or polar station. Yet it may be a good analogue, at least for some of the effects of capsule living. A. J. W. Taylor (e.g., 1987) has posited that the well-known slowdown in cognitive performance in the Antarctic is a matter of changed tempo, the perception that there is plenty of time to fill, not a matter of deteriorated ability. This phenomenon has its counterparts in small, isolated communities, such as remote farms and ranches or mining, logging, and fishing camps (cf. Haggard, 1973).

One more illustration will suffice. This is the occurrence of altered states of consciousness, specifically the impression that another entity is physically present and supportive, which has been reported by people floating in life rafts, climbing mountains, and working in polar regions—as well as by tribal youths during initiation ceremonies and by religious hermits. The commonality of the experience has been ignored because the settings are so disparate that few researchers had noticed this effect; yet, the phenomenon raises important questions about the analogous effects of such situations on psychological and neurological functioning (Suedfeld & Mocellin, 1987).

## Principle 4: Research Should Look at Systematic Links Between Personality Factors and Experience

Considerable research has addressed the issue of optimal personality characteristics for work in unusual environments. Perhaps we should have taken warning from 15 years of fruitless attempts to predict so simple a behavior as tolerance of laboratory sensory deprivation, which was essentially abandoned after it had exhausted the range from psychoanalytic to psychometric approaches (Zubek, 1973).

We may note that many people who seem attracted to a particular extreme environment have had experience in others. Tom Wolfe's *The Right Stuff* (1979), with all its glib superficiality, made that point and has been supported by a great deal of historical evidence. Environmental psychologists have neglected new developments in personality theory that focus on how the individual tends to perceive and respond to difficult—that is, unusual, hazardous, or challenging—environments.

I have mentioned sensation seeking as one candidate, but we have not found polar crews to show a consistent or unusual level of sensation seeking. However, we have yet to test the potential contributions of Farley's concept of the Type T personality (1986), the thrill seeker; Kobasa's (e.g., Kobasa & Puccetti, 1983) characterization of the hardy individual; Kern's (1966) contrast, put to impressive use by Keinan (1986), between the confidence attitude that one can cope with challenges in the environment and the despair attitude that leads to a focus on danger and possible injury, rather than on how to deal with the former and avoid the latter; or Apter's (1982) distinction between being goal oriented and viewing the process by which the goal is reached as a hindrance (telic dominance) versus attending to and enjoying the process as well as the goal it leads to (paratelic dominance). Would we find that successful astronauts, polar explorers, and lone voyagers show a high representation of Type Ts, or hardy, confidence-oriented, paratelic individuals? It would be useful to find out, to use personality measures that actually have something to say about how the individual tends to experience the kinds of environments that interest us.

Or we might use multidimensional measures, such as the NEO (neuroticism–extraversion–openness) Personality Inventory (e.g., McCrae & Costa, 1987), with its factors of surgency (dominance, activity); agreeableness; neuroticism; conscientiousness; and openness to experience. Would the "optimal" members of a task-oriented, structured group in space or the Antarctic show a different pattern on these scales from the "optimal" solitary adventurer? I suspect so. On a group level, Fiedler and Garcia's (1987) updating of the contingency theory of leadership (Fiedler, 1967) could be useful; it goes beyond a list of desirable characteristics for a small-group leader to considering characteristics that may or may not lead to effectiveness depending on circumstances.

## Principle 5: Experience Is Continuous and Integrated

An extreme and unusual environment, be it space or a polar region, may be drastically different and separate from all other environments in which the person has been. But experiences are not encapsulated and isolated from the rest of one's life. They comprise an integrated component of the total life experience of the individual; they are shaped by, and in turn help to shape, the cognitive, affective, perceptual, personality, memory, and other psychological variables that make up the psychological repertoire.

Accordingly, research on such experiences should not be confined to the episode itself. Understanding the impact of an experience requires comparisons of how the individual behaves before, during, and after the focal segment of his or her life. Some former prisoners, for example, suffer from posttraumatic stress symptoms (in some cases, of a psychotic severity); others find that the experience strengthens them and gives meaning to their subsequent life. Studying such differences may call for the use of data sources that have been relatively seldom used by psychologists, such as biographical information and content analysis of documents produced by the individual.

I wonder why there seems to have been so little research published about the long-term impact of the spaceflight experience. The ranks of former astronauts include a United States senator, a Christian missionary searching for Noah's Ark, and a prominent advocate of research on psychic and other paranormal phenomena, just to list some of the most dramatic developments. Spaceflight itself could be a peak experience that reorganizes one's view of the universe; it could be a disillusioning anticlimax; it could be a high point after which everything else seems boring and trivial; and so on. Are there patterns of how the experience is integrated into one's subsequent life? Would we find a similar range of later interests and activities among an equivalent group of military test pilots and other matched controls who have not been in space?

While astronauts are one example, the same problem exists in more mundane cases. Very rarely do we find follow-up data on people who have been in unusual environments; our interest seems to extend only to the period of the actual experience. For example, the diaries and other accounts of single-handed voyagers, explorers, castaways, shipwreck victims, and so on almost always end within a few days of their return to the normal environment. But even in some of these accounts, there is a glimmering of a long-term change in personality, beliefs, philosophy; psychologists, at least, should be interested in these. But we don't seem to be—with the exception of research on posttraumatic stress disorders, we ignore how these experiences are integrated into later life.

Environmental psychology must face the problem of integrating environmental and psychological factors in studying and understanding experiences. This is perhaps particularly difficult when we deal with experiences that occur in dramatic and challenging environments, whose observable features are so compelling to the researcher that the importance of the *person* in the person–situation transaction tends to be overlooked. But it is also particularly important then, since such situations may evoke the widest range of interactive patterns.

The contributions made when we do attack this issue are potentially great: more rigorous and therefore more valid research paradigms, a wide and diverse data base, deeper understanding of what happens, and consequently, the opportunity for more effective design, selection, training, and evaluation.

## References

Altman, I. (1973). An ecological approach to the functioning of socially isolated groups. In J. E. Rasmussen (Ed.), *Man in isolation and confinement* (pp. 241–269). Chicago: Aldine.

Apter, M. J. (1982). *The experience of motivation: The theory of psychological reversals.* London: Academic Press.

Bexton, W. H., Heron, W., & Scott, T. H. (1954). Effects of decreased variation in the sensory environment. *Canadian Journal of Psychology, 8,* 70–76.

Bluth, B. J., & Helppie, M. (1986). *Soviet space stations as analogs.* (2nd ed.) (NASA Grant Report NAGW-659). Washington, DC: National Aeronautics and Space Administration.

Brownstein, R., & Moos, R. H. (1976). Environment and man: Perspectives from geography. In R. H. Moos (Ed.), *The human context: Environmental determinants of behavior* (pp. 36–54). New York: Wiley.

Brunswik, E. (1956). *Perception and the representative design of psychology experiments.* Berkeley, CA: University of California Press.

Chaikin, A. (1985, February). The loneliness of the long-distance astronaut. *Discover,* 20–30.

Connors, M. M., Harrison, A. A., & Akins, F. R. (1986). Psychology and the resurgent space program. *American Psychologist, 41,* 906–913.

Farley, F. (1986, May). The big T in personality. *Psychology Today, 20,* 44–52.

Fiedler, F. E. (1967). *A theory of leadership effectiveness.* New York: McGraw-Hill.

Fiedler, F. E., & Garcia, J. E. (1987). *New approaches to effective leadership: Cognitive resources and organizational performance.* New York: Wiley.

Flaherty, B. E. (Ed.). (1961). *Psychophysiological aspects of space flight.* New York: Columbia University Press.

Grassian, S., & Friedman, N. (1986). Effects of sensory deprivation in psychiatric seclusion and solitary confinement. *International Journal of Law and Psychiatry, 8,* 49–65.

Haggard, E. A. (1973). Some effects of geographic and social isolation in natural settings. In J. E. Rasmussen (Ed.), *Man in isolation and confinement* (pp. 99–143). Chicago: Aldine.

Harrison, A. A. (1986). On resistance to the involvement of personality, social and organizational psychologists in the U.S. space program. *Journal of Social Behavior and Personality, 1*, 315–324.

Helmreich, R. L. (1983). Applying psychology in outer space: Unfulfilled promises revisited. *American Psychologist, 38*, 445–450.

Keinan, G. (1986). Confidence expectancy as a predictor of military performance under stress. In N. E. Milgram (Ed.), *Stress and coping in time of war: Generalizations from the Israeli experience* (pp. 183–196). New York: Brunner/Mazel.

Kern, R. P. (1966). *A conceptual model of behavior under stress with implications for combat training* (Technical Report Number 66-12). Washington, DC: Human Resources Research Office.

Kobasa, S. C., & Puccetti, M. C. (1983). Personality and social resources in stress resistance. *Journal of Personality and Social Psychology, 45*, 839–850.

Lazarus, R. S., & Folkman, S. (1984). *Stress, appraisal, and coping.* New York: Springer.

Lilly, J. C. (1956). Mental effects of reduction of ordinary levels of physical stimuli on intact healthy persons. *Psychiatric Research Reports, 5*, 1–9.

Lilly, J. C. (1977). *The deep self.* New York: Simon & Schuster.

McCrae, R., & Costa, P. T., Jr. (1987). Validation of the five factor model of personality across instruments and observers. *Journal of Personality and Social Psychology, 52*, 81–90.

Mocellin, J. S. P. (1987, under editorial review). Levels of anxiety on board of two expeditionary ships.

Mocellin, J. S. P., & Suedfeld, P. (1987, June 12–15). *Reactions to the polar regions: A content analysis of the writings of polar voyagers in the Heroic Era and today.* Paper read at the Seventh International Congress on Circumpolar Health, Umea, Sweden.

Petrie, A. (1979). *Individuality in pain and suffering* (2nd ed.). Chicago: University of Chicago Press.

Solomon, P., Kubzansky, P. E., Leiderman, P. H., Mendelson, J., Trumbull, R., & Wexler, D. (Eds.). (1961). *Sensory deprivation.* Cambridge, MA: Harvard University Press.

Streufert, S., & Swezey, R. W. (1985). Simulation and related research methods in environmental psychology. In A. Baum & J. E. Singer (Eds.), *Advances in environmental psychology: Vol. 5: Methods and environmental psychology* (pp. 99–117). Hillsdale, NJ: Lawrence Erlbaum.

Suedfeld, P. (1968). Isolation, confinement and sensory deprivation. *Journal of the British Interplanetary Society, 21*, 222–231.

Suedfeld, P. (1980). *Restricted environmental stimulation: Research and clinical applications.* New York: Wiley.

Suedfeld, P. (1987). Extreme and unusual environments. In D. Stokols & I. Altman (Eds.), *Handbook of environmental psychology, vol. 1* (pp. 863–887). New York: Wiley.

Suedfeld, P., & Kristeller, J. L. (1982). Stimulus reduction as a technique in health psychology. *Health Psychology, 1*, 337–357.

Suedfeld, P., & Mocellin, J. S. P. (1987). The "sensed presence" in unusual environments. *Environment and Behavior, 19*, 33–52.

Suedfeld, P., Ramirez, C. E., Deaton, J., & Baker-Brown, G. (1982). Reactions and attributes of prisoners in solitary confinement. *Criminal Justice and Behavior, 9*, 303–340.

Taylor, A. J. W. (1987). Personal communication.

Taylor, A. J. W., & Shurley, J. T. (1971). Some Antarctic troglodytes. *International Review of Applied Psychology, 20*, 143–148.

Taylor, S. E. (1983). Adjustment to threatening events: A theory of cognitive adaptation. *American Psychologist, 38*, 1161–1173.

Vernon, J. (1963). *Inside the black room.* New York: Potter.

Winkel, G. H. (1985). Ecological validity issues in field research settings. In A. Baum & J. E. Singer (Eds.), *Advances in environmental psychology: Vol. 5: Methods and environmental psychology* (pp. 1–41). Hillsdale, NJ: Lawrence Erlbaum.

Wolfe, T. (1979). *The right stuff.* New York: Farrar, Straus, Giroux.

Zubek, J. P. (Ed.). (1969). *Sensory deprivation: Fifteen years of research.* New York: Appleton-Century-Crofts.

Zubek, J. P. (1973). Behavioral and physiological effects of prolonged sensory and perceptual deprivation: A review. In J. E. Rasmussen (Ed.), *Man in isolation and confinement* (pp. 9–83). Chicago: Aldine.

Zuckerman, M. (1979). *Sensation seeking: Beyond the optimal level of arousal.* Hillsdale, NJ: Lawrence Erlbaum.

# 14

# Environmental Design Cybernetics:
# A Relativistic Conceptual Framework
# for the Design of Space Stations
# and Settlements

WOLFGANG F. E. PREISER

A general definition of the field of cybernetics is "the science of effective organization" with the critical elements of control and communication, as well as feedback, all of which depend on the flow of information. According to von Foerster et al. (1974), "the name cybernetics derives from the Greek word meaning 'steersman' and was chosen to show that adaptive control is more like steersmanship than dictatorship" (p. 2).

These principles could be usefully applied to the emerging field of space station/settlement design through adaptive controls in which design is intended to support the crews' or occupants' missions. Environmental design cybernetics, then, can be seen to be analogous to biological organisms or physical machines in terms of how they are functioning and how their behavior is controlled, since "both possess a sensor that feeds information into a decision maker which then regulates the output or behavior" (von Foerster et al., 1974, p. 3).

This chapter is divided into three sections, dealing with philosophical issues, a conceptual framework, and environmental design parameters.

Two earlier, different versions of this chapter were published under the titles "A Conceptual Approach Towards Linking Human Behavior and Physical Environment" (in R. J. Borden (Ed.), *Human Ecology–A Gathering of Perspectives*. Washington, DC: Society for Human Ecology, 1986) and "The Habitability Framework: A Conceptual Approach Towards Linking Human Behavior and Physical Environment" (in *Design Studies, 4*(2), April 1983, pp. 84–91).

## Philosophical Issues

This chapter will not address the issue of whether space stations and extra-terrestrial communities should be established or not. Rather, the creation of such communities will be taken for granted as described in the National Aeronautics and Space Administration (NASA) design study on "Space Settlements" (Johnson & Holbrow, 1977). Certain considerations and limitations in the programming and design of such environments will be discussed. Some basic differences will be pointed out that set the design development of extraterrestrial environments apart from past technological achievements such as the railroads: their original prototypes were modeled after the horse-drawn carriage, adapted to rails. Thus, they evolved from existing images. The prophecy that the speed of railroads would harm their passengers physically and mentally did not deter the railroads' proponents.

In the case of space stations or settlements, no such analogy exists. Earthbound experiences possibly allowing for extrapolation to conditions in space and their effects on humans are limited to isolated and hostile environments, such as Antarctica, in which technological means are used to compensate for such phenomena as sensory deprivation and "cabin fever." Our inexperience concerning the effect of living in space settlements is considerable. A first consideration will be a programming and design philosophy that treats the creation of environments as a continuous experiment and cyclic process with learning feedback (see Figure 14.1) and subsequent adaptations occurring periodically (Studer, 1970). This contrasts with the current and typical Earthbound building delivery process, which is finished-product oriented and which stops at the time of occupation of a facility.

A second consideration refers to the fact that space settlers will find a situation that is the reverse of that traditionally encountered in the colonization of new territories, i.e., the problem of how to humanize an entirely artificial, sophisticated, man-made environment versus the task of cultivating a rough, but basically habitable, natural environment. Seventeenth century settlers emigrating to the New World cut their ties to the old one and came equipped with the basic means to grant them self-sufficiency. The opposite will be the case in space settlements, which will require a continuous lifeline and communication with Earth.

A third consideration relates to the potential of space stations and settlements to become truly humane communities, as expressed in their environmental design characteristics. Sponsorship and political/philosophical orientations of space settlements will provide for international participation under relatively high-density living and working conditions. Therefore, a "homogenization" effect as envisioned by de Chardin (1969) may be the by-product of forced communality, that is, increased interdependence and co-operation among occupants. Greater heterogeneity, increased cultural diversity, and appropriate "cultural niches" to accommodate these requirements will be needed in the design of extraterrestrial environments. A newly found

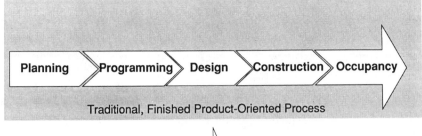

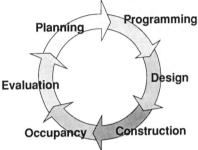

Evolutionary, Cybernetic Feedforward Process

FIGURE 14.1. Evolutionary building delivery cycle vs. traditional process.

sense of ecology, a nonexploitative, dynamic-equilibrium-oriented utilization of resources, is envisioned. The considerations outlined above may imply that in the long run space stations and settlements could become model communities for those of us remaining on "Spaceship Earth."

## The Performance Framework

This section outlines the elements and theoretical basis for *environmental design cybernetics*, that is, various strategies to achieve desirable habitability or facility performance. One of these strategies is postoccupancy evaluation. Other strategies, as part of the facility delivery process, include the planning, programming, designing, simulating, and occupancy of facilities.

The systems approach (Miller, 1978) appears appropriate in this area of endeavor—it is linking in holistic fashion diverse phenomena that influence relationships between people and their surroundings, including physical and social environments.

New directions have also emerged in the field of environmental design, partially in response to real-world failures of various architectural theories and manifestos. *Differentiation*, not universal solutions, in the built environment is being promulgated as a way to solve problems in the future. Such differentiations are based on the recognition that there are different user types, each with special requirements concerning the built environment; that there are different types of places, each with setting-specific requirements; that there are different types of requirements for environments; and that there are different activities that occur in the same environments at different times.

In addition to the complexities of the building delivery process, today's environmental designers have to respond to an ever-increasing avalanche of materials, information, codes, and regulations, all of which affect the quality of environments resulting from this process.

The cybernetic nature of the emerging evolutionary and cyclic facility delivery process is depicted in Figure 14.1 above. This is a process that only now is beginning to be accepted by major client organizations in the public and private sectors.

In the attempt to meet occupant needs better in the built environment, some possible, new professional roles have emerged. They range from research, programming, and documenting of occupant needs and building functions to systematic evaluation of facilities once constructed and in use (Preiser, 1989; Preiser, Rabinowitz, & White, 1988). Feedforward loops of information that pertain to occupant needs in the design and guidance literature and management of change during a facility's life cycle are further areas of professional specialization.

The quality of certain military and nonmilitary environments in terms of occupant needs has been termed "habitability." Habitability is the degree of fit between human goals and cultural characteristics, on the one hand, and the performance characteristics of the environment that is to support them, on the other.

Habitability is environmental quality as perceived by the facility's occupants. Different occupant groups (e.g., regular users, management, maintenance personnel, visitors, and so forth) may perceive the qualities of the same facilities in different ways, depending upon their respective objectives and relationships or interactions within a given sociocultural context and time.

The term "habitability" is derived from "habitat," that is, the kind of place that is natural for the life and growth of an organism (Flexner, 1987). The French-language definition of habitability further amplifies the notion of environmental quality of space for human use. The United States Navy has engaged in shipboard habitability research (Altman and Haythorn, 1967) aimed at improving living and working conditions in submarines, among other places. Also, the United States Army Corps of Engineers sponsored a similar program with the aim of improving the quality of training and housing facilities on military installations.

On the other hand, NASA's definition of habitability research deals with acceptability and human environment fit. NASA defines habitability as a measure of the degree to which the environment promotes productivity and well-being.

The goal of environmental design is to achieve a steadily higher level of performance and, implicitly, quality of the resulting environments. Therefore, the term "performance" refers to those characteristics of an occupied facility that support human activities in terms of individual, group, or organizational goals.

Environmental design performance includes the following considerations:

- Performance strives toward an ecologically sound and humane built environment.
- Performance is related to health/safety/security; function and productivity; as well as psychological comfort and satisfaction of the occupants of a facility.
- Performance is not an absolute but a relativistic concept, subject to different interpretations in different cultures, economies, and social contexts. Thus, building performance (quality) may be perceived differently over time by all those interacting with the same facility or facilities, e.g., owners, occupants, maintenance and management personnel, and visitors.

Environmental design is goal oriented. It can be represented by a basic cybernetic system model or framework with the goal of achieving high-quality performance. (See Figure 14.2). The performance framework conceptually links the overall goal, namely, of achieving habitability, or environmental quality, with the following elements of the system:

1. Performance criteria are explicitly stated so that perceived and objectively measured performance can be measured and tested or evaluated (National Research Council, 1987).
2. The effector represents the "mover," or actor, in the cybernetic framework: that is, the act of planning, programming, designing, constructing, occupying, and evaluating an environment or facility.
3. The outcomes are the objective, physically measurable characteristics of the built environment that result from the facility delivery process: that is, its physical dimensions, lighting levels, thermal performance, and so on.
4. The measured performance is the actual performance and quality of the resulting environment as perceived by those occupying or assessing the environment, referring to the subjective measures of those occupants.

Any number of subgoals for achieving environmental quality can be related to the basic system through modified effectors, outcomes, and performance. Thereby, the outcome becomes the subgoal (or Gss) of the subsystem with respective criteria, effectors, and performance of the subsystem. The total outcome of combined basic systems and subsystems with subgoals is then evaluated by comparing the actual performance with the performance criteria, as in the basic system.

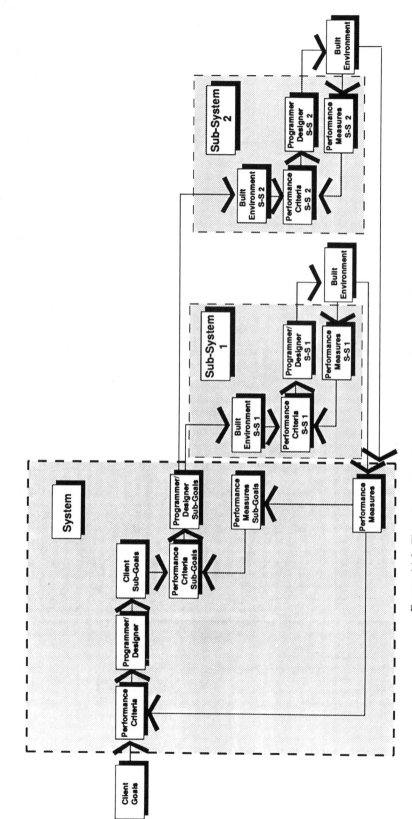

FIGURE 14.2. The cybernetic performance framework: system with subsystems.

# Performance Levels

Subgoals of building performance may be structured hierarchically into three performance levels: (1) the basic health/safety/security level; (2) the function and efficiency level; and (3) the psychological comfort and satisfaction level.

For purposes of this discussion, the performance framework allows one to systematically relate three interacting forces to one another: setting types, occupant types, and occupant needs. Each of these can be seen in parallel hierarchical orders of scale, in ascending numbers of occupants, as well as in levels of human requirements. In order to adequately program and design space stations and settlements, it will be necessary to analyze the interdependencies of the aforementioned forces in a matrix–like fashion by considering the following characteristics.

## *Settings*

Settings range from the workstation, or proximate environment scale, to ensembles of settings in rooms and, further, to assemblies of rooms in facilities and facility complexes. Setting characteristics, then, are defined by environmental descriptor categories relating primarily, but not exclusively, to human sensory input modes including luminous, acoustic, olfactory, tactile, thermal, magnetic and radiation environments, as well as spatial-visual–esthetic environments. Setting types to be considered should, at least, include the 13 archetypal places identified by Spivak (1973), namely, those serving to shelter, sleep, mate, grow, feed, excrete, store, provide territory, play, route, meet, compete, and work.

## *Occupants*

Occupants are differentiated into whether they are individuals, groups, or entire organizations. Occupant human growth and developmental levels according to these life-cycle phases should be considered, i.e., infancy, childhood, adolescence, courting–mating, reproduction–child care, middle life, and aging–maturity. Occupant needs relating to habitability should be considered at three habitability levels roughly parallel to Maslow's (1948) human needs hierarchy, ranging from physical security to self-actualization. More specifically, the three habitability levels are

1. *Health, safety and security level*: preventing death, injury, and disease due to design and material characteristics. Providing secure environments.
2. *Functional and task performance level*: Providing conditions conducive to the performance of a job, for the proper functioning of living environments, and so forth.

3. *Psychological comfort and satisfaction level*: Providing conditions conducive to fostering sensory stimulation, territorial integrity, speech privacy, proximity to valued resources (such as views), expression of individuality, and so forth.

It can be assumed that facility programming will be handled in a like manner, with the highest priority given to the physical, survival-oriented health, safety, and security level. Since atmospheric conditions in the totally enclosed environments of space stations and settlements are to resemble those on Earth, it would seem appropriate to gear environmental design toward meeting relevant occupational health and safety codes now accepted in advanced industrialized nations. Adjustments of such codes and standards can be expected, for example, concerning permissible luminous or radiation levels, without creating health hazards for occupants of outer space environments.

It can also be assumed that programming and design guidance at the functional and task performance level of habitability will follow Earth-based standards of efficiency of environments, dealing with work flow and particular human-factor-related requirements for a given setting within space settlements. Such guidance abounds, ranging from generic information sources such as the *Architectural Graphic Standards* (Ramsey & Sleeper, 1970) to facility-specific *Design Guides*, including those issued by the Department of the Army (1976a, 1976b). As with codes and standards that aim to safeguard the health and safety of occupants of environments, the functional, performance-oriented guidance literature provides spatial and material criteria and information. While material choices are expected to be limited to those that are lightweight and that can either be grown in space settlements (e.g., bamboo), or extracted from minerals contained in the Moon (e.g., aluminum or glass), the Earthbound performance criteria referred to above will be valid and useful to a certain extent.

Of greatest concern to programmers and designers should be the third level of habitability, namely, the short-term and long-term impact of space settlements on the psychological comfort and satisfaction of their occupants. This aspect of environmental design has been largely ignored in recent history, as the sad condition and image of our built environment demonstrates. The repetition of inhumane, discontinuous, and hard environmental design that we commonly face today should be avoided at all costs in space stations and settlements.

## Environmental Design Parameters

In programming environments, it is useful to document performance requirements on a setting-by-setting basis so that the designer can match these requirements with hardware specifications (National Research Council,

1986). Typically, such requirements include criteria concerning the thermal, luminous, visual, and acoustic environments, among others. Reference is rarely made to human requirements such as "privacy," which may entail the acoustic, spatial–visual, and olfactory environments to varying degrees, and at the same time.

In this section, environmental design parameters for space stations and settlements will be identified that are based upon human needs at the psychological comfort and satisfaction level of habitability. Tentative design solutions for the identified issues are suggested. At this time, such solutions can be speculative at best, based upon similar phenomena observed in Earthbound environments. Table 14.1 lists expected occupant needs in space, environmental design parameters, as well as solutions ranging from general considerations to those in specific settings.

While it is likely that the first generation of pioneers in space stations and settlements will be highly motivated and idealistic individuals, as in experimental communities and in some cooperative housing developments, the successive generations may be much less mission oriented. Rather, later generations may be less amenable to endure hardships, inconveniences, and sensory deprivation caused by features of environmental design.

The greatest deprivation will be the absence of natural phenomena such as weather, clouds, seasons, diurnal cycles, the animated environment, and natural sounds, smells, and sights. Highly valued places and views such as riverfronts or hilltops will be nonexistent. Preferred resources and status within society will have to find new ways, or information-based "currencies," of expression, that is, other than the space-related ones.

Other phenomena, for example, synchrony, body sway, and eye contact, are apparently made very difficult in space because of lack of a base surface to relate to. This may require a guidance system for alignment of people sharing a similar task or activity such as dining or socializing.

The confines of the expected extraterrestrial environments will require optimal use of space for production of agricultural and other products, as well as for human living. It can be expected that curtailment or substitution of certain human activities will need to be considered. Also, less space-consuming activities will have to be devised or rediscovered, implying a possibly more sedentary, information-oriented approach to recreation, including watching television or interacting with computers. There may be an economy of information rather than material goods, due to space and payload limitations.

According to Connors, Harrison, and Akins (1986), the notion of multipurpose spaces is a must, due to lack of space and the high cost of space stations. That could be combined with the idea of rotating cylinder layers that could be brought into view depending on the functions and activities being carried out at a given time. Therefore, the same location in the station could take on multiple functions if such a layered arrangement could be solved technically.

TABLE 14.1. An overview of environmental design parameters.

| Phenomena in space settlements | Occupant needs (psychological comfort and satisfaction level) | Environmental design parameters and solutions |
| --- | --- | --- |
| 1. Perfectness and inhumaneness of entire man-made environment in space | Need for flexibility and adaptation; add-on capability | Superstructures, permitting fill-in and completion by occupants |
| 2. Provision and control of environments by sponsoring agency | Need to identify with entire space station or settlement, reduction of alienation | Involvement and active participation of occupants in the process of environmental programming and design |
| 3. Relative scarcity of building materials and facilities | Conservation attitude, valuing of resources | Recycling of materials, reuse of facilities |
| 4. Relative small size and variety of facilities | Engagement in a variety of purposes and activities | Design for multiple types of uses and time shifts in usage |
| 5. Absence of organic materials (wood, animal products, etc.) | Need to relate to natural things in all sensory modes | Simulation or substitution of natural materials |
| 6. Absence of natural cycles of day and night | Need to psychologically relate to biorhythm and cycles | Simulation of day and night or provision of hermetically closed, appropriate environments |
| 7. Absence of the ordered "randomness" of seasons in natural settings | Need to stimulate humans at appropriate levels | Computerized, programmed variations of environmental displays |
| 8. Size and location of individual territory | Expression of status and place in dominance hierarchy | Providing appropriately sized territories for each individual |
| 9. Boundaries of individual and group territories | Need for definition and defense of territories | Marking of living and other areas through partitions, walls, signs, symbolic lines, etc. |
| 10. Spatial distribution and density of occupants | Control of crowding and overpopulation | Devising culture-differentiated criteria for space per occupant |
| 11. Body buffer zones (culture and health dependent) | Need for spatial integrity of an individual's privacy | Devising spatial, acoustic, luminous, olfactory, etc., barriers to protect individuals from intrusion |

TABLE 14.1. *Continued*

| Phenomena in space settlements | Occupant needs (psychological comfort and satisfaction level) | Environmental design parameters and solutions |
| --- | --- | --- |
| 12. Distances maintained in private, social, and public interactions | Need for communication among individuals and groups | Provide settings with culturally differentiated distances and arrangements for social interactions |
| 13. Proportions and relationships of spaces and artifacts | Need for esthetic considerations in a wholistic sense, based on human perception | Providing culture-related forms, spaces, dimensions, materials, and articulated settings |
| 14. Variability of space | Need to identify with work and living environments, i.e., personalization | Providing means to facilitate modification (e.g., flexible furnishings, exchangeable surfaces, etc.) |
| 15. Quantity and quality of the luminous environment | Need to relate to the "outdoors and sunlight" for psychological relief from monotony of totally controlled environments; changing stimuli are needed in luminous environment (following biological rhythms); need for full daylight spectrum | Providing windows and glazing between activity settings; simulating varying colors and displays (clouds, birds) in the artificial, projected sky; providing mirrored sunlight |
| 16. Quantity and quality of the acoustic environment | Need to experience natural sounds such as rainfall, wind, and thunder and from the animal world; protection against acoustic reverberation | Simulating Earthbound, natural sounds of playing recorded, randomized sound sequences over an omnipresent public address system; providing acoustically softened surfaces on the inside of the space station |
| 17. Quantity and quality of the olfactory environment | Need to experience the natural smells, e.g., from seasonal vegetation, etc. | Substituting and/or introducing odors and scents though a pipe distribution system |
| 18. Quantity and quality of the tactile environment | Need to experience natural materials, varied surface textures, degrees of hardness and abrasion | Simulating organically derived materials, as realistically as possible |
| 19. Quantity and quality of the thermal environment | Need to experience Earth-like thermal and climatic conditions | Providing air-conditioning systems for protection from solar greenhouse effect |
| 20. Quantity and quality of the magnetic and radiation environments | Need to experience gravity and spatially orienting equilibrium; need for protection from hazardous radiation—X-ray, ultraviolet, and so forth | Providing of one-gravity; providing environmental coding systems (colors, shapes) to avoid disorientation; shielding from radiation |

There is also the danger that our "plastic" world of today will be replicated in space settlements, i.e., environments without natural materials, thereby creating psychologically deprived occupants in sterile settings. Here the introduction of cultural, symbolic, esthetic decor in space stations is suggested as a means to reduce boredom and to increase identity of occupants with stations. So-called "distractors" will be required, including windows, pictures, designs (maybe landscape designs or simulations), or miniaturizations, as well as books, movies, and recreation activities.

Since space stations and settlements will be structures covering the entire life space of a community, it will be possible to create an "architecture without buildings" in the traditional sense with possibilities of pneumatic or lightweight structures within space stations and the consideration of new curvilinear geometries instead of the traditional rectangular ones that have been considered so far.

The design of environments will occur on a setting-by-setting basis, not necessarily with the customary roofs and enclosures, but with the ethologically evolved principles of human space use in mind. In this context, McBride (1980) observed that "there can be no social order without spatial order." Most of the psychological principles listed below in Table 14.2 stem from our animal past. If violated, they can cause discomfort, stress, and eventually, destruction of the human organism. For example, settings for withdrawal behavior, i.e., places or means to create privacy and personal space, are seen to be critical for space stations. These fall under the category of distancing devices, and they also include temporary barriers such as screens, filters, and masks (Imagine the temporary change in the cast of characters, using masks!), apart from doors and walls.

## Epilogue

Environmental design parameters and solutions for some of the phenomena expected in space stations and settlements are outlined above. It is suggested that the initial, shakedown phase closely follow Earthbound experiences and

TABLE 14.2. Effects of space on human behavior.

| Spatial concept | Behavioral concept |
| --- | --- |
| 1. Territorial space | Dominance hierarchy; status expression |
| 2. Personal space | Privacy; maintenance of integrity and security of individuals through withdrawal |
| 3. Space boundaries | Territorial defense; social order, security and control |
| 4. Proxemic space | Communication; access to valued resources |
| 5. Spatial density | Crowding; distribution of resources |
| 6. Spatial scale | Functionality in relationship to task; anonymity (e.g., in high rises) |
| 7. Sociofugal versus sociopetal space | Dispersion or attraction of people |

specifications. This is to minimize the discontinuity and negative psychological effects on the occupants of archetypal places (Spivak, 1973), which have not been discussed here. They include public as well as private places, e.g., for food acquisition. The "suitaloon" proposed by ARCHIGRAM's Michael Webb (Cook, 1970), while apparently providing for the ultimate in self-actualization, lacks necessary body activation and could eventually produce perceptually blind individuals.

In the well-known "kitten experiment" (Held & Hein, 1963), the inability to move prohibited one kitten from becoming perceptually alert and from functioning normally. By analogy, it is feared that the envisioned space stations and settlements may limit human movement to such a degree that similar, perceptual impediments may occur.

Finally, each of the environmental design parameters alluded to above will require simulation and in-depth study. Conditions in space will require control of placement and movement of occupants in a fashion hitherto unknown. Mastering these controls will be the challenge of designing human habitats in space.

*Acknowledgements.* Graphics for Figures 14.1 and 14.2 were produced by Denise Matysiak of Architectural Research Consultants, Inc., Albuquerque, New Mexico. The figures are from W. F. E. Preiser, J. C. Vischer, and E. T. White (Eds.), *Design Intervention: Toward a Humane Architecture* in press. New York: Van Nostrand Reinhold, 1990. Reproduced with the permission of Van Nostrand Reinhold, Publishers, New York.

Special thanks are owed to Professor Emeritus Heinz von Foerster, formerly Director of the Biological Computer Laboratory, University of Illinois, for his mentorship and inspiration regarding the introduction of cybernetic concepts into the field of environmental design.

## References

Altman, I., & Haythorn, W. W. (1967). The ecology of isolated groups. *Behavioral Science, 12*, 169–182.

Connors, M. M., Harrison, A. A., & Akins, F. R. (1985). *Living aloft: Human requirements for extended spaceflight* (NASA SP-483). Washington, DC: National Aeronautics and Space Administration.

Cook, P. (1970). *Experimental architecture.* New York: Universe Books.

de Chardin, T. (1969). *The future of man.* New York: Harper & Row.

Department of the Army. (1976a). *Design guide: Recreation centers* (DG 1110-2-132). Washington, DC: Office of Engineers, Military Construction Directorate, Engineering Division.

Department of the Army. (1976b). *Design guide: U.S. Army service schools* (DG 1110-3-105). Washington, DC: Office of Engineers, Military Construction Directorate, Engineering Division.

Flexner, S. E. (Ed.). (1987). *The Random House dictionary*. New York: Random House.

Held, R., & Hein, A. (1963). Movement produced stimulation in the development of visually guided behavior. *Journal of Comparative and Physiological Psychology, 56*, 872–876.

Johnson, R. D., & Holbrow, C. (Eds.). (1977). *Space settlements–A design study* (SP-413). Washington, DC: National Aeronautics and Space Administration.

Maslow, A. H. (1948). A theory of human motivation. *Psychological Review, 50*, 370–398.

McBride, G. (1980). Personal communication.

Miller, J. G. (1978). *Living systems theory*. New York: McGraw-Hill.

National Research Council. (1986). *Programming practices in the building process–Opportunities for improvement*. Washington, DC: National Academy Press.

National Research Council. (1987). *Post-occupancy evaluation practices in the building process–Opportunities for improvement*. Washington, DC: National Academy Press.

Preiser, W. F. E. (Ed.). (1989). *Building Evaluation*. New York: Plenum.

Preiser, W. F. E., Rabinowitz, H. E., & White, E. T. (Eds.) (1988). *Post-occupancy evaluation*. New York: Van Nostrand Reinhold.

Ramsey, C. G., & Sleeper, H. R. (1970). *Architectural graphic standards*. New York: Wiley.

Spivak, M. (1973). Archetypal place. In W. F. E. Preiser (Ed.), *Environmental design research: Volume 1: Selected papers* (p.33). Stroudsburg, PA: Dowden, Hutchinson and Ross.

Studer, R. G. (1970). The dynamics of behavior–contingent physical systems. In H. M. Proshanksy, W. H. Ittelson, & L. G. Rivlin (Eds.), *Environmental psychology: Man and his physical setting*. New York: Holt, Rinehart and Winston.

von Foerster, H., et al. (Eds.). (1974). *Cybernetics of cybernetics* (Report No. 73.38). Urbana: University of Illinois, Biological Computer Laboratory.

# 15

# Small Groups and
# Confined Microsocieties

JOSEPH V. BRADY AND MARY A. ANDERSON

The era of the brief visit and speedy return from space is over. The day of the lone astronaut strapped in a one-man capsule has passed. The now and future exploration of space will be accomplished by teams who will live aloft for extended periods in space laboratories, workstations, interplanetary probes, and settlements beyond the Earth's atmosphere. A common feature of these diverse endeavors in space will be the isolation of human participants in confined extraterrestrial microsocieties for lengthy time intervals.

The biological needs of man in space have been addressed from the beginning in order to maximize survival. In contrast, little attention has been directed towards behavioral requirements and social considerations (Connors, Harrison, & Akins, 1985). Conditions that were tolerable over the short term for one or two astronauts will not be compatible with long-term residency involving larger groups of space explorers. To promote the survival and effective functioning of isolated microsocieties, attention must be directed toward biobehavioral investigations with small groups. A primary focus of such efforts must be upon the development of research-based technological, organizational, and sociological support of the human biobehavioral repertoire under conditions of extended isolation and confinement (National Academy of Sciences, 1987).

Beyond consideration of spacecraft design and specific sensorimotor requirements, the interactive physical and biobehavioral features of space environments must provide for configuration of the *sociopolitical organization of space-dwelling groups*. The solution to this problem will doubtless depend upon input from many scientific disciplines and upon several levels of conceptual and methodological analysis. The emerging state of knowledge in this area is probably limited to the information base of those public agencies that serve as the storehouse for the provisioning of expeditionary forces of various kinds (e.g., space crews, military teams, labor groups, and so forth). Initial expeditionary efforts have always been characterized by authoritarian structure because of serious environmental hazards, uncertainties, and minimum provisioning found in such undertakings. So it will be for the foreseeable future with space exploration. The frequent sequelae of such expeditions, however, are the establishment of extended or permanent settlements and the eventual evolution of independence. This evolution develops because, though originally the "senders" are exclusively responsible for the consequences of the activity, pay explicit fees, and demand absolute control over operational performances, gradually, as larger numbers of individuals are transported to established settlements, the needs and aspirations (rewards) of the "sent" become progressively dominant relative to the needs of the "senders." This evolving relationship in the reinforcement matrix between the "senders" and "sent" is the fountainhead for evolution of social structure and governmental policy as expressed in empire, colony, and emergent independent states. The process has filled history books with a major portion of human activity and suffering throughout time. The costly lessons learned from the exploration and inhabitation of Antarctica, for example, cannot be ignored in our plans for extended space occupancy. Formal programs of investigation to understand this evolution and the dynamics of biosocial organization, as influenced by internal and external contingencies, must provide the focus of any space life science research agenda (Brady, 1990).

The complexities of research initiatives that must take into account a wide variety of possible space settlements are imposing. The conceptual and methodological problems associated with designing, establishing, and maintaining functional human and ecological systems require, in the first instance, an approach at the most fundamental scientific level, with subsequent work moving toward more complex situations on the basis of accumulated data. While such an approach will benefit the larger society by supplying an analysis of procedures for effectively promoting biosocial and ecological stability, the immediate results are far more likely to be useful in the management of small, semipermanent, isolated groups such as those involved in operational missions or space research. *What must ultimately be determined is how to maintain a synthetic biobehavioral ecosystem.* This requires, at a minimum, specification of how biosocial and nonsocial environments influence individual health and performance. An environment can then be synthesized that reliably produces and maintains appropriate repertoires with respect to other members of the biosocial milieu, life-support system, and work activities.

# Background

Between the Soviet and United States manned space programs, people have now spent some 4,000 days in space. All crews, whether one man or a small group, have been under virtually continuous control of a ground command. Already there have been examples of minor rebellion and defiance as some crewmembers have expressed their exasperation with exacting schedules. The need for technological developments in human group maintenance within a biosocial environment that will sustain and satisfy larger numbers of people under isolated, confined, and stressful conditions is urgent. The development of such a technology would be greatly facilitated by a research methodology that provided for simulations of expected environmental conditions and the systematic experimental analysis of biobehavioral interactions over extended time periods. *The conceptual framework and methodological approach to the management of a biobehavioral ecology emerging within the context of such an analytic and synthetic orientation would be explicitly experimental in nature. Scientific and pragmatic considerations would dictate compliance with procedures of established effectiveness in other areas of natural science.*

Developments over the past several decades in experimental and applied behavior analysis have given detailed attention to the controlling relations between the environment and biobehavioral processes and suggest an investigative approach to solving many, if not all, of the methodological problems that have constrained previous studies in this critical domain. The inductively derived principles that have resulted provided a generalized *operational* account of the observable, manipulatable, and measurable antecedent and consequent environmental events that bear functional relations to the behavior of both individuals and groups. Such controlling environmental–biobehavioral interrelations are termed contingencies of reinforcement, and by their systematic manipulation, behavior can be demonstrated to change in orderly ways. Experimental analysis based upon these contingency management procedures has been shown to have widespread success in, and reliability for, the control of behavior across both phyletic lines and biobehavioral repertoires from the simple to the complex. While attempts are frequently made to distinguish between applied and basic research, such a differentiation is largely unwarranted, since the methodology involves highly controlled experimental procedures but the results have immediate utility in the management of small-group behaviors in isolated and confined microsocieties, as well as other stressful environments. The approach, then, is neither purely basic nor purely applied research but, instead, partly both (Johnston & Pennypacker, 1980). Optimal control over important variables must be complemented with a high accuracy of measurement under human laboratory conditions to pursue major research questions with widely varying goals using the species of primary interest without sacrifice of methodological rigor. *Without an experimentally derived functional account of individual behavioral variability, a natural science of behavior cannot exist. And without a natural science of behavior, the social sciences will necessarily remain in their current status as disciplines of less than optimal precision or utility.*

## Definitional and Conceptual Considerations

Behavior may be defined as some portion of an organism's interaction with the environment resulting most commonly in detectable displacement in space over time and measurable change in some aspect of the environment. Viewed in this transactional context, *behavior is not specifiable in the absence of a relationship between a living organism and a changing environment.* From a biobehavioral perspective, the environment may be the organism itself, i.e., the interactions of interest may occur inside the skin. Behavior is considered detectable as a physical event in space and time, with both private observation and observation of private events treated as potentially legitimate scientific activities. Closely related and of equal importance is the inclusion of verbal behavior within the definition of behavior, and evidence adduced to date demonstrates the utility of a behavioral account of both private events and verbal behavior (Epstein, Lanza, & Skinner, 1980; Hefferline & Perera, 1963; Hefferline, Keenan, & Harford, 1959).

The conceptual basis of such an experimental analysis of complex behavioral repertoires has its roots in *environmentalism*, which has two main features. The first is that *knowledge comes from experience* rather than from innate ideas, divine revelation, or other obscure sources. And the second is that *action is governed by consequences* rather than by instinct, reason, will, beliefs, attitudes, the currently fashionable "cognitions," or a myriad of other explanatory fictions. Taken together, these two constructs about human nature—the experiential basis of knowledge and the governance of action by consequences—define a philosophy of social optimism that says that if you want people to be a certain way or do certain things, circumstances can be arranged. The coalescence of these two ideas appears to have taken place in late 19th century England—the influence of Darwin and the legacy of Locke—and can be seen to date the emergence of modern behaviorism. Their influence upon the spiritualists and mentalists, not to mention the more contemporary systems theorists, has been less apparent than one might have hoped. But their impact is now beginning to find expression in the growing need to develop a biobehavioral technology that is capable of providing the kind of life support that long-term space occupancy initiatives will require (National Academy of Sciences, 1987).

The research on small groups and confined microsocieties, which provides the title for this chapter, is a direct outgrowth of an effort to combine this conceptual framework for an experimental analysis of behavior with the naturalistic goals of ethological observation to systematically study more complete repertoires of human performance. The origins of this approach and the rationale for methodological development within the framework of the experimental analysis of behavior coincided with the growing commitment to a human presence in extraterrestrial environments. A science-based technology of human behavior is as essential to ensure the success of such space-age initiatives as is the science-based physical engineering technologies that make them possible (Brady, 1990).

## Methodological Considerations

Against a background of extensive laboratory research and experimentally derived behavior analysis principles, a human laboratory facility (Figure 15.1) has been designed and constructed at the Johns Hopkins University School of Medicine for the purpose of maintaining small groups of 3 to 6 individuals in a programmed environment for extended periods (i.e., weeks to months) of continuous residence (Brady, Bigelow, H. H. Emurian, & Williams, 1975). Briefly, this specially designed, live-in laboratory consists of three individual rooms connected by a hallway to a large social area and a smaller work room or "duty station." Each individual unit has a bed, kitchenette, shower, toilet, table, desk, chair, intercom, and microcomputer connected to a central communications system. The social area has two couches (convertible to bunk beds), a table, kitchen, and bathroom. The smaller, work area is equipped with computerized performance tasks, exercise devices, and the like. A corridor between these residential laboratory areas

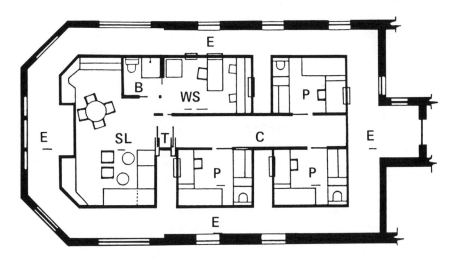

FIGURE 15.1. Diagrammatic representation of the overall floor plan of the programmed environment and its arrangement within the external building shell.

and the external building shell permits transfer of supplies and materials through two-way storage facilities accessible from both sides. Remotely controlled solenoid locks on the doors and cabinets throughout the environment are interfaced with a computer system that provides for programming, monitoring, and recording of access to experimental facilities and resources.

A discursive rationale and a working model were developed for the application of this continuously programmed environment to space–science–related human biobehavioral research on the basis of extended experimental control, objective recording, and the maintenance of realistic and naturalistic incentive conditions. Within this context, contingency management procedures have provided an effective methodology for experimental control, manipulation, and measurement of both individual and group behavior. Well over 200 male and female volunteers have participated in a series of naturalistic, biosocial interaction studies varying in length from several days to several weeks of continuous residence in this programmed environment laboratory.

Early studies readily established the important contributions of explicitly programmed social contingencies in maintaining group cohesion and preventing group fragmentation and performance deterioration (H. H. Emurian, C. S. Emurian, Bigelow, & Brady, 1976; H. H. Emurian, C. S. Emurian, & Brady, 1978). The interacting role of appetitive and aversive motivational conditions as determinants of performance effectiveness and morale was also analyzed experimentally (Brady & H. H. Emurian, 1978). And the effects of joining and leaving an operational group by individual participants under varying environmental conditions have been investigated in a series of substitution and replacement experiments focused upon both the behavioral and physiological consequences of such manipulation (H. H. Emurian, Brady, Meyerhoff, & Mougey, 1981).

The results of these studies emphasized the importance of motivational factors in the maintenance and enhancement of work productivity and social habitability in such progressively autonomous, confined microsocieties. Conceptually, the research undertaken to extend the experimental analysis of these critical productivity and autonomy processes appeals to a person's own natural behavioral dispositions as a basic motivational determinant. Traditionally, experimental studies of human motivation have generally emphasized the effects of "extrinsically" defined rewards like food or money. Under the special conditions of extended isolation in confined microsocieties likely to be characteristic of future space operations, more refined procedures will be required to motivate human participants. In this latter regard, the thrust of current laboratory initiatives directs attention to those "intrinsically" valuable activities that characterize the ordinary human repertoire with a view to the structuring or patterning of these activities to optimize individual productivity and cooperative group interactions (Brady, Bernstein, Foltin, & Nellis, 1988).

In geographically remote, increasingly autonomous, confined microsocieties for which the coming space age must be prepared, many of the environmental conditions that maintain productive work performances and amicable behavioral interactions will be in short supply. The raw excitement of such pioneering ventures is unlikely to sustain motivation long enough to accomplish extended missions. The experimental approach to be described is based upon the all-but-axiomatic observations that behavioral interactions with a high probability of occurrence can be used to strengthen or increase the frequency of low-probability behaviors.

Systematic experimental analysis of the fundamental principles upon which this useful observation is based was initially reported by Premack (1965, 1971) with laboratory animals and has only recently been extended in human research settings. In its simplest form, the principle involved is based upon the observation that the relative value of different activities can be assessed by quantifying the amount of time devoted to the items in a menu of available activities under unrestricted conditions. Furthermore, the outcome of a contingency between any two of these activities can be predicted from this differential probability during free access. That is, the activity that consumed more time (high probability) will function to strengthen or enhance the activity that consumed less time (low probability). These relationships obtain under programmatic conditions that require an increase in the frequency or quality of the low-probability performance in order to gain access to the high-probability activity.

It is commonplace to observe that individuals and groups will work long and hard to engage in selected activities generally judged to be pleasant. From an experimental perspective, it has now been demonstrated that a set of such pleasurable activities can be identified in advance of their being used as rewards by assessing the relative value of the activities in a behavioral hierarchy. Under conditions of unrestricted access to a wide range of activities, those on which the most time is spent will function as reinforcers (i.e., rewards) when access to them is made available only after a specified amount of time is spent in a less valued activity. Generalization of these relationships to work environments has presented recurrent problems, however, because the reported studies with humans have invariably used activities chosen by the subjects themselves (e.g., preferred hobbies, reading materials, and the like). The kind of tasks found in most work settings are not as inherently valuable, however, and it has not been clear that these general motivation principles apply to sets of assigned or required activities. It has been the objective of these initial extensions of this behavioral technology (Brady et al., 1988) to assess the functional properties of the kind of performance tasks typical of a work environment (e.g., a space station or Antarctic colony).

## Procedural Approach

A workplace environment was simulated in the programmed human laboratory by following two strategies. First, a set of repetitive activities was arbitrarily established as the subjects' response repertoire. These activities resemble the kinds of things people do in an unstimulating work environment. Previous laboratory research with preferred activities simulated an exciting workplace, so a set of activities devoid of apparent value was created. Second, the subjects were required to engage in this set of activities for an extended work period. In this context, the baseline and contingency procedures to be described below were implemented.

Subjects spent part of each day working alone and another part interacting with two other people living under the same conditions. There were experimental procedures operating during both individual and social periods of the day, but the current report will focus upon the results obtained during the individual work periods.

Four groups of 3 male subjects each were recruited and screened in accordance with procedures previously described in detail (Brady & H. H. Emurian, 1978). They lived continuously in the programmed residential environment for periods up to a month. Each subject was alone in his individual room for 6 hours per waking day, and for 9 hours per waking day he also had access to a common social area that all subjects could use simultaneously. All behavior was monitored through high-resolution, color video cameras and was categorized and recorded by trained observers using a microcomputer program developed for observation of ordinary human behavior (Bernstein & Livingston, 1979). The reliability of the observers and the microcomputer program were assessed with repeated scoring of videotaped samples of behavior, and agreement was greater than 90%.

Each subject's repertoire of activities was categorized and defined using a combined criterion of manual contact and/or head orientation. The categorization was discussed with each subject to be certain that the boundaries corresponded to the subjects' perceptions of their activities and were clearly understood for the purpose of later verbal identification. There was a standard set of work-like activities available in the individual room during the period each subject was alone. There were two tasks performed at a computer keyboard with a video screen. One, called VIGI, involved vigilant monitoring of a string of numbers for detecting skipped entries in a series, and the other, called DSST, required simple, short-term remembering of a string of digits. There was also a manual task, RUG, that required hooking pieces of wool into holes in a piece of nylon backing. The last task, WORDS, required alphabetizing pieces of paper on which randomly generated nonsense words were printed. Each subject also brought a set of individual hobby activities, and these were normally available only during the period when subjects could gather in the common area.

Experiments began with a baseline period (up to 7 days) during which there was only one restriction on how subjects spent their time. They were free to engage in any of the work-like activities provided, but they had to engage in one of them. The percentage of time devoted to the activities during the initial baseline was used to select the responses for the first contingency condition. Each experimental manipulation was also followed by a baseline period. This work-alone baseline was also compared with a baseline during the private session that included both the work activities and the preferred activities brought into the laboratory by each subject as a check of the assumption that the work activities were without significant inherent value.

Data from the work activities-alone baseline condition immediately preceding each contingency were used to select two activities for which there was a relatively stable preference order. An activity with a high probability (percentage time in baseline) was selected as the contingent response (reward), and an activity with a lower probability was selected as the instrumental response. Performance of the instrumental response was required in order to gain access to the contingent response.

The amount of time available for the contingent response was a constant proportion of the time devoted to the designated instrumental response, and the size of the proportion was learned from experience with the contingency, not from instructions. A minimum amount of instrumental performance was required in order to gain access to the contingent response. Access to the contingent response did not have to be used immediately or all at one time, so the subjects could engage in the response at several different times for short durations or use the time all at once. There was no limit on the amount of time that could be accumulated for the contingent response. As long as the total time on the contingent response did not exceed the credit accumulated by instrumental performance, each subject could alternate between the two responses in any pattern. When the earned time was used, the red light was turned on, and the instrumental performance was again required in order to remove the restriction.

Before the beginning of the experiment, all subjects spent time in the laboratory receiving a full orientation to the living situation and the experimental procedures. Instructions were given explaining communication with the experimenters, use of the microcomputer terminals, the daily schedule, the food schedule, and all of the experimental procedures to be used. A written protocol was provided for each subject to keep for reference during the experiment. There was no deception in the experiment, and subjects were aware of all procedures in advance; they were not told the exact order or duration of the conditions, however, nor were they told how previous subjects in the experiment had performed.

Subjects were awakened at 0900 hours by a signal tone and allowed 45 min to shower, dress, and eat. The interval from 0945 to 1600 hours was the individual activity period. From 1600 until 2300 hours subjects could spend time in the social area engaging in group activities with other subjects. Each group prepared and ate a meal sometime during the social period. At 2300 hours, subjects returned to their private area to prepare for sleep, and the lab was darkened at 2400 hours. Subjects remained in bed in their darkened private room until the 0900-hours wake-up signal.

## Experimental Results

The effect of reinforcement contingencies was straightforward and consistent. The amount of time devoted to the designated *instrumental* responses was greatly *increased* during the contingency periods. For the 9 subjects in the first three groups studied, there were 34 transitions between a baseline condition and a contingency (summing across all 9 subjects), and in 31 of those cases, the contingency produced an increase in the response over baseline levels. Figures 15.2 and 15.3 show the percentage of time devoted to the instrumental response for two typical subjects (Subject 1, Experiment 1, and Subject 1, Experiment 2), averaged across baseline (Base) and contingency (Cntgy) conditions over the course of a 12- and 18-day experiment, respectively.

Figure 15.4 shows the contingent response levels for Subject 3, Experiment 3 during the private session under conditions that compared the work-alone baseline (Base 2) with a baseline that included both the work activities and the preferred activities brought into the laboratory by each subject (Base 1).

The amount of time devoted to the designated *contingent* responses was consistently *reduced* during the contingency periods. For the 9 subjects in the first three groups studied, there were 34 transitions between a baseline condition and a contingency (summing across all 9 subjects), and in 33 of

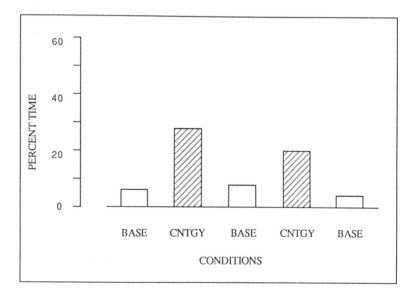

FIGURE 15.2. Percentage of time devoted to the designated instrumental response for Subject 1, averaged across the 12-day course of Experiment 1. BASE = baseline; CNTGY = contingency.

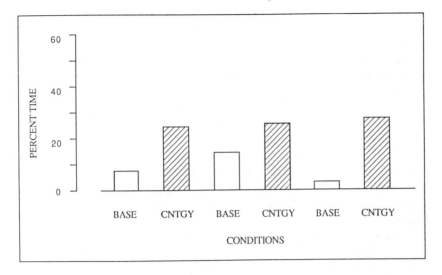

FIGURE 15.3. Percentage of time devoted to the designated instrumental response for Subject 1, averaged across baseline (BASE) and contingency (CNTGY) conditions over the 18-day course of Experiment 2.

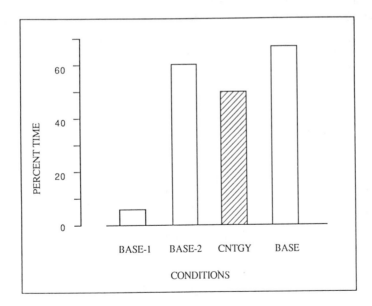

FIGURE 15.4. Percentage of time devoted to the designated contingent response for Subject 3, averaged across the baseline that included both preferred and work activities (BASE-1), the work activities-alone baselines (BASE-2 and BASE), and the contingency (CNTGY) over the course of Experiment 3.

those cases, the contingent response was lower during the contingency period. Figures 15.5 and 15.6 show the percentage of time devoted to contingent response for two typical subjects (Subject 1, Experiment 1, and Subject 1, Experiment 2), averaged across baseline (Base) and contingency (Cntgy) conditions over the course of a 12-day and 18-day experiment, respectively. The data summarized in these two figures show that the magnitude of the indicated decreases was generally substantial and that the effect was consistently reliable.

Figure 15.7 summarizes the results of Experiment 4 in the form of mean percentage of time devoted to both instrumental (left three bars) and contingent (right three bars) activities under baseline and contingency conditions averaged across all three subjects. The results of Experiment 4 were entirely consistent with the findings described for Experiments 1, 2, and 3, reflecting a marked *increase* over baseline in *instrumental* activity (left three bars, Figure 15.6) and a significant *reduction* below baseline in *contingent* activity (right three bars, Figure 15.6) under contingency conditions.

## Discussion

The results of these experiments show clearly that a time-based model of value applies to work-like performances as well as it does to self-selected or preferred recreational activities. Even when the activities have low status in

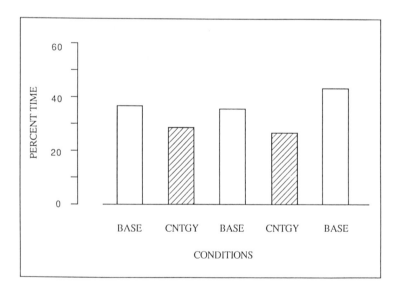

FIGURE 15.5. Percentage of time devoted to the designated contingent response for Subject 1, averaged across baseline (BASE) and contingency (CNTGY) over the 12-day course of Experiment 1.

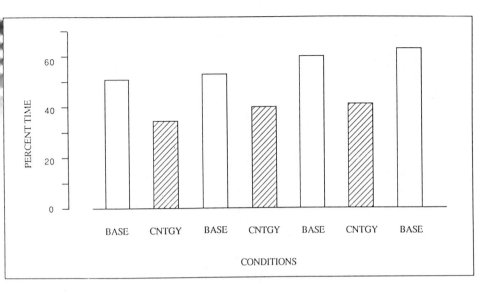

FIGURE 15.6. Percentage of time devoted to the designated contingent response for Subject 1, averaged across baseline (BASE) and contingency (CNTGY) conditions over the 18-day course of Experiment 2.

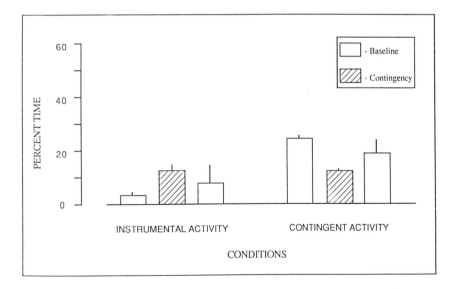

FIGURE 15.7. Mean percentage of time devoted to instrumental (left three bars) and to contingent (right three bars) activities under baseline (open bars) and contingency (hatched bars), averaged aross all three subjects in Experiment 4.

the repertoire, an assessment of time devoted to them under baseline conditions yields orderly predictions of their value under a contingency. These results generally confirm the potential for application of the model to workplace settings including those involving spaceflight operations and Antarctic expeditions. These results also support the position that a baseline estimate is a relative rather than an absolute measure of the value of a performance. Forcing all of the activities above their normal level of performance did not alter the utility of the hierarchy for making predictions about contingencies. As long as relative preference can be described quantitatively, a response deprivation calculation can make an accurate prediction about the outcome of a contingency.

The procedure used in the laboratory could be readily extended to many kinds of work environments, including spaceflight settings. The main requirement is a variety of work alternatives within the range of skills that a particular individual can master. It could be difficult to maintain high levels of performance when there is limited availability of the usual consequating conditions (e.g., money) for high-quality contributions. In addition, personnel turnover to open positions for transfer or promotion are limited in isolated and confined microsocieties. The alternative would be to offer brief access to more preferred activities as a reward for performing a required job well. This could be used until more permanent shifts in assignment can be made. This strategy requires a reasonably precise estimate of each person's ideal distribution of time across all those jobs for which he or she is qualified. It may not be easy to accumulate sufficient preflight baseline data, but a careful verbal assessment of time distributions could work for establishing contingencies that meet the response deprivation criterion (Bernstein, 1985).

Again, it seems worth emphasizing that the utility of this approach may be the most relevant in operational mission settings that are devoid of the usual kinds of consequences that are effective in the workplace and where major human factor concerns focus upon productivity. Certainly, where space mission participants are engaged in extended-duration flight operations, there will be a need for special attention to the conditions under which quality performances can be maintained in a setting characterized by a progressively developing/emerging autonomy. The benefits of the kinds of structured sequences investigated in the current study might even be considered in crisis situations that involve emergency functions. Certainly, extending such research settings to the numerous ground simulations conducted in advance of actual flight missions could provide for accurate baseline determinations essential to structuring an effective work maintenance plan. In remote situations likely to be impoverished in many ways, the use of time-based principles for identifying appropriate work maintenance conditions could make an important contribution to long-term productivity in space and Antarctic environments.

# References

Bernstein, D. J. (1985). Correspondence between verbal and observed estimates of reinforcement value. In L. J. Parrott & P. N. Chase (Eds.), *Psychological aspects of language: The West Virginia lectures.* New York: Thomas.

Bernstein, D. J., & Livingston, C. (1979). A micro-computer system for collection and analysis of long-term observational data. *Behavioral Research Methods and Instrumentation, 14,* 231–235.

Brady, J. V. (1990). Toward applied behavior analysis of life aloft. *Behavioral Science, 35,* 11–23.

Brady, J. V., & Emurian, H. H. (1978). Behavior analysis of motivational and emotional interactions in a programmed environment. In R. Dienstbier & D. M. Hasson (Eds.), *Nebraska Symposium on Motivation, Vol. 26.* (pp. 81–122). Lincoln: University of Nebraska Press.

Brady, J. V., Bigelow, G. E., Emurian, H. H. , & Williams, D. M. (1975). Design of a programmed environment for the experimental analysis of social behavior. In D. H. Carson (Ed.), *Man-environment interactions: Evaluations and applications: Social ecology* (pp. 187–208). Milwaukee: Environmental Design Research Association.

Brady, J. V., Bernstein, D. J., Foltin, R. W., & Nellis, M. J. (1988). Performance enhancement in a semi-autonomous confined microsociety. *The Pavlovian Journal of Biological Science, 23,* 111–117.

Connors, M. M., Harrison, A. A., & Akins, F. R. (1985). *Living aloft: Human requirements for extended spaceflight* (NASA SP-483). Washington, DC: National Aeronautics and Space Administration.

Emurian, H. H., Emurian, C. S., & Brady, J. V. (1978). Effects of a pairing contingency on behavior in a three-person programmed environment. *Journal of the Experimental Analysis of Behavior, 29,* 319–329.

Emurian, H. H., Emurian, C. S., Bigelow, G. E., & Brady, J. V. (1976). The effects of a cooperation contingency on behavior in a continuous three–person environment. *Journal of the Experimental Analysis of Behavior, 25,* 293–302.

Emurian, H. H., Brady, J. V., Meyerhoff, J. L., & Mougey, E. H. (1981). Behavioral and biological interactions with confined microsocieties in a programmed environment. *Proceedings of the Fifth Princeton/AIAA/SSI Conference on Space.* New York: American Institute of Aeronautics and Astronautics.

Epstein, R., Lanza, R. P., & Skinner, B. F. (1980). Symbolic communication between two pigeons (*Columba livia domestica*). *Science, 207,* 543–545.

Hefferline, R. F., & Perera, T. B. (1963). Proprioceptive discrimination of a covert operant without its observation by the subject. *Science, 139,* 834.

Hefferline, R. F., Keenan, B., & Harford, R. A. (1959). Escape and avoidance conditioning in human subjects without their observation of the response. *Science, 130,* 1338–1339.

Johnston, J. M., & Pennypacker, H. S. (1980). *Strategies and tactics of human behavioral research.* Hillsdale, NJ: Lawrence Erlbaum.

National Academy of Sciences. (1987). *A strategy for space biology and medical science.* Washington, DC: National Academy Press.

Premack, D. (1965). Reinforcement theory. In D. Levine (Ed.), *Nebraska Symposium on Motivation, Vol. 13.* Lincoln: University of Nebraska Press.

Premack, D. (1971). Catching up with common sense on two sides of a generalization: Reinforcement and punishment. In R. Glazer (Ed.), *The nature of reinforcement*. New York: Academic Press.

# 16

# Applications of Living Systems Theory to Life in Space

JAMES GRIER MILLER

Earth, as far as we know, is the only planet in our solar system on which living systems have ever existed. Since Earth's primeval atmosphere lacked free oxygen and therefore had no ozone layer to protect primitive cells and organisms from the Sun's killing radiation, life evolved in the sea for the first 2 billion years. The biological activity of primitive algae is considered a major factor in creating our oxygen atmosphere, making it possible to colonize land. Now the human species is contemplating a second great migration, this time into space.

Planning for extraterrestrial living requires a reorientation of the long-range strategic purposes and short-range tactical goals and objectives of contemporary space programs. The primary focus must be upon the human beings who are to inhabit the projected space settlements. This implies a shift in thinking by space scientists and administrators so that a satisfactory quality of human life becomes as important as safety during space travel and residence. Planners are challenged not only to provide transportation, energy, food, and habitats but also to develop social and ecological systems that enhance human life.

As clear a vision as possible of human organizations and settlements in space and on extraterrestrial bodies in the 21st century should be gained now. The National Commission on Space (1986) began by depicting the human future on the space frontier. Behavioral scientists, particularly those with a general systems orientation, can contribute uniquely to this process. Their research can improve strategic and programmatic planning focused upon human needs and behavior. The results should prove to be the drivers of the mechanical, physical, and biological engineering required to create the space infrastructure.

When we envision extraterrestrial stays of long duration, we must plan for quite different social phenomena than we have seen in space missions up to now. Astronauts have lived on space stations for periods of a few weeks or months at the most. The great majority of missions have been relatively brief. Such missions have required the daring and initiative of carefully selected and highly trained astronauts equipped to accomplish limited goals. If people are to remain permanently in settlements far from Earth, however, they cannot endure the inconvenient, difficult, and uncomfortable working and living conditions that have been the lot of the highly trained and motivated professionals who have gone into space over the past 30 years. Months and years in a space environment are an entirely different matter (Connors, Harrison, & Akins, 1985). Motivation diminishes over time, and long-continued discomforts are hard to bear.

No place on Earth closely resembles the conditions in outer space, on the Moon, or on other celestial bodies. The harsh environmental stresses and the isolation that must be faced by people who winter-over in Antarctica, however, are similar in many ways. Antarctica may be the best place within Earth's gravity field to analyze the problems of life in space and even to put a space station simulator or to model a lunar outpost. Also, it is a good place to develop plans for continuous monitoring of human behavior under rigorous conditions, by procedures such as those based on living systems theory that will be outlined below. Alternatives include doing space station research at other locations, such as the simulators at Marshall Space Flight Center in Huntsville, Alabama, or McDonnell Douglas Corporation in Huntington Beach, California, or at Ames Research Center at Moffet Field, California.

## Synopsis of Living Systems Theory

Living systems theory (LST) is an integrated conceptual approach to the study of biological and social living systems, the technologies associated with them, and the ecological systems of which they are all parts. It offers a method of analyzing systems, living systems processes analysis, that has been used in basic and applied research on a variety of different kinds of systems (J. G. Miller, 1955a,b; 1978).

Since 1984, my colleagues and I have been examining how LST can contribute to the effectiveness of space planning and management. During a National Aeronautics and Space Administration (NASA) Summer Study at the California Space Institute in La Jolla, California, the research focused upon strategic planning for a lunar base (McKay, in press). Since then, a team of behavioral and other scientists has explored ways in which a living systems analysis could be employed by NASA to enhance the livability of the space shuttle and eventually of the space station. Developed by an interdisciplinary group of senior scientists, the LST approach to research and theoretical writing differs significantly from that commonly followed in a number of ways.

## Compartmentalization of Science

Modern science suffers from structural problems that have their roots in such factors as the organization of universities by departments and the emphasis of separate disciplines. Although the rewards of academic life are based on becoming expert in a specialty or subspecialty, scientists from all disciplines should realize that they are contributing to a mosaic and that their work fits, like a piece of a jigsaw puzzle, into an overall picture. In the real world of daily affairs, whether one is dealing with computers and information processing or with housing, finance, legislation, or industrial production, the problems are always interdisciplinary. This is also true of space enterprises. Each major project needs the skills of engineers, lawyers, economists, computer scientists, biologists, or social scientists in different combinations.

## Inductive General Theory

There are two major stages in the scientific process: first, the inductive stage; and second, the deductive stage. The inductive stage is logically prior. Scientists begin the first stage by observing some class of phenomena and identifying certain similarities among them. Then they consider alternative explanations for these similarities and generate hypotheses to determine which explanation is correct.

A goal of science that has been recognized for centuries is the development of both special theories of limited scope and general theories that unify or integrate special theories and cover broader spheres of knowledge. It is usually necessary to start with special theories that deal with a limited set of phenomena. Middle-range theories concerned with a greater number of phenomena come later. Ultimately, a body of research based upon these leads to general theories that include a major segment of the total subject matter of a field or several fields. The desirability and usefulness of general theories are more widely acknowledged in some disciplines, like mathematics and physics, than in others. Unfortunately, many students of science, and even senior scientists, have not been taught about this goal and are unaware of it.

Voluntary scientific self-discipline in the mature sciences leads researchers to prefer to carry out studies that test hypotheses that distinguish critically among alternative special theories, middle–range theories, and ultimately general theories. The goal of research on LST is to collect data to make deductive tests of hypotheses derived from inductive, integrative theory.

## Common Dimensions

If scientists or engineers from different fields are to work together, it is desirable that the dimensions and measurements they use be compatible. Experimenters in physical and biological sciences ordinarily make their measurements using dimensions identical to those used by other scientists in those fields or using other units that have known transformations to them. It should eventually be possible to write transformation equations to reduce dimensions of any of the disciplines of physical, biological, or social science into common dimensions that are compatible with the centimeter–gram–second system of measurement so that specialists in different fields can communicate precisely. Investigators studying LST attempt to use such dimensions whenever it is possible.

Comparable dimensions for living and nonliving systems are increasingly useful as matter–energy and information-processing technologies become more sophisticated and are more widely employed throughout the world. The design of person–machine interfaces, for example, is more precise and efficient when both sides are measured comparably. Engineers and behavioral scientists are able to cooperate in joint projects much more effectively than they ordinarily have in the past. Such comparability of dimensions is a main theme of the LST space research program.

## Coexistence of Structure and Process

It is important not to separate functional, that is, process, science from structural science. Psychology and physiology are process sciences at the level of the organism, and sociology and political science are process sciences at the level of the society. Gross anatomy and neuroanatomy are structural sciences at the level of the organism, and physical geography is a structural science at the level of the society.

A psychologist or neurophysiologist, however, is inevitably limited if she or he cannot identify the anatomical structure that mediates an observed process, and an anatomist can have only a partial understanding of a structure without comprehension of its function. Consequently, whenever a process has been identified but the structure that carries it out is not known, it should be an insistent goal of science to identify the structure. The opposite is also true.

## Biosocial Evolution

On the basis of a mass of supporting scientific evidence, LST asserts that over the course of the last approximately 3.8 billion years, a continuous biosocial evolution has occurred, in the overall direction of increased complexity. It has so far resulted in eight *levels* of living systems: cells, organs, organisms, groups, organizations, communities, societies, and supranational systems. Each succeeding level is composed principally of systems at the level below. Cells have nonliving molecular components; organs are composed of cells; organisms are composed of organs; groups are composed of organisms; society is composed of groups; and so on. Systems at higher levels are *suprasystems* of their component, lower level systems. Systems at lower levels are *subsystems* of the higher level systems.

Through a process of *fray-out* (Figure 16.1) larger, higher-level systems evolved with more and more complex components in each subsystem than those below them in the hierarchy of living systems. Fray-out can be likened to the unraveling of a ship's cable. The cable is a single unit, but it can separate into the several ropes that compose it. These can unravel further into finer strands, strings, and threads.

## Emergents

The fact that systems at each level have systems at the level next below as their principal components does not mean that it is possible to understand any system as just an accumulation of lower level systems. A cell cannot be described by summing the chemical properties of the molecules that compose it, nor can an organism be described by even a detailed account of the structure and processes of its organs. LST gives no support to reductionism. At each higher level of living systems there are important similarities to the lower levels, but there are also differences. Higher level systems have emergent structures and processes that are not present at lower levels. It is this increased complexity that makes the whole system greater than the simple sum of its parts and gives it more capability. Larger and more complex than lower level systems, higher level systems can adapt to a greater range of environmental variation, withstand more stress, and exploit environments not available to less complex systems.

## The Subsystems of Living Systems

Because of the evolutionary relationship among them, all living systems have similar requirements for matter and energy, without which they cannot survive. They must secure food, fuel, and other necessary substances. They must process their inputs in various ways to maintain their structure, reproduce, make products, and carry out other essential activities. The metabolism of matter and energy is the energetics of living systems. Input, processing, and output of information are also essential in living systems.

As shown in Figure 16.2, LST identifies 20 essential processes that, together with one or more components (Table 16.1), constitute the 20 subsystems of living systems. Similar variables can be measured in each subsystem at all levels. These are such aspects as quantity, quality, rate, and lag in flows of matter, energy, or information.

**Level**

Cell
Organ

Organism

Group

Organization

Community

Society

Supranational
System

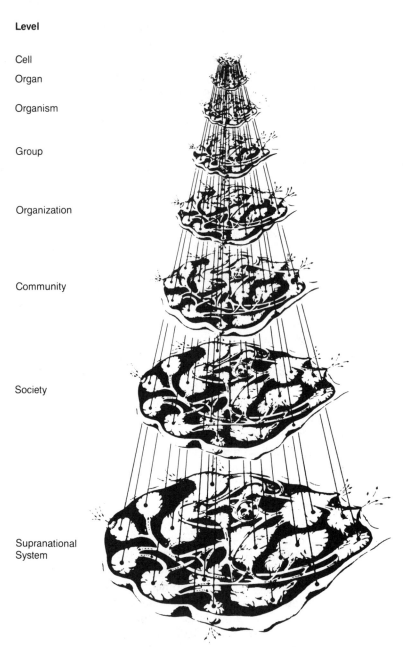

FIGURE 16.1. Fray-out. From J. G. Miller and J. L. Miller, 1990, Introduction: The Nature of Living Systems, *Behavioral Science, 35*, p. 158. Used with permission.

With the exception of the two subsystems of the learning process, which seem to have evolved only in animal organisms, all 20 processes appear to be present at each of the eight levels, although they may not be present in all types of systems at a given level. Bacteria, which are cells, for example, have no motor subsystems, but many other types of cells have motor components and can move about in the environment or move parts of the environment with relation to them. If a system lacks components for a given subsystem or part of it, it may *disperse* the processes to a system at the next or a lower level. Symbiosis and parasitism are examples. It is also possible for systems that lack a given process to use an alternative process to achieve a similar effect.

Figure 16.3 shows symbols designed to represent the levels, subsystems, and major flows in living systems. They are intended for use in simulations and diagrams and are compatible with the standard symbols of electrical engineering and computer science. They can also be used in graphics and flow charts.

## Adjustment Processes

Living systems of all kinds exist in an uncertain environment to which they must adapt. Excesses or lack of necessary matter–energy or information inputs can stress them and threaten their continued well-being or even their existence. In the midst of flux, they must maintain steady states of their numerous variables.

Each system has a hierarchy of values that determines its preference for one internal steady state rather than another, that is, its *purposes*. These are comparison values that it matches to information inputs or internal transductions to determine how far any variable has been forced from its usual steady state. A system may also have external *goals*, such as finding and killing prey or reaching a target in space.

All living systems have *adjustment processes*, sometimes called "coping mechanisms," that they can use to return variables to their usual steady states. These are alterations in the rates of other aspects of matter, energy, or information flows. Subsystems also match the state of each variable they control with a comparison signal and use adjustment processes to correct deviations from it. In general, more adjustment processes are available to higher level systems than to those at lower levels.

Countless small adjustments take place continually as a living system goes about its essential activities. Minor deviations can often be corrected by a single component of one subsystem. More serious threats are countered by a greater number of all subsystems. Severe deviations from steady state constitute pathology that a system may not be able to correct. All adjustment processes are used at some cost to the system. Ordinarily, a system that survives chooses the least costly of its alternatives.

## SUBSYSTEMS WHICH PROCESS BOTH MATTER-ENERGY AND INFORMATION

1. *Reproducer*, the subsystem which carries out the instructions in the genetic information or charter of a system and mobilizes matter, energy, and information to produce one or more similar systems.

2. *Boundary*, the subsystem at the perimeter of a system that holds together the components which make up the system, protects them from environmental stresses, and excludes or permits entry to various sorts of matter-energy and information.

## SUBSYSTEMS WHICH PROCESS MATTER-ENERGY

3. *Ingestor*, the subsystem which brings matter-energy across the system boundary from the environment.

4. *Distributor*, the subsystem which carries inputs from outside the system or outputs from its subsystems around the system to each component.

## SUBSYSTEMS WHICH PROCESS INFORMATION

11. *Input transducer*, the sensory subsystem which brings markers bearing information into the system, changing them to other matter-energy forms suitable for transmission within it.

12. *Internal transducer*, the sensory subsystem which receives, from subsystems or components within the system, markers bearing information about significant alterations in those subsystems or components, changing them to other matter-energy forms of a sort which can be transmitted within it.

13. *Channel and net*, the subsystem composed of a single route in physical space, or multiple interconnected routes, over which markers bearing information are transmitted to all parts of the system.

14. *Timer*, the subsystem which transmits to the decider information about time-related states of the environment or of components of the system. This information signals the decider of the system or deciders of subsystems to start, stop, alter the rate, or advance or delay the phase of one or more of the system's processes, thus coordinating them in time.

5. *Converter*, the subsystem which changes certain inputs to the system into forms more useful for the special processes of that particular system.

6. *Producer*, the subsystem which forms stable associations that endure for significant periods among matter-energy inputs to the system or outputs from its converter, the materials synthesized being for growth, damage repair, or replacement of components of the system, or for providing energy for moving or constituting the system's outputs of products or information markers to its suprasystem.

7. *Matter-energy storage*, the subsystem which places matter or energy at some location in the system, retains it over time, and retrieves it.

8. *Extruder*, the subsystem which transmits matter-energy out of the system in the forms of products or wastes.

9. *Motor*, the subsystem which moves the system or parts of it in relation to part or all of its environment or moves components of its environment in relation to each other.

10. *Supporter*, the subsystem which maintains the proper spatial relationships among components of the system, so that they can interact without weighting each other down or crowding each other.

15. *Decoder*, the subsystem which alters the code of information input to it through the input transducer or internal transducer into a "private" code that can be used internally by the system.

16. *Associator*, the subsystem which carries out the first stage of the learning process, forming enduring associations among items of information in the system.

17. *Memory*, the subsystem which carries out the second stage of the learning process, storing information in the system for different periods of time, and then retrieving it.

18. *Decider*, the executive subsystem which receives information inputs from all other subsystems and transmits to them information outputs for guidance, coordination, and control of the system.

19. *Encoder*, the subsystem which alters the code of information input to it from other information processing subsystems, from a "private" code used internally by the system into a "public" code which can be interpreted by other systems in its environment.

20. *Output transducer*, the subsystem which puts out markers bearing information from the system, changing markers within the system into other matter-energy forms which can be transmitted over channels in the system's environment.

FIGURE 16.2. The 20 critical subsystems of a living system. From J. G. Miller and J. L. Miller, 1990, Introduction: The Nature of Living Systems, *Behavioral Science, 35*, p. 159. Used with permission.

TABLE 16.1. Selected major components of each of the 20 critical subsystems at each of the eight levels of living systems, Part 1. From J. G. Miller and J. L. Miller, 1990, Introduction: The Nature of Living Systems, *Behavioral Science, 35*, pp. 160–161. Used with permission.

| | Subsystem | | | |
|---|---|---|---|---|
| Level | Reproducer | Boundary | Ingestor | Distributor |
| Cell | DNA and RNA molecules | *Matter-energy and information:* outer membrane | Transport molecules | Endoplasmic reticulum |
| Organ | Upwardly dispersed to organism | *Matter-energy and information:* capsule or outer layer | Input artery | Intercellular fluid |
| Organism | Testes, ovaries, uterus, genitalia | *Matter-energy and information:* skin or other outer covering | Mouth, nose, skin in some species | Vascular system of higher animals |
| Group | Parents who create new family | *Matter-energy:* inspect solders. *Information:* television rules in family | Refreshment chairman of social club | Father who serves dinner |
| Organization | Chartering group | *Matter-energy:* guards at entrance to plant. *Information:* librarian | Receiving department | Assembly line |
| Community | National legislature that grants state status to territory | *Matter-energy:* agricultural inspection officers. *Information:* movie censors | Airport authority of city | County school bus drivers |
| Society | Constitutional convention that writes national constitution | *Matter-energy:* customs service. *Information:* security agency | Immigration service | Operators of national railroads |
| Supranational system | United Nations when it creates new supranational agency | *Matter-energy:* troops at Berlin Wall. *Information:* NATO security personnel | Legislative body that admits nations | Personnel who operate supranational power grids |

TABLE 16.1. *Continued*

| | | Subsystem | | | |
|---|---|---|---|---|---|
| Converter | Producer | Matter–Energy storage | Extruder | Motor | Supporter |
| Enzyme in mitochondrion | Chloroplast in green plant | Adenosine triphosphate | Contractile vacuoles | Cilia, flagellae, pseudopodia | Cytoskeleton |
| Gastric mucosa cell | Islets of Langerhans of pancreas | Central lumen of glands | Output vein | Smooth muscle, cardiac muscle | Stroma |
| Upper gastrointestinal tract | Organs that synthesize materials for metabolism and repair | Fatty tissues | Sweat glands of animal skin | Skeletal muscle of higher animals | Skeleton |
| Work group member who cuts cloth | Family member who cooks | Family member who puts away groceries | Mother who puts out trash | Driver of family car | Birds that build nests |
| Operators of oil refinery | Factory production unit | Stockroom personnel | Janitorial staff | Crew of company jet | Building and repair and maintenance personnel |
| City stockyard organization | Bakery | County jail officials | City sanitation department | City transit authority | Maintenance crew at capitol building |
| Nuclear industry | All farmers and factory workers of a country | Guards at national armory | Export organizations of a country | Trucking industry | Officials who operate national public buildings and lands |
| EURATOM, CERN, IAEA | World Health Organization | International storage dams and reservoirs | Downwardly dispersed to societies | Operators of United Nations motor pool | People who maintain international headquarters buildings |

continued

TABLE 16.1. Selected major components of each of the 20 critical subsystems at each of the eight levels of living systems, Part 2

| | Subsystem | | | |
|---|---|---|---|---|
| Level | Input transducer | Internal transducer | Channel and net | Timer |
| Cell | Receptor sites on membrane for activation of cyclic AMP | Repressor molecules | Pathways of mRNA, second messengers | Fluctuating ATP and NADP |
| Organ | Receptor cell of sense organ | Specialized cell of sinoatrial node of heart | Nerve net of organ | Heart pacemaker |
| Organism | Sense organs | Proprioceptors | Hormonal pathways, central and peripheral nerve nets | Suprachiasmatic nuclei of hypothalamus |
| Group | Lookout of gang of thieves | Group member who reports members' attitudes to group decider | Person-to-person communication channels among group members | Mother who wakens other family members on time |
| Organization | Secretaries who take incoming calls | Factory quality-control unit | All users of corporate phone network | People who operate factory whistle |
| Community | Representatives who report from state capital to local voters | Neighborhood watch groups | Telephone linesmen in city | Caretakers of clock on city hall tower |
| Society | Foreign news services | Public opinion polling organizations, voters | Telephone and communications organizations | Legislators who decide on time and zone changes |
| Supranational system | UN Assembly hearing speaker from non-member territory | Speaker from member country to supranational meeting | Universal Postal Union (UPU) | Personnel of Greenwich observatory |

TABLE 16.1. *Continued*

| | Subsystem | | | | |
| --- | --- | --- | --- | --- | --- |
| Decoder | Associator | Memory | Decider | Encoder | Output transducer |
| Molecular binding sites | Unknown | Unknown | Regulator genes | Structure that synthesizes hormones | Presynaptic membrane of neuron |
| Second echelon cell of sense organ | None found—upwardly dispersed to organism | None found—upwardly dispersed to organism | Sympathetic fibers of sinoatrial node of heart | Presynaptic region of output neuron | Presynaptic region of output neuron |
| Sensory nuclei | Unknown neural components | Unknown neural components | Components at several echelons of nervous system | Temporo-parietal area of dominant hemisphere of human cortex | Larynx |
| Member who explains rules to team | Parents who teach good behavior | Father who stores family records | Parents, family council | Writer of group communication | Jury foreman |
| Foreign language translation group | People who train new employees | Filing department | Top executives, department heads, middle managers | Annual report writers | Public relations department |
| Attorney general of state who interprets law | City school teachers | Operators of central police computer | Governor, legislators, judges of state | Writers of city ordinances | Representatives from state to national legislature |
| Cryptographers | All teaching institutions of a country | Keepers of national archives | Voters and officials of national government | Drafters of treaties | National representatives to international meetings |
| Simultaneous translation staff of supranational organization | FAO units that teach farming methods in Third World nations | Librarians of UN libraries | Council of Ministers of the European Communities | UN Office of Public Information | Top official who announces decisions of supranational body |

continued

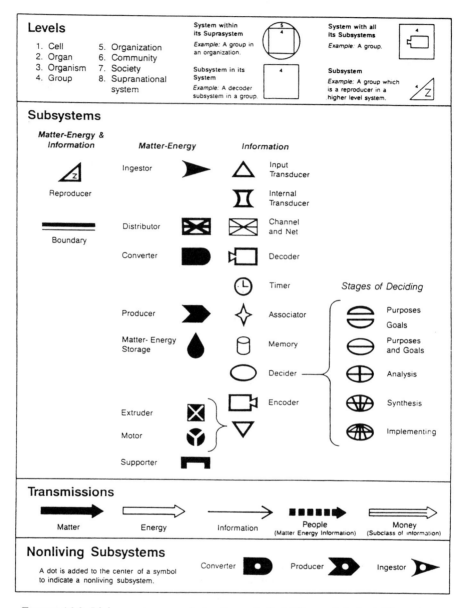

FIGURE 16.3. Living systems symbols. From J. G. Miller and J. L. Miller, 1990, Introduction: The Nature of Living Systems, *Behavioral Science, 35*, p. 162. Used with permission.

## *The LST Research Strategy*

Because of the similarities that exist across all levels of life, empirical cross-level comparisons are possible and are the sort of basic research that is the most characteristic of living systems science. Since the evolution of the levels has occurred in physical space–time, their comparable subsystems and variables can ultimately be measured in centimeter–gram–second or compatible units. The following strategy is used to analyze systems at any given level. It has been applied in systems as different as psychiatric patients and organizations.

1. Identify and make a two- or three-dimensional map of the structures that carry out the critical subsystem processes in the system being studied.
2. Identify a set of variables in each subsystem that describe its basic processes. At levels of the group and below, these represent aspects of the flows of matter, energy, and information. At levels of the organization and above, it has proved useful to measure five, instead of three, flows: MATFLOW (materials), ENFLOW (energy), COMFLOW (person-to-person, person-to-machine, and machine-to-machine communications information), PERSFLOW (individual and group personnel), and MONFLOW (money or money equivalents).
3. Determine the normal values of relevant variables of every subsystem and of the system as a whole and measure them over time, using appropriate indicators. The normal values of numerous variables have been established for human organisms. A physician can make use of reliable tests and measurements and accepted therapeutic procedures to discover and correct pathology in a patient. Similar information is not available to the specialist who seeks to improve the cost-effectiveness of an organization. Studies that make it possible to generalize among organizations are few, with the result that the usual values of most variables are unknown at the organization and higher levels. This makes it difficult to determine to what extent an organization's processes deviate from "normal" for systems of its type. Pathology in an organization may become apparent only when deviation is so great that acceptance of the organization's products or services declines or bankruptcy threatens.
4. Take action to correct dysfunctional aspects of the system and make it healthier or more cost-effective by, for example, removing a psychiatric patient from an unfavorable environment, altering the structure or process of a work group, or introducing nonliving artifacts (like computers or faster transport equipment) into an organization.

We propose applying the above strategy to evaluating the cost-effectiveness of the operations of a crew of a space station, tracking the five categories of flows through its 20 subsystems, identifying its strengths and dysfunctions, and recommending ways to improve its operations. Later, a similar approach could be applied to a mission to Mars, a lunar settlement, and perhaps other human communities in space.

## Application and Validation of LST

If LST is to have validity and utility, confirmation of its hypotheses is essential (J. G. Miller, 1986a). The first test of an LST hypothesis was a cross-level study of information input overload at five levels of living systems, carried out in the 1950s (J. G. Miller, 1978, pp. 121–202). It confirmed that comparable information input–output curves and adjustment processes to an increase in rate of information input would occur in systems at the level of cell, organ, organism, group, and organization. Numerous other quantitative experiments have been done on systems at various levels to test and confirm cross-level hypotheses based on living systems theory (e. g., Lewis, 1981; Rapoport & Horvath, 1961).

LST has been applied to physical and mental diagnostic examinations of individual patients and groups (Kluger, 1969; Koluch, 1970) and psychotherapy of individual patients and groups (J. G. Miller & J. L. Miller, 1983). An application of living systems concepts to families described the structure, processes, and pathologies of each subsystem as well as feedbacks and other adjustment processes (J. G. Miller & J. L. Miller, 1980). A subsystem review of a real family (Bell, 1986) was carried out in a videotaped interview that followed a schedule to discover which members were included in each of several subsystems, how the family decided who would carry out each process, how much time was spent in each, and what problems the family perceived in each process.

Research at the level of organizations includes a study of some large industrial corporations (Duncan, 1972); general analyses of organizations (Alderfer, 1976; Berrien, 1976; Lichtman & Hunt, 1971; Merker, 1982, 1985; Noell, 1974; Reese, 1972; E. M. Rogers & R. A. Rogers, 1976); an explanation of certain pathologies in organizations (Cummings & DiCortiis, 1973); and studies of accounting (Swanson & J. G. Miller, 1986), marketing (Reidenbach & Oliva, 1981), and management accounting and marketing (Weekes, 1983). The largest application of LST has been a study of the performance of 41 United States Army battalions (Ruscoe et al., 1985).

Several researchers have used LST as a framework for modeling, analysis, and/or evaluation of community mental health activities and health delivery systems (Baker & O'Brien, 1971; Bolman, 1967; Burgess, Nelson, & Wallhaus, 1974; Newbrough, 1972; Pierce, 1972 ). LST has also provided a theoretical basis for assessing program effectiveness in community life (Weiss & Rein, 1970). After a pretest of comparable methods of evaluation, a study of public schools in the San Francisco area was carried out (Banathy & Mills, 1985). The International Joint Commission of Canada and the United States has been employing living systems theory as a conceptual framework for exploring the creation of a supranational electronic network to model the region surrounding the border separating those two countries (J. G. Miller, 1986b).

It is too early to make a definitive evaluation of the validity of living systems theory. It is possible to say, however, that the theory has proved useful in conceptualizing and working with real systems at seven of the eight levels. (Studies of the eighth level, the organ, have not so far been carried out, but these will be undertaken in the future.) In addition, most published articles that have addressed living systems issues have been supportive of the theory.

## Proposed LST Space Research

It appears probable that a space station that is now in the planning stage at NASA will become a reality in the next few years. It would be a prototype for future extraterrestrial communities on the Moon and on Mars.

The crew of such a station would include not only astronauts but also technicians and other personnel. They would spend a much longer time in the space environment than crews of space vehicles have spent in previous missions.

Our research would use LST process analysis to study a space station, identify its strengths and dysfunctions, evaluate the performance of personnel, and recommend ways to improve the cost-effectiveness of its operations. A prototypical space station and its subsystems are presented in Figure 16.4.

Until the space station is in operation, we would study human activities on modules of a simulated space station. The method used in this phase could later be applied to a space station and eventually to extraterrestrial communities on the Moon or on Mars.

The basic strategy of LST process analysis of organizations is to track the five flows (matter, energy, personnel, communication, and, if applicable, monetary information) through the 20 subsystems and observe and measure variables related to each. We would measure such variables as rate of flow of essential materials; lags, error rates, and distortion in information transmissions; timeliness of completing assigned tasks; and costs in time and resources of various activities. We plan to collect both subjective and objective data.

Subjective data would consist of responses by personnel to questions about their activities related to the variables under study. Questions would be presented and answered on computer terminals. Responses would be collected in a centralized knowledge base for analysis by an artificial intelligence expert system.

Our research design also includes the use of objective indicators or sensors to monitor flows in all subsystems and components and measure them on a real-time basis. A time series of data about them would be transmitted or telemetered to the knowledge base in the computer.

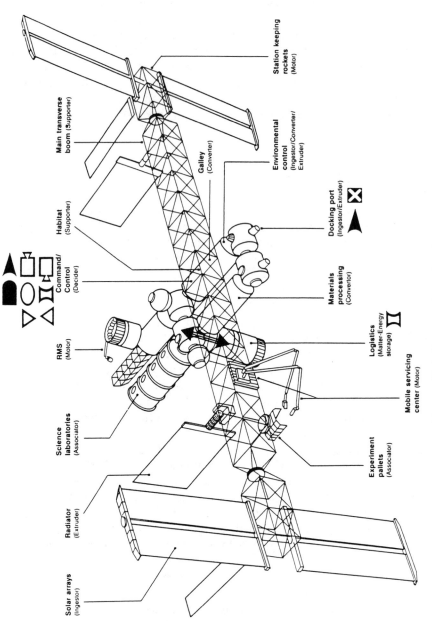

FIGURE 16.4. Space station subsystems.

In addition to standard measures of units of energy, quantities of material, bits of information, and the usual personnel records, we plan to make use of a novel technical innovation to monitor the movements of personnel and materials. It consists of badges similar to the ordinary identification badges worn by personnel in many organizations. Each badge contains an infrared transponder in the form of a microchip that, on receipt of an infrared signal from another transponder on the wall, transmits a stream of 14 characters that identify the person or object to which the badge is attached. With this equipment, it is possible to locate in 0.7 s any one of up to 65,000 persons, or materials such as equipment, furniture, weapons, ammunition, or food. If desired, the phone nearest to a person's current location can be rung in another 0.3 s.

In this way, many aspects of processes such as the response time of personnel to questions or commands, the average time spent in various activities, the patterns of interactions among people, and the movement of equipment to different parts of the space station can be measured without unduly distorting the day-to-day activities of the system.

All the data on the five major flows, from questionnaires and objective indicators, would be stored in a single computer. Such data could help NASA officials evaluate effects of changes in policy or procedures on space station operations. In addition, measurements of variables over time make it possible to determine norms for them and to identify deviations that may show either special strengths or dysfunctions. With such information, a computerized artificial intelligence expert system can analyze the relationships among the different variables of the five major flows and suggest ways to improve the space station's effectiveness.

In a real space situation, use of monitoring would be of value in many ways. It could identify and report technological or human problems as they occurred. Badges would make it easy for each spacefarer to be found at all times. The officer of the watch would be able to see instantly the location of all crewmembers with active badges on a video-type screen. In addition, the computer could be programmed to present possible solutions to problems and even to initiate necessary steps to assure continuation of mission safety and effectiveness in the event of in-flight emergencies and breakdowns.

Analyzing such flows in subsystems of the space station would provide experience with a novel system for monitoring both living and nonliving components of other future space habitations. This experience could well lead to use of similar methods on manned missions to the Moon or to Mars.

For instance, sometime in the next century such procedures could be applied to a lunar outpost, a community that would include men, women, and children. A wide range of professional interests, expertise, abilities, and perhaps cultures might be represented in the lunar community. Residents would live for long times under at least six ft of regolith (extraterrestrial "earth"), which would provide protection from solar radiation, solar flares, and other lunar hazards.

A lunar outpost might have designated areas for a command center, habitation, a generating station, solar power, storage, a small nuclear-powered energy plant, lunar mines for regolith ore mining, a solar furnace to use the direct rays of the Sun for smelting ore and heating the station, a recycling system for oxygen and hydrogen, a farm, a waste disposal area, and lunar rovers to transport materials and people on the surface of the Moon from one part of the community to others, as well as for travel outside the immediate area. The five flows through the 20 subsystems are diagrammed comparably to those of the space station shown in Figure 16.3. In sum, I suggest that living systems theory provides a general, tested, and useful theory for guiding much of the life sciences research that must be completed as we move into the 21st century.

## References

Alderfer, C. P. (1976). Change processes in organizations. In M. D. Dunnette (Ed.), *Handbook of industrial and organizational psychology* (pp. 1592–1594). Chicago: Rand McNally.

Baker, F. & Obrien, G. (1971). Intersystem relations and coordination of human service organizations. *American Journal of Public Health, 61*, 130–137.

Banathy, B. S., & Mills, S. R. (1985). The application of living systems process analysis in education. *ISI Monograph 85-7.*

Bell, R. A. (1986). Videotape and script. Personal communication.

Berrien, F. K. (1976). A general systems approach to organizations. In M. D. Dunnette (Ed.), *Handbook of industrial and organizational psychology* (pp. 42–43). Chicago: Rand McNally.

Bolman, W. M. (1967). Theoretical and community bases of community mental health. *American Journal of Psychiatry, 124*, 7–21.

Burgess, J., Nelson, R. H., & Wallhaus, R. (1974). Network analysis as a method for the evaluation of service delivery systems. *Community Mental Health Journal, 10*(3), 337–345.

Connors, M. M., Harrison, A. A., & Akins, F. R. (1985). *Living aloft: Human requirements for extended spaceflight* (NASA SP-483). Washington, DC: National Aeronautics and Space Administration.

Cummings, L. L., & DiCortiis (1973). Organizational correlates of perceived stress in a professional organization. *Public Personnel Management, 2*, 277.

Duncan, D. M. (1972). James G. Miller's living systems theory: Issues for management thought and practice. *Academic Management Journal, 15*, 513–523.

Kluger, J. H. (1969). Childhood asthma and the social milieu. *Journal of the American Academy of Child Psychiatry, 8*, 353–366.

Koulouch, F. T. (1970). Hypnosis in living systems theory: A living systems autopsy in a polysurgical, polymedical, polypsychiatric patient addicted to Talwin. *American Journal of Clinical Hypnosis, 13*(1), 22–34.

Lewis, F. L., II. (1981). Conflicting commands versus decision time: A cross-level experiment. *Behavioral Science, 26*, 79–84.

Lichtman, C. H., & Hunt, R. G. (1971). Personality and organization theory: A review of some conceptual literature. *Psychological Bulletin, 75*, 285–287.

McKay, M. F. (in press). *Strategic planning for a lunar base.*

Merker, S. L. (1982). Living systems as a management tool. *Proceedings of the Twenty-Sixth Annual Meeting of the Society for General Systems Research*, 886–888.

Merker, S. L. (1985). Living systems theory: A framework for management. *Behavioral Science, 30*, 187–194.

Miller, J. G. (1955a). Living systems: Basic concepts. *Behavioral Sience, 10*, 193–236.

Miller J. G. (1955b). Living systems: Structure and process. *Behavioral Science, 10*, 337–379.

Miller, J. G. (1978). *Living Systems*: New York: McGraw-Hill.

Miller, J. G. (1986a). Can systems theory generate testable hypotheses? From Talcott Parsons to living systems theory. *Systems Research, 3*, 73–84.

Miller, J. G. (1986b). A living systems analysis of a Canada/U.S. boundary region. In P. T. Haug, G. L. Bandurski, & A. L. Hamilton (Eds.), *Toward a transboundary monitoring network: A continuing binational exploration I* (pp. 132–144). Washington, DC: U. S. State Department, International Joint Commission U.S.A. and Canada.

Miller, J. G., & Miller, J. L. (1980). The family as a system. In C. E. Hofling & J. L. Lewis (Eds.), *The family: Evaluation and Treatment* (pp. 141–184). New York: Brunner/Mazel.

Miller, J. G., & Miller, J. L. (1983). General living systems theory and small groups. In H. I. Kaplan & B. J. Sadock (Eds.), *Comprehensive Group Psychotherapy* (pp. 33–47). Baltimore: Williams & Wilkins.

National Commission on Space. (1986). *Pioneering the space frontier: Our next fifty years in space*. New York: Bantam Books.

Newbrough, J. R. (1972). Community psychology. *American Psychologist, 27*, 770.

Noell, J. J. (1974). On the administrative sector of social systems: An analysis of the size and complexity of government bureaucracies in the American states. *Social Forces, 52*, 549–558.

Pierce, L. H. (1972). Usefulness of a system approach for problem conceptualization and investigation. *Nursing Research, 21*, 509–517.

Rapoport, A., & Horvath, W. J. (1961). A study of a large sociogram. *Behavioral Science, 6*, 279–291.

Reese, W. G. (1972). An essay on administration. *American Journal of Psychiatry, 128*, 69–72.

Reidenbach, R., & Oliva, T. A. (1981, Fall). A framework for analysis. *Journal of Marketing*, 42–52.

Rogers, E. M., & Rogers, R. A. (1976). *Communication in organizations* (pp. 29–58). New York: Free Press.

Ruscoe, G. C., Fell, R. L., Hunt, K. T., Merker, S. L., Peter, L. R., Cary, J. S., Miller, J. G., Loo, B. J., Reed, R. W., & Sturm, M. I. (1985). The application of living systems theory to 41 U. S. Army Battalions. *Behavioral Science, 30*, 1–56.

Swanson, G. A., & Miller, J. G. (1986). Accounting information systems in the framework of living systems theory and research. *Systems Research, 4*, 253–265.

Weekes, W. H. (1983). *A general systems approach to management accounting*. Salinas, CA: Intersystems Publications.

Weiss, R. S., & Rein, M. (1970). The evaluation of broad-aim programs: Experimental design, its difficulties, and an alternative. *Administrative Science Quarterly, 15*(1), 97–109.

# Part III Isolation and Confinement Effects

## Introduction

To some extent, spaceflight, polar, and undersea environments share similar environmental attributes and produce similar kinds of psychological effects. The chapters in this section focus on the cognitive, emotional, and behavioral consequences of isolation and confinement.

One of the earliest behavioral findings in Antarctica was Mullin's discovery of spontaneous trance states. Arreed Barabasz describes these states and Mullin's and subsequent studies, showing how isolation and confinement can produce significant and sometimes quite dramatic alterations in consciousness as measured by standardized instruments, including tests of hypnotizability. Marianne Barabasz offers preliminary data from two pilot investigations. This research shows that increases in mental absorption (imperviousness to distracting events) and imaginative involvement (the ability to get involved in fantasy) accompany prolonged Antarctic living.

Donna Oliver presents her own original research on psychological adaptation to Antarctica. Some minor psychological problems were noted during the austral winter, and there was evidence suggestive of a "midwinter slump." Follow-up interviews revealed temporary adjustment problems on return to the "real world." Despite this, two standardized psychological tests showed a *decrease* in pathology and an *increase* in self-actualization during the winter, and many participants subsequently described wintering-over as one of the best experiences of their lives. Next, Sybil Carrère, Gary Evans, and Daniel Stokols offer the preliminary results of a longitudinal study of stress in Antarctica. Both the chronic qualities of the environment such as wind speed and acute social and environmental events such as the arrival of the summer crew were related to physiological and psychological measures throughout the winter. Results suggest that Antarctica is not simply a static source of stress but a dynamic environment whose impact varies from individual to individual.

Lawrence Palinkas summarizes a series of studies that examined the health and service records of enlisted Navy personnel who took part in the Operation Deep Freeze (Antarctic) Program. Results indicate that the overall illness rate for the winter-over group was significantly *lower* than that of the control group. Then, International Biomedical Expedition to the Antarctic researchers Ian Hampton and Rainer Goldsmith discuss the stress-inducing and other properties of extreme cold temperatures and both natural and experimentally induced processes of cold adaptation.

Research in isolated environments shows a tendency for negative emotions and behavior to peak during the third quarter of the sojourn. Robert Bechtel and Amy Berning suggest that this is a more general phenomenon than was previously supposed. They then identify and discuss several hypotheses that may account for this effect. To conclude this section, Mary Connors reviews environmental elements that make communication in space different from communication on Earth. Among the salient issues discussed by Connors are the roles of liaisons, or boundary-role persons; the relationships of crewmembers to principal investigators in the conduct of tele-science; crew–ground control and crew–family communications; person-machine communications; and the optimal use of mass media.

# 17

# Effects of Isolation on States of Consciousness

ARREED F. BARABASZ

The first systematic psychological studies of Antarctic personnel were conducted by Mullin and his psychologist colleagues Connery and Wouters during the 1958 International Geophysical Year. Subjects consisted of 85 men who were nearing the end of their wintering-over isolation period at a number of stations. One of the most exciting and dramatic discoveries of this work provided the basis for my own line of research over the past 10 years. Mullin, Connery, and Wouters (1958) found that 30 of their 85 subjects reported having experienced "absentmindedness" and "wandering of attention." The response was noted only after several months in Antarctic isolation. The investigators concluded that the change in alertness or awareness was "a striking phenomenon" requiring further study (Mullin, 1960, p. 324). In a few cases the reaction was considered so extreme as to take the form of a "fugue state." The individual would recall leaving his quarters, but nothing thereafter until he "came to" later in some other part of the station wondering how he got to that area and why he was there. Since the occurrence of fugue-like, or dissociative, trance states under conditions of restricted environmental stimulation (REST) is consistent with E. R. Hilgard's (1977, 1979) neodissociation theory of hypnotic phenomena, it seemed appropriate to explore the possibility of an increase in hypnotic susceptibility as a consequence of Antarctic living.

Hypnosis has been subjected to controlled scientific investigation for over 30 years and has been accepted by the American Psychological Association, the American Medical Association, and the American Psychiatric Association. Hypnosis, defined as *the responsive state achieved following a typical hypnotic induction or its equivalent* (E. R. Hilgard, R. L. Atkinson, & R. C. Atkinson, 1979, p. 597) may be conceptualized as a specialized form of imagination or concentration. While hypnosis does not involve sleep in any form, the hypnotic state does produce identifiable electroencephalogram (EEG) components that demonstrate an attentional shift (A. F. Barabasz & Lonsdale, 1983; Crawford, Kitner-Triolo, & Clark, 1988; Spiegel, Cutcomb, Ren, & Pribram, 1985). In hypnosis, the the subject focuses his or her mind in a very special fashion. This form of concentration makes it possible to become absorbed into fantasy, so absorbed one can feel as if he or she is experiencing it in reality (E. R. Hilgard, 1965). Both positive and negative auditory, olfactory, and visual hallucinations can occur in hypnosis. These phenomena can be tested by standardized instruments such as the Stanford Hypnotic Susceptibility Scales (Weitzenhoffer & E. R. Hilgard, 1959, 1962). Consistent with the spontaneous dissociative phenomena discovered by Mullin (1960) in winter-over Antarctic personnel, this investigator (A. F. Barabasz, 1988) found hypnosis to occur spontaneously in highly hypnotizable subjects exposed to laboratory REST.

The first pilot study of hypnotizability in Antarctica also considered the possibility of psychophysiological changes (A. F. Barabasz, 1978, 1980a). Engstrom (1976) suggested that the restriction of sensory experience may be basic to hypnosis. Engstrom noted that becoming hypnotized may include subjects' predisposition to restrict sensory input because of lower levels of cortical arousal. Even in active, alert, hypnotic conditions (Banyai & E. R. Hilgard, 1976), where subjects remained at a high level of physiological arousal and subjects' focused attention occurred in an apparent state of alertness, subjects' gaze appeared unfocused. These subjects reported that they could simply "tune other things around me out" (Banyai & Hilgard, 1976, p. 220).

Consistent with notions of an attentional shift in hypnosis, early laboratory studies targeted waking, eyes-closed EEG alpha density and hypnotizability (Cooper & London, 1976; Edmonston & Grotevant, 1975; Engstrom, 1970; E. R. Hilgard & J. R. Hilgard, 1975; London, Hart, & Leibovitz, 1968; Morgan, MacDonald, & E. R. Hilgard, 1974; Morgan, McDonald, & MacDonald, 1971; Nowlis & Rhead, 1968), and those studies failing to show such a correlation (Dumas, 1976; Dumas & Morgan, 1975; Evans, 1972; Galbraith, London, Leibovitz, Cooper, & Hart, 1970). The purpose of the first Antarctic pilot study was to investigate the stability of EEG alpha and hypnotizability.

All nine men wintering-over at New Zealand's Scott Base, 1976–1977, served as subjects. Subjects were tested in Antarctica, after an initial adjustment period to the environment and, again, immediately following the long, dark winter. In order to preserve the naivete of subjects with respect to the hypnosis focus of the study, modified items from the Barber Suggestibility Scale (or BSS) of Barber and Glass (1962) were used to measure hypnotizability. This instrument allows assessment of hypnotic susceptibility without the necessity of exposing subjects to a hypnotic induction. Contrary to the high level of stability of hypnotic talent under normal living conditions (E.

R. Hilgard, 1965; J. R. Hilgard, 1979), significant increases in hypnotizability appeared following winter-over. The project also showed increases in EEG alpha densities that correlated with hypnotizability using a new skin-conductance-based correction of psychophysiological arousal. These results appear in Tables 17.1 and 17.2. The findings remain open to question because of the very limited range of hypnotic responsiveness tapped by the modified Barber Scale, the small number of subjects available, and the lack of criterion data beyond that of hypnosis test scores.

In a separate study of the same subject group at Scott Base, the possibility of shifts in responsiveness to suggestion was investigated using transient olfactory stimulation, eight channels of EEG averaged evoked potential (AEP) measures, and skin conductance (A. F. Barabasz & Gregson, 1979).

After exposure to relaxation instructions, subjects were asked to keep their eyes closed and were told that they would be exposed to six odorants. Subjects were asked to breathe through their nose only, without making any

TABLE 17.1. Percent-alpha and hypnotizability correlations for Antarctic wintering-over party.[a]

| Period | Total | Percent-alpha |
|---|---|---|
| Prewinter isolation | .21 | .61* |
| Postwinter isolation | .58* | .86** |

[a]Data from the *International Journal of Clinical and Experimental Hypnosis, 28,* 69. Copyright 1980 by the Society for Clinical and Experimental Hypnosis.
*$p < .05$
**$p < .01$

TABLE 17.2. Alpha density $t$-test results for winter-over party.[a]

| Contrast | N | X Percent-Alpha | S.D. | t Value |
|---|---|---|---|---|
| Prewinter total alpha | 9 | 32.00 | 15.44 | 4.78* |
| Postwinter total alpha | 9 | 44.22 | 18.81 | |
| Prewinter SC[b]-corrected alpha | 9 | 38.33 | 17.17 | 3.53* |
| Postwinter SC[b]-corrected alpha | 9 | 49.44 | 21.54 | |

[a]Data from the *International Journal of Clinical and Experimental Hypnosis, 28,* 70. Copyright 1980 by the Society for Clinical and Experimental Hypnosis.
[b]SC, skin conductance.
*$p < .01$

effort to sniff forcibly, while stimuli were presented. Four standard research-grade odorants were quasi-randomly drawn afresh for each subject. Two suggested (i.e., nonexistent) stimuli were also employed. Real and suggested stimuli initially were presented to subjects on exhalation, by the technique of holding the ends of sterile glass rods approximately 1 cm beneath the nose, for a silent count of 5 s. Event marking was actuated on inhalation. Stimuli were introduced by the instruction "Here is odor number_____," followed by "O.K." upon removal of the rod from proximity to the nose. At least 1 min elapsed between any two successive presentations. Despite marked interindividual differences among the nine subjects, multivariate analysis of variance findings indicated consistent trends. Skin conductance (or SC) showed significant responses for real and suggested odorants pre- and post-wintering-over in contrast to tonic skin conductance levels in the absence of olfactory stimulation. Significant EEG AEP amplitudes for real and suggested odorants were evidenced prior to wintering-over in contrast to baseline recordings. After wintering-over, EEG AEP amplitudes showed significant increases for real odorants but a significant decrease for suggested stimuli. The most dramatic activity was evidenced in hypnosis at the temporal sites. The apparent AEP shifts in response to suggested stimuli following winter-over living in Antarctica support Mullin's (1960) discovery of increased responsiveness to suggestions and studies demonstrating measured increases in hypnotizability (A. F. Barabasz, 1978, 1980a).

These preliminary data must be viewed with caution because evoked-potential data analysis was limited to the standardized peak analysis method (Shimizu, 1966) due to budgetary considerations in this New Zealand study. The tedious hand score procedure only accounted for those EEG pen deflections greater than 4 mm.

The utility of EEG AEP measures in identifying the hypnotic state was subsequently supported by highly controlled laboratory studies using computerized averaging techniques (A. F. Barabasz & Lonsdale, 1983; Spiegel, Cutcomb, Ren, & Pribram, 1985). This discovery, of the greatest nonlateralized activity in the temporal region during hypnosis, has been independently verified and greatly extended in the study of cerebral blood flow in hypnosis and waking conscious states (Crawford, Skolnick, Benson, R. E. Gur, & R. C. Gur, 1985).

The striking preliminary finding of apparent increases in hypnotizability following wintering-over isolation, supported by the EEG AEP data, led to additional pilot studies featuring Antarctic summer field party isolation as the focus. Studies reviewed by Zubek (1969) demonstrated short-term sensory restriction to have significant effects on primary suggestibility and EEG alpha. Antarctic summer field research teams face isolation conditions that are similar in certain aspects to the restriction of environmental stimulation imposed by winter-over conditions. These include loss of diurnal variation (24 hours of daylight per day), anosmia due to low ambient working temperatures, and a high degree of restriction of contact with the outside world.

The summer field project used seven scientific personnel assigned to biology project field sites located in the dry valleys about 100 km from McMurdo Station. Subjects were tested for hypnotizability using the Stanford Hypnotic Clinical Scale (SHCS) of Morgan and J. R. Hilgard (1975). As in the winter-over studies, subjects were tested in Antarctica after an initial adjustment period. The nonfunded status of the study and logistic limitations prevented immediate postisolation testing at the field site location and limited the type of hypnotizability scale to the short, five-item SHCS. Follow-up testing was completed 3 months after subjects returned to their usual activities at Virginia Polytechnic Institute and State University. Such follow-up data were not available for the winter-over pilot investigations. Contrary to the winter-over data, the follow-up SHCS scores did not show increases in hypnotizability. Such adaptive responses to Antarctic living may have been evident had immediate on-site, postisolation testing been possible. Such a finding seems particularly likely since the laboratory REST study involving 6 hours of isolation (A. F. Barabasz, 1982) showed significant increases in measured hypnotizability, which were shown to be generalizable to changes in responsiveness to suggestions for analgesia. Furthermore, the Tellegen Absorption Scale scores administered to the same summer subjects showed significant increases in the personality variable "absorption," or imperviousness to distracting events.

# Summary

Exposure to Antarctic isolation may enhance hypnotizability. Increases in hypnotizability bring increases in individuals' capacity and probability of experiencing a variety of phenomena. These include positive or negative hallucinations (E. R. Hilgard, 1965; Weitzenhoffer & E. R. Hilgard, 1962), changes in the perception of odors (A. F. Barabasz & Gregson, 1978, 1979; Weitzenhoffer & E. R. Hilgard, 1962), increases or decreases in vigilance performance (A. F. Barabasz, 1980b), dissociative, or fugue, states (Mullin, 1960), and increases in deep imaginative involvement and absorption (M. Barabasz, A. F. Barabasz, & Mullin, 1983). These phenomena have the potential to facilitate, degrade, or endanger human performance in Antarctica and, by analogy, in outer space environments. The instances of "bizarre imagery" occurring in space travelers (Bluth, 1979), for example, might be understood through the controlled study of hypnotizability and absorption in Antarctica. The findings would have implications for environmental designs and personnel selection. The data would also contribute to the empirical knowledge base underlying the use of artificially restricted environments to increase hypnotizability for clinical applications.

## References

Banyai, E. I., & Hilgard, E. R. (1976). A comparison of alert hypnotic induction with traditional relaxation induction. *Journal of Abnormal Psychology, 85*, 218–224.

Barabasz, A. F. (1978). Electroencephalography, isolation, and hypnotic capability at Scott Base. *New Zealand Antarctic Record, 1*, 35–42.

Barabasz, A. F. (1980a). EEG alpha, skin conductance and hypnotizability in Antarctica. *International Journal of Clinical and Experimental Hypnosis, 28*, 63–74.

Barabasz, A. F. (1980b, August). *Imaginative involvement and hypnotizability in Antarctica*. Paper presented at the 10th Annual Congress of the Australian Society for Clinical and Experimental Hypnosis, Hobart, Tasmania.

Barabasz, A. F. (1982). Restricted environmental stimulation and the enhancement of hypnotizability: Pain, EEG alpha, skin conductance, and temperature responses. *International Journal of Clinical and Experimental Hypnosis, 30*, 147–166.

Barabasz, A. F. (1988, August). *Spontaneous hypnosis in flotation restricted environmental stimulation*. Paper presented at the 11th International Congress of Hypnosis and Psychosomatic Medicine. The Hague.

Barabasz, A. F., & Gregson, R. A. M. (1979). Antarctic wintering-over, suggestion and transient olfactory stimulation: EEG evoked potential and electrodermal responses. *Biological Psychology, 9*, 285–295.

Barabasz, A. F., & Lonsdale, C. (1983). Effects of hypnosis on P300 olfactory-evoked potential amplitudes. *Journal of Abnormal Psychology, 92*, 520–526.

Barabasz, M., Barabasz, A. F., & Mullin, C. S. (1983). Effects of brief Antarctic isolation on absorption and hypnotic susceptibility: Preliminary results and recommendations. *International Journal of Clinical and Experimental Hypnosis, 31*, 235–238.

Barber, T. X., & Glass, L. B. (1962). Significant factors in hypnotic behavior. *Journal of Abnormal and Social Psychology, 64*, 222–228.

Bluth, B. J. (1979). Consciousness alterations in space. In *Space Manufacturing 3: Proceedings of the 4th Princeton/AIAA Conference* (pp. 525–532). New York: American Institute of Aeronautics and Astronautics.

Cooper, L. M., & London, P. (1976). Children's hypnotic susceptibility, personality, and EEG patterns. *International Journal of Clinical and Experimental Hypnosis, 24*, 140–148.

Crawford, H., Skolnick, B., Benson, D., Gur, R. E., & Gur, R. C. (1985, August). Regional cerebral blood flow in hypnosis and hypnotic analgesia. Paper presented at the 10th International Congress of Hypnosis and Psychosomatic Medicine, Toronto.

Crawford, H. J., Kitner-Triolo, M., & Clark, S. (1988, November). *EEG activation patterns accompanying induced happy and sad moods: Moderating effects of hypnosis and hypnotic responsiveness*. Paper presented at the Annual Scientific Meeting of the Society for Clinical and Experimental Hypnosis, Ashville, NC.

Dumas, R. A. (1976). *Operant control of EEG alpha and hypnotizability*. Doctoral dissertation, Stanford University, Palo Alto, CA. (Ann Arbor: University Microfilms No. 76-25, 991)

Dumas, R., & Morgan, A. (1975). EEG asymmetry as a function of occupation, task, and task difficulty. *Neuropsychologia, 13*, 219–228.

Edmonston, W. E., & Grotevant, W. R. (1975). Hypnosis and alpha density. *American Journal of Clinical Hypnosis, 17,* 221–232.

Engstrom, D. R. (1970). *The enhancement of EEG-alpha production and its effects on hypnotic susceptibility.* Doctoral dissertation, University of Southern California, Los Angeles. (University Microfilms No. 70-26, 521)

Engstrom, D. R. (1976). Hypnotic susceptibility, EEG-alpha, and self-regulation. In F. E. Schwartz & D. Shapiro (Eds.), *Consciousness and self-regulation: Advances in research,* (pp. 173–221). New York: Plenum.

Evans, F. J. (1972). Hypnosis and sleep: Techniques for exploring cognitive activity during sleep. In E. Fromm & R. E. Shor (Eds.), *Hypnosis: Research developments and perspectives* (pp. 43–83). Chicago: Aldine-Atherton.

Galbraith, G. C., London, P., Leibovitz, M. P., Cooper, L. M., & Hart, J. T. (1970). EEG and hypnotic susceptibility. *Journal of Comparative and Physiological Psychology, 72,* 125–131.

Harrison, A. A. (1986). On resistance to the involvement of personality, social, and organizational psychologists in the U. S. space program. *Journal of Social Behavior and Personality, 1,* 315–324.

Hilgard, E. R. (1965). *Hypnotic susceptibility.* New York: Harcourt, Brace & World.

Hilgard, E. R. (1977). *Divided consciousness: Multiple controls in human thought and actions.* New York: Wiley.

Hilgard, E. R. (1979). Consciousness and control: Lessons from hypnosis. *Australian Journal of Clinical and Experimental Hypnosis, 7,* 103–116.

Hilgard, E. R., & Hilgard, J. R. (1975). *Hypnosis in the relief of pain.* Los Altos, CA: Kaufmann.

Hilgard, E. R., Atkinson, R. L., & Atkinson, R. C. (1979). *Introduction to psychology.* New York: Harcourt, Brace, Jovanovich.

Hilgard, J. R. (1979). Imaginative and sensory-affective involvement in everyday life and in hypnosis. in E. Fromm & R. E. Shor (Eds.), *Hypnosis: Developments in research and new perspectives* (2nd ed.) (pp. 483–517). New York: Aldine.

London, P., Hart, J. T., & Leibovitz, M. P. (1968). EEG alpha rhythms and susceptibility to hypnosis. *Nature, 219,* 71–72.

Morgan, A. H., & Hilgard, J. R. (1975). Stanford Hypnotic Clinical Scale (SHCS). In E. R. Hilgard & J. R. Hilgard (Eds.), *Hypnosis in the relief of pain* (pp. 209–221, Appendix A). Los Altos, CA: Kaufmann.

Morgan, A. H., McDonald, P. J., & MacDonald, H. (1971). Differences in bilateral alpha activity as a function of experimental task, with a note on lateral eye movements and hypnotizability. *Neuropsychologia, 9,* 459–469.

Morgan, A. H., MacDonald, H., & Hilgard, E. R. (1974). EEG alpha: Lateral asymmetry related to task, and hypnotizability. *Psychophysiology, 11,* 275–282.

Mullin, C. S. (1960). Some psychological aspects of isolated Antarctic living. *American Journal of Psychiatry, 117,* 323–326.

Mullin, C. S., Connery, H., & Wouters, F. (1958). *A psychological-psychiatric study of an IGY station in Antarctica* (Project Report). United States Navy, Neuropsychiatric Division of the Bureau of Medicine and Surgery.

Nowlis, D. P., & Rhead, J. C. (1968). Relation of eyes-closed resting EEG alpha activity to hypnotic susceptibility. *Perceptual and Motor Skills, 27,* 1047–1050.

Shimizu, H. (1966). Binary addition of peak time for electroencephalic audiometric responses. *Journal of Speech and Hearing Research, 9,* 313–316.

Spiegel, D., Cutcomb, S., Ren, C., & Pribram, K. (1985). Hypnotic hallucination alters evoked potentials. *Journal of Abnormal Psychology, 94,* 249–255.

Weitzenhoffer, A. M., & Hilgard, E. R. (1959). *The Stanford Hypnotic Susceptibility Scale: Forms A and B.* Palo Alto, CA: Consulting Psychologists Press.

Weitzenhoffer, A. M., & Hilgard, E. R. (1962). *The Stanford Hypnotic Susceptibility Scale: Form C.* Palo Alto, CA: Consulting Psychologists Press.

Zubek, J. P. (1969). *Sensory deprivation: Fifteen years of research.* New York: Appleton Century Crofts.

# 18

# Imaginative Involvement in Antarctica: Applications to Life in Space

Marianne Barabasz

This chapter focuses on preliminary data obtained from two Antarctic pilot investigations. The first study investigated changes in imperviousness to distracting events, a personality variable termed *absorption*, as assessed by objective test measures. Absorption can also be defined as the capacity for deep imaginative involvement. The second pilot investigation employed structured interviews to assess changes in imaginative involvement.

Several investigations, cited by E. R. Hilgard (1965, 1979), have demonstrated hypnotic susceptibility to be a stable trait. Contrary to the findings of high stability obtained with subjects exposed to normal living conditions, a recent investigation found significant increases in hypnotic susceptibility following exposure to wintering-over in Antarctica (A. F. Barabasz, 1980). This change appears to be a unique adaptation to the isolation of Antarctic living. The observation of this adaptation to restricted environmental stimulation has been further supported by preliminary Antarctic electroencephalogram research (A. F. Barabasz & Gregson, 1979) and well controlled laboratory studies (A. F. Barabasz, 1982; A. F. Barabasz & Kaplan, 1989).

Josephine R. Hilgard (1970) found that imaginative involvements outside of hypnosis, often originating in early childhood, were related to hypnotic capability as an adult. She hypothesized that the ability to develop one or two strong areas of imaginative involvement sufficed as "pathways into hypnosis." (p. 173). She noted, however, that very highly susceptible subjects commonly had a number of areas of imaginative involvement.

J. R. Hilgard (1970, 1974) investigated differences between subjects with high hypnotic capacity and subjects with low hypnotic capacity on ratings of imaginative involvement. Highly hypnotizable subjects had significantly more imaginative involvement than did subjects with low hypnotic capability. J. R. Hilgard concluded that the results of this study added to the evidence that imaginative involvements play a central role as background factors for hypnotic susceptibility.

Anecdotal reports and systematic behavioral observations of Antarctic personnel experiencing wintering-over and/or summer isolation (A. F. Barabasz & Gregson, 1979; Mullin, 1960) indicate increases in the savoring of sensory experiences and the imperviousness to distraction associated with deep imaginative involvement. J. R. Hilgard (1974) suggested that the capacity for deep imaginative involvement is the bridge to higher hypnotic susceptibility. Increased capability for deep imaginative involvement as a result of exposure to the Antarctic environment may be related to the observed increases in hypnotizability. The current studies were aimed at determining the effects of Antarctic isolation on these phenomena.

## Study 1: Absorption

### Subjects

Subjects volunteered for both the absorption (Study 1) and imaginative involvement (Study 2) projects. The seven subjects consisted of male scientific personnel ranging in academic qualifications from bachelor of science to doctoral level. The subjects were members of the phycology research team studying the fresh water lakes in the Dry Valleys of Antarctica more than 100 km from McMurdo Station. The subjects lived in individual pup tents separated from each other by at least 20 m. The tent material was yellow and translucent, providing what was essentially a ganzfeld field illuminated by 24 hours of sunlight per day. The subjects spent 3 weeks in field site isolation and a total of 3 months in Antarctica. At the field site, total isolation was broken only by (a) a bi-weekly mail drop; (b) daily scheduled radio contact with McMurdo Station; and (c) supply drop-offs at 5-day intervals during which helicopters did not remain long enough to shut down.

### Procedure

Absorption was assessed by a measure developed by Tellegen and Atkinson (1974) using the 34-item scale from Tellegen's Differential Personality Questionnaire. The scale measures openness to absorbing experiences. Subjects are presented with 34 absorbing experiences, for example, "When listening to organ music or other powerful music, I sometimes feel as if I am being lifted into the air"; "I like to watch cloud shapes change in the sky"; "While watching a movie, a T.V. show, or a play, I may become so involved that I forget about myself and my surroundings and experience the story as if it were real and as if I were taking part in it." For each statement, subjects indicate if this is mostly true or mostly false. It was intended to obtain data in Antarctica prior to and immediately following field site isolation and in a follow-up session, after subjects returned to the United States, 6 months later. Logistical difficulties complicated by the unfunded status of this preliminary project precluded data collection immediately following field site isolation. Preisolation and follow-up data were collected by different investigators as part of a more general assessment program that also involved interviews aimed at evaluating Antarctic adjustment.

## Results

Absorption scale scores for preisolation and follow-up were analyzed by analysis of variance. A significant increase in absorption scores was found (preisolation mean = 10, S.D. = 3.3; follow-up mean = 19, S.D. = 2.5; $F = 25.00, p < .003$).

The absorption scale (Tellegen & Atkinson, 1974) provides information about subjects' openness to absorbing experiences in a wide variety of areas, e.g., listening to music, watching a film. As noted above, Josephine R. Hilgard (1970, 1974) suggested that the capacity for deep imaginative involvement in one or two areas may suffice as the bridge to hypnosis. In order to evaluate changes in level of imaginative involvement, possibly occurring in only one or two areas, a second pilot investigation was conducted.

## Study 2: Imaginative Involvement

Group One (long-term isolation) consisted of a nine-man wintering-over party at New Zealand's Scott Base, Antarctica. This group was composed of scientific technicians, engineers, a mechanic, and an electrician. Consistent with J. R. Hilgard's (1974) description of low hypnotizable individuals, these subjects were considered to be predominantly objective, matter-of-fact, reality-oriented, analytic people. The Antarctic tour of duty lasted approximately 12 months at the base. Group 2 consisted of the same seven-man, summer scientific field team that participated in the first study. The control group consisted of 10 New Zealand university students.

## Procedure

Group 1 (long-term isolation) subjects were interviewed at Scott Base, Antarctica, prior to and immediately following the winter-over period. A New Zealand psychologist conducted formal interviews to assess emotional adjustment. This made it possible to obtain imaginative involvement information informally in both pre- and post-winter over periods. Quasi-nondirective interview techniques were used. Selective reflection, silence, acceptance of relevant information, and summary clarification counseling leads were used to stimulate further elaboration of imaginative involvement material.

Notes were not taken during the interviews, but details were summarized in written records as soon as possible after each interview. To assess potential treatment effects of the interview procedure, 10 New Zealand university students (controls) were subjected to the same procedure using the same intervening period of time as Group 1. Group 2, (short-term isolation) subjects were interviewed only after their return to the United States. Despite the inability to obtain preisolation interviews, this group of subjects was included in the current study because of the lack of data on brief Antarctic isolation and to provide a preliminary basis for comparison with the wintering-over isolates. Essentially, the same interviewing techniques were employed as for Group 1. Situational variables, however, required a more formal orientation and a more frequent use of direct questions. Notes were taken during these interviews. Undoubtedly, these subjects were more clearly aware of the imaginative involvement focus of the interview than Group 1 or control subjects.

## Results

Interview records were assessed for the level of imaginative involvement by averaging the scores from two independent raters who were blind with respect to group identity and data collection period. Low to high imaginative involvement was rated on a 1- to 7-point scale for each record. Interrater reliability for the total of 45 rated interviews was .76. Areas of involvement considered for scoring were based on the work of J. R. Hilgard (1974), including mental space travel, reading, creativity, daydreaming, and savoring of sensory experiences.

Nonparametric statistical tests were chosen because it could not be assumed that imaginative involvement would be normally distributed among subjects volunteering for Antarctic duty. Means and standard deviations are, however, of interest and are shown in Table 18.1.

Imaginative involvement scores, pre- versus post-wintering-over, for

TABLE 18.1. Means and standard deviations (S.D.) for imaginative involvement.[a]

| Group | N | Preisolation X | Preisolation S.D. | Postisolation X | Postisolation S.D. |
|---|---|---|---|---|---|
| Controls | 10 | 1.8 | 1.3 | 1.7 | 1.5 |
| Group 1 | 9 | 1.5 | 1.0 | 4.8 | 1.4 |
| Group 2 | 7 | — | — | 4.8 | 1.6 |

[a]Data from the *International Journal of Clinical and Experimental Hypnosis, 32,* 288. Copyright 1984 by the Society for Clinical and Experimental Hypnosis.

Group 1 subjects and for the control subjects were analyzed using Wilcox-on's Matched Pairs Signed Ranks Test. Group 1 subjects showed a significant increase ($T = 0$, $N_{s-r} = 9$, $p < .001$) in imaginative involvement pre- to post-wintering-over. No significant increases were found for control subjects between the interview periods ($T = 4$, $N_{s-r} = 5$, $p < .05$).

Imaginative involvement scores for Group 2 subjects were contrasted with those of the control and Group 1 subjects (post-isolation) using the median test. Group 2 subjects showed a significantly greater level of imaginative involvement than the control group subjects ($\chi^2 = 7.16$, $p < .01$) and no significant differences in imaginative involvement compared with the post-isolation scores of Group 1 subjects ($\chi^{*2} = .24$, $p < .05$).

## Discussion

The results of these preliminary investigations appear to support the view that subjects exposed to either short- or long-term Antarctic living conditions demonstrate unique adaptations.

Subjects exposed to both forms of Antarctic isolation demonstrated substantial increases in imaginative involvement. These subjects consistently noted increases in experiential absorption. Following Antarctic isolation, subjects noted "I could block things out easier"; "More vivid daydreams"; "Much more impressionable than at home because of fewer distractions"; "Concentrate on what was there better and get absorbed in it better"; "Could make my own stories, live them in my mind as if they were real life"; and "When reading books on telekinesis, I felt almost like I had the powers out there." "The same thing happened to the other guys when reading, it was difficult to get one's attention. They'd have to call my name two to three times." "After being weathered in, if he was reading a book you'd have to hit him to get his attention." These reactions may be related to childhood hypnosis by way of the breaking of reality ties. The restricted environmental stimulation situation included disruption of diurnal experiences combined with a lack of varied responsibilities for rational action. Responses led quickly from voluntary behavior (e.g., deciding to read a book) to a level of imaginative involvement and fantasy evocation (A. F. Barabasz, 1984; E. R. Hilgard, & J. R. Hilgard, 1982, personal communication; J. R. Hilgard, 1970, 1974) to the warding off of intrusion by others. In the case of summer field team members, subjects chose to place their one-man pup tents 20 m or more apart. Similarly, winter-over party members sometimes isolated themselves from the other base members by moving their sleeping equipment to laboratories and sometimes not being seen, except for meals, for periods lasting up to 3 days.

The standardized paper-and-pencil absorption scale measures supported the imaginative involvement findings. The content validity aspect of the absorption scale, viewed on an item-by-item basis, was also entirely consistent with the imaginative involvement interview data.

Consistent with laboratory observations under conditions of restricted environmental stimulation (A. F. Barabasz, 1982; A. F. Barabasz & Kaplan, 1989), the interview material and absorption scale data seem to reflect internally generated imaginative activity. The phenomenon might be related to a regression to primary process thinking (Gill & Brenman, 1959). The isolation of Antarctic living may have revived the mental processes available to these subjects as children (E. R. Hilgard & J. R. Hilgard, 1982, personal communication). Alternatively, the imaginative activity might be the result of learning through practice of a dissociative reaction (E. R. Hilgard, 1977, 1979) that was initiated by subjects as one of several behaviors attempted in an effort to cope with the reduced external stimulation. Regardless of the theoretical basis, it would seem obvious that such adaptive responses need further study because of their significant implications for both Antarctic and spaceflight operations.

## References

Barabasz, A. F. (1980). EEG alpha, skin conductance and hypnotizability in Antarctica. *International Journal of Clinical and Experimental Hypnosis, 28*, 63–74.

Barabasz, A. F. (1982). Restricted environmental stimulation and the enhancement of hypnotizability: Pain, EEG alpha, skin conductance, and temperature responses. *International Journal of Clinical and Experimental Hypnosis, 30*, 147–166.

Barabasz, A. F. (1984). Antarctic isolation and imaginative involvement: Preliminary findings. *International Journal of Clinical and Experimental Hypnosis, 32*, 296–300.

Barabasz, A. F., & Gregson, R. A. M. (1979). Antarctic wintering-over, suggestion and transient olfactory stimulation: EEG-evoked potential and electrodermal responses. *Biological Psychology, 9*, 285–295.

Barabasz, A. F., & Kaplan, G. (1989). Effects of restricted environmental stimulation (REST) on hypnotizability: A test of alternative techniques. In D. Waxman, D. Pederson, I. Wilke, & P. Mellett (Eds.), *Hypnosis: The fourth European congress at Oxford* (pp. 139–145). London: Whurr.

Gill, M. M., & Brenman, M. (1959). *Hypnosis and related states: Psychoanalytic studies in regression*. New York: International Universities Press.

Hilgard, E. R. (1965). *Hypnotic susceptibility*. New York: Harcourt, Brace & World.

Hilgard, E. R. (1977). *Divided consciousness: Multiple controls in human thought and actions*. New York: Wiley.

Hilgard, E. R. (1979). Consciousness and control: Lessons from hypnosis. *Australian Journal of Clinical and Experimental Hypnosis, 7*, 103–116.

Hilgard, E. R., & Hilgard, J. R. (1982). Personal communication.

Hilgard, J. R. (1970). *Personality and hypnosis: A study of imaginative involvement*. Chicago: University of Chicago Press.

Hilgard, J. R. (1974). Imaginative involvement: Some characteristics of the highly hypnotizable and non-hypnotizable. *International Journal of Clinical and Experimental Hypnosis, 22*, 138–156.

Mullin, C. S. (1960). Some psychological aspects of isolated Antarctic living. *American Journal of Psychiatry, 117*, 323–326.

Tellegen, A., & Atkinson, G. (1974). Openness to absorbing and self–altering experiences ("Absorption"), a trait related to hypnotic susceptibility. *Journal of Abnormal Psychology, 83*, 268–277.

# 19

# Psychological Effects of Isolation and Confinement of a Winter-Over Group at McMurdo Station, Antarctica

Donna C. Oliver

In all the world there is no desolation more complete than the polar night. It is a return to the Ice Age—no warmth, no life, no movement. Only those who have experienced it can fully appreciate what it means to be without the sun day after day, week after week. Few men unaccustomed to it can fight off its effects altogether, and it has driven some men mad. (Lansing, 1959, p. 51)

The accounts of early explorers (Amundsen, 1912; Byrd, 1938; Cherry-Garrard, 1922; Lansing, 1959; Scott, 1905; E. Wilson, 1966) and most modern psychological studies (Gunderson, 1974a, 1974b) emphasize the negative or pathological problems of psychological adjustment to Antarctic isolation and confinement. The well-described "winter-over syndrome" (Strange & Klein, 1974) includes symptoms of depression, hostility, sleep disturbance, and impaired cognition (Gunderson, 1974a, 1974b).

This study explores the positive and negative psychological changes in an Antarctic winter-over group using a variety of psychological techniques, including standardized tests, questionnaires, interviews, and personal observations by the author. Unlike most previous studies, the current study shows significant positive psychological changes in winter-over participants that may be as important as the better known, negative problems of isolation and confinement.

## Methods

### Study Site

Antarctica is a natural laboratory for the study of isolation and confinement in human groups (Shurley, 1974). Today, a handful of stations are occupied by transient populations either periodically or throughout the year. Even the largest station is a tiny outpost on an extensive, cold, and monotonous landscape. This study was conducted in the largest Antarctic township, the U.S. McMurdo Station. The summer period began in October 1976 for most of the winter-over participants. During the summer, there was considerable turnover of station personnel, with many airplane arrivals and departures and visits from several ships. The station population was as high as 800 persons during the peak period of summer research and support activities. The winter-over period began in February and ended in September 1977. During this 7-month period, the station was closed to direct contact with nonwinter persons except by radio. There were only 78 winter-over personnel.

## Subjects

The 1977 winter-over group was composed of 9 civilians and 69 military persons. Most civilians were scientists. The military subgroup included 2 officers, 31 administrative and technical persons (ad–techs), and 36 skilled tradesmen of the Navy Seabees. The mean time in the Navy was 12 years. Group ages ranged from 20 to 45 with an average of 31 years; 64% were married, and 52% had children. The investigator was the only woman. Thirty-one persons (6 civilians) volunteered and completed all the tests and questionnaires. Reasons for other personnel not participating in the tests and questionnaires were quite variable (Oliver, 1979).

## Standardized Tests

Three standardized tests were given to the winter-over subjects: the Myers–Briggs Type Indicator (MBTI), the Personal Orientation Inventory (POI), and the Minnesota Multiphasic Personality Inventory (MMPI) (Table 19.1).

The MBTI was given once, at the beginning of the winter, to characterize the personality types of the winter group. The MMPI and POI were given three times: at the beginning (March), middle (June), and end (August) of the winter-over period. The MMPI may be the most frequently used standardized psychological test (Buros, 1972; Mitchell, 1985). It investigates traits that are characteristic of disabling psychological abnormality (Hathaway & McKinley, 1967). This study used the standard 4 validity and 10 clinical scales as well as 13 of the special MMPI scales (see Oliver, 1979). The POI assesses changes in values, attitudes, and behavior relevant to Maslow's (1968) concept of the self-actualizing person (Mitchell, 1985). Since the standardized tests were scored after the winter, when subjects returned home, personal observations and interviews on the ice were not influenced by the test results. Changes in MMPI and POI scores over time were tested by means of analysis of variance (or ANOVA).

TABLE 19.1. Components of the research design showing the number of times each technique was used and the number of subjects involved.

| | Times administered | Number of Subjects |
|---|---|---|
| Psychological tests | | |
| Myers–Briggs Type Indicator | 1 | 31 |
| Minnesota Multiphasic Personality Inventory | 3 | 31 |
| Personal Orientation Inventory | 3 | 31 |
| Questionnaires | | |
| Demographic Questionnaire | 1 | 31 |
| Winter-Over Status Questionnaire | 6 | 31 |
| "Real World" Interview | Periodically for 1 year | 29 |
| Personal narratives | | |
| Written observations of group behavior | Continuous | 78 |
| Case study (written self-observations) | Continuous | 1 |
| Taped interviews | Periodically for 5 months | 12 |

## Questionnaire

The questionnaire was modified from a questionnaire used in earlier Antarctic studies (Gunderson, 1976, personal communication). It was used to assess changes in behavior and attitudes that were reported in earlier investigations concerning aggressive behavior, sleep cycles, dreams, paranoia, alcohol consumption, job satisfaction and performance, and appetite (Oliver, 1979). The questionnaire was administered six times during the winter at approximately 1 month intervals.

## Personal Narratives

Personal narratives can play an important role in psychological science (Allport, 1942; Taylor, Robinson, & McCormick, 1986). The author kept a detailed journal of daily observations and impressions throughout the winter. Many informal interviews were recorded in the journal, and 12 formal interviews (with open-ended questions) were taped. Observations and interviews involved both individuals who did and did not volunteer to complete the tests and questionnaires. The primary techniques, the number of times they were administered, and the number of subjects involved are shown in Table 19.1.

## Results

### Standardized Tests

The MBTI indicated that a variety of personality types was present in the winter-over group. No single type dominated (Oliver, 1979). Fifty-two percent of the subjects were extroverts, and 48% were introverts on the Extroversion–Introversion Index. Sixty-one percent perceived primarily through intuition and 39%, through sensing, on the Sensing–Intuition Index. Fifty-eight percent judged principally by thinking and 42%, by feeling, on the Thinking–Feeling Index. And finally, 68% dealt with the outer world through a judging process and 32%, through a perceptive process, on the Judgment–Perception Index (see Oliver, 1979). Therefore, the study group was split fairly evenly in each index dichotomy. A future paper will evaluate the relationship between personality type and psychological change during the winter and will compare the personality types of the winter-over group to other populations.

Statistically significant changes in the MMPI scores showed a general move away from psychological pathology as the winter progressed (Table 19.2). There was a significant decrease in Dependency and Paranoia, suggesting that subjects became more self-sufficient and trusting. The surprising result is the absence of change in most MMPI scores. Some of these are expected to increase and others, to decrease, if there was an overall negative adjustment to Antarctic isolation and confinement (Table 19.3). None of the MMPI test profiles showed questionable validity on the four validity scales, using standard guidelines (Lachar, 1974).

There were two significant changes in POI scores during the winter, and both indicated an increase in self-actualization (Table 19.2). There was an increase in Existentiality (the ability to react without rigid adherence to principles) and Capacity for Intimate Contact. The latter scale was a measure of the individual's motivation and capacity for intimate contact, not an indicator of the quality or quantity of intimate contact during the Antarctic winter.

## Questionnaire

The responses to the questionnaire showed no statistically significant changes over the winter (Oliver, 1979). Nevertheless, sleeping problems and negative responses to the dominant mood question peaked during the

TABLE 19.2. Significant changes in MMPI[a] and POI[b] subscales from tests given at the beginning, middle, and end of winter.

| Significant decrease in MMPI subscales | | Significant increase in POI subscales | |
| --- | --- | --- | --- |
| Subscale | ANOVA[c] probability level | Subscale | ANOVA probability level |
| Dependency | .011 | Existentiality | .0001 |
| Paranoia | .02 | Capacity for Intimate Contact | .0002 |

[a]MMPI, Minnesota Multiphasic Personality Inventory.
[b]POI, Personal Orientation Inventory.
[c]ANOVA, analysis of variance.

TABLE 19.3. MMPI[a] subscales that showed no significant change among scores of tests given at the beginning, middle, and end of the winter.

| Unchanged MMPI subscales | ANOVA[b] probability level |
|---|---|
| Expected increase | |
| Maladjustment | .69 |
| Aggression | .35 |
| Repression | .80 |
| Prejudice | .69 |
| Anxiety | .38 |
| Addiction Proneness | .34 |
| Hypochondriasis | .09 |
| Depression | .13 |
| Hysteria | .51 |
| Psychopathic Deviate | .18 |
| Masculinity–Femininity | .32 |
| Psychasthenia | .66 |
| Hypomania | .16 |
| Schizophrenia | .18 |
| Social Introversion | .17 |
| Expected decrease | |
| Responsibility | .45 |
| Control | .19 |

[a]MMPI, Minnesota Multiphasic Personality Inventory.
[b]ANOVA, analysis of variance.
*Note:* Subscales are divided into those expected to increase and those expected to decrease as predicted by the winter-over syndrome.

midwinter, when there were also the lowest number of responses to the question about having unusually happy moments. These nonsignificant patterns are consistent with a number of the negative symptoms of the winter-over syndrome. The author is currently evaluating questionnaire results with a statistical approach designed to assess the midwinter slump, or the "third-quarter phenomenon."

## Observations and Interviews

The researcher's observations and interviews indicated a distinct qualitative change in group morale during the year at McMurdo Station (Figure 19.1). This pattern also corresponded with the results from the standardized tests and questionnaires. When the wintering personnel arrived at the station in October 1976, they shared the facility with hundreds of other persons. At first, their morale seemed high, but they were eventually fatigued by crowded living conditions and demanding work schedules. A camaraderie developed among the winter crew as the station closing was awaited. A winter-

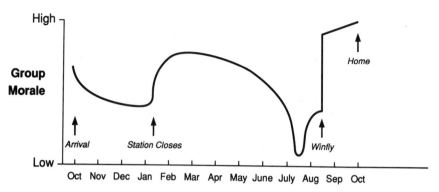

FIGURE 19.1. Changes in group morale.

over pride developed during the late-summer season. Hence, the group morale gradually declined until the late summer and rose during the period of winter expectation (Figure 19.1).

In early February, when winter isolation began, the group morale soared (Figure 19.1). The summer activities were exhausting and routine. The winter was envisioned as a calm, favorable change. The group morale peaked after station closing (February 19) and remained high through Sun-Down Day festivities (April 21). A large part of this change was undoubtedly related to the suddenly relaxed and uncrowded atmosphere after the station closed. By May and June, the routines of the personnel were firmly established. Some mentioned that the sterility of the environment, lack of different stimuli, monotony of routine, and total absence of sunlight and of fresh food were beginning to "get to them." Discussions of sleep problems, boredom, and homesickness increased. It was common to discuss dreams of sunny beaches, fresh food, home, and women. The range of daily events had narrowed and become routine. The group reached the midwinter slump in group morale before July (Figure 19.1). The slump ended as the group prepared for "winfly" (station opening with the first flight after the winter) and the attendant fresh food, mail, new faces, and the last phase of the Antarctic tour. With the arrival of the first plane, the winter group crystallized into a close-knit unit. They had passed the winter, and a new sense of group pride emerged. Although the intruders were not taken into the group and resentment was commonly expressed, their presence raised the winter group morale and unity. As the mid-October departure approached, the group morale improved even more (Figure 19.1), and nostalgic discussions of the long year were common.

Adjustment problems and "culture shock" to home and new surroundings were common after departure from the Antarctic. Interviews with winter group members at home and discussions with two Navy Detachment Alpha (winter) commanding officers revealed that many winter participants experienced difficulty adjusting to home (Table 19.4). In many cases, the Antarctic experience was considered a return to a simple and more enjoyable life-style. Marital difficulties, financial problems, sleep disturbances, or the activities of a complicated culture seemed to overwhelm them. Within 6 months of their return, most of the interviewed group had adjusted to their new surroundings. Furthermore, almost every member of the winter party considered his Antarctic stay as one of the best experiences of his life (Table 19.4), and almost half wanted to winter-over again.

## Discussion

It is unclear how the size of the McMurdo Station may have influenced the results of the current study. Much of the previous work was done at the smaller Antarctic bases, especially the South Pole Station (e.g., McGuire & Tolchin, 1961; Natani & Shurley, 1974). Nevertheless, a few earlier studies were performed at McMurdo Station, and their results were generally similar to the conclusions from the smaller stations (Gunderson, 1974a), where pathology and problems of adjustment to isolation were emphasized.

Several lines of evidence indicate that the positive aspects of the winter-over experience are worthy of study along with negative psychological changes (Oliver, 1979; Palinkas, 1986,a,b). Emphasis on negative behavioral patterns was a necessary outcome of developing methods for screening and selecting Antarctic personnel. While the majority of studies focused on pathology or adjustment problems, the positive nature of the winter-over experience has been recognized (Mullin, 1960; Taylor & Shurley, 1971; Wilson, 1965). Nevertheless, positive psychological changes were seldom considered a dominant feature of isolation and confinement in Antarctica. In the current study, positive psychological changes were indicated by the four significant subscale changes on the POI and the MMPI (Table 19.2). All of these scale changes (decreased Dependency and Paranoia and increased Existentiality and Capacity for Intimate Contact) suggested an improvement in the capacity or desire for better interpersonal relationships.

Perhaps the most convincing evidence of positive psychological changes was the remarkably large number of persons who considered the winter-over stay among the best experiences of their life (Table 19.4). They did not deny that wintering was accompanied by physical and psychological discomforts; however, in some respects they felt that they had grown stronger.

The apparent lack of widespread psychopathology during the winter is contrary to the common conception of Antarctic summer personnel and many researchers. They believe the winter-over experience is basically negative and may cause permanent psychological damage. This view may be supported by the winfly period, when the winter-over members become highly territorial and commonly express contempt for the winfly newcomers. This negative behavior, combined with the pale and often scruffy look

TABLE 19.4. Results of follow-up questionnaire of 29 winter-over subjects (Responding to the questions, Did you have adjustment problems when you returned home
after the Antarctic winter? and How would
you rank the value of the winter-over experience?).

| Adjustment problems | |
| --- | --- |
|     Great difficulty | 12 |
|     Some difficulty | 14 |
|     No difficulty | 3 |
| Value of winter experience | |
|     One of worst | 1 |
|     Bad | 1 |
|     Good | 10 |
|     One of best | 17 |

of the winter crew, probably helps to fuel persistent rumors of pathology.
The tall tales told by many ex-winterers to naive, unsuspecting listeners
undoubtedly help to perpetuate the negative impression.

A relatively unexplored problem among winter groups is acclimation into
the main culture, or "rapid reentry stress." In a matter of days, the winter
participant moves from a simple life, where most of the basic needs are
provided, to the complexities and economic and social realities of the real
world. Most of the group experienced a variety of temporary adjustment
problems when they returned home (Table 19.4). Although these problems
did not appear to be serious, they were apparently more serious than the
adjustment problems occurring in the winter.

The winter-over syndrome is characterized by depression, hostility, sleep
disturbance, and impaired cognition (Strange & Klein, 1974). Although
these problems were not revealed by the POI or MMPI, the questionnaire
trends (not statistically significant), interviews, and the author's personal
observations indicated that sleep disturbance ("big eye") and impaired cognition ("driftiness") were common in the midwinter. Some of the winter-
over-syndrome problems are clear from the following journal entry by the
author (journal entry of August 13, 1977, after 250 days in Antarctic isolation):

I have a slight headache and feel as if my mind has been anesthetized. I have only
been out of bed for ten hours so my condition is not due to physical exhaustion.
Perhaps I have not been eating properly due to our diet, or maybe I need the sun's
rays. But, it is more likely that I am suffering from "Big Eye" and "Driftiness." I
seem to go in cycles of feeling energetic to dulled to energetic. I am usually an
attentive listener when friends talk to me. I have noticed lately that I sometimes cut
them off and stare into space and then float back not knowing what they said. Oh,
well, it is not really serious, just not optimal for doing much more than surviving.

But I would like to feel awake and alert. Perhaps because of this my coffee intake has about tripled. I became curious about everyone else so during the day I took a verbal survey of 36 guys and asked how much coffee they consumed. Three of them drink from 35 to 50 cups and six of them reported drinking between 20 and 25 cups per day!

My level of alertness is way under par. No matter how much I sleep I frequently feel tired. My motivation and level of production are also way down. I laugh at myself and say that my attention span must be equivalent to that of a kindergartner. Both my recent and remote memory are lacking. I sometimes forget simple vocabulary words that I have known for perhaps twenty years. Or, I walk to get something and forget what it is two seconds later.

My sense of time is geared only by the clock. My perception of being rested/tired, alert/sleepy is not a clue to the time because I am almost always dragged out. Of course, the twenty-four hour cyclic light/dark outdoor conditions are not present here and are of no help. Making mealtimes is the only restricting regulatory time-keeper.

I believe that movies, dreams, and daydreams become more important here because they are one of the few sources of variety. Also, more of my otherwise non-consciously remembered memories come to the forefront of my awareness. I quite frequently have very, very vivid flashbacks. I enjoy the warm, comfortable ones, and have an opportunity to "work through" those which are hassling. At home this happens less frequently because many new, demanding stimuli come and go and come and go and occupy my attention.

The positive psychological changes during the winter may be related to a sense of accomplishment. There was a common perception that the winter was both difficult and worthwhile. The hardships that are characterized by the winter-over syndrome were considered worth taking for the reward. Almost every participant ranked the winter stay among one of the best experiences of his life (Table 19.4), and, remarkably, over half of the personnel expressed an interest in spending another winter in Antarctica.

*Acknowledgments.* This study was indirectly supported by a grant from the National Science Foundation (Division of Polar Programs) to Paul K. Dayton at the Scripps Institution of Oceanography. Paul's support and enthusiasm were essential. William D. Wilkins, the other members of my dissertation committee, and E. K. Eric Gunderson and Walter Wilkins made many helpful suggestions. Harley Baker completed a second, independent statistical analysis, and John S. Oliver helped with all aspects of the study. I thank him and my other Antarctic companions.

## References

Allport, G. W. (1942). *The use of personal documents in psychological science*. New York: Social Science Research Council.

226     Donna C. Oliver

Amundsen, R. (1912). *The South Pole* (2 vols.). London: John Murray.
Buros, O. K. (Ed.). (1972). *The seventh mental measurements yearbook.* Highland Park, NJ: Gryphon Press.
Byrd, R. E. (1938). *Alone.* New York: Putnam.
Cherry-Garrard, A. (1922). *The worst journey in the world: Antarctic 1910-1913.* London: Scott Polar Research Institute and Blandford Press.
Gunderson, E. K. E. (1974a). Introduction. *Antarctic Research Series, 22,* 1-4.
Gunderson, E. K. E. (1974b). Psychological studies in Antarctica. *Antarctic Research Series, 22,* 115-131.
Gunderson, E. K. E. (1976). Personal communication.
Hathaway, S. R., & McKinley, J. C. (1967). *Minnesota Multiphasic Personality Inventory Manual.* New York: Psychological Corporation.
Lachar, D. L. (1974). *The MMPI: Clinical Assessment and Automated Interpretation.* Los Angeles: Western Psychological Services.
Lansing, A. (1959). *Endurance: Shackleton's incredible voyage.* New York: McGraw-Hill.
Maslow, A. (1968). *Toward a psychology of being.* New York: D. Van Nostrand.
McGuire, F., & Tolchin, S. (1961). Group adjustment at the South Pole. *Journal of Mental Science, 107,* 954-960.
Mitchell, J. V., Jr., (Ed.). (1985). *The ninth mental measurements yearbook.* Lincoln: The University of Nebraska Press.
Mullin, C. S. (1960). Some psychological aspects of isolated Antarctic living. *American Journal of Psychiatry, 117,* 323-325.
Natani, K., & Shurley, J. T. (1974). Sociopsychological aspects of a winter vigil at South Pole Station. *Antarctic Research Series, 22,* 89-114.
Oliver, D. M. (1979). *Some psychological effects of isolation and confinement in an antarctic winter-over group.* Doctoral dissertation, United States International University, San Diego. (University Microfilms No. 80-00, 243)
Palinkas, L. A. (1986a). Health and performance of Antarctic winter-over personnel: A follow-up study. *Aviation, Space and Environmental Medicine, 57,* 954-959.
Palinkas, L. A. (1986b). Long-term effects of environment on health and performance of Antarctic winter-over personnel (Report 85-48). San Diego: Naval Health Research Center.
Scott, R. F. (1905). *The voyage of the* Discovery (2 vols.). London: Thomas Nelson and Sons.
Shurley, J. T. (1974). Antarctica is also a prime natural laboratory for the behavioral sciences. In O. G. Edholm & E. K. E. Gunderson (Eds.), *Polar human biology*: The proceedings of the SCAR/IUPS/IUBS Symposium on human biology and medicine in the Antarctic (pp. 430-435). Chicago: Year Book Medical Publications.
Strange, R., & Klein, W. (1974). Emotional and social adjustment of recent U.S. winter-over parties in isolated Antarctic stations. In O. G. Edholm & E. K. E. Gunderson (Eds.), *Polar human biology*: The proceedings of the SCAR/IUPS/IUBS symposium on human biology and medicine in the Antarctic (pp. 410-416). Chicago: Year Book Medical Publications.
Taylor, A. J. W., & Shurley, J. T. (1971). Some Antarctic troglodytes. *International Review of Applied Psychology, 20,* 143-148.
Taylor, A. J. W., Robinson, R. D., & McCormick, I. A. (1986). Written personal

narratives as research documents–The case for their restoration. *International Review of Applied Psychology, 35*, 197–208.

Wilson, E. (1966). *Diary of the Discovery expedition*. London: Blanford.

Wilson, O. (1965). Human adaptation to life in Antarctica. In J. Van Meigheim, P. van Oue, & J. Schell (Eds.), *Biogeography and ecology in Antarctica* (Monographiae Biologicae Vol. 15, pp. 690–752). The Hague: W. Junk.

# 20

# Winter-Over Stress: Physiological and Psychological Adaptation to an Antarctic Isolated and Confined Environment

SYBIL CARRÈRE, GARY W. EVANS, AND DANIEL STOKOLS

The isolated and confined environment (ICE) is an area of environmental stress that has received very little attention by U.S. investigators. Understanding the physical and psychological components of ICEs is important because many people are exposed to these settings. Naval submarines routinely go on 60-day patrols where outside communication is extremely limited. Oil companies employ professional divers who are required to remain in hyperbaric chambers for a month at a time. Research and business require the maintenance of isolated stations in both polar regions that can be isolated for 6 to 9 months at a time. The space station proposed by the National Aeronautics and Space Administration will confine and isolate its inhabitants for extended periods, as well.

Much of the psychological research conducted in field ICEs has focused on group dynamics and changes in behavior (Earls, 1969; Johnston & Dietlein, 1977; Oliver, 1979; Radloff & Helmreich, 1968). Rivolier (1974) has conducted one of the few field studies that examines on-going interactions between the physical environment and human behavior. Using an Antarctic research station as an ICE, Rivolier found no relationship between outside temperature and residents' mood, but he noted increased psychological and somatic complaints on those days when weather conditions were rated best or worst. His findings underscore the importance of research that treats an ICE as a setting in which there are dynamic environmental factors that interact in their influence on human well-being. This study uses inhabitants of a winter Antarctic research station to examine human adaptation to a dynamic, long-term ICE. The environment's influence is charted by weekly measurements of both changes in the environment and fluctuations in the physiological and psychological indicators of stress.

Isolated and confined environments include both social and physical components. Isolation is primarily a psychosocial concept in that the individual is separated from his or her social network (Rasmussen, 1973). Isolation involves a reduction in sensory and social input (Zubek, 1973). When individuals are separated from their normal social network, abnormal behavior can occur (Suedfeld, 1974). Isolation can sometimes have a physical component when the isolation is imposed by geographical or other physical boundaries. However, it is the psychological response to the reduction in social and sensory stimuli that seems to generalize across situations in which individuals are socially isolated.

Confinement is a salient physical dimension of the ICE setting. In confined environments, individual mobility is restricted in some manner, usually because of limited physical space. Confinement in ICEs is often caused by harsh exterior environments that limit or prohibit activity outside the built habitat. In the space laboratory, vacuum and extreme temperatures found in outer space created a harsh exterior. In Antarctica, the harsh weather conditions, dangerous ice formations, and unusual day/night cycles restrict movement outside buildings.

Both physical and social aspects of the ICE can combine to make it stressful to its inhabitants. Behavioral changes associated with stress have been recorded in ICEs and include declines in alertness and mental functioning; low motivation; increases in somatic complaints such as sleep disturbances, digestive problems, and symptoms of colds and flu; social withdrawal; self-reports of depression and hostility; group splintering and polarization; feelings of helplessness; and psychotic episodes (Edholm & Gunderson, 1973; Natani & Shurley, 1974; Rasmussen, 1973; Suedfeld, 1974; Weybrew & Noddin, 1979).

Physical sources of stress can include crowding, irregular or unnatural light cycles, noise, fluctuating or extreme temperatures, poor air ventilation, sterile and monotonous surroundings, the novelty of the setting, and the physical threat to life of the exterior environment. Social stressors associated with an ICE include the loneliness associated with being separated from one's normal social network, a reduction in privacy, the necessity of forced interaction with the other members of the ICE, dependence on a limited community of individuals for one's social needs with no control over who may be included in that group, and limited ability to help loved ones with problems that may arise.

These physical and social elements of the ICE constitute the ambient qualities of the setting that can make it chronically stressful to the inhabitant. Chronic stressors are those phenomena that require the individual to respond over a long period of time to a perceived threat from the environment. These stressors are not subject to control.

Acute stressors also take place in ICEs. Acute stressors are discrete events taking place over a short period of time. The emergency evacuation of the South Pole Station, described by Natani and Shurley (1974), is such an event. Other acute stressors that might occur in an ICE include an injury to one of the residents or a breakdown in life-sustaining equipment such as occurred in the space laboratory. Acute stressors interact with the ambient qualities of the ICE and amplify the psychological and physiological responses to the chronic stress of the setting (Fleming, Baum, Davidson, Rectanus, & McArdle, 1987). Other discrete events of a positive nature, such as a party or good news from the outside world, may reduce the stress associated with the ambient qualities of the ICE setting.

This research examines the social and physical factors, both chronic and acute, that modify human adaptation in an Antarctic ICE during the winter season. The information presented in this chapter represents a preliminary analysis of the data on adaptation. It is part of a larger study that examined human adaptation, behavioral adjustment, and the use of the built environment at a U.S. research station in Antarctica. This study uses multiple measures of stress to develop a robust picture of what individuals exposed to a long-term ICE are experiencing.

Antarctic ICEs have qualities that moderate the level of stress experienced by their residents, including weather, arrival of new people at the station, length of stay in the ICE, and special events occurring at the study site. Each of these factors interacts with the others to create a setting that changes in quality over the course of the winter season. The role that each of these independent variables is thought to play will be discussed in more detail below.

There are long-term costs of adapting to the chronic stress of the ICE. Environments that are perceived to be stressful place a demand on individuals. Over time, it is believed, the cost of adapting to that stressful situation manifests itself through physiological arousal and negative mood changes (Cohen, Evans, Stokols, & Krantz, 1986). For these reasons, length of stay in a long-term confined and isolated environment was expected to be associated with increases in blood pressure, catecholamines, and negative moods.

The harsh weather conditions in Antarctica may moderate stress because poor weather conditions can confine individuals indoors for extended periods. Strong winds were the major weather element that prevented people from going outside at Palmer Station, the setting for this study. Restriction of movement to the limited indoor environment has been associated with self-reports of negative moods (Harrison & Connors, 1984; Radloff & Helmreich, 1968). We hypothesized that high winds would be associated with increased levels of physiological arousal and negative mood reports.

Special events such as parties and holiday celebrations add a bit of pleasant novelty in an otherwise very predictable environment. A lot of time, effort, and planning go into making these events take place. Such efforts include food preparation, the manufacturing of costumes, scavenging through station supplies for presents, unusual presentations, and room decorations. Effort elicited by the special events was expected to result in increases in blood pressure, catecholamines, and positive mood reports.

At the end of the winter, the summer crew for the following year arrived at the station. The 2 weeks of overlap between the winter-over crew and the new summer crew marked an influx of new people, crowded station conditions, and increased environmental stimuli, and the new crew impinged upon personal territory as indicated by anecdotal reports. We expected that this period would be negative and would elicit increases in all of the physiological measures. Self-reports of anxiety and hostility were also expected to increase during this period.

## Methods

The research was conducted at Palmer Station, Antarctica, during the mid-1980s. The station is located on Anvers Island near the Antarctic Peninsula at 64° 46′ South, 64° 3′ West. Palmer Station is situated on a rocky peninsula on the glacier-covered island. The winter period extended from late April until the third week of November. During this period, temperatures ranged between 19° and −17° C. The winds were often extreme. At one point during the winter, the winds were in excess of 80 kn. The shortest period of light experienced at the research setting during the winter was 4 hours of indirect light in June.

### Subjects

Nine of the 12 inhabitants of Palmer Station, who wintered during the months between May and November, were the subjects for this research. Four of the participants were scientists conducting winter research at the station. The remainder of the subjects were support personnel responsible for the day-to-day operations of the facility. All of the participants were males. Ages ranged between 26 and 43. Only one of the subjects had not attended college. Several of the winter-over personnel in the study had previous experience in Antarctica (four), and three of those individuals had wintered-over previously. All subjects were provided a detailed overview of the study design and purpose. Specific hypotheses were not included in the handout.

### Data Collection

Physiological measures included twice-a-week measures of blood pressure and weekly urinary catecholamine samples (collected over an 8-hour waking period). The Bipolar Profile of Mood States, or POMS, (Lorr & McNair, 1984), a brief adjective checklist, was used as a self-report measure of positive and negative mood states. Embedded within the measure were subscales. The subscales used in this study measured degree of anxiety, level of hostility, and level of depression. Self-reports of mood were measured three times a week. A journal was kept by the on–site investigator to record stressors and positive events that took place over the winter.

## Statistical Analysis

*ARIMA* time-series analyses were used to address the concern that changes in outcome measures over time might be due to autocorrelation in the error terms rather than the strength of the independent variables. ARIMA refers to a time series statistical analysis approach that responds to error in time-ordered data points due to *auto*regressive, *integrative* (nonstationary), and *moving average* terms (McCleary, Hay, Medinger, and McDowall, 1980). Interrupted time-series analyses and bivariate time-series analyses were used to evaluate the relationship of the independent and dependent variables. The reader is referred to McCleary, Hay, Medinger, and McDowall (1980) and Carrere (1990) for a description of the techniques used in time-series analyses. The data for the study participants were aggregated by week.

# Results

## Chronic Qualities of the Setting

No significant increases were observed in any of the physiological or psychological outcome measures over the $6^{1/2}$ months of winter. There was an increase in self-reports of anxiety over time [$t(26) = 1.47, p < .10$ (one-tailed)]. This increase was marginal when the autocorrelation between the observations was removed.

In contrast to the hypotheses of the research, high winds were associated with significant decreases in epinephrine, $t(25) = 2.38, p < .05$ (two-tailed), and norepinephrine, $t(25) = 2.36, p < .05$ (two-tailed). Systolic blood pressure also decreased during periods of high wind, but the relationship was marginal: $t(25) = 1.95, p < .1$ (two-tailed). Depression did increase, as predicted, during the high-wind periods: $t(26) = 2.18, p < .05$ (one-tailed).

## Acute Qualities of the Setting

During the weeks that festivities took place, there was a significant increase in epinephrine, $t(25) = 1.77, p < .05$ (one-tailed). Norepinephrine levels were marginally above the mean, $t(25) = 1.68, p < .10$ (one-tailed). There were no significant increases in systolic or diastolic blood pressure. Self-reports of anxiety, hostility, and depression did not differ significantly from the winter means for these measures.

The arrival of the summer crew for the following year was associated with a significant increase in both systolic blood pressure, $t(25) = 3.55$, $p < .005$ (one-tailed), and diastolic blood pressure, $t(26) = 2.65$, $p < .025$ (one-tailed). No significant increases in catecholamines, anxiety, hostility, or depression were found for this time period.

## Discussion

Outcomes of this study suggest that the Antarctic ICE is not just a static source of stress but, rather, a dynamic environment in which a large number of acute and chronic forces impinge upon the individual. These acute and chronic environmental factors may be positive or negative in the meaning they have for individuals. Subsequently, the physiological and psychological outcomes of these forces can differ significantly from each other. In addition, the results indicate that individuals are able to adapt to the unique qualities of an ICE. There does not appear to be an on-going cost of coping with the confinement and isolation of Antarctica, as reflected in the lack of increases in stress levels over the course of the winter.

The data suggest that changes in outcome measures are a compilation of effects that include the chronic characteristics of the Antarctic station as well as acute events. What individuals experience in an ICE is not just a reflection of time spent in confinement and isolation.

In addition, none of the environmental forces at play in the ICE operates alone. There is an overlay of chronic conditions and acute events at any one point. Individuals respond to the interaction of these chronic and acute environmental factors. For example, high wind speeds were associated with decreases in catecholamines and systolic blood pressure and increases in self-reports of depression. However, intervening events changed these patterns of outcomes when parties or social events took place during periods of high winds. These special occasions allowed people to interact differently, stepping away from day-to-day relations and putting forward a more playful side. During the weeks in which festivities took place, catecholamine levels were above the winter mean levels. In contrast to the influence of high winds alone, blood pressure levels and reports of depression were not lower than average during those weeks that special events took place. This pattern of outcomes for the parties reflects time periods that are scattered throughout the winter period, implying the strength of these discrete events' influence on the chronic quality of the weather for the ICE residents.

In addition, the profiles of outcomes for the environmental factors differ. While the physiological outcome measures were lower for periods of high winds and reports of depression were elevated, there was a different pattern of outcomes for the time period at the end of the ICE tenure, when the exchange of crews took place. Both systolic and diastolic blood pressure levels were elevated during these last two weeks of the study. This time period during the exchange of crews is a type of acutely stressful event that may be common in many ICEs. Journal entries for this time period help to place this event in context. People felt invaded and overwhelmed by the new inhabitants. Work areas of the station that were set aside for individual winter crew use now had to be shared and turned over to new people. Sites that could be counted on for solitary refuge were no longer available. The influx of new people required changes in the arrangement of the dining room and recreational room furniture and more rigid rules for the uses of these areas. In general, the station took on a more institutional ambience. The sensitive nature of this time period was also reflected in the steps taken by incoming station management to ease the process. The summer crews were instructed to "take it easy" with the winter crew. Efforts were also made to minimize the time that the winter crew would remain at the station to train the new personnel before leaving for the United States.

One of the beliefs about Antarctic ICEs is that they are stressful environments that place a tremendous demand on residents. Several investigators have questioned this assumption. Suedfeld (1980) and Oliver (1979) have suggested that ICE settings may have a positive effect on inhabitants. Some aspects of their proposal have been supported by their research. Oliver (1979) points to Antarctic winter-overers who have used their experience to enhance their self-growth. Suedfeld (1987) reports the use of restricted environmental stimulation settings in many forms of therapy. Individuals in our study demonstrated no on-going costs of coping with the Antarctic ICE. Journal entries again place these results in context. Several of the winter-over residents sought out the Antarctic experience as a challenge and an adventure. Others saw the experience as a way to enhance their careers and to earn money. In self-selecting to go to Antarctica for the winter, all of the residents balanced the benefits of the experience against the costs and found that the positive aspects of the winter in Antarctica outweighed the negative. It is possible that ICEs may only be stressful for individuals who have been placed in them against their will, such as for the elderly in convalescent hospitals or for military personnel in some circumstances. Future research could examine the role of self-selection in the stressful impact of ICEs.

This research emphasizes the importance of treating the ICE as a dynamic environment that changes as a function of the fluctuating influences of different social and physical environmental forces. The ICE of Antarctica is not a static, oppressive setting that never changes.

Future research on ICEs should examine the dynamic qualities of these settings. The interaction of acute and chronic forces in the ICE should be explored further to determine those physical and social factors that have similar outcomes across ICEs. Information about coping styles and behaviors that reduce any of the stress that might be associated with an ICE could prove useful in both the training of ICE personnel and schedule programming for these settings. It would also be useful to learn more about the adaptation and adjustment processes that individuals go through in making the transitions to and from the low-stimulus environment of Antarctica. Oliver's (1979) interviews with former winter-over residents indicate that the adjustment back to the high-stimulus environment of the United States may be more difficult than the adjustment to the Antarctic.

On a methodological note, longitudinal ICE studies that utilize frequent outcome measures should employ time-series techniques that remove the correlation between time-ordered observations due to error. Because this form of error is systemic in nature, it tends to inflate $t$ and $F$ statistic values. The use of statistics that do not remove this systematic error can often result in misrepresentations of the data.

Antarctic research offers valuable information that it may be possible to generalize to other isolated and confined settings, such as space and underwater habitats. In addition, Antarctica may prove to be a research setting that serves to broaden our theoretical understanding of more fundamental human processes. For example, longitudinal studies of stress and arousal processes have been limited by the expense, logistics, and methodological constraints of monitoring subjects over long time periods. Studying these processes in Antarctica allowed the use of a nonlaboratory setting in which we were able to control for many extraneous variables present in most other applied field settings. Future research projects in Antarctica should utilize these unique qualities of the setting to examine theoretical questions that generalize beyond ICEs to principles of human behavior.

*Acknowledgements.* This research was supported by National Science Foundation Grant DPP86-08969 and National Aeronautics and Space Administration Grant NAG-287. This project received additional support under National Science Foundation Grant DPP85-40817, awarded to Dr. William S. Hamner, and from Dr. Neil Grunberg at the Uniformed Services University of the Health Sciences, Bethesda, Maryland. We thank Maria Mercado and Carol Jones for assistance with the data analysis. We gratefully acknowledge the cooperation of the study participants.

# References

Carrere, S. (1990). *Physiological and psychological patterns of acute and chronic stress during winter isolation in Antarctica*. Doctoral dissertation, University of California, Irvine.

Cohen, S., Evans, G. W., Stokols, D., & Krantz, D. (1986). *Stress and the environment*. New York: Putnam.

Earls, J. H. (1969). Human adjustment to an exotic environment: The nuclear submarine. *Archives of General Psychiatry, 20*, 117–123.

Edholm, O. G., & Gunderson, E. K. E. (Eds.). (1973). *Polar human biology: The proceedings of the SCAR/IUPS/IUBS symposium on human biology and medicine in the Antarctic*. London: William Heinemann Medical Books Ltd.

Fleming, I., Baum, A., Davidson, L. M., Rectanus, E., & McArdle, S. (1987). Chronic stress as a factor in physiologic reactivity to challenge. *Health Psychology, 6*, 221–237.

Harrison, A. A., & Connors, M. M. (1984). Groups in exotic environments. In L. Berkowitz (Ed.), *Advances in experimental social psychology*, (Vol. 18, pp. 49–87). New York: Academic Press.

Johnston, R. S., & Dietlein, L. F. (Eds.). (1977). *Biomedical results from Skylab.* Washington, DC: National Aeronautics and Space Administration.

Lorr, M., & McNair, D. M. (1984). *Manual of Profile of Mood States.* San Diego: Educational and Industrial Testing Service.

McCleary, R., Hay, R. A., Jr., Medinger, E. E., & McDowall, D. (1980). *Applied time series analysis for the social sciences.* Beverly Hills: Sage.

Natani, K., & Shurley, J. T. (1974). Sociopsychological aspects of a winter vigil at South Pole Station. In E. K. E. Gunderson (Ed.), *Human adaptability to Antarctic conditions. Antarctic Research Series*, (Vol. 22, pp. 89–114). Worcester, MA: Heffernan Press.

Oliver, D. M. (1979). *Some psychological effects of isolation and confinement in an Antarctic winter-over group.* Doctoral dissertation, United States International University, San Diego. (University Microfilms No. 80-00, 243)

Radloff, R., & Helmreich, R. (1968). *Groups under stress: Psychological research in SEALAB II.* New York: Appleton-Century-Crofts.

Rasmussen, J. E. (Ed.). (1973). *Man in isolation and confinement.* Chicago: Aldine.

Rivolier, J. (1974). Physiological and psychological studies by continental European and Japanese expeditions. In E. K. E. Gunderson (Ed.), *Human adaptability to Antarctic conditions. Antarctic Research Series*, (Vol. 22, pp. 55–70). Worcester, MA: Heffernan Press.

Suedfeld, P. (1974). Social isolation: A case for interdisciplinary research. *The Canadian Psychologist, 15*, 1–15.

Suedfeld, P. (1980). *Restricted environment stimulation.* New York: Wiley.

Suedfeld, P. (1987, August). *Distress, no stress, antistress, eustress: Where does REST fit in?* Presidential address, Third International Conference on REST, New York.

Weybrew, B. B., & Noddin, E. M. (1979). Psychiatric aspects of adaptation to long submarine missions. *Aviation, Space, and Environmental Medicine, 50*, 575–580.

Zubek, J. P. (1973). Behavioral and physiological effects of prolonged sensory and perceptual deprivation: A review. In J. E. Rasmussen (Ed.), *Man in isolation and confinement.* (pp. 9–84) Chicago: Aldine.

# 21

# Group Adaptation and Individual Adjustment in Antarctica: A Summary of Recent Research

LAWRENCE A. PALINKAS

It seems paradoxical that a continent that historically has been without indigenous human inhabitants should serve as an ideal laboratory for the social and behavioral sciences. Nevertheless, there has been a growing recognition that the human experience in Antarctica permits detailed study of certain behavioral principles pertinent to all human groups, regardless of size and complexity (Gunderson, 1974; Pierce, 1985; Shurley, 1974). In fact, certain features of this experience are paradigmatic of the human factors associated with long-term missions in space. Particularly relevant to the task of planning for these missions are the relationship between group adaptation and individual adjustment and the effect of this relationship on human health and performance under conditions of prolonged isolation in an extreme environment.

The objective of this chapter is to report on some recent studies, conducted on archival data at the Naval Health Research Center (NHRC), that address these issues. In doing so, I wish to highlight three salient themes of this research: (1) its relevance for the space program; (2) its interdisciplinary nature; and (3) the need for developing a comprehensive program of additional behavioral and social research in the Antarctic.

Throughout the 1960s and early 1970s, NHRC was a major center of psychological research in the Antarctic. Several studies conducted by Dr.

Report No. 87-24, supported by the Naval Medical Research and Development Command, Bethesda, Maryland, under Research Work Unit RE 000 000 REIMB. The opinions expressed in this chapter are those of the author and do not reflect the official policy or position of the Department of the Navy, the Department of Defense, or the U.S. Government.

Eric Gunderson and his colleagues examined the emotional effects of prolonged isolation; criteria measures of adaptation such as physical and mental health, task performance, and social compatibility; and individual and group predictors of successful adaptation. This research provided valuable input into the methods used to screen Operation Deep Freeze candidates and has contributed to the overall record of health and performance characteristic of Antarctic expeditions since the early 1960s.

In 1983, the NHRC received a request from the Naval Medical Research and Development Command to reexamine some of these data in order to advise the National Aeronautics and Space Administration (NASA) regarding the application of the Antarctic winter-over experience to their proposed space station program. Of particular interest was the extension of these earlier studies to include follow-up assessments of personnel who had wintered-over in the Antarctic. The objective of these assessments was to determine the effects of prolonged isolation in an extreme environment on health and performance in the short term (i.e., during the mission itself) and in the long-term (i.e., postmission) follow-up. It was hoped that such research could contribute to NASA's space station program in four respects. First, it would lead to the development and modification of methods used to screen the best qualified candidates with an emphasis on traits necessary for coping with prolonged isolation. Second, it would contribute to the development of a training program designed to enhance skills and resources useful in coping with stress. Third, it would suggest changes in organizational frameworks to enhance performance during long-term missions while minimizing any adverse effects of prolonged isolation. Finally, it would identify the means for minimizing any adverse long-term consequences of prolonged isolation through periodic assessment of postmission health and performance.

Most of the research to date on the effects of prolonged exposure to the Antarctic environment has focused on the physiological changes that have occurred at the end of the winter-over period. A number of studies (for instance, Dick, Mandel, Warshauer, Conklin, & Jerde, 1977; Meschievitz, Raynor, & Dick, 1983; Muchmore, Tatem, Worley, Shurley, & Scott, 1974; Muchmore, Parkinson, & Scott, 1983; Parkinson, Muchmore, & Scott, 1979) have noted the outbreaks of upper respiratory infections and colds among winter-over personnel at the opening of a station each year. These are attributed to the immunosuppressed state of winter-over personnel due to the climate, psychological stress, and absence of viral agents (Muchmore, Blackburn, Shurley, Pierce, & McKown, 1970; Williams, Climie, Muller, & Lugg, 1986). Sleep studies have also demonstrated that south polar plateau subjects lose all stage IV sleep as well as significant amounts of stage III and rapid eye movement (or REM) sleep. The restoration of a standard sleep-electroencephalogram (or EEG) pattern has required as long as 24 months after return from a year in the Antarctic (Natani & Shurley, 1974).

Winter-over personnel are also believed to experience emotional problems upon their return to the outside world. Oliver's (1979) study of personnel who wintered-over at McMurdo Station in 1977 reported feelings of isolation and problems with readjusting to the larger society for periods as long as 12 months after returning to the United States. In addition, there have been some anecdotal reports among Australian winter-over personnel of attempted suicides, severe depression, and alcohol abuse upon their return from the Antarctic (Lugg, this volume).

The impact of living and working under such conditions may be felt more dramatically after the experience itself. One working hypothesis for behavioral scientists, therefore, is that the risk for illness and disease subsequent to the winter-over experience may be similar to the risk for illness after a stressful life event or series of life events, such as posttraumatic stress disorders among Vietnam combat veterans (Figley, 1978), the risk of myocardial infarction after death of spouse (Helsing & Szklo, 1981), or the risk of a stroke after loss of a job (Brenner & Mooney, 1982). To examine this possibility, we at the NHRC conducted a series of follow-up studies to determine whether winter-over personnel were indeed at risk for physical and mental disorders in both the short term and long term and what, if any, factors (social, psychological, environmental) moderated the relationship between the winter-over experience and subsequent health and performance.

## Follow-Up Studies of Operation Deep Freeze Volunteers: Methodology

The subjects for our studies were 2,724 enlisted Navy men who volunteered to winter-over in Antarctica between 1963 and 1974 (Palinkas, 1986). All of these individuals were evaluated by screening teams, each consisting of a clinical psychologist and psychiatrist, and found to be acceptable for winter–over duty. The study population was divided into two groups on the basis of whether or not they actually wintered-over at one of six small stations between 1963 and 1974. Because of the specific needs for personnel with certain qualifications at each station, only 328 of these individuals actually wintered-over during this period. The remainder were assigned to other duty stations throughout the world during the austral winter.

Records of screening evaluations of the study subjects were compiled into a computerized file at the NHRC. The Operation Deep Freeze file contains biographical and service history information and screening results on 4,557 military and civilian applicants from this period. However, only Navy enlisted personnel were selected for follow-up because of the availability of medical and service history data on these individuals. The NHRC maintains an Inpatient Medical Data file containing records on all hospitalizations for all active-duty Navy personnel for the period 1965–1984 and an Enlisted Service History file containing service history information on all enlisted personnel during this period, as well (Garland et al., 1987). These two files were searched for all medical and service history information on the Navy enlisted personnel identified from the Operation Deep Freeze file.

A 15-year period from 1965 through 1979 was established for follow-up, based on the period of time for which medical and service history information was available for both groups at the time the study was conducted. The start date for participation in the study was established as January 1, 1965, or the year an individual was evaluated for the Operation Deep Freeze program if after this date. Withdrawal was defined as the date of last discharge from the Navy or December 31, 1979, whichever came first. The mean length of follow-up for study subjects was 6.1 years for the winter-over group, 5.3 years for the control group, and 5.4 years for the entire population.

The subjects were young (mean = 26.1 years) enlisted men with a mean paygrade of 4.9, reflecting that of 2nd class petty officers, and had served an average of 7 years in the service in the Navy at the time they were screened for the Operation Deep Freeze program. Most (71.0%) of the subjects were high school graduates; 15% had one or more years of college. Slightly over half (50.5%) of the subjects were blue collar personnel; the remainder were classified in administrative-clerical (23.4%), electronic-technical (15.2%), medical (6.7%), and apprentice (3.8%) occupational categories.

The health status of our subjects at entry into the study was assessed by responses to the Cornell Medical Index (CMI) scales. A comparison of CMI scores obtained from winter-over personnel and the control group found no significant differences between winter-over and control personnel on any of the questions except that winter-over personnel were heavier drinkers (CMI No. 144, $\chi^2 = 5.57$, $p < .02$); complained more of constant coughing (CMI No. 22, $\chi^2 = 4.59$, $p < .03$); and were more likely to have had hepatitis (CMI No. 62, $\chi^2 = 4.78$, $p < .03$). The control group, on the other hand, complained more of frequent urination (CMI No. 104, $\chi^2 = 5.07$, $p < .03$).

Disease incidence was defined on the basis of the first inpatient admission for all diagnoses for each subject. Inpatient medical data included all first hospitalizations for all diagnoses that occurred after entry into the study (i.e., subsequent to screening for Operation Deep Freeze). Diagnoses were in accordance with the Eighth Revision, International Classification of Diseases Adapted for Use in the United States (ICDA-8). First hospitalization rates for 16 ICDA-8 diagnostic categories were calculated using person-years at risk as the denominator.

# Health and Performance of Antarctic Winter-Over Personnel: A Follow-up Study

The first study conducted with these data compared personnel who wintered-over in the Antarctic with the control group to determine whether they were at risk for illness and injury upon their return. Given the stressful nature of the winter-over experience, we expected that the winter-over groups would have a significantly higher rate of first hospitalizations than the control group. Both groups were compared on a series of performance indices as well as on rates of all-cause first hospitalizations and rates for each of the 16 selected ICDA-8 categories.

The rate of total, or all-cause first, hospitalizations for the winter-over group was 21% less than the rate for the control group ($p < .05$). The winter-over group had significantly fewer first hospitalizations for neoplasms; endocrine, nutritional, and metabolic diseases; and diseases of the musculoskeletal system than the control group. Differences observed in the remaining diagnostic categories failed to attain statistical significance at the .05 level, although observed lower rates among the winter-over group for mental disorders and accidental and violent injuries are at the .10 level (Palinkas, 1986).

The results indicated that the winter-over experience did not seriously impair the long-term health and performance of enlisted Navy personnel. In fact, the experience appeared to be related to a reduced risk of subsequent disease incidence for certain diagnostic categories. To explain this observed relationship, we entertained several different possibilities. For instance, although not statistically significant, the lower rates of mental disorders and accidental injuries among the winter-over group might indicate that the Operation Deep Freeze screening program effectively eliminated candidates with high-risk psychological profiles. Similarly, the lower rates of other disease categories may indicate that the winter-over group was healthier than the control group at the time of screening. However, psychiatric suitability did not discriminate between winter-over and control groups, because both were composed of individuals who were evaluated by a screening team as suitable for winter-over duty. Other factors, such as the need for a certain occupational skill at a particular research station and the previous experience of the applicant, are used in the final determination as to who does winter-over. Our examination of CMI responses indicated that the health status of both groups at the time of screening was similar except in those instances where the winter-over group appeared to have a less favorable health profile (i.e., greater alcohol consumption, complaints of constant coughing, history of hepatitis) than the control group.

Differences in age and education may also account for the observed differences in rates of first hospitalization. However, the incidence rates were age adjusted to control for the possibility of a spurious relationship. Education may have been a factor in accounting for the observed differences; however, while other studies have indicated an inverse relationship between education and disease risk, our results suggest a direct relationship, with the better educated control group exhibiting the higher rates of first hospitalization.

Finally, we considered the possibility that the results may have simply been a representation of the "healthy worker effect," a phenomenon commonly observed in studies of occupational health where the observed differences in rates between workers in certain occupations and the general population are due to the fact that not only are persons who are selected for employment on the average healthier than the general population but also that once they become employed, they tend to have better economic circumstances and better access to medical care; they also may make changes in their life-style that are conducive to better health (Kelsey, Thompson, & Evans, 1986). However, both groups were employed as enlisted Navy personnel; both were in similar occupations; and follow-up occurred only during the period of active-duty service. Moreover, when rates of first hospitalizations were adjusted for occupational differences (using the categories of blue collar versus all other occupational groups), the observed differences between the winter-over and control groups remained. Similarly, because both groups are composed of volunteers, self-selection of highly motivated winter-over personnel does not explain the observed differences.

## A Longitudinal Study of Disease Incidence

One of the issues not specifically addressed by this long-term follow-up study was the previously reported instances of stress and illness observed during the first year after wintering-over in the Antarctic. The observation that winter–over personnel did not exhibit significantly higher rates of disease incidence than the control group over a long period of time did not necessarily invalidate the possibility that the former were at increased risk during the period of time when struggling to return to their former jobs and renew relationships with family, friends, and co-workers. It was hypothesized that perhaps a more sensitive indicator of the relationship between prolonged isolation and disease risk would be to examine the rates of first hospitalization by selected time intervals small enough to observe the health status of winter-over personnel within the first year or two upon their return from the Antarctic. We therefore conducted a study to determine whether winter-over personnel were at risk for first hospitalizations during the first year subsequent to returning from Antarctica.

A survival analysis method was adopted to calculate rates of first hospitalization by 6-month intervals subsequent to being screened for the Operation Deep Freeze program. Because the number of cases among the winter-over group within these 6-month intervals was too small to permit the calculation of statistically valid rates for each diagnostic category, only all-cause first hospitalization rates were used in this study.

The rate of total first hospitalizations for all diagnoses for the winter–over group during the first two 6-month periods of study participation was significantly lower than the rate for the control group. The rate for the winter-over group displayed a steady increase, however, reaching a peak during the fifth interval, which was about 27 months after entry into the study and 9 months after the end of winter-over duty. With the increase in the rate of total first hospitalizations, the risk of hospital admissions in the winter-over group relative to the control group also increased, reaching a peak at the same time (i.e., 9 months after the winter-over period). However, this relative risk was not statistically significant. Moreover, the rate of total first hospitalizations among the winter-over group for the remainder of the study period (Months 30 to 180) was significantly less than the rate for the control group (Palinkas, 1987).

Despite the observed increase in rates during the first year upon returning from Antarctica, the incidence of first hospitalizations among those who wintered-over was still no greater than that of the control group. This suggests that the experience is not associated with either short-term or long-term disease/injury risk.

One possible explanation for these results is that the harshness of the environment, combined with the processes of psychosocial adjustment to prolonged isolation, minimize the risk of disease both in the short term, and, in the context of adaptation to stressful life events, in the long term as well. Previous research has attributed the low incidence of infectious disease and diseases of the respiratory system among Antarctic personnel during the austral winter as the result of prolonged isolation in a relatively sterile and disease-free environment (Allen, 1974; Meschievitz et al., 1983; Muchmore et al., 1983; Parkinson et al., 1979). This would help to account for the smaller rates of first hospitalizations during the intervals of Antarctic duty. In addition, despite the presence of the psychological symptoms of the winter-over syndrome, the microcultures of Antarctic research stations support and promote values, rules for behavior, and personality traits in individual members, enabling them to adapt to isolation and perhaps also promoting health on a long-term basis as well (Palinkas, 1989; Taylor, 1974). The significantly lower rate of total first hospitalizations among the winter-over group after the fifth interval (27 months after entry into the study and 9 months after returning from the Antarctic) would appear to suggest such a long-term benefit from this process of adaptation. This process may also begin immediately upon selection for winter-over duty, which would account for the significantly lower rates during the 6-month period prior to Antarctic duty. Hence, the process of psychosocial adjustment may have long-term as well as short-term benefits for one's health and well-being.

## Personality and Disease Incidence

The third study to be reviewed examined differences in personality traits of winter-over and control groups in an effort to explain the observed differences in rates of first hospitalizations. Because the two groups were similar with respect to their clinical evaluations, the differences cannot be attributed to the screening process. However, it is possible that the differences in rates of disease incidence were due to differences in personality characteristics moderating the relationship between a prolonged stressful life event (the winter-over experience) and a subsequent long-term risk for disease incidence. Thus, two questions emerged from this earlier research: (1) Do the winter-over and control groups exhibit different personality traits? and (2) Do these traits predict for long-term disease incidence as defined by first hospitalization for a specific disease?

The personality characteristics and interpersonal needs of study subjects were measured by two scales originally employed to screen prospective candidates for winter-over duty during this period and to predict for performance on the ice (Palinkas, Stern, & Holbrook, 1986). The first inventory was the Fundamental Interpersonal Relations Orientation-Behavior or FIRO-B (Schutz, 1958). This questionnaire was designed to assess how an individual acts in three areas of social interaction (Inclusion, Affection, and Control) in terms of the behavior the individual expresses toward others (expressing) and how he wants others to behave toward him (wanting). The second set of scales and rating measures utilized in the study was developed especially for the Antarctic screening program on the basis of qualities believed to be desirable in winter-over personnel (Ford & Gunderson, 1962). Factor analysis was employed to identify highly intercorrelated clusters of inventory items that appeared to represent meaningful psychological attributes (Gunderson & Mahan, 1966). Four of the test scales measured common psychological needs: Achievement, Autonomy, Nurturance, and Order. The content of these four scales is generally similar to the content of the corresponding Edwards Personal Preference Schedule (or EPPS) scales (Edwards, 1959), although the format of the items was entirely different.

In this study, each of the 10 scales was examined independently. In order to determine the effect of these personality characteristics on risk for first hospitalization, the subjects were divided into two groups for each personality measure on the basis of whether their scores fell above or below the median. None of the differences in mean personality scores between the two groups were statistically significant; hence, the differences in rates of first hospitalization observed in the previous studies could not be explained by differences in personality tests.

Because the number of first hospitalizations in each diagnostic category was too small to yield meaningful results, the Cox proportional hazards model (Lee, 1980) was used to assess the independent effects of demographic and personality characteristics on risk of all-cause first hospitalizations. When all demographic and personality factors were combined in one model, age and education were significant predictors, with personnel 26 years and older exhibiting the highest relative risk. After controlling for the demographic characteristics and winter-over experience, only Control-Expressed ($p < .01$) and Achievement ($p < .05$) were significant independent predictors of first hospitalization. Our results also indicated that those who wintered-over in Antarctica had a significantly decreased risk for subsequent all-cause first hospitalizations than the control group. This difference cannot be attributed to differences in personality, age, or education (Palinkas et al., 1986). How, then, do we explain this positive effect of a prolonged stressful experience?

Other studies (Palinkas, 1989; Taylor, 1974) have suggested that winter-over personnel learn from their experience in Antarctica, becoming more independent and self-reliant. The fact that the winter-over personnel have significantly fewer hospitalizations throughout their enlisted careers when contrasted with the control group suggests that the lessons learned in coping with the stressful Antarctic environment may be utilized in coping with other stressful experiences as well. If, in fact, this is the case, then stressful life events may not always result in illness, because individuals with certain personality characteristics in certain social and environmental contexts may learn from their experience and develop coping styles and social resources enabling them to cope with subsequent events, thereby reducing the risk for illness in the long term. This may help to explain the low-order correlations found in most studies of stressful life events and illness (Rabkin & Struening, 1976; Schroeder & Costa, 1984).

It is not surprising that both the winter-over experience and a high need for expressed control were significant predictors of improved health status. The winter-over experience addresses the issue of the limits of one's control over his or her physical and social environment. All winter-over personnel must learn to cope with limited control over their environment. They are dependent upon their physical shelters to withstand the harsh climate and must interact with the same group of people for 8 months at a time. Removal from this environment during this period is not possible. Natani and Shurley (1974, p. 110) hypothesize that under these conditions, "the independent individuals who volunteered for Antarctic duty also have developed a strong need for behaviors that give them positive feedback about their own self-control, control over their fate, and control over their environment."

These behaviors may also be utilized in coping with other stressful environments and life events. A sense of control over the environment has been implicated as a moderator of stress in several different studies. Studies that have applied Rotter's (1966) notion of locus of control have generally found that individuals with an external locus of control are at greater risk for physical and psychological disorders than individuals with an internal locus of control (Johnson & Sarason, 1978; Seligman, 1975). Evidence produced by Seeman and Seeman (1983), for example, showed that the sense of control is associated with (1) practicing preventive health measures, e. g., diet, exercise, alcohol moderation; (2) making an effort to avoid the harm in smoking (by quitting, trying to quit, or simply not smoking); (3) being more sanguine about early medical treatment for cancer; (4) achieving higher self-ratings on general health status; and (5) reporting fewer episodes of both chronic and acute illness. The concept of mastery used by Pearlin and Schooler (1978) also includes notions of control, as does the concept of potency used by Ben-Shira (1985) and Kobasa's (1979) concept of hardiness.

Thus, while a need for control itself does not explain the difference in rates of first hospitalization between the winter-over and control groups, a synergistic relationship involving the individual need for control, the station microculture that reinforces this need and identifies strategies for meeting it, and the process of adaptation and adjustment to the stress associated with the winter-over experience may be responsible for the significantly reduced risk for subsequent disease and injury.

## Future Directions

The findings of these studies are constrained by a number of limitations. Nevertheless, the results of these studies do have relevance for the space program with respect to the objectives outlined earlier. For instance, they suggest that certain personality characteristics such as need for achievement, internal locus of control, and social compatibility should be assessed in a screening program designed to select individuals for extended missions in space. The experience in Antarctica can also be incorporated into a training program for these individuals. Such a training program would help to "inno-culate" them (cf. Meichenbaum, 1985) from potential adverse consequences of prolonged isolation, including significant decrements in health and performance. The human experience in the Antarctic also suggests that certain organizational structures may help to improve health and performance. The microcultures of Antarctic research stations may serve as a model for the organization of long-term, manned space missions. These station microcultures provide or identify appropriate strategies for coping with the stress associated with the extreme environment and social isolation. These strategies include the types and networks of available social support; the emphasis placed on certain psychological resources such as an internal locus of control and self-reliance; and the commitment to the assigned task and to the social group.

Finally, our results suggest that there are no adverse long-term effects of prolonged isolation with respect to health and performance. However, participants of long-term missions in space should be closely monitored during the first year subsequent to mission completion in order to identify potential decrements in health and performance and initiate corrective or therapeutic measures. In addition, the process of readjustment itself may produce a positive benefit in terms of long-term health and performance. Follow-up assessment, using more sensitive measures of adaptation than hospital admissions or numbers of promotions and demotions, could determine whether a positive benefit is derived from the combined experience of prolonged isolation and reintegration into society, what form this benefit may assume, and what its mode of operation may be.

The studies described in this chapter by no means satisfy the requirements of each of these objectives. However, they do suggest certain lines of inquiry for additional research. First, studies are required to provide an update of the human experience in the Antarctic necessary for an evaluation of social, cultural, and psychological factors influencing the processes of adaptation and adjustment. Second, new data obtained from ethnographic and longitudinal studies could be compared with archival data available at NHRC to determine whether the adjustment experience has indeed changed in the past 20 years. Third, research is needed to determine whether and how the winter-over experience reduces the risk of neoplasms; endocrine, nutritional, and metabolic disorders; and diseases of the musculoskeletal system. Fourth, research is necessary to evaluate the lessons learned from the winter-over experience and the extent to which these lessons reduce the risk of subsequent illness. Fifth, the social and psychological characteristics that facilitate the acquisition and utilization of social supports to cope with stress in the Antarctic should be identified.

To pursue these lines of inquiry, however, a comprehensive program of social and behavioral research in the Antarctic is essential. An understanding of the processes of adaptation and adjustment requires the perspective and methods of several different disciplines, including psychology, sociology, psychiatry, human ecology, and anthropology. The concept of coping, for instance, represents an area for the potential cross-fertilization of approaches in examining the role of personality, social support, environmental resources and demands, and values and rules of behavior composing the station microcultures as moderators of the relationship between prolonged isolation and health and performance.

A comprehensive program must also reflect both theoretical and applied interests and be flexible enough to attain scientific results without undue interference with routine operations. Such objectives can only be met by the establishing and maintaining of an active dialogue among all concerned parties. As the studies summarized by this chapter suggest, however, the potential benefits from this dialogue and the research it supports are enormous.

*Acknowledgements.* The author would like to thank Dr. Frank Garland and Dr. Eric Gunderson for their critical reading and editorial suggestions.

## References

Allen, T. R. (1974). Common cold epidemiology in Antarctica. In O. G. Edholm & E. K. E. Gunderson (Eds.), *Polar human biology: Proceedings of the SCAR/IUPS/IUBS symposium on human biology and medicine in the Antarctic.* (pp. 123-124). Chicago: Heinemann.

Ben-Shira, Z. (1985). Potency: A stress-buffering link in the coping–stress–disease relationship. *Social Science and Medicine, 21*, 397-406.

Brenner, M. H., & Mooney, A. (1982). Economic change and sex-specific cardiovascular mortality in Britain, 1955-1976. *Social Science and Medicine, 16*, 431-442.

Dick, E. C., Mandel, A. D., Warshauer, D. M., Conklin, S. C., & Jerde, R. S.

(1977). Respiratory virus transmission at McMurdo Station: Isolation of rhinoviruses from common colds during the winter fly-in period, 1976. *Antarctic Journal of the United States, 12,* 2–6.

Edwards, A. L. (1959). *A manual for the Edwards Personal Preference Schedule (rev. ed.).* New York: Psychological Corporation.

Figley, C. (Ed.). (1978). *Stress disorders among Vietnam veterans: Theory, research and treatment.* New York: Brunner/Mazel.

Ford, K. A., & Gunderson, E. K. E. (1962). Personality characteristics (EPPS) of Antarctic volunteers (Report No. 62-18). San Diego: Navy Medical Neuropsychiatric Research Unit.

Garland, F. C., Helmkamp, J. C., Gunderson, E. K. E., Gorham, E. D., Miller, M. M., McNally, M. S., & Thompson, F. A. (1987). A guide to the computerized medical data resources of the Naval Health Research Center (Report No. 87-13). San Diego: Naval Health Research Center.

Gunderson, E. K. E. (1974). Psychological studies in Antarctica. In E. K. E. Gunderson (Ed.), *Human adaptability to Antarctic conditions* (pp. 115–131). Washington, DC: American Geophysical Union.

Gunderson, E. K. E., & Mahan, J. L. (1966). Cultural and psychological differences among occupational groups. *Journal of Psychology, 62,* 287–304.

Helsing, K. J., & Szklo, M. (1981). Mortality after bereavement. *American Journal of Epidemiology, 114,* 41–52.

Johnson, J. G., & Sarason, I. G. (1978). Life stress, depression and anxiety: Internal-external control as a moderator variable. *Journal of Psychosomatic Research, 22,* 205–208.

Kelsey, J. L., Thompson, W. D., & Evans, A. S. (1986). *Methods in observational epidemiology.* New York: Oxford University Press.

Kobasa, S. C. (1979). Stressful life events, personality, and health: An inquiry into hardiness. *Journal of Personality and Social Psychology, 37,* 1–11.

Lee, E. T. (1980). *Statistical methods for survival data analysis.* Belmont, CA: Wadsworth.

Meichenbaum, D. (1985). *Stress inoculation training.* New York: Pergamon.

Meschievitz, C. K., Raynor, W. J., & Dick, E. C. (1983). Cold severity, duration, and epidemiology in persons emerging from isolation compared to newly arrived persons at McMurdo Station. *Antarctic Journal of the United States, 18,* 232–234.

Muchmore, H. G., Blackburn, A. B., Shurley, J. T., Pierce, C. M., & McKown, B. A. (1970). Neutropenias in healthy men at the south polar plateau. *Archives of Internal Medicine, 125,* 646–648.

Muchmore, H. G., Tatem, B. A., Worley, R. A., Shurley, J. T., & Scott, N. (1974). Immunoglobulins during south polar isolation. In O. G. Edholm & E. K. E. Gunderson (Eds.), *Polar human biology: Proceedings of the SCAR/IUPS/IUBS symposium on human biology and medicine in the Antarctic* (pp. 135–140). Chicago: Heinemann.

Muchmore, H. G., Parkinson, A. J., & Scott, E. N. (1983). Respiratory virus infections during the winter at the South Pole. *Antarctic Journal of the United States, 17,* 229–230.

Natani, K., & Shurley, J. T. (1974). Sociopsychological aspects of a winter vigil at South Pole Station. In E. K. E. Gunderson (Ed.), *Human adaptability to Antarctic conditions* (pp. 89–114). Washington, DC: American Geophysical Union.

Oliver, D. M. (1979). Some psychological effects of isolation and confinement in an

Antarctic winter-over group. Doctoral dissertation, United States International University, San Diego. (University Microfilms No. 80-00, 243)

Palinkas, L. A. (1986). Health and performance of Antarctic winter-over personnel: A follow-up study. *Aviation, Space, and Environmental Medicine, 57*, 954–959.

Palinkas, L. A. (1987). A longitudinal study of disease incidence among Antarctic winter-over personnel. *Aviation, Space, and Environmental Medicine, 58*, 1062–1065.

Palinkas, L. A. (1989). Sociocultural influences on psychosocial adjustment in Antarctica. *Medical Anthropology, 10*, 235–246.

Palinkas, L. A., Stern, M. J., & Holbrook, T. L. (1986). A longitudinal study of personality and disease incidence among Antarctic winter-over volunteers (Report No. 86-25). San Diego: Naval Health Research Center.

Parkinson, A. J., Muchmore, H. G., & Scott, L. V. (1979). Parainfluenzavirus upper respiratory infections at McMurdo Station during the austral summer 1975–1976. *Antarctic Journal of the United States, 14*, 186–187.

Pearlin, L. I., & Schooler, C. (1978). The structure of coping. *Journal of Health and Social Behavior, 19*, 2–21.

Pierce, C. M. (1985). Social science research in high latitudes. *Journal of Clinical Psychology, 41*, 581.

Rabkin, J., & Struening, E. (1976). Life events, stress, and illness. *Science, 194*, 1013–1020.

Rotter, J. B. (1966). Generalized expectancies for internal versus external control of reinforcement. *Psychological Monographs: General and Applied, 80* (1, Whole No. 609).

Schroeder, D. H., & Costa, P. T. (1984). Influence of life event stress on physical illness: Substantive effects or methodological flaws? *Journal of Personality and Social Psychology, 46*, 853–863.

Schutz, W. C. (1958). *FIRO: A three-dimensional theory of interpersonal behavior.* New York: Holt, Rinehart & Co.

Seeman, M., & Seeman, T. E. (1983). Health behavior and personal autonomy: A longitudinal study of the sense of control of illness. *Journal of Health and Social Behavior, 24*, 144–160.

Seligman, M. (1975). *Helplessness: On depression, development and death.* San Francisco: Freeman.

Shurley, J. T. (1974). Antarctica as a primary natural laboratory for the behavioral sciences. In O. G. Edholm & E. K. E. Gunderson (Eds.), *Polar human biology: Proceedings of the SCAR/IUPS/IUBS symposium on human biology and medicine in the Antarctic* (pp. 430–435). Chicago: Heinemann.

Taylor, A. J. W. (1974). The adaptation of New Zealand research personnel in the Antarctic. In O. G. Edholm & E. K. E. Gunderson (Eds.), *Polar human biology: Proceedings of the SCAR/IUPS/IUBS symposium on human biology and medicine in the Antarctic* (pp. 417–429). Chicago: Heinemann.

Williams, D. L., Climie, A., Muller, H. K., & Lugg, D. J. (1986). Cell-mediated immunity in healthy adults in Antarctica and the subantarctic. *Journal of Clinical and Laboratory Immunology, 20*, 43–49.

# 22

# International Biomedical Expedition to the Antarctic: Physiological Studies in the Field

IAN F. G. HAMPTON AND RAINER GOLDSMITH

Seen from the physiologist's point of view, the Antarctic is a cold desert, a large portion of which is at a considerable altitude and a place where life requires more than ordinary physical effort. The environment therefore challenges the physiological mechanisms for conserving heat and water and the cardiorespiratory and muscular processes involved in exercise at normal and reduced partial pressures of oxygen.

The physiological program on the International Biomedical Expedition to the Antarctic (IBEA) addressed all of these problems and was designed with several aims in mind, but before listing these, it is necessary to define terminology. A physiologist thinks of an environmental factor such as cold weather in physical terms, as a stress which produces a strain in the body, in this case cooling of the tissues, to which the body then responds by shivering. A psychologist, on the other hand, regards the cooling as the stress and the factor that produced it, the weather, as the stressor. In the hope that it will avoid confusion, we shall use the term *mixed stimulus* in place of stress (physiology) or stress (psychology) to describe any environmental factor which produces a disturbance in the body. The disturbance we shall call the *effective stimulus*, for strain (physiology) or stress (psychology), and this will produce responses as in the example above. The responses may engender adaptations, physiological or psychological, which by feedback may modify the effective stimulus (by physiological mechanisms) or by behavioral means

In preparing this report, the authors have drawn heavily on the work of many other scientific contributors to the International Biomedical Expedition to the Antarctic. They are too numerous to acknowledge individually here; a full list may be found in the official report of the expedition (Rivolier, Goldsmith, Taylor, & Lugg, 1988).

(clothing and so on) modify the mixed stimulus (psychological mechanisms).

The physiology program was designed with several objectives: first, to characterize the expedition members in terms of their responses to various mixed stimuli, such as heat, cold, and exercise, to aid comparison with the subjects of other studies; second, in the event that adaptations would occur as a result of exposure to the Antarctic environment, to try to measure some of the effective stimuli that produced them; and third, to test whether adaptive changes could be detected and to examine whether the procedure of artificial acclimation had conferred any benefits. This chapter describes the second of these: an accompanying one deals with the first and third, while the context of the physiological studies and the background and overall organization and objectives of the expedition may be found elsewhere (Rivolier, Goldsmith, Taylor, & Lugg, 1988). This chapter will review the climatological background to the studies and the physiological stimuli and responses produced, with the exception of effects due predominantly to altitude.

## The Physiological Studies

### The Environment

First, how cold was it? An accurate determination of the cold mixed stimulus in real life is impossible to achieve, as it depends upon a multiplicity of factors which are incapable of being measured simultaneously. In qualitative terms, few would deny that temperature and wind are important factors, particularly when taken together. Weather data were collected via an automatic weather station (Cimel Electronique) mounted on the roof of the laboratory trailer, 2.8 m above the snow surface. Continuous records were made of shade temperature (dry bulb), temperatures from inside a blackened globe (15-cm diameter) and a cylinder (8-cm diameter, 24-cm height), radiation by solarimeter, air movement by anemometer, and, separately, atmospheric pressure by aneroid barometer. The data were logged, and every 24 hr, the apparatus was interrogated to give hourly averages computed from 8 samples/hr (temperature), samples every 4 s (solarimeter), and total revolutions in the hour (anemometer). Subjective evaluations were made once daily, by an experienced observer, of cloud cover, sunshine, drifting snow, and the like, who then categorized the weather as good, medium, or bad.

In 71 days of records, there was no hour which was completely calm, and, although this was the austral summer, for more than 50% of the time temperatures were below $-20°$ C or winds above 45 km/hr; often these two conditions occurred together. Mean values and ranges were as follows: shade temperature, $-14.4°$ C ($1.7°$ to $-28.9°$ C); wind velocity, 10.6 m/s (0.3 to 22.3 m/s); and radiation gain, 114.2 W/m². Drifting snow was observed on

32 days; 3 days were blizzards. By making some assumptions, the investigators found it possible to estimate an overall index of the cold stimulus. The best known of these is the Wind Chill Index (Siple & Passel, 1945), and calculations of this showed that for more than 70% of the time in the field it exceeded 1,600 W/m², the level which has been suggested as the threshold for danger of cold exposure (Wilson, 1967). Indeed, the mean value over the whole period in the field was above this level at 1,620 W/m². Despite these figures, the subjective, but formal, assessments of the weather judged that it was bad for only 18% of the time, 32% being medium, and 50% good.

## Skin Temperature

The effect of the cold on the body (effective stimulus) was assessed by recording skin temperatures from precise locations on the forehead, chest, back, hand and thigh, sites on both clothed and exposed areas chosen to be correlates of the "microclimate" to which the men were exposed. These measurements were stored on tape in a miniature four-channel recorder (Medilog, Oxford Instruments) carried on a waist belt. One channel served to record the five surface temperatures, a second served to multiplex the signal, and a third recorded a time signal of 1Hz. The temperatures were transduced by matched thermistors mounted in polyethylene holders and attached to the body by double-sided sticky tape. A plug-in unit of known resistances was used to calibrate the system. Recordings were made over 48 hr at a time, randomly spaced over the period in the field.

The tapes were returned to the United Kingdom for analysis. The analogue signals were converted to temperatures using the calibrations and stored in a computer as mean temperatures for 1 min. The records were then automatically plotted and printed. Faulty records were eliminated by visual inspection and the remaining data used to calculate derived values. In total, good data were gathered on each man for approximately 10 to 15% of the total time in the field. For gross analysis, the temperatures were divided into those from peripheral regions, which may have been unclothed at times, and those from the trunk and into two intensities, classed as cold (for the extremities, less than 15° C; for the trunk, less than 20° C) and cool (extremities, between 15° and 20° C; trunk, 20° to 30° C). In addition, temperatures from sleep as opposed to the waking day were examined, and those recorded during days spent traveling were separated from those during work at a static base.

Mean values calculated for each site showed that the men were in general significantly warmer at night than during the day ($p < .001$), by amounts varying from 1.4° C on the back to 8.5° C on the forehead. In general, the nighttime temperatures on the chest (range, 33.3° to 33.7° C) did not reach the levels (mean, 34.9° C) observed in temperate climates (Goldsmith & Hampton, 1968). There were relatively few complaints of feeling cold at night, which suggests that living in this severe climate may have led to some habituation. Daytime temperatures were similar on traveling and nontraveling days, ranging from 24.7° C on the forehead to 33.0° C on the back. In general, temperatures were in the cool and cold zones more frequently during traveling on motorized toboggans than at base camps (approximately 7% compared to 5% of the time), while in the extreme cases of face and thigh, the frequency of occurrence of the low values of effective stimulus was more than double. As the number of days spent traveling and at base were in the ratio of 1 : 3.5, mean time/temperature integrals for the two types of days are similar. From the data it can be predicted that, during the time spent in the field, temperatures in the "unclothed" regions would have been cool for about 130 hr (face) and 40 hr (hand) and cold for 22 hr (face) and 13 hr (hand). Corresponding values for the back, chest, and thigh would have been 100 hr and 6 hr, 110 hr and 9 hr, and 140 hr and 10 hr, respectively. These frequencies of occurrence of different temperatures, and the estimates of mean levels and the lengths of time for which they were present, are parameters of the "dose" of cold, or the effective stimulus to adapt. It is interesting to speculate whether the changes seen in the laboratory studies result from the daily but short exposures to low temperatures or from the longer, accumulated dose of mild cold and whether the local and general cooling had differential effects. In these, as in all other observations reported here, there was no evidence of adaptation occurring in the field or of differences between artificially acclimated and nonacclimated men.

## Thermal Discomfort

Although measurements of temperature give objective indications of heat loss or gain, they do not necessarily tell the whole story. Thermal balance depends on a multitude of factors, some of them not easily quantified or inferred. It could be that how a person feels is a better indicator of body cooling or heating; so it was felt that it would be valuable to make formal records of the comfort and discomfort of expedition members. This was done using the Bedford "comfort vote" technique (Bedford, 1936); each man recorded his thermal sensations on a 7-point scale, and related factors, twice daily at randomly preset times between 0700 hours and 1900 hours. Every 7 or 8 days, he also completed such questionnaires at about hourly intervals. A total of 1,969 valid votes were cast, 60% of them in tents or trailers (indoors) and 40% of them outdoors.

Analysis of the data showed a failure to achieve thermal balance (comfort) on 19% of occasions outdoors. Of these, 15% were too warm and 4% too cold: the men were sweating in 9%, and shivering in 2% of records. Discomfort was mainly from overheating and sweating from the trunk, from cold-induced numbness and pain for the face and hands, and from both heat and cold for the feet. Thermal comfort results from an appropriate balance between the effects of the climate, clothing, and physical activity: in practice, it is frequently difficult to achieve this. As the weather became colder, the men wore more clothes and were more active. These adjustments were successful in maintaining the same range of comfort of the trunk as earlier, at the cost of overheating during exercise in some cases, but did not prevent the face, hands and feet from feeling proportionally much colder. Maintaining the same range of comfort when body temperatures were lower would be evidence of habituation to the new conditions.

## Heart Rate and Patterns of Activity

An important element of the plan for IBEA laid down that the environment (mixed stimulus) would be physically demanding. Part of this demand was expected to be the level of physical work required from the men in the field. Heart rate ($f_c$) is one correlate of the level of work, particularly in the absence of other factors that tend to elevate it. It was therefore planned that the $f_c$ in all men would be measured over a representative sample of the time in the field. Heart rates were derived from electrocardiogram signals (ECG) from self-adhesive, pregelled, bipolar chest electrodes and recorded on a fourth channel of the Medilog (vide supra, temperatures). Since the recordings were made simultaneously with the temperatures, the same basic protocol was followed. Upon their return to the United Kingdom, the tapes were processed by computer using a x64 real-time playback. A detector of the QRS wave produced a pulse for each ECG, and the number of these in each minute was counted. The data were plotted and printed and erroneous recordings eliminated by visual inspection. The records were then filtered to remove as much noise as possible with minimal loss of data. The data have been analyzed in a manner similar to the temperatures, zones of 100 to 120 beats/min and of above 130 beats/min being chosen to represent medium and hard work, respectively. An average of 15.5 recordings per man was obtained, representing a sample of nearly 23% of the time spent in the field. Following the elimination and filtering of the data, the final usable sample represented about one seventh of the total time.

Although mean daytime $f_c$ was significantly higher during traveling than at camp (94.8 compared to 88.4 beats/min, $p < .001$), the analyses show similar mean heart rates during the following nighttime periods (68.6 compared to 69.6 beats/min), indicating that there was no spillover of the day's activities. A convenient way of comparing the physical activity required in different occupations is to calculate the ratio of day-to-night heart rates. By this criterion, these men were slightly more active in the static camps (ratio = 1 : 1.27) than men with sedentary occupations (1 : 1.14); during travel, the ratio (1 : 1.38) was almost at the level found for workers in a steel mill (1 : 1.40). The proportion of time with elevated $f_c$ in the two zones was higher during traveling than at base, though the total length of time spent with $f_c$ elevated was much longer while at base because of the greater number of days spent at base.

Other uses of $f_c$ involved matching it with visual records of precise activities noted by a separate observer. This has allowed the building up of profiles of the distribution of heart rates among different activities and subjects, allowing many different comparisons to be made and the creation of a data base of human activity patterns.

## Oxygen Consumption

The expedition set out to measure the oxygen consumption of men carrying out their normal activities during periods of time selected at random during specially designated days, thus allowing the estimation of energy expenditure by indirect calorimetry. A miniature respirometer (MISER, P. K. Morgan) was used to measure the volume of expired air over timed periods, while taking aliquots for later analysis of oxygen content. The subjects breathed through inspiratory and expiratory valves in a face mask which was well insulated from the environment to prevent the valves from freezing. Downstream, an axial gas meter recorded volume: at isovolumetric intervals, an electronic control box activated a sampling valve, and an aliquot was taken into a small evacuated canister. The apparatus switched itself off after a preset volume had been expired and recorded the total time and the expired volume. All of the apparatus was worn beneath the clothing to keep the components and batteries well above freezing temperatures. Analysis of the expired air was carried out later on a modified paramagnetic oxygen analyzer calibrated on air and after total evacuation. Oxygen consumption was converted to energy expenditure on the assumption that 1l of oxygen was equal to 21 kJ. Measurements were carried out on men at three preset times during the second day of heart-rate recordings.

There were many technical problems with this study, which partly frustrated the objectives, but over 100 satisfactory measurements were made. These showed that shoveling snow, a not uncommon occupation, required 420 to 490 W of energy; helping in a snow sampling pit, 350 to 400 W; and walking over the rough snow surfaces, only a little less. Driving the motorized toboggans varied between 150 and 300 W. The mean energy expenditure was 211 W (S.D. = 85 W).

The apparatus was cumbersome and prevented the subjects from carrying out their duties in a normal fashion. Thus, the samples did not represent normal, habitual activity, and the mean value for all measurements is about three times as large as might be expected for values made in resting men and could lead to predictions of rather high levels of daily energy expenditure. In addition, one of the reasons for the limited number of samples was because, on many days, the inclement weather kept the men confined to their tents and no readings were taken in that location. Despite the patchy sampling, it seemed clear that outdoor activities, although somewhat infrequent, did require high levels of energy expenditure, ensuring that the men did work hard occasionally and probably harder than they would habitually be required to do in their work at home.

## Daily Fluid Balance

The questions of interest were, how much do people sweat in Antarctica? Is it enough to adapt them to heat? How much water condenses in their clothing? How dehydrated do they get? Fluid balance was assessed over a period of 8 to 10 hr during the day, every 7 or 8 days, by nude and clothed body weighings morning and evening and by weighing and measuring food, drink, urine, and feces. A total of 98 observations was made on 11 men.

Nonrenal water loss (i.e., due to respiration and sweating) averaged 73 g/hr (S.D. = 33 g/hr), about three times that lost in a nonsweating person at rest in normal temperatures. High values up to 158 g/hr were recorded, which would be sufficient to adapt to heat! Clothing weight changed by an average of +69 g/day (S.D. = 264 g/day), ranging from a loss of 760 g to a gain of 1,000 g. The clothing lost weight on 44% of the observations, presumably from drying out on a fine day after being wet by bad weather. Food intake and fluid intake and output were very variable, depending upon circumstances. Averages were 399 g (S.D. = 315 g), 790 g (S.D. = 390 g), and 638 ml (S.D. = 418 ml), respectively. Calculations showed that, on average, dehydration occurred during the day, amounting to 537 g (S.D. 607 g) and ranging from −1,150 g (i.e., overhydration) to extreme values of 2,230 g. These represent a mean loss in body mass of 0.74% (S.D. = 0.85%, with a range from a gain of 1.5% to a loss of 3.4%).

## Sleep

In other studies, various changes in the parameters of the electroencephalograph (EEG) during sleep have been found to occur during sojourns in Antarctica and have been related to diverse psychophysiological disturbances in the polar environment. This expedition offered a good opportunity to examine the effects of what was designed to be a taxing experience in the field. The six men who did not participate in the artificial acclimation study acted as the subjects in these experiments. EEG electrodes were applied at positions Cz and O1-Pz on shaved areas of the scalp. In addition, ocular and myographic electrodes were applied to appropriate positions on face and chin. Recordings were made on Medilog recorders, and the tapes were returned to France for analysis.

Compared to the control measurements in Sydney, the results showed that there were no significant changes in the duration of the stages of sleep, although there was a trend for an increase in stage II and decreases in stages III and IV. The percentage of stage II sleep was significantly increased ($p <$ .05) in the field, whereas the percentage of stage IV sleep decreased significantly ($p <$ .05), and a similar trend was seen in stage III sleep. Latencies of occurrence of stages III and IV were significantly increased ($p <$ .01 and $p <$ .05, respectively). Paradoxical sleep latency was slightly decreased but failed to reach significant levels. Latency to the first awakening was slightly less in the field, a mean of 347 min compared to 362 min in the control period.

Many successful records were obtained under these difficult conditions. It seemed that the stimulus of the fieldwork induced an increase in light sleep (stage II) and an accompanying increase in the latency of deep, slow-wave sleep (stages III and IV), which is not altogether consistent with previous findings.

## Conclusions

Physiological responses to life in cold climates have been of interest because of their importance for more than 40 years, but there is still no consensus as to their nature and extent. Perhaps technology, even as undeveloped as that possessed by the Eskimo, but particularly in the advanced forms of clothing and shelter available to us today, is sufficient to prevent the presence of an adequate effective stimulus. Perhaps humans from temperate climates are already maximally adapted, so no further changes may be expected. What is certainly true is that earlier studies have been fragmented or specialized in their approach and have used differing methodologies which make comparisons difficult. This has hindered the accumulation of knowledge.

This experiment was planned to be holistic in its approach, and the purpose of the physiological studies in the field was to provide a quantitative background for the laboratory-based studies. The measurements showed the environment to be taxing in all the areas of investigation, but preacclimation did not appear to confer benefits in terms of the effective stimuli induced.

## References

Bedford, T. (1936). *The warmth factor in comfort at work*. (Report No. 76). London: Industrial Health Research Board.

Goldsmith, R., & Hampton, I. F. G. (1968). Nocturnal microclimate of man. *Journal of Physiology, 194*, 32–33P.

Rivolier, J., Goldsmith, R., Taylor, A. J. W., & Lugg, D. J. (1988). *Man in the Antarctic: the scientific work of the International Biomedical Expedition to the Antarctic*. London: Taylor and Francis.

Siple, P. A., & Passel, C. F. (1945). Measures of dry atmospheric cooling in subfreezing temperatures. *Proceedings of the American Philosophical Society, 89*, 177–199.

Wilson, O. (1967) . Objective evaluation of Wind Chill Index by records of frostbite in the Antarctic. *International Journal of Biometeorology, 11*, 29–32.

# 23

# The Third-Quarter Phenomenon: Do People Experience Discomfort After Stress Has Passed?

ROBERT B. BECHTEL AND AMY BERNING

During the cold regions study project (Bechtel & Ledbetter, 1976), a number of anecdotes were encountered that did not get into the final report because of a lack of hard data. These anecdotes were supplied by chaplains, school teachers, police officers, and base commanders to the effect that the hardest part of the winter seemed to be in February, *after* the peak of winter cold had passed. The chaplains claimed that marital counseling reached a peak at this time, the police remembered more accidents and assaults, and base commanders thought there were more absences.

Unfortunately, the pressure of the research did not allow the collection of pertinent data on site, and an opportunity was missed. Yet, if this phenomenon has any reality, it should appear in data collected at other sites and under similar circumstances. A literature search did reveal data that not only seemed to confirm the hypothesis for cold regions but also seemed to show that it was a general characteristic of finite-time stressful situations.

In their review of the literature on groups in exotic environments, Harrison and Connors (1984, p. 56) reveal that "Typically, mood and morale reach nadir somewhere between the one-half and two-thirds mark of the mission." Vinograd (1974) and Lebedev (1980) are cited as supporting this conclusion. Since the third quarter begins after the one-half mark and is centered near the two-thirds mark, let this be called the *third-quarter phenomenon* for the sake of convenience. The question remains whether additional data can be found that either contradict or support this phenomenon.

In their book *Living Aloft: Human Requirements for Extended Spaceflight* (Connors, Harrison, & Akins, 1985), the authors quote from Rohrer (1961) as identifying three broad stages of reaction to prolonged isolation. These are a first stage of heightened anxiety, a second stage of settling down to routine marked by depression, and *a third stage of anticipation marked by emotional outbursts, aggressiveness, and rowdy behavior*, which may be detrimental to the mission because of its disruptive nature.

An important feature of this third stage is that it seems to depend more on the relative rather than the absolute passage of time. That is, the sequence remains the same regardless of the length of the mission.

Supporting data are quoted by Connors et al. (1985), coming from a 1-year stay in Antarctica, a 30-day submarine mission, a McDonnell Douglas 90-day-simulation study, and a fallout shelter study that involved 1- and 2-week periods of confinement.

But the literature is more extensive. Earls (1969) studied sailors on a nuclear submarine and reported a "half-way" syndrome that was a "low point" in the group's morale. Actually, Earls's data show this to occur after the half-way point, indicating that it is in the third quarter.

Gunderson and Nelson (1963, p. 1112) show that for 90 men on two Antarctic expeditions,

. . . reporting sleep difficulties, feeling blue, and feeling irritable was considerably higher during the mid-winter period (after three to four months of isolation) than during the pre-winter period (at the end of the Antarctic summer, near the close of an active period of preparation for an oncoming winter) in both expeditions, although irritability did not reach a high point until the end of winter in the second expedition. . . . Responses shifted toward the "severe" end of the scale from pre-winter to mid-winter more frequently than expected by chance on many of the 54 items (on a questionnaire) studied. Change occurred most frequently on items reflecting sleeplessness, depression, irritability, and anxiety.

Since the data Gunderson and Nelson present are recorded only at the pre-, mid- and postwinter periods, it is not clear whether the peak of change occurred at the third quarter or exactly at the midwinter midpoint. These data are reported because they are typical of many studies that do not collect data for the four quarters of a stay. The conclusions from these studies must remain in limbo, because they do not directly support the hypothesis. Also, please note the rise in irritability in the second expedition. These data are also ambiguous because it cannot be known whether the increase is coming from the third quarter.

Palmai (1963), however, seems clear in the interpretation of his data: "Analysis of sample discussions for each quarter indicates that there is a significant increase of negative social and emotional feeling in these discussions in the third quarter of the year, with some recovery in the fourth quarter" (p. 367).

Popkin, Stillner, Osborn, Pierce, and Shurley (1974, p. 652) report staring and "drifting" behavior:

Eleven subjects (50%) reported staring themselves. Occurrence was again a mid-to-late winter phenomenon. This phenomenon lasted between 1 and 90 minutes with

85% lasting less than 20 minutes. The staring was usually associated with leisure activity and the men were typically seated.

Thus, it would seem that not only in cold regions but also in other situations of isolation and stress there is a discomfort period that occurs in the third quarter of the stay. But the existence of this phenomenon raises many questions. First, what is the cause of the breakdown in psychological control that seems to characterize this period? Is it the release from pressure that comes from anticipating the end of the isolation? Rohrer (1961) seems to imply an anticipation. But why should an anticipation be accompanied by discomfort? Does not anticipation of a happy end usually bring pleasant phantasies? The evidence from all sources makes it clear that this is a decidedly negative release of emotion. Does this occur because these negative emotions are the result of repressing negative feelings prior to the third period? Such a hypothesis might have credibility if it were not for the expression of depression in Rohrer's second stage. Nevertheless, one could argue that it is the less acceptable emotions that are repressed and come out after the reason for repression becomes less salient. Let us call this the "release from repression" hypothesis.

A second hypothesis suggests that the release of negative emotion is due to the body's relaxation from stress. Without the extra energy from adrenaline, the isolated person is less able to control emotions. This can be called the "release from pressure" hypothesis.

The opponent-process theory of acquired motivation was introduced by Richard Solomon in 1974 (Solomon, 1980; Solomon & Corbit, 1974). Briefly, it posits that continuous presentation of an unconditioned stimulus (in this case, perhaps adrenaline in response to a stressful situation) produces a tolerance level or even habituation. Then, when the stimulus is withdrawn (i.e., adrenaline flow decreases), the organism undergoes a withdrawal syndrome that becomes a secondary motivation. In simplest terms, by this theory, the human feels uncomfortable when the accustomed flow of adrenaline ceases and wants to restore the state that resulted from adrenaline flow. This would account for the variety of symptoms experienced and reported in the literature.

Still a fourth hypothesis is one proposed by Martin Orne (1987), the "father" of demand characteristics in an environment. Orne discovered that subjects in stimulus deprivation experiments experienced "going crazy" (hallucinations) about two thirds of the way through the experiments regardless of the length of the experiments. One experiment was for 2 weeks, a second for 1 week, and a third for only 24 hours. Despite the researchers' claims that subjects did not know the length of the experiment, Orne surreptitiously recorded the secretary who signed up the subjects and determined that, by careful questioning of the secretary, subjects had indeed searched out the length of time they would be confined without making the secretary specify the exact time.

A demand characteristic interpretation specifies that the subject knows the length of time the ordeal will last and has some idea of the kind of behavior expected. This "idea" of what is expected can be completely idiosyncratic on the part of the subject. What is important is that he/she forms the idea and produces the behavior before it is too late to disappoint the experimenter. In the Antarctic situation and at the space station, it might be possible to predict that *nothing* will occur if the demand characteristics are such that nothing is expected of the subjects. Thus, a high demand characteristic of any environment can be a person (experimenter, doctor) whose presence and/or manner would lead anyone to anticipate normal behavior was expected.

This short review is not enough to firmly establish the third-quarter phenomenon as a universal entity. Much future work must be done to establish or disconfirm its existence in a variety of situations. The most that a short chapter like this can do is to point out the possibility of the existence of the phenomenon and to plead for more research.

A final word must be addressed to the design consequences of the third-quarter phenomenon. It should be obvious that not only designers of space and terrestrial expedition habitats but also planners, city managers, law enforcement personnel, architects, and landscape architects have a stake in such knowledge. Many of the existing isolated sites have to retrofit their designs in order to accommodate the third-quarter discomforts. One strategy at Fort Wainwright in Alaska was to have a February "breakaway" and fly out the wives of personnel to Anchorage for a short vacation. Other strategies are to increase the amount of indoor private space so that personnel can withdraw during this period. This suggests the radial design of Izumi (1965), which allows choice of public and private spaces. Still other strategies are to lighten schedules, have celebrations, or create distracting tasks. There are, of course, no fixed rules. Ideally, if the demand characteristics are responsible for the phenomenon, it could be eliminated entirely. Yet, for the immediate future, each situation has its own limitations in time, expense, and space available. The important aspect is that if one has the knowledge of when the phenomenon is likely to occur, one can plan for it in both social programming and design considerations.

## References

Bechtel, R. B., & Ledbetter, C. B. (1976). *The temporary environment: Cold regions habitability*. Hanover, NH: Cold Regions Research and Engineering Laboratory.

Connors, M. M., Harrison, A. A., & Akins, F. R. (1985). *Living aloft: Human requirements for extended spaceflight*. (NASA SP-483). Washington, DC: National Aeronautics and Space Administration.

Earls, J. H. (1969). Human adjustment to an exotic environment. *Archives of General Psychiatry, 20*, 117–123.

Gunderson, E. K. E., & Nelson, P. (1963). Adaptation of small groups to extreme environments. *Aerospace Medicine, 34*, 1111–1115.

Harrison, A. A., & Connors, M. M. (1984). Groups in exotic environments. In L. Berkowitz (Ed.), *Advances in experimental social psychology Vol. 18*, (pp. 50–88). New York: Academic Press.

Izumi, K. (1965). Psychosocial phenomena and building design. *Building Research, 2*, 9–11.

Lebedev, V. (1980). Stages of psychological adaptation under altered conditions of existence. *So Voprosy Psikhologii, 4*, 50–59.

Orne, M. (1987, August). *Demand characteristics in REST and health psychology.* Invited lecture to the Third International Conference on REST.

Palmai, G. (1963). Psychological observations on an isolated group in Antarctica. *British Journal of Psychiatry, 109*, 364–370.

Popkin, M., Stillner, V., Osborn, L., Pierce, C. M., & Shurley, J. T. (1974). Novel behaviors in an extreme environment. *American Journal of Psychiatry, 131*, 651–654.

Rohrer, J. (1961). Interpersonal relationships in isolated small groups. In B. Flaherty (Ed.), *Psychological aspects of manned spaceflight*. New York: Columbia University Press.

Solomon, R. (1980). The opponent-process theory of acquired motivation. *American Psychologist, 35*, 691–712.

Solomon, R., & Corbit, S. (1974). An opponent-process theory of motivation. *Psychological Review, 81*, 119–145.

Vinograd, S. (Ed.). (1974). *Studies of social group dynamics under isolated conditions*. St Louis: Washington University Medical Center.

# 24

# Communication Issues of Spaceflight

MARY M. CONNORS

Before examining the communication issues of spaceflight, we might find it useful to try to understand what is implied by "communication" and "communication issues." In ordinary speech, the term "communication" is used to describe a variety of activities, and its particular meaning can be understood only by reference to the context in which it is used. Among communication professionals, there is a similar ambiguity of meaning. For instance, the distinction between "communication" as an activity and the elements that constitute communication (e.g., the message, the transmission link, the supporting hardware, and so forth) or between communication activity and the industry as a whole is frequently blurred. In addition, over the years, communication theorists and researchers have significantly changed their view of what drives communication activity. During one period, the initiator, or sender, of the message was thought to be primary (Lasswell, 1948); later, the emphasis shifted to the receiver (Bauer, 1964). Still later, a convergent view emerged that posits communication to be a shared information orientation involving both the sender and the receiver (Schramm, 1971).

While definitions that are both broad enough to satisfy the need for a comprehensive concept and narrow enough to be descriptive and useful continue to elude us, there are significant areas of agreement. For instance, it is generally agreed that communication involves the *movement of information*. Further, communication can best be thought of as a *process* rather than an event; as *dynamic* rather than static; and as somehow *interactive*, not just imposed or administered. It should also be emphasized that communication bears a particular, though not an exclusive, *relationship to language*. Communication should also be thought of as a *fundamental human activity*, one that gives form to any social group, whether that group be composed of two individuals or whether it be a family, a corporation, or a nation. While concurring with these descriptions, we will, for our purposes, view communication primarily as a coming together in understanding, and communication issues as those factors that influence this coming together.

With this brief introduction, we can begin to explore the communication issues of space. When considering these issues, we must not overlook general concerns (i.e., communication issues as they would exist in any group), but more particularly, we must consider communication issues that follow from the special environment of space. This environment includes weightlessness, the noise level and transmission characteristics of the atmosphere, the amount of information that must be conveyed via mediated modes of communication, and the possible influences of language and other cultural differences.

In the current chapter, we will explicate communication issues related to extended spaceflight from the perspective of human factors, or behavioral science (vs. an engineering, or hardware, approach). Specifically, we will look at communication between and among members of the flight crew, communication between the flight crew and the ground, and some examples of the psychological or psychodynamic aspects of space communication.

## Intracrew Communication

Issues of communication among members of a spaceflight crew have both verbal and nonverbal components. Within the spacecraft, lift-off and reentry are accompanied by very high noise levels that can hinder verbal communication. However, these phases are brief and therefore tolerable. More important, the cruise phase of the flight is accompanied by a background noise level that, although much lower, is still about equal to that of a busy office. This cruise noise level has been identified as sometimes interfering with the communication process during spaceflight (Kelly, 1987; Willshire & Leatherwood, 1985). In addition, there can be transmission characteristics associated with the internal ambience of the spacecraft that contribute to miscommunication. Although not a problem on all flights, artificial atmosphere can influence verbal communication if, for instance, the ambient gas mixture modifies normal voice characteristics or if the internal pressure of the craft causes audio signals to dissipate at a rate different from that on Earth. Problems in verbal communication were particularly noted on Skylab, America's largest space vehicle. Here the astronauts reported that their voices dropped off quickly and that they had to shout to be heard (Johnson, 1974). When devising warning systems or determining how to present critical information, planners must take into account the potential loss in verbal or auditory communication capability within the spacecraft. Providing supplementary visual information or building other forms of redundancy into the system may be required to offset communication loss.

At the same time that astronauts may not be able to hear each other as well in flight as they would on the ground, nonverbal cues accompanying verbal messages may also be distorted. In space, gesturing cues are altered, at least during the initial adaptation period. Facial expression also changes in space. Without the pull of gravity, fluid floats to the upper region of the body, resulting in a redness and puffiness of the face that can hide expression. Distancing cues are also affected. On Earth, an individual rests by staying still and must exert energy to move from one location to another. In spaceflight, the opposite is true. When, as in the case of space, one cannot easily hold his body placement, distancing cues lose their meaning. There are also losses introduced by the angle at which one space traveler approaches another. On Earth, while walking or sitting upright, one has easy visual access to the facial expressions of others. In space, depending on the angle of approach, one may be looking at an upside-down face or a pair of shoes, in which case facial expression has no communication value.

A communication issue that will become increasingly important in future spaceflight is language diversity. As we move to explore the near planets and beyond, it is almost inevitable that flight costs will demand multinational sponsorship and result in crews drawn from divergent cultures. In difficult and demanding situations, even skilled multilinguals can miscommunicate. And, over the long term, language/cultural differences can result in a basic failure to connect, e.g., a failure to understand the humor and other subtleties of language on which so much human interaction depends.

Intracrew communication patterns are sensitive measures of how effectively groups are functioning. Kanki, Lozito, and Foushee (1989) have shown that communication patterns can distinguish high-performance from low-performance teams. From this observation, it can be inferred that communication not only is an important process in itself but also might serve as a measure of how well other activities in space are being accomplished.

## Crew–Ground Communication

While significant intracrew communication differences can be identified, the major communication differences of spaceflight occur between the crew and the ground. All communication external to the spacecraft must be conducted through media, i.e., by audio, video, or computer/telegraphic means. The sheer volume of such information constitutes the single most distinguishing feature of space communication and leads to numerous efficacy issues. The following are among the more significant intergroup questions for spaceflight. How does the fact of mediated communication influence the communication process? What types of information need to be transmitted in the space setting? What modes of transmission best accommodate the various categories of information? What other considerations should be included in the planning process?

## Mediated Communication

Led by efforts of the Communications Study Group of the British Post Office, the 1970s saw a focused effort to understand the dynamics of mediated interactive communication. This same decade saw the emergence of the field of teleconferencing, a field that placed a new emphasis on group communication as opposed to individual or mass communication (Connors, 1973). The results of studies published over the last 15 years have brought us well along the road to understanding the dynamics of mediated communication and, especially, the differences in dynamics between mediated and direct communication. Clearly, mediated communication lacks the richness and redundancy of face-to-face communication. Direct communication travels across channels so numerous and so interconnected that their influence may go unacknowledged. Mediated communication passes along preselected and (relatively) narrow channels. For instance, full-motion video, although the medium most akin to direct communication, still allows us to see only what is selected on the camera at the moment. (A few attempts have been made to address this limitation [Brown, Geller, Goodnow, Hoecker, & Wish, 1980; Sticha, Hunter, & Randall, 1981]. However, providing simultaneous, relational views tends to greatly complicate design and operations and has rarely been adopted in practice.) While direct communication is information rich, mediated communication remains information limited. And, in general, while direct communication tends to be free flowing or random access, mediated communication often requires one or more "gatekeepers" who, either technically or substantively, process and interpret information for others in the group.

Although direct communication is usually the standard with which mediated communication is compared, direct communication is not always to be preferred (George, Coll, Strickland, Patterson, Guild and McEown, 1975; Noll, 1976). On the contrary, the various media bring their own unique qualities to the exchange, sometimes by focusing what might in a face-to-face meeting be a nondirected and nonprofitable discussion (Champness, 1973; Williams & Holloway, 1974) or else by providing the psychological distancing necessary to place an appropriate emphasis on the value of the arguments rather than on the status of the presenter (Hiltz, 1975; Hiltz & Turoff, 1976; Short, Williams, & Christie, 1976). The important point is not that mediated communication is better or worse than direct communication but that communicating via media is not the same as communicating directly and that these differences must be known, understood, and accommodated.

## Information to Be Transmitted

Having underscored the implications of mediated communication, we must understand the nature of the information being exchanged. For the space application, "information" must be viewed very broadly. At one point in the

TABLE 24.1. Categories of communication
activities.

---

Person-to-person media (group media)
  Flight support
  Mission support
    On-board experimentation
  Private
    Medical
    Family and friends
  In-flight training
Mass media
  Movies
  Radio/audio recordings
  Television/video recordings
  Newspapers
  Books

---

flight, the information required may be navigational coordinates; at another time, it may be the reassuring sound of a child's laugh. The general categories of communication activities expected for spaceflight are given in Table 24.1.

This table outlines two general classes of information: person-to-person (or group) communication and mass media. Person-to-person communications are generally interactive and require full-duplex channels. They may be thought of as supporting the flight itself (e.g., control, environmental, life support, monitoring, and so forth), the mission of the flight (satellite deployment or recapture, observations from space, on-board experiments), private communications (exchanged with physicians, attorneys, accountants, friends, and relatives), and in-flight training (noncritical spacecraft tasks, crew back-up capability, career development). Mass media are either carried on board or transmitted from the ground. Although less demanding from a transmission perspective, quantity will be high, since we can assume that space travelers will want to enjoy the benefits of the full range of mass media.

## Modes of Transmission

Questions concerning the form in which information is sent and the method by which it is received, searched, and displayed are among the most pressing human engineering issues of long-duration spaceflight. The popular image of the interior of a spacecraft is one of flashing, moving, multicolored indicators. The implied message is that limitless amounts of information can be displayed in this psychedelic manner with no significant problems resulting. In reality, there are several limitations to this scenario. First, for the foreseeable future at least, there is a limit to the power that can be made available for driving sophisticated displays. Whether this power is very strictly limited (e.g., the upcoming Space Station *Freedom*) or more liberally dispersed, power will remain a scarce commodity. But, there is another, more compelling reason why visual displays may supply only a partial solution to the information-deprived space traveler. The human observer can absorb only so much information at a time, and the information he or she is able to absorb is influenced by how it is presented. The environment of a "glass cockpit" has not resolved these problems on the modern aircraft, and cannot be expected to resolve them on future generations of spacecraft. In terms of the value of information itself, we know that astronauts already have suffered data overload and have complained that much of the "information" reaching them was of no consequence (Helmreich, Wilhelm, Tanner, Sieber, & Burgenbach, 1979). We must strive to ensure that astronauts receive not just data, but useful information, and that the information provided is presented in ways that will allow them to absorb, process, and apply it.

As there are significant differences between direct and mediated communication, so are there significant differences between modes of mediated communication. Media may be thought of in the broadest terms as computer/telegraphic, audio, or video based, with video further divided into (two-directional or one-directional) freeze frame, limited motion, compressed motion, and full motion. Table 24.2 demonstrates the verbal and nonverbal cues available with each broad media category (from Connors, Harrison, & Akins, 1985; following Kaplan and Greenberg, 1976). Differences between media express themselves in the efficacy with which a particular medium handles certain kinds of tasks. As can be inferred from Table 24.2 and as numerous studies have shown (see Johansen, Vallee, & Spangler, 1979), a simple conveyance of information can be handled by virtually any means. As communication becomes more complex (Connors & Swift, 1988; Connors, Lindsey & Miller, 1976) or as it includes more personal or emotional elements such as persuasion or bargaining, only certain media will suffice. This latter requirement has been identified as a need for "presence" (Morley & Stephenson, 1969; Short et al., 1976), a need generally satisfied only by direct communication or by broad-band, full-motion, interactive video.

TABLE 24.2. Communication as a function of medium.[a]

| Cue | Video | Audio | Computer/Telegraphic |
|---|---|---|---|
| Proxemic (distancing or placement) | — | — | — |
| Kinesic (facial expression and gestures) | X | — | — |
| Paralinguistic (amplitude, rate, and tenor of speech) | X | X | — |
| Linguistic (written or spoken word) | X | X | X |

[a]From M. M. Connors, A. A. Harrison, and F. R. Akins, 1985, *Living Aloft: Human Requirements for Extended Spaceflight* (NASA SP-483). Washington, DC: National Aeronautics and Space Administration.

From this brief analysis, it can be seen that media selection for spacecraft is not a simple procedure and that planning for effective and efficient communications requires, at a minimum, a clear understanding of all the elements of the tasks to be performed.

Delays introduced by distance cannot be reduced (by any known means) to less than those implicit in the speed of light. Therefore, a variable of paramount importance to communication researchers or advisors is space-flight destination. For instance, a multiyear flight of an manned, Earth-orbiting spacecraft is likely to introduce far fewer communication problems than a 1-year flight to Mars. As distance from Earth increases, time delays, at first inconsequential, will quickly render verbal exchange difficult. At greater distance, true interaction will be replaced by sequential monologues. Farther out, only one-way communication will be possible, although timely responses may still be expected. At still greater distances, one-way communication with significant response delay will be the only possibility. The particular distances/delays that result in changing interaction patterns and behaviors and the requirement for new system designs are part of the needed research base.

## Other Considerations

As indicated above, the preferred mode of exchanging information with the crew and the preferred method of displaying information to the crew will shift with the task being performed and with the distance from the source. All expected events of each mission should be analyzed as part of the communication planning process. One activity that could have particular significance for communication planning is the conduct of remote research or telescience. Telescience allows a ground-based experimenter to direct his on-board experiment, requiring the space crew to have little or no involvement. Here, the communication system needed is one that will allow the experimenter to query the system, to receive data on demand, and to interactively influence the conduct of the experiment based on the data received. Such an arrangement implies two-way data and, probably, one-way video from the spacecraft to the ground. If, instead, one were to assume a collaborative approach between the ground-based experimenter and an on-board crew-member, then two-way data, voice, and video might be indicated.

Time aloft can also be a driving variable in selecting communication links. To date, the United States has flown relatively short-duration flights. The U.S. flights have provided one-way video, allowing us to see the astronauts at work and to experience with them the sights of space and the visual images of satellites being deployed, telescopes being put in place, and so forth. The Soviet Union has stretched cosmonaut time in space to roughly a year, and the Russian program has included two-way video between the spacecraft and the ground. The intimacy supplied by the capability of seeing important persons on the ground may be a luxury on a short flight; it becomes far more important to the stability and health of a crew on a long-duration flight.

The mass media lend themselves to transmission from ground to spacecraft for all missions, since the delays involved are of little consequence in this unidirectional process. The questions here are ones of storage and, particularly, of display. As alluded to above, a plethora of screens displaying visual material is impractical. Some other method needs to be devised to provide space travelers the ease of access to written materials that is available through paper-based media. One possibility would be a functional equivalent that would allow "print" to be applied to "paper" that could later be recycled. If such a system could be developed (and ignoring for the moment the difficulties imposed by a closed environment), a limited amount of base material could be stored on board, and the astronaut could request that a book or magazine be copied from an on-board data base or from a data base on the ground. Alternatively, an electronic book might be developed. The essential elements are that the person should be able to "hold" the material and scan it. Since computer scanning (i.e., scanning or search via specific physical locations, word strings, or other discrete and predefined criteria) represents only one small subset of human scanning, a satisfactory electronic book might ultimately be more difficult to develop than recyclable hard copy. If recyclable hard copy, electronic books, or some other acceptable method of displaying large amounts of printed material could be developed, it would be a boon to long-duration spaceflight, and, more generally, to the terrestrial world of electronic information systems.

## Psychodynamics of Space Communication

Communication issues introduce a number of questions that have a direct impact on the way crewmembers relate to one another and to those on the ground. The following are examples of some of the significant interpersonal issues for long-duration spaceflight: formal versus informal networks; boundary roles between groups; the relationship of crewmembers and principal investigators; contact with family and friends; and the allocation of responsibilities between crew and ground, between people and machines. To address these and other communications questions requires the active participation of communication researchers, planners, and others interested in the communication dynamic.

### Formal versus Informal Networks

In most organizational settings, communication is conducted through both formal and informal networks. When formal networks fail to yield desired results, workers revert to informal channels, i.e., to identifying and working through those individuals who, regardless of their official position or job description, are able to get the job done. Informal networks are chosen—they are not imposed—and they often result in more efficient as well as more satisfying contacts. In space, communication will be largely limited to predetermined, formal channels. This restriction places a heavy burden on the researcher and the planner to try to anticipate the requirements of the space traveler, i.e., to meet both rational and emotional needs, and to provide mechanisms that will help crewmembers, not only in theory but also in fact. Since the planner cannot fully anticipate how events will develop, he or she should, wherever possible, include a safety valve or "work-around." One way to do this is to provide access to broad-based networks such as the worldwide telephone system, national/international electronic mail networks, and so on.

## Boundary Roles

When two or more groups work together to accomplish a task, certain individuals must act as buffers between the differing interests. These individuals are formally known as boundary-role persons (Adams, 1976), or more simply, as liaisons. The primary tasks of such individuals are to interpret the interests and concerns of each side to the other in a way that will allow the activity to progress smoothly. Two groups frequently have conflicting goals and almost always have at least some conflicting perceptions. When one group is also isolated and confined, thinly disguised or even open hostility toward the outside group can result. In spaceflight, the role of boundary-role persons is especially demanding. Both on board the spacecraft and on the ground, these individuals must interpret the ground personnel to the crew and the crew to the ground personnel, filtering out any potentially disruptive elements in the exchange. In both cases, these individuals must be carefully selected and trained against the dangers of conveying too much information (e.g., passing along negative responses that are only transient expressions of frustration) or too little information (e.g., assuming personal control over information intended for the group). The persons filling this role on board the spacecraft will be in particular need of support since, like all liaisons, they are in danger of being identified with the interests of the outside group and, potentially, of being excluded from the crew activities. Within a space crew, such exclusion would constitute an intolerable situation.

## Crewmember/Principal Investigator Relationships

As mentioned above, there is considerable interest in the possibilities of remote science or telescience. In addition to influencing facility/equipment planning, telescience could also influence social dynamics. From a strictly experimental standpoint, arguments might be offered that telescience places control of the experiment directly in the hands of the responsible individual, freeing the experimenter from dependence on the availability of on-board crew support and freeing crewmembers for other mission activities. However, the benefits possible from actively involving crewmembers in space research should also be taken into account. First, there could be positive benefits to the research itself from a collaborative approach. Telescience, no matter how well planned, will lack a certain flexibility, and variables that are not expected prior to flight could be forever excluded. Second, there could be positive benefits from collaboration both to crewmembers and to the mission as a whole. For long-duration flights, it will be necessary to occupy the crew with meaningful work; on-board experimentation would be a leading candidate to fill this need. Although it might be possible to combine the advantages of remote experimentation and on-board support, it would be expected that maximum crew support will be given only if the crewmember feels fully a part of the research effort. To do this, he or she would need to understand and appreciate the purpose of the experiment, contribute to its final design and execution, and benefit in some way from participation, e.g., by sharing authorship of the resulting reports. The psychodynamics as well as the engineering and operational aspects of spaceflight research need to be considered and evaluated before informed mission decisions can be made.

## Contact with Family and Friends

Most observers believe that on long-duration flights, contact between space crewmembers and their families and friends back home will be an important requirement for emotional stability and sound mental health. The Soviets have made use of full-duplex communication channels, not only for the substantive exchange of information but also for emotional support. However, questions still remain. How much of such communication is beneficial to the crew and to the family? Under what conditions should this communication be encouraged? It has been found that as flight progresses, space travelers make ever-greater use of opportunities for outside contact (Gazenko, Myasnikov, Ioseliani, Kozerenko, & Uskov, 1979). This use could reflect positive factors such as more free time, greater ease with living in space, and anticipation of reestablishing home contacts; or it could reflect a disenchantment with on-board life and/or a need for outside contact and stimulation. When we more fully understand the dynamics of outside contact and its effects on the on-board life of the space crew, we will be prepared to offer better recommendations on how such channels might be constituted and used.

## Allocation of Responsibilities

One of the most significant issues for future spaceflight—and one with direct communication impact—is how responsibilities are to be distributed between the spacecraft and the ground and between human and automated systems.

As noted above, the distance traveled from Earth will affect the distribution of tasks. In order for responses to be made in a timely manner, many of the decisions that are now made — and controls that are now initiated — from the ground will have to be made and initiated by the space crews or their on board systems. The necessity for making decisions on board the spacecraft introduces new requirements for expertise to be immediately available to the space crew. On-board data bases, expert systems, and other intelligent aids will be required to help replace the expertise now resident on the ground. As we move towards increased automation, we must do so with great caution.

As tasks are redistributed, new questions of interpersonal dynamics may be expected to surface (Connors, 1989; Statler and Connors, 1990). There is ample evidence that changing the level of automation changes the dynamics of how the crew functions. For instance, it has been observed that the level of human communication within an aircraft cockpit decreases as the influence of automated systems increases. More generally, decreasing the human involvement and increasing the role of automated systems often results in the substitution of one problem for another and, frequently, a larger one for a smaller one (Wiener, 1988).

However, since interplanetary flight will require greater crew autonomy than an Earth-orbiting flight requires, advanced missions must include a high level of on-board automation. The challenge is to direct our efforts towards assuring that increased crew autonomy is accomplished without compromise to safety or productivity. The assignation and implementation of tasks between the crew and the ground, between the human operator and the robotic operator, between ground-based computer systems and on-board computer or expert systems are among the most demanding, emerging questions for future spaceflight research.

## Conclusion

Communication issues of space that need to be addressed include those activities and concerns that exist in any organization but, more important, those activities and concerns that are specific to spaceflight. Among the latter are issues related to the environment of the spacecraft and issues arising from the need to communicate with the ground. Significant questions also relate to the psychodynamics of communication, i.e., the way in which the communication process influences relationships among crewmembers and with those on the ground. These issues need to be considered from a broad behavioral science perspective, an approach that is essential to ensuring task effectiveness, social acceptability, and efficient use of resources.

# References

Adams, J. S. (1976). The structure and dynamics of behavior: Organizational boundary roles. In M. D. Dunnette (Ed.), *Handbook of organizational and industrial psychology* (pp. 1175–1199). Chicago: Rand McNally.

Bauer, R. (1964). The obstinate audience. *American Psychologist, 19*, 319–328.

Brown, E. F., Geller, V. J., Goodnow, J. E., Hoecker, D. G., & Wish, M. (1980). Some objective and subjective differences between communication over two videoconferencing systems. *IEEE Transactions on Communications, 28*, 759–764.

Champness, B. (1973). *The assessment of users' reactions to contravision* (Paper No. E/73250/CH). London: Communications Study Group.

Connors, M. M. (1973). *Teleconferencing systems: Current status and effects on user population.* Unpublished manuscript, Stanford Univerisity, Communications Department, Palo Alto, CA.

Connors, M. M., (1989, July). *Crew systems dynamics: Combining human and automated systems.* SAE Technical Paper Series No. 891530, 19th Intersociety Conference on Environmental Systems, San Diego.

Connors, M. M., & Swift, D. A. (1989). Freeze frame video: A users' evaluation. International Teleconferencing Assn. (ITCA) Yearbook.

Connors, M. M., Lindsey, G., & Miller, R. H. (1976). *The NASA teleconferencing system: An evaluation.* NASA TM-X-74160 National Aeronautics and Space Administration–Ames Research Center.

Connors, M. M., Harrison, A. A., & Akins, F. R. (1985). *Living aloft: Human requirements for extended spaceflight* (NASA SP-483). Washington, DC: National Aeronautics and Space Administration.

Gazenko, O. G., Myasnikov, V. I., Ioseliani, K. K., Kozerenko, O. P., & Uskov, F. N. (1979). *Important problems of space psychology: As evidenced by Salyut-6–Soyuz manned missions.* Paper presented at the XXVII International Congress of Space Medicine. Manila, Phillipines, Oct. 8-12.

George, D. A., Coll, D. C., Strickland, L. H., Patterson, S. A., Guild, P. D., & McEown, J. M. (1975). *The wired city laboratory and educational communication project, 1974-1975.* Ottawa: Carleton University.

Helmreich, R., Wilhelm, J., Tanner, T. A., Sieber, J. E., & Burgenbach, S. (1979). A critical review of the life sciences project management at Ames Research Center for the Spacelab Mission Development Test III (NASA TP-1364.). Mountain View, CA: National Aeronautics and Space Administration.

Hiltz, S. R. (1975). *Communications and group decision making: Experimental evidence on the potential impact of computer conferencing* (Research Report No. 2). Newark, NJ: New Jersey Institute of Technology, Computer Conferencing and Communications Center.

Hiltz, S. R., & Turoff, M. (1976). *Potential impacts of computer conferencing upon managerial and organizational styles.* Newark, NJ: New Jersey Institute of Technology, Computer Conferencing and Communications Center.

Johansen, R., Vallee, J., & Spangler, K. (1979). *Electronic meetings: Technical alternatives and social choices.* Reading, MA: Addison-Wesley.

Johnson, C. C. (1974). Skylab experiment M487: Habitability/Crew quarters. In W. C. Schneider & T. E. Hanes (Eds.), *The Skylab results, Advances in the astronautical sciences, 31, part 1.* (pp. 315–333). Tarzana, CA: American Astronomical Society.

Kanki, B. G., Lozito, S., & Foushee, H. C. (1989). Communication indexes of crew coordination. *Aviation, Space, and Environmental Medicine, 60*(1), 56–60.

Kaplan, Kalman J. and Greenberg, Carl I. (1976). Regulation of interaction through architecture, travel and telecommunications. Environmental Psychology and Nonverbal Behavior, 1(1).

Kelly, A. (1987). *Communication in space: A questionnaire for astronauts and cosmonauts.* Palo Alto, CA: Stanford University, Communications Department.

Lasswell, H. (1948). The structure and function of communication in society. In L. Bryson (Ed.), *The communication of ideas* (pp. 37–51). New York: Harper.

Morley, I. E., & Stephenson, G. M. (1969). Interpersonal and inter-party exchange: A laboratory simulation of an industrial negotiation at the plant level. *British Journal of Psychology, 60*, 543–545.

Noll, A. M. (1976). Teleconferencing communications activities. *Communications Society, 14*, 8–14.

Schramm, W. (1971). The nature of communication between humans. In W. Schramm & D. F. Roberts (Eds.), *The process and effects of mass communication* (pp. 3–53). Urbana: University of Illinois Press.

Short, J. A., Williams, E., & Christie, B. (1976). *The social psychology of communications.* London: J. Wiley & Sons Ltd.

Statler, Irving C. and Connors, Mary M. (1990). Issues on combining human and non-human intelligence. Proceedings of the Space Operations, Applications and Research Conference (SOAR '90) Albuquerque, N.M., June 26–28, in press.

Sticha, P. J., Hunter, G. M., & Randall, L. S. (1981). *Research into teleconferencing* (Report No. TR-80-9-314). McLean, VA: Decisions and Designs, Inc.

Wiener, E. L. (1988). Cockpit automation. In E. L. Wiener & D. C. Nagel (Eds.), *Human factors in aviation* (pp. 433–461). New York: Academic Press.

Williams, E., & Holloway, S. (1974). *The evaluation of teleconferencing: Report of a questionnaire study of users' attitude to the Bell conference television system* (Paper No. P/74247/WL). London: Communications Study Group.

Willshire, K. F., & Leatherwood, J. D. (1985). *Astronaut survey of shuttle vibroacoustic environment* (PIR No. SD-6). Hampton, VA: National Aeronautics and Space Administration–Langley Research Center, Structures Directorate, Acoustics Division.

# Part IV.  Interventions and Outcomes

## Introduction

In this final section, we feature chapters that propose means for improving the fit between people, on the one hand, and isolated and confined settings, on the other. Techniques include (1) selection, or choosing crews on the basis of abilities, motives, and interests; (2) training, or advance preparation for a mission; and (3) engineering, that is, arranging environments to accommodate the behavioral propensities of their human occupants. "Environments" is used here in the most general sense and includes social and cultural as well as physical dimensions.

The first two chapters in this section, by Jean Rivolier and his associates, focus on selection. The first of these discusses assessments made during the International Biomedical Expedition to the Antarctic, and the second proposes an improved, comprehensive, psychobiological approach for personnel selection and training. These procedures are designed to prepare a winter-over crew for an Antarctic simulation of an extended-duration, manned space mission and space itself. Next, Kirmach Natani describes how neurometric measures may be useful for selecting individuals for work in isolated and confined environments. His analysis suggests that exercise of the antigravity muscles may be one key to maintaining the highest levels of cognitive and psychomotor performance.

In the following chapter, Arlene Levine describes how long-duration space missions can lead to chronic and episodic stress and discusses stress amelioration techniques through training in meditation and yoga. According to Levine, progressive muscle relaxation, biofeedback, and self-hypnosis may be of use on tomorrow's space missions. Douglas Raybeck reminds us that Western cultures, particularly those of Northern Europe and North America, place a strong emphasis on personal privacy. Life in situations where territories are ill-defined or where crowding is rife can produce stress and conflict. Raybeck reviews several solutions to the problems of crowding that have been devised by various cultures throughout the world, including the Malays, Indonesians, Japanese, and Arabs, and assesses the applicability of these solutions to extraterrestrial living.

There follows a series of chapters that address issues in environmental design. Yvonne A. Clearwater and Richard G. Coss describe their experimental work, which demonstrates the potential utility of various esthetic countermeasures to reduce stress, relieve boredom, and enhance the habitability of stimulus-impoverished, confining habitats. Richard Haines discusses the role of windows. Haines, originator of the Window Dimensions—WINDIM—model, notes that although windows may be points of structural weakness, they serve so many important psychological and other functions that they still need to be incorporated in outer space and analogous habitats. The concluding chapter on environmental design, by Paul Klaus, proposes that introducing microenvironments—miniature living representations of landscapes—will have important stress-reducing properties and improve the quality of life in polar and outer space settings.

The final contributed chapters in this book address mechanisms for regulating conflict among people and between groups. Don Scott notes that the informal, community-based, conflict-resolution system in San Francisco's Visitacion Valley District has worked for over a decade to help neighbors live in peace with one another. Characterized by simplicity, this program, which has inspired similar programs elsewhere, may be easily adapted for "keeping the peace" in Antarctica and outer space. Harry Almond notes that competition for territory and resources in previously uninhabited areas provides a base for international friction and conflict. He describes some of the pitfalls and loopholes that exist in Antarctic and space law and shows ways in which international agreements and treaties in Antarctica can be improved and extended to regulate people and nations in outer space. Finally, F. Kenneth Schwetje reviews some of the constraints that Antarctic and space environments are likely to place upon our normal legal and judicial processes. He offers the Uniform Code of Military Justice as a possible prototype for application in outer space.

# 25

# The International Biomedical Expedition to the Antarctic: Psychological Evaluations of the Field Party

JEAN RIVOLIER, GENEVIEVE CAZES, AND IAN MCCORMICK

Psychological studies of IBEA participants were conducted to test the efficacy of various methods of psychological assessment and to explore the effects of field conditions on psychological functioning. The research design was longitudinal and involved testing before, during, and after the expedition. Through this research, we hoped to (1) identify the determinants of adaptation to the Antarctic environment; (2) identify new and efficient means for ameliorating the problems that arise in the field; and (3) sharpen selection procedures for future space missions.

## Procedures

Before and after the mission, tests were conducted by two psychologists who did not accompany the field party to Antarctica. Prior to departure, they established prognoses on each member of the field team and on the team as a whole; these prognoses were kept secret from the field team, including the field psychologist. The reassessment following the field party's return provided the opportunity to validate the prognoses. Most of the tests used during the pretest and posttest are classical, and it is not necessary to describe them in detail (Table 25.1). These traditional techniques were supplemented by special biographical and motivational questionnaires and through observing the members of the field party interacting with one another in a clinical setting.

Premission prognoses and postmission outcomes were then related to psychological data collected in the field. These data were obtained from three sources: observations made by a trained psychologist who accompa-

TABLE 25.1. Psychological instruments used during the
International Biomedical Expedition to the Antarctic.

Pretest measures
  *Individual measures*
    Clinical interview
    Medical questionnaire
    Biographical questionnaire
    Motivational questionnaire
    Recent life change questionnaire
    Family questionnaire
    Wechsler Adult Intelligence Scale (WAIS)
    Thematic Apperception Test (TAT)
    Rorschach Psychodiagnostics
    Minnesota Multiphasic Personality Inventory (MMPI)
    Rosenzweig Frustration Test
    Gottschalk Content Analysis Scale
    MacKay's Self Report Inventory
    Hopkins's Symptom Checklist
    Videotaped Interpersonal Distance Measure
    Cognitive Test
  *Group measures*
    Matrix of Interindividual and Intraindividual Processes in Group
    Group Dynamic Measure
En route measures
    Psychologist's observations
    Daily diaries
    Self-reports and peer reports
    Relational Grid and Group Interaction Measurements
    Free discussions (tape recorded)
Posttest measures
  *Individual measures*
    Interview
    Unstructured personal account
    Sociability and leadership questionnaire
    MacKay's Self Report Inventory
    Hopkins's Symptom Checklist
    Videotaped Interpersonal Distance Measure
    Family questionnaire
  *Group measures*
    Matrix of Interindividual and Intraindividual Processes in Group
    Group Dynamic Measure

nied the expedition, self-reports, and peer evaluations. Instruments used
during the field phase included standard psychometric measures (Table
25.1); diaries; medical, mood, and sleep questionnaires; adaptability questionnaires; the relational grid, a measure of group interaction; and, once or
twice, MacKay's Self Report Inventory, Hopkins's Symptom Checklist, Ro-
senzweig's Picture Frustration Test, a Family Questionnaire, and a General
Field Questionnaire.

# Data Analysis

The quantity and diversity of data precluded a conventional clinical analysis. Instead, observations were organized within a framework consisting of preselected and antecedent and consequent variables. There were three antecedent variables, or causes: *C1*, which related to the living environment (variations in the weather and so forth); *C2*, which related to the working environment (logistical and scientific tasks); and *C3*, consisting of the proximal (field) and distal (home) psychological environments. There were four consequent variables, or effects. *V1* consisted of personal reactions: variations in mood including sadness, depression, worry, emotional withdrawal, apathy, and so forth. *V2* consisted of social reactions to the leader and to peers: irritability, aggression, social withdrawal, and so forth. *V3* consisted of physical and psychosomatic reactions such as somatic problems, psychophysiological responses, and accidents. *V4* consisted of "occupational reactions," that is, variations in motivation and work performance.

# Results

Although we cannot present the results in detail, we can provide an overview of the highlights (see Table 25.2 and Fig. 25.1). On the whole, the quantitative data suggest that the subjects did well during the field expedition. There was, however, considerable scattering of scores, and the generally positive picture suggested by the standardized tests is tempered by frequent reports of boredom, weariness, homesickness, bad temper, anxiousness, and difficulties posed by separation from one's family.

Using the "limit of confidence" of two standard deviations from the mean, we found no statistical differences between subjects who were very well adapted and those who were not. Subjects' ratings of themselves tended to be more positive than peer ratings of them, and the positive pictures presented by the quantitative self-ratings were not always supported by accompanying written narratives. The observer felt that the greatest number of difficulties were experienced at the beginning and end of the traverse; the subjects felt that the greatest number of difficulties occurred at the end. The most trouble-free period centered around the halfway mark, Day 55.

There were interpersonal difficulties within the team. Scores for leadership were generally lower than those for sociability, but the officially designated leader did receive the highest leadership scores. Displays of bad temper and open hostility were infrequent; there were, however, latent tensions, and the social climate was generally disagreeable. Some participants were highly unpopular with their peers, and one was undeniably isolated. There was some factionalism along national lines; a subgroup of three subjects of the same nationality was not very well accepted by several other members of

TABLE 25.2. Quantitative values for variable $V_1$ (personal reactions) from different instruments.[a]

| $V_1$-Personal reactions | $M_1$ | | $M_2$ | | $M_3$ | | Reference Scale → Good | Bad |
|---|---|---|---|---|---|---|---|---|
| | m | σ | m | σ | m | σ | | |
| Adaptability questionnaire ($\Sigma T_3$) | 2.03 | 1.31 | | | 1.48 | 1.01 | 0→5 | |
| Adaptability questionnaire (day 87) | 1.73 | 1.27 | 1.75 | 0.75 | 1.36 | 0.81 | 0→5 | |
| General field questionnaire | | | | | | | | |
| Q.5 Psychologically | | | | | 1.20 | 0.75 | 0→5 | |
| Q.13 Separation with family | | | | | 1.73 | 1.27 | 0→5 | |
| Self-report of mood and sleep | | | | | | | | |
| Q.1 % answers "rather low morale" | | | | | 4.2 | | | |
| Family questionnaire | | | | | | | | |
| Q.5 Coping with partner's absence | | | | | 2.6 | 1.2 | 5→1 | |
| Q.4 Coping if accident in family | | | | | 2.9 | 1.3 | 5→1 | |
| Q.1 Anxious about injury of your partner | | | | | 3.4 | 0.92 | 5→1 | |
| Q.2 Anxious about partner failing to return | | | | | 4.4 | 1.21 | 5→1 | |
| Q.6 Confident that relationships will stand the strain of separation | | | | | 4.7 | 0.47 | 5→1 | |

[a]From J. Rivolier, R. Goldsmith, D. L. Lugg, and A. J. W. Taylor (Eds.), 1988, *Man in the Antarctic*. London: Taylor and Francis. Copyright 1988 Taylor and Francis. Used with permission.

the team. This intergroup conflict was manifested in irritability, aggressiveness, and a lack of mutual aid.

An analysis of the MIPG data revealed some uneasiness surrounding the group structure and concerns about rejection by one's peers. Subjects tended

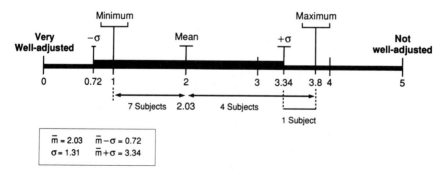

FIGURE 25.1. Values of the variable $V_1$ from the adaptability questionnaire (observer) and for $T_3$. (From J. Rivolier, R. Goldsmith, D. L. Lugg, and A. J. W. Taylor (Eds.), 1988, *Man in the Antarctic*. London: Taylor and Francis. Copyright 1988 Taylor and Francis. Used with permission.)

to be rather defensive and tended to deny or project their hostilities (for example, by accusing others of failing to communicate). Almost all diaries reported, with regret, the superficial nature of human relationships, hyperindividualism, and a lack of team cohesiveness.

With the exception of one subject, there were few physical (somatic) problems. However, there were many complaints about fatigue and some complaints about poor sleep and cold sensitivity.

There were important difficulties in the sphere of work. Most of these related to housekeeping tasks. Making and breaking camp, working with food, and other chores were painful, but conducting scientific work was fun and gratifying. Not all participants remained eager throughout, and those with an excessive work load became hyperactive or tense. Low performance was rationalized through criticizing the equipment or the organization of the expedition, and expressing doubts about the value of the work itself.

# Discussion

## *On the Methods*

Can we be satisfied with an observer's observations alone, or must we take into consideration data from other sources, such as test results, self-ratings, and peer nominations? There is a good correlation between the observer's reports and the reports of a subject's peers, but subjects tend to be lenient in their self-evaluations. One possibility, in an international expedition such as this, is that the observer belonged to the majority subgroup and that his observations reflected the opinions of this subgroup, with the result that his reports lacked objectivity. We consider it unwise to rely on an observer's reports alone.

Our research used both objective and open-ended instruments and generated both quantitative and qualitative data. Each approach and each type of data offers advantages and disadvantages. Without doubt, because they provide general and diversified data, the adaptability questionnaire and the general field questionnaire were essential. Additionally, the preferred relationships questionnaire and the group interaction measure, an unrivaled technique for evaluating group dynamics, were essential for understanding social phenomena. Diaries were a rich and important source of data, but it is quite exceptional that all participants would be willing to provide them, as they did for the International Biomedical Expedition to the Antarctic (IBEA). Global measures were useful but tended to flatten individual differences, especially over time.

We recognize limitations in our procedure of organizing results according to $V_1$-$V_4$. Additionally, we were forced to make certain arbitrary decisions and use procedures that could mask important forms of variability. For example, as a result of summation procedures, a subject with many minor

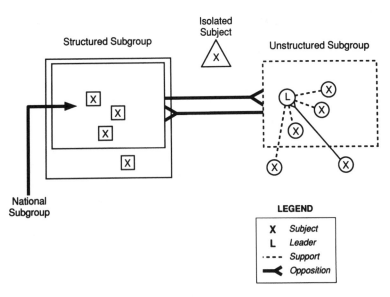

FIGURE 25.2. Qualitative valuations of the social reactions ($V_2$) from group interaction questionnaire (observer). (From J. Rivolier, R. Goldsmith, D. L. Lugg, and A. J. W. Taylor (Eds.), 1988, *Man in the Antarctic*. London: Taylor and Francis. Copyright 1988 Taylor and Francis. Used with permission.)

problems could receive the same overall adjustment score as a subject who had one major problem. However, our procedures have heuristic value. They make possible the definition of a limited number of key problem areas and facilitate the integration of data from many different sources.

A longitudinal, or diachronal, approach is imperative. Reliance on posttest data or after-the-fact reports masks underlying dynamics and leaves cause and effect in the dark.

## On the Results

Behind the apparently "happy ending" of the expedition are certain facts that should not remain hidden. These include (1) severe maladaptation on the part of one member, who had to be sent back home; (2) the development of opposed subgroups along national lines; and (3) clear maladjustment on the part of one-third of the team. By some measures, problems were the most pronounced at the beginning and, more particularly, at the end of the traverse. Despite the lack of open clashes, social relationships were not too good. Two subjects showed hyperaggressivity and hypercriticism; one experienced difficulties getting along with the leader, and one person remained isolated and lonely. However, high motivation to succeed prevented the disintegration of the group.

From the time of his arrival, the subject who had to be evacuated showed unusual problems on variables V1, V3, and V4. Initially, the trained observer noted little more than fatigue and worry, but half of this subject's peers described him in their diaries as preoccupied, strained, sad, tired, and lacking enthusiasm for work. He did not like the food, felt cold, slept badly; he got depressed, felt homesick, had difficulty in accepting separation from his family and friends, and reported the feeling that "he has fallen into a trap." He felt unused to the camping and work conditions, was very uncomfortable and anxious, and did "not understand why people come to the Antarctic."

One objective of the experiment was to ascertain whether undergoing special training for the cold with icy baths could enhance resistance to stress (see Hampton and Goldsmith, this volume). Based on psychology, we found no difference between the group that had been acclimated to cold baths and the group that had not.

## On the Causes of Stress

There were several causes of stress. Perhaps predominant was a difficulty for many participants to understand the common goals of the different subgroups and to focus too narrowly on their own personal research specialty. A second source of stress was an initial lack of appreciation of the rigors of the living and working conditions. Some participants were not aware of the difficulties that they would encounter. Did some of them hide the truth from themselves before departure, refuse to see, knowing that a full recognition of the realities would cause them to drop out, to forego the mission?

Disrupted family relationships formed another cause of stress. The separation itself was uncomfortable. Participants were not concerned about the continuation of their respective partner's attachment and fidelity, but they did worry about their partner's ability to deal with accidents or other problems that might arise in the course of the separation. The separation itself was also uncomfortable. Why this anxiety about the family back home? Could it be a way to express personal anxiety in a group where failure may not be tolerated? It may also be a justification through an interposed object (introprojection) of their boredom or their reluctance to be on the expedition.

Factionalism, or the emergence of a hypocritical national subgroup, was another important cause of perturbation. The problem did not center on language but, rather, on nationality, a way of life, a point of view, a particular attitude that had a slight connotation of imperialism.

Achieving the appropriate level of tension or motivation is essential. If there is too little, then the results are boredom, frustration, and depression. If there is too much, then there is too much anxiety, irritability, and grumbling about others.

## Conclusions

Many of our observations are consistent with earlier findings. We find the classical underlying causes of maladaptation (frustration, deception, dread, culpability) and, also, the classical manifestations in terms of attitudes, feelings, personalities, and roles. Individual coping mechanisms include criticism, justification, denial, displacement, projection, and somatization. Group coping mechanisms include self-satisfaction, eagerness to succeed, and scapegoating. Not all of these group mechanisms were comfortable for all group members.

Some of those who really kept good self-control (in the sense that they avoided severe clashes) showed a lack of psychological maturity. Conscious realization of the situation was almost nonexistent. This lack of appreciation of the realities of the situation made it difficult for subjects to distance themselves from the stressors, and they suffered. This was also true for the subjects who gave their best for the success of the expedition. They developed anxiety, became meddlesome, and tried to take over other people's tasks.

There are three general lessons to be learned from the psychological studies of the IBEA. In that expedition, there was no preselection; the idea was to include a range of people to see what would happen. Perhaps the first lesson is that psychological selection is an absolute necessity. Conventional methods of psychological selection are imperfect and by our estimate result in a 30% error rate, but this is better than the error rate associated with no psychological selection at all. Selection procedures should be multipronged and multifaceted and address psychophysiological, cognitive, and emotional variables (see Rivolier, Bachelard, & Cazes, this volume). It is particularly important to assess coping capacity, and we need to include interpersonal or group behaviors.

A second lesson is that advance preparation is essential. Both the logistical and scientific aspects of the mission must be hammered out in detail and clearly understood. Each participant must understand the overall scientific goals of the mission. The group cannot be assembled at the last minute; instead, it must meet repeatedly prior to departure. We recommend that the group practice living and working together in different and difficult environments. Equipment, materials, and procedures should be tested and tasks well rehearsed prior to departure.

Finally, we repeat — after many others — that motivation is the key to success. Unfortunately, motivation encompasses many different things in psychology, and it is not easy to identify and manipulate the key determinants. Maximizing motivation remains an essential research problem, and we are working on it.

# 26

# Crew Selection for an Antarctic-Based Space Simulator

JEAN RIVOLIER, CLAUDE BACHELARD, AND GENEVIEVE CAZES

The current chapter proposes an improved, comprehensive, psychobiological approach to crew selection and training. These procedures are designed for selecting a winter-over crew for an Antarctic simulation of a long-duration, manned space mission.

## Selection

People vary in their ability to withstand prolonged periods of isolation, confinement, and hardship. At one end of the continuum are those who are unable to adapt and who quickly yield to the trying conditions; at the other end of the continuum are those who not only resist the environmental pressures but also overcome the difficulties and even thrive. Case histories of men and women in mountains, on the seas, in the deserts, and in other demanding environments provide many illustrations of weakness and helplessness at one end of the continuum and a strong ability to cope at the other end of the continuum.

Certain personality structures and personal styles seem to distinguish those who cope with environmental stress from those who do not. The differences between individuals who cope and those who do not exist at several levels, including the cognitive, psychophysiological, and biological. All too often, selection procedures tend to focus on one of these levels (for example, the cognitive) while ignoring the others. On the basis of our knowledge of psychology and medicine and our experience working with the French Polar Expeditions, the European Space Agency (ESA), and other agencies related to exotic environments, we propose research intended to evaluate a comprehensive, multipronged approach to selecting crewmembers for an Antarctic-based outer space simulator. Possible predictors include measures of (1) cognitive style; (2) attention; (3) emotionality and anxiety; (4) defensiveness; (5) global behaviors; and (6) psychobiological functioning.

## Cognitive Style

Differences in people's information processing may be important determinants of their ability to adapt to isolation and confinement. Measures of cognitive style assess characteristic differences in the ways that people process information. Some people are flexible and open to new ways of viewing things; other people are not. This openness and flexibility may confer an advantage in dealing with new or unusual circumstances.

One important variable is field dependence, or the extent to which the person relies on an external frame of reference for interpreting the world. This can be assessed by the Embedded Figure Test, the more complex Tridimensional Embedded Figure Test, and the Rod and Frame Test. Other variables include reflection versus impulsivity (as assessed by the Matching Familiar Figure Test); categorization (Kagan's Conceptual Style Test); spatial estimation (the Paper Folding Test, Kohs' Cubes, or the French version of Koh's Cubes — Bonnardel's Cubes); and perceptual flexibility (Stroop Color-Word Test, Necker's Cube Test and other ambiguous figures tests). In each case, a flexible, open, unconstrained style that makes it possible to abandon old perspectives and develop new ones should encourage adaptation to novel conditions and, hence, facilitate adaptation to isolation and confinement.

## Studies of Attention

As noted in other chapters in this volume (A. F. Barabasz, chapters 3 and 17; M. Barabasz; Oliver) there have been many reports of "driftiness," or inability to concentrate, in Antarctica and, to a lesser extent, in outer space. Consequently, measures of attention may help us identify people who are likely to adapt. Although over a hundred years old, reaction-time tests of neural functioning may be useful, especially sophisticated, sensitive reaction-time tests. We suggest tests of short-term memory (ability to recollect a succession of figures or letters, for example) and also the ability to rapidly detect subtle differences between two lengthy sequences of numbers. In our opinion, many of the best known pencil-and-paper tests (e.g., Benton; Thurstone; and Zazzo) lack sufficient sensitivity.

## Studies of Emotionality and Anxiety

Both physiological and psychological measures can help us distinguish between emotional, anxiety-prone individuals and those who are likely to remain calm and emotionally controlled under high stress. Physiological measures related to emotionality and anxiety include heart and respiratory rates; muscle tonus; electrodermal resistance (a function of sweating); saliva pH; and catecholamines. Of the psychological measures, we prefer Spielberger's State–Trait Anxiety Indicator (or STAI) to the Taylor Manifest Anxiety Scale or the Cattell Anxiety Scale.

## Studies of Defense Mechanisms

Defense mechanisms can be harmful or useful in extreme situations. It depends on the defense mechanism. We use the Defense Mechanism Test of Kragh and the Defense Mechanism Inventory of Ihilevich and Gleser.

## Studies of Global Behaviors

Many global behaviors should affect adaptation to spaceflight environments. Decisions involving risk is one prominent consideration. A standard procedure for assessing risk-taking propensities is Kogan and Wallach's Choice Dilemma Procedure. However, potential crewmembers are likely to find this test less realistic and engaging than Fourcade and Bremond's TD 9. This latter instrument includes nine useful quantitative scales based on three clusters of items: choice items, action items, and person-versus-environment items. Many computerized tests and games can also be used for assessing decision making under risk.

Crowding is an important feature of some Antarctic and spaceflight environments, and people's tolerance for the approach of others may be an important consideration. There are several ways for separating people who can live in close quarters from those who respond to others' approaches with aggressiveness and territoriality. These include paper-and-pencil tests, the manipulation of figurines, and observations of real-life behaviors. Of particular use is the Videotaped Measure of Interpersonal Distance, developed in New Zealand.

Of course there are many other critical global qualities. Many key characteristics can be explored through interviews. Our procedures involve presenting subjects with real or imaginary situations and then asking them to describe how they would react. Through doing this systematically, we can look beyond specific responses and explore underlying personal qualities. For example, through these systematic interviews, we are able to explore resistance to the physical and mental demands of the environment, imagination, concentration, combativity, sociability, and so forth.

## Psychobiological Studies

Stress can be assessed through hormones and metabolic markers. Another selection procedure would involve subjecting candidates to stressful circumstances and then measuring catecholamines, cortisol, renin, prolactin, the stimulating hormones, and so forth. Prolonged exposure to stress can also have an adverse impact on immunological responses. Physiological measures of stress reveal adaptability and coping and are, hence, measures of personality.

Here we have focused upon individual selection. Each person's characteristics have to be studied in relation to those of the other members of the team, his or her position within the team, and the specific goals of the expedition.

## An Antarctic Simulator of a Spaceflight Environment

An Antarctic simulator would help make it possible to (1) identify stressors and stress symptoms associated with extended-duration spaceflight; (2) explore the relationship of personality traits to coping with isolation and confinement; and (3) assess and validate selection and training procedures. The study site itself should be close to the South Pole Station. Among the advantages of this location are (1) a very harsh climate that discourages movement outside the habitat; (2) extended periods of darkness forcing reliance on artificial lighting that can duplicate the lighting conditions expected in space; (3) high accessibility by airplane from McMurdo Station during the summer months; (4) high isolation from McMurdo Station during the winter months, the presumed period for the core portion of the study; and (5) a measure of safety provided by the proximity of South Pole Station.

### Organization

The number and gender of participants should depend upon anticipated spaceflight requirements. We suggest using people who do not know each other prior to the beginning of the exercise (a requirement that would eliminate established couples). We recommend subjects between the ages of 25 and 35, drawn from an international pool. Participants should be volunteers and, as in the case of the IBEA, serve simultaneously as researchers and subjects. Participants' occupations should be the same as those required of the potential space crew.

It is possible to envisage, depending on financing and logistics, the establishment of a large base that closely mimics a space station, a camp consisting of special heavy-duty tents or cabins, or something in between. Trips outside of the habitat should be prohibited, except as such trips mimic expected extravehicular activities. Light–dark cycles, food, work assignments, and leisure activities should all mimic those expected in space, with the exception that safety must be preserved at all times.

## *Program Outline*

Research should encompass selection, training, and the performance period in Antarctica.

### Selection

Selection would have two goals: (1) to select members of the winter-over team and (2) to compare various methods of selection with a view to their future application to selecting space crews. At the individual level, selection criteria must relate to the behaviors required of all team members and also to the specific behaviors required of individual participants. At the group level, selection must yield a collectivity of people who can live and work together as a team. It is essential to conduct dynamic group selection, using such methods as role playing and T-groups. Ideally, one should be able to observe the group in real-life situations (for example, in a remote mountain hut or on a yacht) or, at the very least, performing real tasks. Audiovisual recordings that can later be analyzed are useful here.

### Preparation and Training

Here, too, it is essential to work with individuals and with the entire group. The people chosen are considered to have a reserve of positive traits to help them cope with conditions of stress. It is essential that they put these resources to full use.

The first stage consists of making them aware of their personal resources. This is a period of education and explanation. For example, the individual is made to understand how he processes information and how he could process it more effectively. By recalling past experiences and their consequences, the resulting failure or success, and the way these situations were "lived," the individual is taught to make the best use possible of his skills and to control the situation.

Of course, everyone has weaknesses. These must be highlighted, and mere explanation is insufficient here. The individual must develop new patterns of behavior by being trained and taught behavioral or cognitive restructuring techniques. The training may be accompanied by the acquisition of learned methods of emotional control and relaxation.

Group work seems indispensable. Besides training people to work together, it is essential to give the group a structure. Two aspects of this training are worth noting here. First, difficulties of comprehension and potential problem areas need to be identified. The group will function only when a common language has to be found. Second, the group acquires a real perception of itself. Group members must have a collective awareness of the unit of which they are a part, its channels of communication, its hierarchies, values, and aims. This goes beyond the simple issue of prior logistic and scientific information.

Studies During the Stay

Studies during the stay should focus on stress, that is, on the impact of the situation on the thinking and behavior of individuals. The aim is to relate these observations to the information gathered before departure, particularly to the methods of selection and preparation used, in order to identify the cause of difficulties and assess how people cope and adapt.

Various studies could be conducted by monitoring adaptation on the basis of the four variables: psychological, social, physical, and occupational (see Rivolier, Cazes, & McCormick, this volume). Information gathered in the field must remain confidential and be neither read nor used until the end of the stay.

We recommend multiple methods. Psychological observations could be active and direct (by self) or indirect (by peers, by observer), qualitative, quantitative, sociometric, standardized, or specially devised. People may be subjected to questionnaires at various times during the stay, but extensive outside investigations should not be used, since they can cause disturbance that should be considered as a deviation from the norm. Passive techniques consist essentially in recording conversations or sequences of events. It may be noted that personal diaries are a relatively unrestricted and very useful source of information.

Psychophysiological studies should focus on three areas: the study of mental performance and fatigue (alertness, cognition, logic); the study of emotions and their control; and the study of sleeping patterns (and dreams).

Biological studies should relate essentially to hormones and immune defenses. Other substances produced mainly by the metabolism of lipids might also be monitored. Medical studies include the study of pathology, nutrition, physical fitness, and the menstrual cycle.

This project requires the approval of the National Science Foundation and would benefit from the support of ESA, the National Aeronautics and Space Adminstration, and the Scientific Committee on Antarctic Research.

# The Psychophysiology of Adaptation and Competence: Altered States of Consciousness During Antarctic Wintering

Kirmach Natani

Antarctic wintering on the polar plateau tends to produce a syndrome that has been clinically described as a combination of sleep disturbance, the reappearance of symptoms of old chronic diseases, general lassitude, sluggishness, and reduced working capacity coupled with irritability and apathy as well as occasional groundless fears—i.e., a "dysadaptation neurosis," according to Soviet sources (Danishevskii, Ponomarev, & Tikhomirov, 1967/ 1970). The resistance of this Antarctic syndrome to quantification and description by a number of commonly used psychometric techniques has been of interest for some time. Psychiatric mental health ratings have had little correlation with actual performance in field settings (Smith, 1966). On the other hand, most field results reported up to the present time have been frustratingly unremarkable, especially with regard to psychological factors. Wilson (1965) reported negative findings in the Antarctic for psychophysiological measures (cold-induced vasodilation [CIVD]) and neuropsychological techniques (critical flicker fusion [CFF]).

Periodic administrations of the Minnesota Multiphasic Personality Inventory (MMPI) have also produced equivocal results. The MMPI only began to yield results consistent with clinical observation when administered under the most extreme Antarctic conditions at the U.S. Plateau Station (Blackburn, Shurley, & Natani, 1973). However, it is noteworthy that the overall picture presented by the MMPI administrations at Plateau was one of significant improvement in psychological adjustment. An explanation for this finding is that, in general, the veterans of isolated duty appear to have benefited from the small-group acculturation experience and have developed an ability to form a complex impression of other individuals that includes tolerance for more deviant behavior in others as well as in themselves. Those individuals who show signs of positive psychological growth from isolated-duty experiences tend to be more mature, tough-minded and realistic, autonomous, and independent of authority (Smith, 1966; Taylor & Shurley, 1971). The negative behavioral aspects of Antarctic wintering appear to be real in those individuals with clinical symptoms, but the measures used to assess the state may have been inappropriate or insensitive. One problem with self-reported responses to items on most psychometric instruments is that they represent highly controlled events. They provide little insight concerning the dynamics of controlling processes occurring within the individual. Teichner (1968) concluded that in order to predict human performance it is necessary to measure controlling processes instead of controlled events. Teichner's work employed physiological stressors, such as hypoxia, and he hypothesized that decrements in performance are related to shifts in attention and response blocking due to inappropriate attentional neural mechanisms. Vaillant (1977) concluded that adaptive ability involves both biological and psychosocial factors. He suggested that the most important biological factor may be the state of the nervous system and the manner in which experience has influenced the development of the brain.

Our work has focused on the problem of insensitive measures as well as the source of individual differences in adaptation strategies and competence. White (1974) defined adaptive competence as an ability to cope with immediate changes in the environment and adjust to long-term changes while maintaining effective performance and continuing psychological growth. From the human engineering point of view, Meister (1985) addressed adaptation in terms of an inherent ability to adopt more efficient response strategies under conditions of increased work load. Meister conceptualized this ability as an individual's "workload resistance" capacity. In an attempt to obtain metrics that would reflect both cerebral status and architecture, as well as provide predictive information related to human performance, we have employed lateralized neuropsychological procedures. Preliminary results suggest that neurometric procedures may be more appropriate than psychometric techniques for both individual evaluation and crew selection (Natani, 1980).

## Evidence for Laterality Effects

CFF is a neuropsychological assessment procedure that was discarded by many clinicians because of low sensitivity to the effects of cerebral lesions (Halstead, 1947). Parsons found that a modified CFF technique provided a sensitive method for the detection of deficits related to cerebral lesions (Parsons, Chandler, Teed, & Haase, 1966). Parsons's modification used a special apparatus for the lateralized perimetric, as opposed to the standard central binocular, presentation of the flickering stimulus light. Guided by Parsons's success in increasing the sensitivity of CFF by lateralizing the test stimuli, we reviewed our own studies and the electroencephalographic (EEG) literature for laterality effects that might be related to the Antarctic dysadaptation syndrome. The sleep EEG data from South Pole Station showed an increase in sleep spindle activity (14 Hz) during the winter that exceeded baseline levels for normal subjects (Natani & Shurley, 1975). This finding was originally attributed to increased levels of stage 2 sleep.

The results of the literature survey suggested another explanation for the spindle activity. There may be a functional correlation among EEG sigma activity (12 to 15 Hz) in the left hemisphere, hypokinesia, and behavior. Sterman (1978) reported that sigma activity, or sensory motor rhythm (SMR), is abundant in quadriplegics and that wrist-cuff restraint of monkeys confined to a chair induces SMR in the EEG coupled with a dazed and motionless behavioral state. Zubek, Pushkar, Sansom, and Gowing (1961) found that extended periods of reduced kinesthetic and sensory stimulation induced the appearance of significant sigma activity in the EEG of human subjects. Zubek (1969) concluded that the adverse and unusual subjective phenomena experienced by his subjects were not due to sensory deprivation but could be attributed directly to their extended confinement in the recumbent position. Zubek also found that the periodic performance of calisthenic exercises by some of his subjects significantly reduced both the subjective reports and the physiological (EEG) effects of the experimental conditions used in his sensory deprivation studies. These findings coupled with evidence for a thalamic source of sigma generation (Thatcher & John, 1977) and the lateralized differentiation of the human thalamus (Oke, Keller, Meffoed, & Adams, 1978) suggested the hypothesis that enhanced sigma activity reflects a functional laterality effect. Thus, significant changes in EEG SMR activity may indicate the presence of subtle neuropsychological deficits that are correlated with the lateral functional organization of the brain and modulated by reduced muscular activity.

## Hypokinesia

The common denominator across these studies that address sensory deprivation, SMR research, and Antarctic wintering is reduced motor activity, or hypokinesia. The reports cited provide support for the hypothesis that a reduction in kinesthetic stimulation may interfere with normal integrated behavior. This view has been expressed by a number of investigators, including Fiske (1961), Held and Freedman (1963), Klein (1970), Thatcher and John (1977), and Riesen (1961). These authors all support the theory that motor activity is important not only in the development of perceptual processes but also in their continued maintenance.

Jones (1965) has taken a related position that suggests that behavior is fixed by the maintenance of postural sets and that postural changes must be accomplished before significant changes in behavior can occur. Others

(Beigel, 1952; Jacobson, 1964; Klein, 1965) have concluded that qualitative changes in mental activity are linked to body position. Their work suggests that the upright body position is important for maintaining the integrity of certain cognitive functions and may be essential to concentrated, disciplined thought in some individuals. The relaxed recumbent position, on the other hand, has been associated with a tendency to remove mental processes from reality concerns while favoring the reception of suggestions and associations of both relevant and irrelevant material. Apparently the normal activity of the antigravity muscles involved in the maintenance of an erect standing posture is essential for the reality-oriented, goal-directed executive thinking associated with high motivation that has recently come to be associated with the cognitive processes of the left hemisphere. One would thus expect to find some subtle behavioral effects related to the postural changes associated with the hypodynamia and hypokinesia found in spaceflight.

Some significant changes in cognitive style have been reported by several astronauts following spaceflight (Rosen, 1976). The relatively short duration of recent spaceflights coupled with extremely busy schedules and the astronauts' training and career experiences that have emphasized the requirement for the maintenance of reality-oriented, goal-directed executive thinking under the most diverse and stressful conditions associated with military flight testing probably prevented the appearance of any significant behavioral effects. However, as in the case of sensory deprivation studies and Antarctic wintering, individual differences in response to the experience of spaceflight have been evident. Even greater individual differences may have been prevented by the in-flight exercise program introduced as a prophylaxis for the adverse effects of the weightless hypodynamia (Dietlein, 1977; Pestov & Gerathewohl, 1975).

## Lateralization and Individual Differences

Individual differences were especially evident in the early studies of water-immersion hypodynamia and hypokinesia (Graveline, Balke, McKenzie, & Hartman, 1961; Graybiel & Clark, 1961). One possible source of these individual differences may be subtle variations in the organization of hemispheric cerebral differentiation in man. Several discrete patterns of cerebral organization may be found in normal right-handed human males. Our exploratory efforts in this area suggest that the most adaptive organization appears to be one that yields no significant differences between the two hemispheres in performance measures on the lateralized tasks used (Natani, 1977). This is apparently the case when both hemispheres are highly differentiated and the individual is capable of swift and flexible alternation between response sets requiring the specialized abilities of the right or left hemisphere. It has occurred to us that in a brain with highly differentiated specialization the right hemisphere may provide a reference system for the stabilization of left hemisphere functions under novel conditions such as hypokinesia that may tend to degrade left hemisphere processes. On the other hand, an organization possessing less differentiation may not provide a point of reference and could also be less efficient from the standpoint of cerebral architecture.

A conceptualization of cerebral organization based upon General Systems Behavior Theory has been developed elsewhere (Shurley, Natani, & Sengal, 1977). The basic premise of this theory is that the environmental stimuli impinging upon the body and personality systems of a given individual from a novel or grossly altered physical environment exert deviation-amplifying influences upon both systems. The magnitude of the deviations in behavior that these external influences may produce will be dependent upon deviation-counteracting forces in the system. Counteracting forces are derived from social and reference group norms as well as other behavioral setting constraints and the physiological bases of behavior resident in the neural organization of the biological system. The physiological sources are derived from both genetic and developmental influences and are certainly not wholly constrained to the simple model suggested here for lateral hemispheric differentiation. We have used lateral cognitive metrics but are aware that there is evidence for serious aberrations of both behavior and personality that may be correlated with vestibular effects (Hubbard, 1973).

Where the functional neural substrate may be different, as outlined above, one would expect to see marked individual differences in performance and adaptation when the environmental supports for cognitive systems are significantly altered, as they may be in long-term spaceflight. A primary human factors problem for future spaceflight will involve the selection of scientists, technologists, and skilled workers who have not had the extensive experience in aviation characteristic of the early astronauts. Our theoretical approach and the evidence available suggest that lateralized neurometric and neuropsychological evaluations may be more sensitive to individual differences correlated with positive adaptation to exotic environments than traditional assessment techniques. Traditional assessment techniques have not focused upon positive individual characteristics relevant to coping with demanding situations in the real world. Selecting for competence in dealing with problems by using social skills and adaptive cognitive styles is relatively new. There appears to be a need for generating a new assessment technology based upon neurometric and neuropsychological tests sensitive to brain function as shaped by an individual's developmental history and other biological determinants of behavior.

## Applied Psychophysiology

The reports reviewed here suggest that exercise of the antigravity musculature may provide prophylaxis for the effects of hypokinesia in a number of situations ranging from the confinement of the polar winter on the Antarctic plateau to the weightlessness of spaceflight. In terms of monitoring the onset of hypokinetic effects, 12 to 15 Hz spindles in the EEG appear to offer considerable potential. In particular, a significant increase in this sigma activity in the left hemisphere may reflect the deterioration of neural representational systems that form the basis for complex cognitive activities. The evidence available suggests that a decrement in sigma activity may indicate cortical hyperexcitability and an absence of inhibitory processes often associated with epilepsy. On the other hand, an abundance of sigma spindles may reflect a dominance of cortical processes by subcortical structures that is accompanied by apathy and cognitive inefficiency associated with decrements in psychomotor coordination and motivation. Hypokinesia in any setting may eventually produce symptoms similar to those seen in some of the men wintering on the Antarctic plateau. Exercises such as those developed to prevent the adverse effects of weightless hypodynamia in spaceflight may offer the best prophylactic measure for the maintenance of adaptive behavior in the polar regions as well as in space.

## References

Beigel, H. G. (1952). The influence of body position on mental processes. *Journal of Clinical Psychology, 8*, 193–199.

Blackburn, A. B., Shurley, J. T., & Natani, K. (1973). Psychological adjustment at a small Antarctic station: An MMPI study. In O. G. Edholm & E. K. E. Gunderson (Eds.), *Polar human biology* (pp. 369–383). London: William Heinemann Medical Books Ltd.

Danishevskii, G. M., Ponomarev, V. N., & Tikhomirov, I. I. (1967/1970). Human acclimatization in the Antarctic. In V. A. Bugaev (Ed.), *Soviet Antarctic Research 1956–1966* (NTIS Report TT 69-55004). Springfield, VA: Clearinghouse for Federal Scientific and Technical Information. (Translated from Russian in 1970)

Dietlein, L. F. (1977). Skylab: A beginning. In R. S. Johnson & L. F. Dietlein (Eds.), *Biomedical results from Skylab* (NASA SP-377). Washington, DC: U.S. Government Printing Office.

Fiske, D. W. (1961). Effects of monotonous and restricted stimulation. In D. W. Fiske & S. Maddi (Eds.), *The functions of varied experience*. Homewood, IL: Dorsey Press.

Graveline, D. E., Balke, B., McKenzie, R. E., & Hartman, B. (1961). Psychobiologic effects of water-immersion-induced hypodynamics. *Aerospace Medicine, 32*, 387–400.

Graybiel, A., & Clark, B. (1961). Symptoms resulting from prolonged immersion in water: The problem of zero G asthenia. *Aerospace Medicine, 32*, 181–196.

Halstead, W. G. (1947). *Brain and intelligence: A quantitative study of the frontal lobes*. Chicago: University of Chicago Press.

Held, R., & Freedman, S. J. (1963). Plasticity in human sensorimotor control. *Science, 142*, 455–462.

Hubbard, D. G. (1973). *The skyjacker: His flights of fancy (Rev. ed.)*. New York: Collier Books.

Jacobson, E. (1964). *Anxiety and tension control*. Philadelphia: Lippincott.

Jones, F. P. (1965). Method for changing stereotyped response patterns by inhibition of certain postural sets. *Psychological Review, 72*, 196–214.

Klein, G. S. (1965). On hearing one's own voice: An aspect of cognitive control in spoken thought. In M. Schur (Ed.), *Drives, affects and behavior, Vol. 2.* New York: International Universities Press.

Klein, G. S. (1970). *Perception, motives and personality.* New York: Knopf.

Meister, D. (1985). *Behavioral foundations of system development* (2nd ed.). Malabar, FL: Krieger.

Natani, K. (1977). Laterality effects in a tachistoscopic optional shift task in young adults. *Dissertation Abstracts International, 38,* 744.

Natani, K. (1980). Future directions for selecting personnel. In T. S. Cheston & D. L. Winter (Eds.), *Human factors of outer space production* (pp. 25–63). Washington, DC: American Association for the Advancement of Science.

Natani, K., & Shurley, J. T. (1975). Extrinsic parameters and the self-regulation of sleep in Antarctica. *Biological Psychology Bulletin, 4,* 16–22.

Oke, A., Keller, R., Meffoed, I., & Adams, R. N. (1978). Lateralization of norepinephrine in human thalamus. *Science, 200,* 1411–1413.

Parsons, O. A., Chandler, P. J., Teed, R. W., & Haase, G. (1966). Comparison of flicker perimetry and standard visual fields in brain-damaged patients. *Acta Neurological Scandinavia, 42,* 207–212.

Pestov, I. D., & Gerathewohl, S. J. (1975). Weightlessness. In M. Calvin & O. G. Gazenko (Eds.), *Foundations of space biology and medicine, Vol. II, Book I* (NASA SP-374). Washington, DC: National Aeronautics and Space Administration.

Riesen, A. (1961). Studying perceptual development using the technique of sensory deprivation. *Journal of Nervous and Mental Disease, 132,* 21–25.

Rosen, S. G. (1976). Mind in space. *USAF Medical Service Digest, 27,* 4–17.

Shurley, J. T., Natani, K., & Sengal, R. (1977). Ecopsychiatric aspects of a first human space colony. In J. Grey (Ed.), *Space manufacturing facilities II (space colonies).* New York: American Institute of Aeronautics and Astronautics.

Smith, M. B. (1966). Explorations in competence: A study of Peace Corps teachers in Ghana. *American Psychologist, 21,* 555–556.

Sterman, M. B. (1978). Biofeedback and epilepsy. *Human Nature, 1,* 50–57.

Taylor, A. J. W., & Shurley, J. T. (1971). Some Antarctic troglodytes. *International Review of Applied Psychology, 20,* 143–148.

Teichner, W. H. (1968). Interaction of behavioral and physiological stress reactions. *Psychological Review, 75,* 271–291.

Thatcher, R. W., & John, E. R. (1977). *Functional neuroscience, Vol. I, Foundations of Cognitive Processes.* Hillsdale, NJ: Lawrence Erlbaum.

Vaillant, G. E. (1977). *Adaptation to life.* Boston: Little, Brown.

White, R. W. (1974). Strategies of adaptation: An attempt at systematic description. In G. V. Coelho, D. A. Hamburg, & J. E. Adams (Eds.), *Coping and adaptation.* New York: Basic Books.

Wilson, O. (1965). Human adaptation to life in Antarctica. In J. Van Meighen, P. Van Oye, & J. Schell (Eds.), *Biogeography and ecology in Antarctica.* (Monographie Biologicae Vol. 15). The Hague: Dr. W. Junk.

Zubek, J. P. (1969). *Sensory deprivation: Fifteen years of research.* New York: Appleton-Century-Crofts.

Zubek, J. P., Pushkar, D., Sansom, W., & Gowing, J. (1961). Perceptual changes after prolonged sensory isolation (darkness and silence). *Canadian Journal of Psychology, 15,* 83–100.

# 28

# Psychological Effects of Long-Duration Space Missions and Stress Amelioration Techniques*

ARLENE S. LEVINE

As we observed the 30th anniversary of the beginning of the "space age," the United States and the Soviet Union were formulating comprehensive plans to extend the human presence into space on a permanent basis. On December 29, 1987, Soviet cosmonaut Yuri Romanenko returned to Earth after a record flight of more than 326 days aboard the *Mir* space station. In recent months, other countries have disclosed plans and concepts for Earth-orbiting space stations and have developed scenarios for human exploration and exploitation of the Moon, Mars, and beyond. One of the three major goals of the National Aeronautics and Space Administration in the 21st century is to "expand human presence beyond the Earth into the solar system" (Ride, 1987, p. 13).

The Ride (1987) report points out that "the prospect of an extended human presence in space on the Space Station, and later, on extended missions to the Moon or Mars, requires a commitment to better understand and respond to biomedical, psychological, and human engineering challenges" (p. 41). This is an important statement and reflects a new direction in thinking. Only very recently have mission planners come to the realization that the extension of human presence into space on a long-term basis will depend on more than engineering, technology, and hardware. While past research and interest in the United States has centered on the medical aspects of human spaceflight, little concern has centered on the psychological and behavioral health of the astronaut. Some of these psychological and behav-

---

*This work was initiated while the author was a National Aeronautics and Space Administration (NASA)/American Society for Engineering Education Summer Faculty Fellow at NASA's Langley Research Center in 1984.

ioral concerns and a strong appeal for behavioral research appear in a recent report to the National Academy of Sciences (Goldberg, 1987).

This chapter addresses the question of psychological stress associated with long-duration space missions and its causes and symptoms and offers some effective ways to ameliorate these stresses.

## Psychological Stress

The psychological and behavioral stresses associated with human space-flight will increase over the coming years as a result of longer duration space missions and the accessibility of spaceflight to the nonprofessional astro-naut. A summary of the durations of U.S. and Soviet manned missions is given in Table 28.1. Note that the emergent space station era and future Mars missions will greatly increase the time for humans in space.

The Soviet Union has logged 12 man-years in space as compared to the United States with less than 5 (Canby, 1986). With their increased experience in manned spaceflight and missions of increased duration came the recognition that the extreme factors of spaceflight and existence in space can cause considerable psychophysiological stress (Parin, Gorbov, & Kosmolinskiy, 1972/1974), stress that may in fact be lethal. Rex Hall, a London analyst of Soviet space activities, believes that several cosmonaut trainees died from stress during training (Canby, 1986). In fact, an irregular heart beat, which may have been brought about by stress, ended the spaceflight of cosmonaut Alexander Laveikin (Maugh, 1987). Laveikin was a passenger on the Soyuz

TABLE 28.1. Manned space missions: Past, present, and future.

|  | Era | Number | Duration |
|---|---|---|---|
| *United States* |  |  |  |
| Mercury | 1961–1963 | 6 | 15 min–34 hr |
| Gemini | 1965–1966 | 10 | 4 hr 53 min–330 hr |
| Apollo | 1968–1972 | 11 | 147 hr–295 hr |
| Skylab | 1973–1974 | 3 | 28–84 days |
| Apollo/Soyuz | 1975 | 1 | 217 hr |
| Space shuttle | 1981–present | 25 | 54 hr–10 days 8 hr |
| Space station | Planned |  | 6 months |
| Mars mission | Planned |  | 3–5 years |
| *USSR* |  |  |  |
| Vostok | 1961–1963 | 6 | 108 min–119 hr |
| Vokshod | 1964–1965 | 2 | 24 hr 17 min–26 hr |
| Soyuz | 1967–1981 | 38 | 20 min–184 days 20 hr |
| Soyuz T | 1980–1986 | 14 | 48 hr–237 days |
| Soyuz TM | 1987–present | 7 | 8 days–366 days |
| Salyut | 1971–1986 | 6 | 6 days–237 days |
| *Mir* | 1986–present | 1 | 8 days–366 days |

TM-2 mission, launched in February 1987, and was replaced on the Space Station *Mir* by Alexander Alexandrov. Because the impacts of such pressures may be so extreme, they require careful consideration. With study, it may be possible to eliminate or ameliorate some of these pressures and their concomitant feelings of stress. The major contributors to stress in extended space missions are listed in Table 28.2.

Isolation can be a significant source of stress during long-duration missions. Isolation during spaceflight is an estrangement from all that is familiar (Berry, 1973). It means a separation from friends, family, and society at large, resulting in a loss of reassurance, affection, respect, and the variety of relationships and roles that one has on Earth (Connors, Harrison, & Akins, 1985).

Confinement with a limited number of individuals adds to the pressures of isolation. These few are not necessarily the spacefarer's choice of traveling companions. This may be as true in space missions as it is in analogous situations such as Antarctic camps, space simulation studies, submarines, and submersibles. There is a feeling of no escape from the environment or the companions. The need for privacy will increase with the duration of the mission.

Weightlessness and microgravity have profound effects on the body and mind. The Soviets believe that after 4 or 5 months, work performance may decline (Canby, 1986). Microgravity and weightlessness may cause other difficulties as well. They can degrade perception, motor skills, reflexes, and coordination. In addition, physiological deconditioning occurs, which includes bone demineralization, muscle (heart and skeletal) atrophy, and fluid shift to the upper torso (Chaikin, 1984; Coleman, 1984; Connors et al., 1985; DeCampli, 1987). The fluid shift causes head stuffiness and intermittent congestion of the inner ear canal (Pogue, 1974).

In addition to the other physical effects of weightlessness, there is the space-adaptation syndrome, which is wholly unlike its Earth–based counterpart. In space, sweating, pallor, and even nausea are frequently absent; instead, loss of appetite occurs, and there is often a knot-in-the-stomach sensation. The voyager often vomits without warning (Chaikin, 1984). Space-adaptation syndrome lasts for several days, sometimes starting as early as 2 to 3 hr after launch. It may last for as long as 5 days before

TABLE 28.2. Sources of stress on long-duration space missions.

Isolation, confinement, and lack of privacy
Weightlessness, microgravity, and space adaptation syndrome
Noise and vibration
Toxic agents
Reduced sensory input, increased sensory input, and boredom
Separation reaction
Fear of equipment failure

habituation occurs. Motion sickness in space was first reported by Frank Borman, mission commander of Apollo 8, in 1968. It is quite common; 4 out of every 10 shuttle astronauts have suffered from it (Chaikin, 1984). Astronaut William Pogue, pilot of the Skylab 3 mission, feels that there is an inverse relationship between motion sickness in one gravity and zero gravity: "Those strongly immune to motion sickness in one-$g$ Earth environments seem more sensitive to vestibular stimulation in zero-$g$, and vice versa" (Pogue, 1974).

Noise and vibration are also stressors. Noise and vibration in the spacecraft are usually caused by equipment, such as pumps, motors, and cabin fans, as well as by hygiene and recreation facilities (Bluth, 1984; Chaikin, 1985). Crewmembers have no escape from the omnipresent noise (Coleman, 1984). The noise level can affect the performance of some crewmembers. It can degrade the ability to detect and discriminate auditory information accurately. It also contributes to fatigue, sleep loss, and irritability (Coleman, 1984).

Astronauts may be exposed to toxic agents, such as continuous, high, ambient radiation dosages. If the spacecraft or station were to encounter a solar storm, the increased radiation levels could be lethal. It has been estimated that the normal exposure will approximate 15 rads/hr; this exceeds the occupational limits for radiation workers in the United States. In the space station, radiation exposure can be controlled by increased shielding as well as by orbital inclination and altitude selection (Coleman, 1984). Light flashes, which were first reported by Apollo 11 crewmembers, may be high-energy, high-atomic-particle radiation perceived in the retina (Berry, 1973). These light flashes occurred during periods of darkness (Connors et al., 1985).

Long-duration missions present the possibility of accumulated toxic chemicals contaminating the breathing atmosphere of the spacecraft. Potential sources for contamination include outgassing of materials such as plastics; liquid or gaseous chemicals escaping from the craft's life-support system; industrial activities and materials processing; chemicals produced by propellant systems, combustion, thermal decomposition, or heat vaporization of various materials; or metabolic by-products produced by the crew (Coleman, 1984).

Sensory input during spaceflight is limited or reduced. The ambience is static over long periods. Boredom sets in. Too little sensory input can be as stressful as too much sensory input. A change in scenery is not possible or is severely limited. Although astronauts enjoy looking out of the spacecraft windows, the variety of views is limited. Cosmonauts who have flown on long-duration flights have experienced this limited input. The Soviets speak of "sensory hunger," or sensory deficiency, and insufficient input of external stimuli (sight, hearing, taste, touch, and feeling) that feed the brain (Parin et al., 1972/1974). U.S. astronauts, on the other hand, because their missions generally have been of shorter duration, suffered from the reverse — sensory overload or excess. There were too many tasks to accomplish in too short a time period, causing some astronauts to function at a subliminal level of anxiety (Pogue, 1974). As the U.S. missions increase in duration, the problems endured by Soviet cosmonauts, such as sensory hunger, will also be encountered by the astronauts.

Another potential source of stress is separation reaction. Jet pilots sometimes experience it when leaving the Earth's "friendly" surface. Some suffer from depression and others from euphoria, and others are unaffected. The Soviet Union recognizes this stress possibility in spaceflight and couples the anxiety of separation from Earth, humanity, and all that a person is accustomed to with the anxiety of confinement (Parin et al., 1972/1974). Polish scientific studies of high-altitude pilots indicated that approximately 35% of the interviewed pilots reported unpleasant responses to the sensation of loneliness and separation from Earth. Other emotional responses, such as uneasiness, stress, lack of confidence, and fear resulting in errors in piloting, illusions, and loss of spatial orientation, were also reported. Increased flight velocity and altitude may exacerbate the situation (Parin et al., 1972/1974).

There is an ever-present fear of equipment failure, which is based on experience and reality. There have been at least 11 reported deaths in space because of equipment failure. In 1967, Vladimir Komarov, the pilot of the first Soyuz spacecraft, was the first space fatality (Canby, 1986). Mechanical failures allowed the spacecraft to tumble out of control. In 1971, the first Salyut crew returned to Earth after a successful mission. The reentry and descent were made in a Soyuz capsule. Because of a valve malfunction, the life-supporting cabin atmosphere escaped, and all three men died (Canby, 1986). The United States lost seven astronauts in the Challenger accident in 1986, when defective seals on the solid rocket booster led to an explosion a little more than a minute into the launch.

There have also been many examples of equipment malfunctions that caused the abort or termination of the mission but not the loss of lives. In 1983, a two-cosmonaut team lifted off in their Soyuz capsule for the Salyut 7 space station. An ensuing fire destroyed the automatic switch for the escape system. The rocket subsequently exploded into flames, but two different ground stations were able to fire the escape capsule, and the cosmonauts escaped unhurt (Canby, 1986). The Apollo 13 mission was terminated in 1970, when an oxygen tank blew up and a second one was ruptured. In addition to the oxygen loss, vital stores of water, propellant, and power were depleted. All three astronauts were returned to Earth safely (Lovell, 1975).

The stresses briefly discussed above have affected the performance and well-being of the crew in a number of ways. These effects are listed in Table 28.3.

Mitigating stress is expected to be a major challenge of future human long-duration missions. However, it is important to note that the elimination of all stress is neither possible nor desirable (Albrecht, 1979). Stress may be

TABLE 28.3. Some effects of stress on long-duration human missions.

Lowered energy and decreased capacity for intellectual pursuits
Impairment of memory
Lowered productivity
Lowered problem-solving ability
Lowered efficiency (both group and individual)
Increased hostility toward other crewmembers
Increased hostility toward ground control
Lowered attentiveness
Fatigue
Anxiety
Sleep disorder
Boredom
Withdrawal and increased need for privacy
Miscommunications
Overconcern with health
Impulsive behavior

situational (and therefore episodic) or chronic. It is the chronic stresses (prolonged arousal) that are of the most concern. They are responsible for the most wear and tear on the body. Episodic stresses (crisis situations) perturb the body but are of short duration. Afterwards the body returns to equilibrium, or homeostasis. It is the chronic stress that may lead not only to a health breakdown but also to decreased capacity to deal with episodic stress (crisis situations). The goal of stress amelioration is not to eliminate all stress so that an individual's stress level is near zero. Rather, it is to bring that stress level to an optimum, or comfortable, level. Too much stress, as well as too little stress, causes discomfort. Humans function at their best at moderate levels of stress.

In addition, it is important to note that not all stress is the product of a crisis situation. In fact, stress can be the result of positive situations. Eustress is the stress of achievement, triumph, and exhilaration, according to Hans Selye, whereas distress is the stress of helplessness, desperation, and disappointment (Albrecht, 1979). However, the body chemistry and reaction are identical whether the stress is eustress or distress. The sympathetic nervous system is activated, whether the stress is triumph, danger, physical exercise, temperature extremes, injury, or infection. These stressors invoke the same general response to stress and the identical biochemical reaction in the body. What is important to note is that chronic stress can lead to a serious health breakdown (Pelletier, 1977). This is a serious concern on a prolonged space mission.

There are several directions to be considered that may be taken to reduce stress on long-duration spaceflights. Astronaut selection, like selection of personnel for all exotic environments (submarines, Antarctica, and so on) continues to exclude those with obvious or potential problems. When stress is considered, it is important that not only the specific stressor but also the individual's "other stressors" (pressures) and his or her reactivity be considered. Some individuals are highly reactive to stress, whereas others appear to be less so. An individual who is highly reactive reacts to everything, small as well as large, whereas someone less reactive responds only to large problems (Albrecht, 1979). Personnel selection certainly alleviates some of the problem; however, there are other measures that can be taken to ameliorate stress.

Some environmental stressors can be lessened by increasing the private living space of an astronaut or cosmonaut. It has been documented that confined or isolated individuals need increased privacy. Other environmental changes that may reduce stress include permitting the occupants to have some input on the decor and layout of the spacecraft and eliminating as much of the excessive noise as possible. Astronaut William Pogue, veteran of the 84-day Skylab mission, stated that rest, relaxation, and entertainment become increasingly important as a mission progresses (Pogue, 1974). Thus, these activities need to be included in long-duration space missions. However, those stressors that cannot be controlled through personnel selection and environmental manipulation can be lessened by training.

There are many training techniques that are effective in ameliorating stress. Group techniques—using group therapy to work out problems—as well as counseling techniques would be very useful for confined individuals. It is important to conduct sessions that outline and explain the results of experimentation in a confined environment and the observations in exotic environments, as well as to relate U.S. and Soviet Union space mission experiences. Historical awareness can serve to forewarn the astronauts about group cohesiveness and the expectation of hostility within the crew and towards ground control. If individuals, both on the ground and in space, are aware that incidents are to be expected, then these incidents can be handled with greater tact because they will not be personalized. Anticipated incidents can be smoothed over more rapidly than if the target of the hostility believes that the animosity is directed towards him. Exercise conducted to hasten postflight, physiological recovery also results in a feeling of well-being (Pogue, 1974). Thus, exercise can be used as a means of stress reduction. In addition, individual reactivity can be controlled by stress amelioration techniques. There are many potential amelioration techniques, including those listed in Table 28.4.

These stress amelioration techniques can affect and regulate a number of bodily functions and processes, including brain waves, heart rate, blood pressure, muscle tension, body temperature, stomach acidity, electrical resistance of the skin, consumption of oxygen, and the rate of respiration.

TABLE 28.4. Psychological stress amelioration techniques.

Yoga, Transcendental Meditation, and the relaxation response
Progressive muscle relaxation
Hypnosis, self-hypnosis, and autosuggestion
Autogenic training
Biofeedback

## Yoga, Transcendental Meditation, and the Relaxation Response

Yoga is the oldest relaxation technique, originating in India thousands of years ago. It consists of both physical and meditative exercises. There are many forms of yoga (which means "union") as it serves to unite the mind and body. Its purpose is to bring about tranquility by the use of breathing exercises, varying body postures, and mental focusing. It can alter physiological functions such as brain waves, metabolism, heart rate, blood pressure, and respiratory rate (Benson, 1976; Culligan & Sedlacek, 1979). Yoga has already been practiced in space by India's first cosmonaut, Rakesh Sharma. Sharma practiced yoga to combat the effects of weightlessness during a mission in the spring of 1984 aboard Salyut 7.

Transcendental Meditation (TM) is a simple yoga technique. TM eliminates all elements from yoga that are deemed nonessential and therefore can be easily learned by Westerners (Benson, 1976). TM involves the use of a Sanskrit word as a mantra, which is chosen for the meditator by a trained instructor. The mantra is repeated continually while the meditator is in a comfortable position. This serves to block extraneous thoughts from entering the meditator's consciousness. TM is practiced twice daily for 20 minutes (Benson, 1976).

The relaxation response technique was formulated by Dr. Herbert Benson while testing the effectiveness of TM to bring about certain physiological changes such as a decrease in blood pressure. He noted that prayer and meditation decrease the activity of the sympathetic nervous system. He considers that all relaxation response techniques are a form of altered states of consciousness (Benson, 1976; Culligan & Sedlacek, 1979).

There are four basic components needed to induce the relaxation response: (1) a quiet environment to eliminate distracting thoughts; (2) a mental device—a word, sound, or phrase repeated silently or aloud or fixed gazing on an object—while a slow rhythm for breathing is established; (3) a passive attitude [distracting thoughts are to be disregarded and one's whole attention redirected to the mental device]; and (4) a comfortable position. Unlike TM, the relaxation response does not require a Sanskrit mantra; instead, any neutral word, sound, phrase, or prayer will do. All serve the same purpose, i.e., thought blocking. The relaxation response would require very little training and would be very simple to practice in space. The only necessary requirement would be a small, quiet, private space and noninterference for 20 min once or twice a day.

## Progressive Muscle Relaxation

Progressive muscle relaxation is a relaxation technique devised by Dr. E. Jacobson (Benson, 1976). It induces relaxation in the body and then in the mind. This technique involves the relaxation of voluntary skeletal muscles in a systematic sequence that starts at the head and progresses to the toes. The technique also requires a passive attitude and/or pleasant mental thoughts or images. Muscles are tensed and held, then relaxed. Relaxation may be achieved by imagining that the muscles are made of jelly. The sequence is repeated several times. This exercise sequence takes about 15 to 20 min. This, too, requires a quiet area for successful use.

## Hypnosis, Self–Hypnosis, and Autosuggestion

Hypnosis is the easiest way to learn relaxation (Albrecht, 1979). This technique increases the subject's receptiveness to suggestions and has been described as an altered state of consciousness. Self-hypnosis is more difficult to master when using book instructions only (Albrecht, 1979). Parin and colleagues (1972/1974) in the Soviet Union consider autosuggestion a very promising technique for preventing stress states during long-duration space missions. A. I. Svyadosh has shown that 2 to 3 months of special exercise can result in a self-induced rise or fall of skin temperature and altered muscle tone and heart rate (Parin et al., 1972/1974). Parin intimates that autosuggestion can eliminate an anxious state, severely reduce neuroemotional stress, and be used to teach oneself to fall asleep or awaken at a desired time.

## Autogenic Training

Autogenic training is a form of autosuggestion developed in Germany over 30 years ago by Dr. H. H. Schultz (Albrecht, 1979; Benson, 1976; Culligan & Sedlacek, 1979). This technique involves six progressive exercises dealing with muscle relaxation and mental images. It is performed in a quiet room in a comfortable, relaxed position with eyes closed and/or with a passive attitude. The subject focuses on feelings of heaviness and sensations of warmth in the limbs. Autogenic training affects heart regulation and breathing. The subject often develops a feeling of coolness in the forehead.

## Biofeedback

This popular relaxation technique is based on the fact that certain physiological activities and functions may be monitored by electrical devices. Subjective feelings (emotions) are associated with the physiological condition and their changes. Relaxation may be achieved by learning to control emotions and hence the physiological state. However, there are disadvantages with this technique, in that only one function can be monitored at a time. In addition, because equipment is needed, this is not a spontaneous or simple technique to apply.

# Conclusion

Soviet researcher V. Parin (Parin et al., 1972/1974) writes, "Problems in space psychology will more and more interest researchers as progress is made in astronautics. This field of science has only just gotten under way, and it has a great future." As the human presence in space increases both in numbers of individuals and in the duration of missions, psychological stress problems will increase. Attention must be given to this problem and to its solution or amelioration without undue delay. Psychological stress amelioration techniques must become an integral and important part of the training program for astronauts. Training in these techniques should begin immediately. Our future in space is just as dependent on the psychological well-being of the astronauts as it is on the hardware and machinery that will carry them into space.

## References

Albrecht, K. (1979). *Stress and the manager: Making it work for you.* Englewood Cliffs, NJ: Prentice-Hall.

Benson, H. (1976). *The relaxation response.* New York: Avon Publishing.

Berry, C. (1973). View of human problems to be addressed for long duration space flight. *Aerospace Medicine,* 1136–1146.

Bluth, B. J. (1984, June 5–7). *Human systems interface for space stations.* Paper No. 84-1115 presented at the AIAA/NASA Space Systems Technology Conference, Costa Mesa, CA.

Canby, T. (1986). Are the Soviets ahead in space? *National Geographic, 170*(4), 420–459.

Chaikin, A. (1984). Sick in space. *Science 84,* 51–55.

Chaikin, A. (1985, February). The loneliness of the long-distance astronaut. *Discover,* 20–31.

Coleman, M. (1984). *Atmospheric contamination control: Space station medical sciences concepts* (NASA Technical Memorandum TM-58255). Washington, DC: National Aeronautics and Space Administration.

Connors, M. M., Harrison, A. A., & Akins, F. R. (1985). *Living aloft: Human requirements for extended spaceflight* (NASA SP-483). Washington, DC: National Aeronautics and Space Administration.

Culligan, M. J., & Sedlacek, K. (1979). *How to avoid stress before it kills you.* New York: Gramercy.

DeCampli, W. M. (1987). Medical problems associated with long-duration spaceflight. In G. L. Burdett & G. A. Soffen (Eds.), *The human quest in space* (pp. 197–220), San Diego: American Astronautical Society, Univelt Publishers.

Goldberg, J. M. (1987). *A strategy for space biology and medical science for the 1980s and 1990s.* Washington, DC: National Academy Press.

Lovell, J. A. (1975). Houston, we've had a problem. In E. M. Cortwright (Ed.), *Apollo expeditions* (pp. 247–263). (NASA SP-350). Washington, DC: National Aeronautics and Space Administration.

Maugh, T. H. (1987, September 28). Cooped up. Los Angeles *Times,* (p. 9).

Parin, V., Gorbov, F., & Kosmolinskiy, F. (1972). Space psychology. In B. Konstantinov & V. Pekelis (Eds.), *Inhabited space part two*. (NASA TTF-820, pp. 29–36). Washington, DC: National Aeronautics and Space Administration. (Translated from Russian in 1974)

Pelletier, K. (1977, February). Mind as healer, mind as slayer. *Psychology Today*, 21–25.

Pogue, W. R. (1974). Three months in space. *Society of Experimental Test Pilots Technical Review, 12*, 203–217.

Ride, S. K. (1987). *Leadership and America's future in space: A report to the administrator of NASA*. Washington, DC: National Aeronautics and Space Administration, Office of Exploration.

# 29

# Proxemics and Privacy: Managing the Problems of Life in Confined Environments

DOUGLAS RAYBECK

Western societies, including the United States, place considerable emphasis on the concept of privacy. Privacy is something to which nearly all Westerners believe they are entitled, and most individuals will go to considerable lengths to establish a territory that they can regard as private, whether this is a house, an apartment, or simply a room. The absence of privacy and the crowding that frequently accompanies such a condition have been blamed for many social ills including greater family friction, increased juvenile delinquency, and the like (Ashcraft & Scheflen, 1976).

Although social scientists have studied privacy (e.g., Altman, 1977, 1979), they have frequently meant different things by it, such as solitude, anonymity, intimacy, secrecy, and control over interpersonal interactions (Russell & Ward, 1982). This chapter will use privacy to refer to the ability to obtain solitude and to regulate access to interpersonal interactions. Further, this chapter recognizes the useful distinction between density, the number of people per unit of space, and crowding, a psychological perception dependent upon environmental, personal, and social factors (Knapp, 1978).

The relevance of a concern with privacy to life in confined environments should be obvious. Problems identified with long-term occupation of confined environments include intellectual impairment, motivational decline, somatic complaints, and undesirable changes in mood (Harrison & Connors, 1984). It is particularly worthwhile to reduce the likelihood and severity of such problems in the context of the long-term occupation of a space station.

This chapter will briefly examine some of the problems encountered by members of American culture that are associated with crowding and the absence of privacy in confined environments. Then the reactions of members of selected other cultures to problems posed by an absence of privacy will be examined, as will their cultural solutions. Finally, in an effort to improve our ability to deal with the problems posed by crowding and an absence of privacy, findings from sociology, psychology, and anthropology on factors that influence the perception of privacy and crowding will be reviewed, and practical steps for alleviating the aforementioned problems will be suggested.

## Privacy and Crowding

The literature on crowding and privacy, while dealing largely with Americans, is not always consistent in its findings (Freedman, Klevansky, & Ehrlich, 1971; Ronchi & Sparcino, 1982). Jonathan Freedman (1975), one of the acknowledged experts on crowding, has persuasively argued that crowding acts as an experiential intensifier. Thus, bad experiences can appear worse and positive ones, better. Unfortunately, often situations of high density tend to promote bad rather than good experiences especially in conditions involving long-term living in confined environments.

Several researchers have noted an association between crowding and social and psychological problems (Ashcraft & Scheflen, 1976; Connors, Harrison, & Akins, 1986; Knapp, 1978; Sommer, 1969). The general argument tends to be that crowding and the absence of privacy act to increase social tension and to exacerbate interpersonal problems. Normally, individuals who are discomfited by a social setting or interpersonal experience have the opportunity to withdraw from interaction, to rest, and to seek a period of isolation and lowered arousal (see Connors et al., 1986). However, in situations where the possibility of privacy is slight, irritations can blossom into aggression, and dislike may be transmuted into hostility.

One study examining interactions among students in both crowded and uncrowded conditions found that the crowded students were significantly more anxious and hostile than the uncrowded ones and that this situation became more marked with time (Zeedyk-Ryan & Smith, 1983). Harrison and Connors (1984) reviewed several studies of groups in confined environments and noted patterns of increasing isolation, territoriality, and intragroup conflicts. Finally, Freedman (1975) carried out a study using a range of adult subjects sorted into mixed-sex, all-male, and all-female groups, who were asked to perform as a jury and render a verdict to a tape-recorded trial case in both a crowded and uncrowded condition. All-male groups gave more severe sentences in the crowded condition and were less well disposed toward one another, while females manifested an opposite pattern. The responses of mixed-sex groups did not differ in either condition and approximated the responses of the all-female groups.

Altman (1979) and other researchers who have examined human behavior in periods of prolonged confinement note that there is a marked increase in territorial behaviors and in social withdrawal (see Harrison & Connors, 1984; Hickson & Stacks, 1985). These behaviors would seem to be the result of both a limited area and the kinds of interpersonal interactions such limits promote. Each of us defines a "personal zone" surrounding our bodies, which is approximately arm's length. We dislike and can be upset by someone invading this space without our explicit or tacit consent (see Hall, 1959, 1969; Sommer, 1969). It has been found that people subjected to interpersonal invasions are less likely to volunteer assistance to others (DeBeer-Keston, Mellon, & Solomon, 1986) and that they are more easily irritated (Hickson & Stacks, 1985).

The difficulties associated with crowding and an absence of privacy seem to stem from at least two features of such environments. First, as Freedman and others (Freedman 1975; Freedman et al., 1971) have argued, crowding acts as an intensifier and seems to increase the arousal level of both humans and animals who have to endure such conditions. Second, as Goffman (1959) would argue, individuals who lack privacy necessarily lack a "backstage" and are continually engaged in manifesting a social performance designed to create a desired impression upon others in the environment. Social withdrawal may be viewed as an attempt to reduce levels of arousal and to achieve a backstage area in which individuals can relax from the demands of social performance.

## Privacy and Crowding in Different Cultures

Virtually all of the information in the preceding section was derived from studies conducted in the United States, a society more concerned with privacy and its maintenance than most. There are many cultures in the world where our concept of privacy would seem not only unusual but also eccentric and even dangerous.

Many societies are composed principally of small social units in which individuals are well known to one another, often related through cross-cutting kinship ties, and continuously involved in face-to-face interactions. In such social units, there is a great deal of interdependence among members, and they are strongly interested in one another's behavior (see Raybeck, 1988). Gossip is a common means of sharing information on the behaviors of others and also serves as an informal sanction to promote conformity on the part of those whose behaviors depart from the normative. In social units of this sort, active participation in the social life of the unit is mandatory, and interconnecting relationships assure the high visibility of unit members.

Many societies composed largely of small social units actually lack a term for privacy, and people who seek to be alone are often regarded with suspicion. Visibility and social participation assure other members of the unit that an individual is acting as a proper member, promoting the interests of the group, and conforming to established customs. Those who withdraw from interaction cannot readily be monitored, and the common assumption is that someone seeks isolation to pursue deviant and unsavory activities. Thus, in several societies, those who seek to be alone are often suspected of being sorcerers, witches, and the like and may be strongly sanctioned if they persist in such a pattern of behavior (see Gregor, 1977; Selby, 1974).

Hunter–gatherers are the simplest societies with which anthropologists are familiar. Such societies consist of small bands that, because of their subsistence adaptation, usually roam over fairly extensive territories. Patricia Draper, studying the !Kung Bushmen in South-West Africa, found that, while their population density was extremely low (approximately one person/10 mi$^2$), they tended to live in extremely dense clusters when establishing camps. The design of the camps tended to produce situations that were equivalent to 30 people occupying one room, and there seemed to be no adverse effects of such crowding (cited in Knapp, 1978). Draper suggests that the !Kung may be able to cope with the pressures of such crowding by escaping when necessary to other bands where they are known and may have relatives. Clearly, the !Kung are able to tolerate and may even prefer densities that would be very difficult for most Westerners to adjust to. The interdependent nature of life in such bands may help to explain this pattern, but it is also clear that the !Kung must possess a distinctive concept of the relationship of self to group, one that permits much closer association and higher visibility than Westerners could readily tolerate (Shostak, 1983; Thomas, 1959).

Thomas Gregor has studied and commented on privacy among the Mehinaku Indians of Brazil (Gregor, 1977). Mehinaku live in small nucleated villages consisting of large thatch structures in which several families reside. Houses usually lack internal partitions, and visibility both within the houses and throughout the village tends to be high. Unlike the !Kung hunter–gatherers, the largely horticultural Mehinaku, it is clear, are concerned about privacy and the effects of crowding.

Part of the reason for the Mehinaku's concern with privacy, in addition to the high density of their living arrangements, involves the Mehinaku propensity for engaging in deviant behaviors including theft and, especially, extramarital relations. Mehinaku reduce their social visibility by following a maze of small paths that can conceal them from others' view, by adding purposeful falsehoods to the gossip network to disguise their behaviors or to misdirect the attention of others, by adopting social conventions that can promote lessened visibility and some degree of privacy, and perhaps most notable, by establishing screened portions of houses behind which individuals undergoing life crises must spend as much as 2 or 3 years in seclusion. Gregor (1977) argues persuasively that one of the major functions of this custom is to reduce "the flow of information and the play of interaction within the village theater" (p. 238).

Edward Hall, perhaps the foremost anthropological authority on cross-cultural proxemics, has noted that Arabs tend to have a distinctive adaptation to the use of space and to privacy (Hall, 1969). Hall notes that Arabs consistently contend for public space by pushing one another about and that they have established comparatively small zones of personal space (see also Watson & Graves, 1966). He explains this by arguing that Arabs possess a sense of self that is distinctive and quite different from that of Westerners. Rather than regarding the person as to some extent congruent with a fleshy envelope as in the West, Arab personhood exists "somewhere down inside the body" (p. 157) where it is not easily reached through bodily contact. Hall argues that this conception of self may well facilitate Arab adaptation to densely populated cities.

Despite their seeming resistance to situations that we would regard as crowded, Arabs prefer homes that are, as perceived by Westerners, quite spacious because they usually lack internal partitions. Hall argues that Arabs do not like to be alone and suggests that this preference may have originally developed as an adaptation to family life in tents. Arabs lack a word for privacy and generally live in conditions where physical privacy (isolation) is not easily obtained. According to Hall, when Arabs wish to be alone they simply stop talking (p. 159). This is a customary means of reducing interaction and is respected by family members and others. Privacy is achieved interpersonally rather than spatially, as would be the case in the West.

The Javanese and Malays of Southeast Asia live predominantly in nucleated rural villages that are characterized, especially in the Javanese case, by high density. Both cultures lack a term for privacy and, for reasons similar to those described above, tend to distrust those who withdraw from interaction with co-villagers. Consequently, Malays and Javanese of both sexes are involved in nearly continuous face-to-face interactions with other villagers. Isolation is undesirable, and there exist a number of village customs that make obtaining isolation difficult even when it may be desired. Houses may be entered by relatives and co–villagers at most times of day, and hosts are expected to display active hospitality. Further, there are periods of active visiting that occur during holidays and nearly every night after the evening meal.

Despite daily immersion in a social context that Westerners would clearly regard as crowded, there is little evidence that this high-density situation is a problem. Members of both cultures have adapted to these living conditions with similar means. These focus principally on conceptions of the self and on a set of supporting cultural constructs that enable the self to manage situations of stress.

The self is viewed as a constructed entity. Newborns are essentially animals who must learn to be humans and whose souls are initially weak. It is the responsibility of parents to produce appropriate "human" contributors to the local society who possess strong souls and who can control their animality (Raybeck, 1975). In this conception, all people have at their core a degree of base emotion that must be tamed and overlaid by cultural experience. Emotionality is both a sign of insufficient development, a weakness of personality if you will, and a phenomenon that can threaten village harmony and the well-being of others.

Not surprisingly, given this conception of selfhood, a great deal of emphasis is placed upon emotional control. People who behave in a courteous, controlled manner toward others are referred to as *halus*, refined and sensitive, while those who speak brusquely or demonstrate an insensitivity to the feelings of others are termed *kasar*, rough and coarse (Raybeck, 1974). Among traditional upper class Javanese, emotional equanimity is highly prized, and it is cultivated through the recognition and practice of several cultural values: emotional and intellectual detachment, patience, and acceptance of circumstances (Geertz, 1960). In both societies, persons who lose their tempers are sanctioned, and there are few offenses graver than directing physical violence against a co-villager or relative (Raybeck, 1986).

The solution to the pressures of crowding and the absence of privacy adopted by Malays and Javanese clearly depend upon conceptions of the self and other background elements of these two cultures. While the emotional control solution seems to work well for the most part, it should be noted that it is not perfect, and it can be brittle. These are the cultures in which *amok* was first identified. *Amok* is a state of emotional abandon in which an individual attacks anyone nearby, usually with deadly consequence. *Amok* seems to occur when individuals who are under pressures of various sorts lose all emotional control and behave in a frenzied fashion that is the antithesis of the cultural ideal.

The Japanese possess a distinctive means for dealing with the pressures and stresses created by crowding and the absence of privacy. Several authorities have noted that Japanese living situations are often crowded and that, at least in some circumstances, the Japanese seem to prefer it that way (Befu, 1971; Dore, 1965; Hall, 1959, 1969). The tolerance by Japanese for comparatively high-density living situations can be traced to culture constructs and to child-rearing patterns.

Nonetheless, it is clear that Japanese can be stressed by situations of high density and that they have an appropriate means of dealing with such pressures. Japanese have been argued to possess barriers of privacy that surround the inner self (Takeuchi, n.d.). Japanese culture has long emphasized the importance of meditation for religious purposes, for periods of deep thought, and as means of dealing with emotional stress (see Dore, 1965). Through meditation, Japanese may retreat inward and obtain respite from a variety of pressures including those occasioned by crowding and the absence of privacy. This solution not only improves the emotional state of the meditator, but also reduces the amount of interaction in the group in which the meditator participates. Finally, unlike the solution to emotional stresses provided by Malay and Javanese societies, there does not seem to be any risk of sudden emotional displays associated with meditation. Indeed, studies in

America, Japan, and elsewhere indicate that meditation is a very effective means of lowering levels of arousal and promoting emotional equanimity (Bagchi & Wenger, 1957; Wallace & Benson, 1972).

It is apparent that cultures such as those of the Javanese, Malays, and Japanese can tolerate and even enjoy densities that most Americans would find very stressful. However, it is also apparent that, even though these societies lack a term for privacy and do not seek it in the same manner that Westerners do, there are limits on everyone's ability to deal with high density and absence of privacy. Crowding may be relative to the cultural context within which it is defined, but it is still capable of acting as a stressor, and there do not seem to be any means to wholly eliminate this problem.

The preceding examples clearly support one of anthropology's basic tenets: human behavior is highly malleable, and through their cultures, people can successfully adapt to a wide range of circumstances. Underlying each of the examples above is a rich cultural background that cannot be treated within the confines of this chapter. However, it should be noted that varying adaptations to the absence of privacy and to crowding reflect such fundamental cultural components as the conception of self and the appropriate relationship of the self to others. These observations emphasize the importance of paying attention to the individuals who are expected to spend prolonged periods of time in confined environments such as space stations, as well as to the nature of the environment itself.

## Factors Influencing Perceptions of Crowding and Privacy

There are a number of influences on the perception of crowding in American culture that are almost wholly due to the environment. There is a good deal of evidence that the nature and design of an environment can markedly influence the attitudes, moods, and performance levels of those who occupy it (see Hayduk, 1983; Russell & Ward, 1982). It has been found that the general pleasantness of an environment can significantly affect the moods of people and their willingness to engage in helpful, altruistic behaviors (Sherrod et al., 1977a; see also Hickson & Stacks, 1985).

The perception of the degree of pleasantness of an environment is affected by several factors. Studies of the influence of color upon environmental perceptions have been reviewed by Knapp (1978) and Hickson and Stacks (1985). There is general agreement that the most arousing colors, red, orange, and yellow, are also perceived as the least pleasant, especially over time. In contrast, green and blue are perceived as quite pleasant and are reported to be less arousing and more restful. Studies of lighting seem to complement these findings, as bright lighting is associated with higher arousal than dim lighting, while red lighting seems to decrease human reaction time and green, to increase it.

The structure of an environment, including size, shape, the amount and location of both fixed and movable objects, and paths of ingress and egress, can markedly influence both the perception of the environment by its occupants and patterns of interaction between them. Rotton, in a recent study (1987), found that people are less tolerant of crowding in rooms with curved rather than straight walls. Schoonhoven, commenting on the placement of work positions in a space station, notes that the locations of workstations bear directly upon patterns of interaction, sometimes involving enforced isolation (Schoonhoven, 1986, p. 281).

Personality considerations are relevant to personnel performance in confined environments. Stone (1986) found that introverts seemed to have greater privacy needs than extroverts and were more sensitive to invasions of privacy. Harrison and Connors (1984) review arguments indicating that versatile individuals who are good self-monitors and who are skilled in both task-oriented and socioemotionally oriented activities may be better performers in space station situations.

Even when people have been chosen for optimum adaptability to a confined environment, problems concerning privacy and the use of available space will remain. One means of trying to reduce these difficulties concerns the establishment and maintenance of spatial norms concerning territorial claims and space use. Harrison and Connors review several studies indicating that those individuals who succeed in adapting to confined spaces for significant durations invariably establish norms regarding interpersonal distances and territorial claims (Harrison & Connors, 1984, pp. 70–71; also see Sommer, 1969). Zimring (1981) reviews several studies that indicate that the absence of privacy and spatial norms "encourages more aggressive boundary-control behavior in public, and encourages withdrawal to limit interaction" (p. 153).

The foregoing variegated considerations are relevant to planning an optimal setting for an extended stay in a space station, and there is strong evidence that supports the importance of yet two additional concerns: gender and perceived control.

Freedman's work on differing gender-based responses to high density was cited earlier. He believes that increased density tends to intensify reactions to an environment (Freedman, 1975, p. 93). There are circumstances where high density may be desirable, such as a cocktail party, but there are clearly others where high density can be irritating and result in a perception of crowding and in increased arousal. Freedman's evidence on differences in response to crowding supports an argument that the sexes tend to view crowded circumstances in dramatically different ways. Women tend to perceive small, comparatively crowded spaces as friendly and sociable, while men tend to find such environments irritating and uncomfortable. Under crowded conditions, women compete less with one another and perceive their co-occupants as more likable than do men. Men, in contrast, seem to find crowded spaces, especially where personal zones are violated, a continuing challenge to patterns of male dominance. Consequently, men respond with greater irritation and hostility than do women. The evidence that women adjust better to crowded environments than do men is consistent, considerable, and persuasive (I. N. Edwards, Booth, & P. K. Edwards, 1982; Epstein, 1981; Harrison & Connors, 1984; Schoonhoven, 1986). It also seems to be the case that mixed-sex groups respond nearly as well to crowded circumstances as do groups of women only (Freedman, 1975). One exception to this pattern of gender difference concerns achievement-oriented teams where males have been found to display a greater degree of cooperative behavior than females, although women cooperate more when the task is socioemotional (Epstein, 1981).

The evidence for the importance of perceived control on the part of environmental occupants is as convincing as that for gender. A large number of psychological studies have found that people respond better to challenging circumstances when they perceive that their actions can influence and even control the situations in which they find themselves. One of the major researchers into perceived control, Drury Sherrod, found that the performance and positive mood of subjects in differing experimental situations increased in direct proportion to the degree of their perceived control over their environments (Sherrod, 1974; Sherrod, Hage, Halpern, & Moore, 1977b). Environments that have been designed to permit users a sense of control have been found to be less stressful than those where occupants perceived themselves to be unable to influence their surroundings (Zimring, 1981). These studies and others like them strongly support the importance of perceived control as a mediator of stress in crowded environments (A. Baum, Singer, & C. S. Baum, 1981; Hickson & Stacks, 1985; Knapp, 1978; Schmidt & Keating, 1979; Sherrod & Downs, 1974; Sommer 1969).

## Practical Recommendations

Having reviewed a variety of psychological and anthropological materials that bear upon crowding, the absence of privacy and environmental design, I want to attempt practical suggestions for improving the ability of people to adapt successfully to confined environments such as that of a space station.

### *Gender*

Much of the evidence cited above indicates that crowding and the inability to withdraw from crowding due to the absence of privacy act as significant situational intensifiers, often producing increased stress. Given the characteristically different responses of the sexes to crowded circumstances, it is desirable that space station personnel be selected to achieve a reasonably balanced sex ratio. The token selection of a woman is of dubious value (see Schoonhoven, 1986, p. 279), and also, evidence suggests that mixed-sex groups can withstand the pressures of crowding much better than all-male groups and that they are better adapted to deal with both task-oriented and socioemotionally oriented responsibilities than are single-sex groups.

## Spatial Norms and Privacy

Space personnel are regularly tested for a variety of characteristics, including personality attributes, compatibility, and so forth. However, given that individuals can vary in the size of their personal zones (A. Baum et al., 1981; Hayduk, 1983) and in their needs for privacy (Stone, 1986), it would seem wise to examine potential space personnel for such characteristics. Failure to do so could result in a mixture of personnel some of whom finding that their comfortable conversational distance is regarded as a spatial invasion by others. Differences can reflect cultural backgrounds, with those from Northern European backgrounds generally needing more space than those from areas such as the Mediterranean and Latin America (Gillis, Richard, & Hagan, 1986; Hall, 1959, 1969), but they can also vary within a cultural tradition and result from early family circumstance (see Hayduk, 1983).

Whatever the characteristics of the personnel, it is clear that establishing spatial norms is an important means to reduce the likelihood of conflict in a confined environment. These norms should be established among personnel well before the actual occupancy of a space station, and they should be integrated into the mock-up space situations that personnel are asked to experience as part of their training.

These norms should deal both with the use of public spaces and with the definition of private territories. Limitations on the size of the space station environment may preclude private living quarters for personnel, but it should still be possible to identify small environmental niches that can be regarded as areas of exclusive use or, at the least, limited use according to a preestablished schedule.

## Design Concerns

There are several straightforward suggestions that can be made on the basis of materials reviewed above. Since people are more likely to perceive crowding in environments with curved walls, where possible—and it often won't be—curved walls should be avoided in favor of straight ones. Since red, orange, and yellow are excitatory colors, associated with increased productivity, portions of the work areas might employ these colors. Similarly, since green and blue are perceived as pleasant and nonexcitatory, it would be desirable to use these in rest areas. As noted below, these recommendations are not for fixed environments.

## Perceived Control

There is a great deal of evidence testifying to the importance of this variable. People who believe they can meaningfully influence their situations are much more resistant to stressors, including crowding, and they perform their responsibilities in a more tenacious and productive fashion. While there will be certain necessary limits on the degree of control afforded space personnel, anything that can increase the perception of control seems to be highly desirable.

Space station personnel should be accorded some control over their tasks and schedules. These individuals are highly motivated and inclined to work diligently in any event, so that giving them some perceived control over their responsibilities is unlikely to diminish their productivity and may well increase it. Indeed, when the crewmembers of Skylab 4 were given a degree of control over their work schedules, tensions were reduced and productivity was not diminished. Similarly, it is desirable that elements of the space habitat be amenable to change and to control by the occupants. Occupants, when at rest, should be able to control their accessibility to interaction, and where areas of exclusive use can be defined, access to these areas should be recognized as within the control of the "owner."

It would be difficult to make changes in the structure of the habitat, and it is likely that there will be little in the way of movable objects. Nonetheless, where possible, it is desirable to construct furnishings, such as workbenches, so that those using them can adjust the height and, perhaps, the orientation of these objects. Also, the colors and appearance of much of the environment can be designed to be controlled by the occupants. Work areas and rest areas can be constructed so that changes in lighting and color can be easily made. This could be accomplished by placing sets of small lights behind translucent wall screens or by something as simple as readily changeable wallpaper. Choice of color for the work space may be rotated through the personnel according to a previously agreed-upon schedule, but rest areas and private niches should be controlled by those using them. These are small and seemingly unimportant alterations, but the evidence is that they will yield significant benefits to space station personnel and will help to maintain and perhaps improve their productivity.

## Meditation

Irrespective of the steps taken to make a space station habitable, spatial limitations will necessarily increase the arousal states of the occupants and the intensity of their interactions. Withdrawal has been found to be a common response to such situations, and it is probably a healthy one, as it represents attempts to reduce levels of arousal to more manageable levels. The preceding review of solutions to crowding and the absence of privacy in various cultures indicates the prevalence of such patterns, and it also suggests an approach that might profitably be adopted by Westerners.

In addition to other cultures that, due to space limitations, have not been reviewed, the Japanese have demonstrated the utility of meditation as a means of obtaining relief from stressful circumstances including those due to crowding. Although readers will likely find this to be the most *outré* recommendation of this chapter, it should be borne in mind that there is good evidence from studies conducted in the United States and elsewhere that meditation greatly increases alpha rhythms associated with restfulness and that it can provide quick relief from stressors (see Bagchi & Wenger, 1957; Wallace & Benson, 1972). Meditation techniques are easily learned and represent a very efficient means of providing, in the absence of physical privacy, a form of psychological privacy that should substantially reduce the stress of life in a crowded environment.

The preceding recommendations may need to be altered or attenuated to adapt to the exigencies of space station design, but a caution would seem to be appropriate. Given the enormous expense of lifting payloads to orbit, engineers and designers have been, and will necessarily continue to be, very concerned with conserving weight and with designing environments that make very economical use of space. Given these concerns, individuals directly involved in the design of a space habitat may be relatively uninterested in recommendations originating within the social sciences (see Connors et al., 1986; Harris, 1986). However, the performance of individuals in such a habitat is and should be of considerable moment. An orbital station that makes efficient use of space but that impedes the actions of its occupants may prove to be far more costly in terms of lost productivity than an environment that is designed to facilitate human adaptation and thus to encourage optimal performance on the part of station personnel.

## References

Altman, I. (1977). Privacy regulation: Culturally universal or culturally specific? *Journal of Social Issues, 33*, 66–84.

Altman, I. (1979). Privacy as an interpersonal boundary process. In M. von Cranach, K. Foppa, W. Lepenies, & D. Ploog (Eds.), *Human ethology: Claims and limits of a new discipline* (pp. 45–132). Cambridge, England: Cambridge University Press.

Ashcraft, N., & Scheflen, A. E. (1976). *People space*. Garden City, NY: Anchor Press/Doubleday.

Bagchi, B., & Wenger, M. (1957). Electrophysiological correlates on some Yogic exercises. *Electroencephalography and Clinical Neurophysiology*, (Suppl. 7), 132–149.

Baum, A., Singer, J. E., & Baum, C. S. (1981). Stress and the environment. *Journal of Social Issues, 37*, 4–35.

Befu, H. (1971). *Japan: An anthropological introduction*. San Francisco: Chandler.

Connors, M. M., Harrison, A. A., & Akins, F. R. (1986). Psychology and the resurgent space program. *American Psychologist, 41*, 906–913.

DeBeer-Keston, K., Mellon, L., & Solomon, L. Z. (1986). Helping behavior as a function of personal space invasion. *Journal of Social Psychology, 126*, 407–409.

Dore, R. P. (1965). *City life in Japan*. Los Angeles: University of California Press.

Edwards, J. N., Booth, A., & Edwards, P. K. (1982). Housing type, stress, and family relations. *Social Forces, 61*, 241-257.

Epstein, Y. M. (1981). Crowding stress and human behavior. *Journal of Social Issues, 37*, 126-144.

Freedman, J. L. (1975). *Crowding and behavior*. New York: Viking.

Freedman, J. L., Klevansky, S., & Ehrlich, P. R. (1971). The effect of crowding on human task performance. *Journal of Applied Social Psychology, 1*, 7-25.

Geertz, C. (1960). *The religion of Java*. New York: The Free Press.

Gillis, A. R., Richard, M. A., & Hagan, J. (1986). Ethnic susceptibility to crowding. *Environment and Behavior, 18*, 683-706.

Goffman, E. (1959). *The presentation of self in everyday life*. New York: Anchor Press/Doubleday.

Gregor, T. (1977). *Mehinaku: The drama of daily life in a Brazilian Indian village*. Chicago: University of Chicago Press.

Hall, E. T. (1959). *The silent language*. Greenwich, CT: Fawcett Publications.

Hall, E. T. (1969). *The hidden dimension*. Garden City, NY: Anchor Press/Doubleday.

Harris, P. R. (1986). The influence of culture on space developments. *Behavioral Science, 31*, 12-28.

Harrison, A. A., & Connors, M. M. (1984). Groups in exotic environments. In L. Berkowitz (Ed.), *Advances in Experimental Social Psychology, Vol. 18*, (pp. 49-87). San Diego, CA: Academic Press.

Hayduk, L. A. (1983). Personal space: Where we stand now. *Psychological Bulletin, 94*, 293-335.

Hickson, M. L., & Stacks, D. W. (1985). *Nonverbal communication: Studies and applications*. Dubuque, IA: Wm. C. Brown.

Knapp, M. L. (1978). *Nonverbal communication in human interaction*. New York: Holt, Rinehart and Winston.

Raybeck, D. (1974). Social stress and social structure in Kelantan village life. In W. Roff (Ed.), *Kelantan: Religion, society and politics in a Malay state* (pp. 225-242). Kuala Lumpur: Cambridge University Press.

Raybeck, D. (1975). *The semantic differential and Kelantanese Malay values*. Unpublished doctoral dissertation, Cornell University, Ithaca, NY.

Raybeck, D. (1986). The elastic rule: Conformity and deviance in Kelantan village life. In S. Carstens, (Ed.), *Cultural identity in northern Peninsular Malaysia* (pp. 55-74). Columbus: Ohio University Press.

Raybeck, D. (1988). Anthropology and labeling theory: A constructive critique. *Ethos, 16*, 371-397.

Ronchi, D., & Sparcino, J. (1982). Density of dormitory living and stress: Mediating effects of sex, self-monitoring, and environmental affective qualities. *Perceptual and Motor Skills, 55*, 759-770.

Rotton, J. (1987). Hemmed in and hating it: Effects of shape of room on tolerance for crowding. *Perceptual and Motor Skills, 64*, 285-286.

Russell, J. A., & Ward, L. W. (1982). Environmental psychology. *Annual Review of Psychology, 33*, 651-688.

Schmidt, D. E., & Keating, J. P. (1979). Human crowding and personal control. *Psychological Bulletin, 86*, 680-700.

Schoonhoven, C. B. (1986). Sociotechnical considerations for the development of the space station. *Journal of Applied Behavioral Science, 3*, 271-286.

Selby, H. (1974). *Zapotec deviance*. Austin: University of Texas Press.

Sherrod, D. R. (1974). Crowding, perceived control and behavioral after-effects. *Journal of Applied Social Psychology, 4*, 171–186.

Sherrod, D. R., & Downs, R. (1974). Environmental determinants of altruism: The effects of stimulus overload and perceived control on helping. *Journal of Experimental Social Psychology, 10*, 468–479.

Sherrod, D. R., Armstrong, D., Hewitt, J., Madonia, B., Speno, S., & Teruya, D. (1977a). Environmental attention, affect and altruism. *Journal of Applied Social Psychology, 7*, 359–371.

Sherrod, D. R., Hage, J., Halpern, P., & Moore, B. S. (1977b). Effects of personal causation and perceived control on responses to an aversive environment: The more control the better. *Journal of Experimental Social Psychology, 13*, 14–27.

Shostak, M. (1983). *Nisa: The life and words of a !Kung woman*. New York: Vintage Books.

Sommer, R. (1969). *Personal space*. Englewood Cliffs, NJ: Prentice-Hall.

Stone, D. L. (1986). Relationship between introversion/extroversion, values regarding control over information, and perceptions of invasion of privacy. *Perceptual and Motor Skills, 62*, 371–376.

Takeuchi, T. (n.d.). Social values and interpersonal interaction. Unpublished manuscript.

Thomas, E. M. (1959). *The harmless people*. New York: Vintage Books.

Wallace, R. K., & Benson, H. (1972, February). The physiology of meditation. *Scientific American*, 84–90.

Watson, O. W., & Graves, T. D. (1966). Quantitative research in proxemic behavior. *American Anthropologist, 68*, 971–985.

Zeedyk-Ryan, J., & Smith, G. F. (1983). The effects of crowding on hostility, anxiety, and desire for social interaction. *Journal of Social Psychology, 120*, 245–252.

Zimring, C. M. (1981). Stress and the designed environment. *Journal of Social Issues, 37*, 145–171.

# 30

# Functional Esthetics to Enhance Well-Being in Isolated and Confined Settings

YVONNE A. CLEARWATER AND RICHARD G. COSS

As the technology for providing living and working settings in space and other remote environments has evolved, the focus of mission planners and facility designers alike has expanded from concerns for survivability to an emphasis on the achievement of human goals and a resulting sense of well-being (Clearwater, 1988). Requirements for habitability—the level of environmental acceptability—change dramatically with circumstances. For short periods of time, almost any arrangement may be viewed as acceptable to highly motivated individuals, as long as they are assured of staying alive and physically fit enough to perform their work. For longer stays, however, conditions must support psychological as well as physical health. In discussion of Soviet aviation ergonomics, Bugayev and Denisov (1976) attribute the quality of systems operations not only to the capabilities of the operator but also to the influence of the environment, the character and conditions of the work, and the interactions of the operator and the machine.

In planning the technology that will transport and house astronauts on longer, more complex, and dangerous space missions, the National Aeronautics and Space Administration (NASA) is taking a more integrated approach to the psychosocial and psychobiological aspects of space facility design and operations than any to date. At NASA–Ames Research Center, we are conducting habitability research to support the human role in space. An area of our habitability research known as "functional esthetics" involves the blending of science, engineering, and art toward ensuring envi-

This research was supported by National Aeronautics and Space Administration (NASA)–Ames Research Center Grant NAG 2-428 (NASA Technical Officer: Y. A. Clearwater) and NASA Training Grant NGT-70018 awarded to R. G. Coss.

ronments that will be both functionally and esthetically supportive of human well-being and productivity under the special conditions of spaceflight. In particular, our investigations are aimed at the development of interior decor elements (color, lighting, graphics, and surface materials) that affect perceived habitability.

Experience has shown that sustained confinement of workers in remote, isolated, high-risk environments analogous to space produces undesirable symptoms, nonadaptive behaviors, and performance decrements associated with stress. Confined groups in settings such as Antarctic research stations, nuclear submarines, and undersea habitats have demonstrated low morale, heightened anxiety, sleep disturbances, fatigue, reduced productivity, hostility, and interpersonal conflict (Connors, Harrison, & Akins, 1985; Evans, Stokols, & Carrere, 1988; Natani & Shurley, 1974).

In space, crewmembers confined to small, austere, machine-dominated settings even on relatively brief tours of duty have experienced performance-degrading effects (Bluth, 1981) similar to those reported in short-term laboratory deprivation experiments, including the emergence of visual disturbances, illusions, and restlessness characteristic of reduced environmental variation (e.g., Hauty, 1964; Heron, Doane, & Scott, 1956; Zubeck, 1973). Under longer conditions of confinement in isolated settings, such as that provided by a 7-month austral winter-over context, Antarctic station crews are reported to experience more serious behavioral disturbances that can include sleep disorders, increased anxiety, irritability accompanied by social withdrawal, and reductions in vigilance that can be hazardous (Natani & Shurley, 1974; Suedfeld, 1980). Weybrew and Noddin (1979) also note that reduction of alertness is a common finding among submarine crews during the monotonous conditions of prolonged submergence.

Soviet experience has shown that long-term confinement in their small Salyut 6 space station engendered prolonged episodes of boredom (Bluth, 1981; Gurovskiy, Kosmolinskiy, & Mel'nikov, 1980). To alleviate the stress of boredom, Soviet cosmonauts spent many off-duty hours at the station windows to obtain spectacular views of the Earth and aurora borealis (Gurovskiy et al., 1980). Similarly, looking out of the window, especially looking back at the Earth, was reported as the most favored off-duty activity by Skylab astronauts (Johnson, 1974). Cosmonauts Berezevoy and Lebedev reported that looking outside for long periods of time replaced watching telecasts of artistic performances and video movies as a form of relaxation (Zubkov, 1982). In 1978, Salyut 6 cosmonauts were provided with a videotape player and numerous videotapes of movies. Videotapes depicting natural scenery in the Soviet Union were found to be especially appealing (Gurovskiy et al., 1980).

Habitability improvements on the subsequent Salyut 7 and *MIR* space stations have been the result, in part, of an evolving process of esthetic experimentation, application, and evaluation in an attempt to provide familiar Earth-reference cues. For example, the soft pastel interior colors used in the Salyut 6 space station interior to create a familiar home-like ambience (Kidger, 1979) were replaced by higher contrasting colors aboard the Salyut 7 space station (Konovalov, 1982) in an attempt to provide the cosmonauts with more ecologically "natural" spatial-orientation cues in the microgravity environment. More specifically, the Salyut 7 station was provided with a well-illuminated white ceiling that, according to Gurovskiy et al. (1980), "will seem to imitate the sky." Research by Barbour and Coss (1988) further demonstrated that disoriented subjects subjectively experienced a vertical body orientation when they viewed various brighter colors in their upper visual fields juxtaposed with darker colors in their lower visual fields. Application of differential brightness to spacecraft interiors could provide a natural "floor–ceiling" relationship that could facilitate the maintenance of the same spatial reference plane that would reduce head turning and body rotation known to induce motion sickness (Oman, Lichtenberg, Money, & Mc-Coy, 1986). Although application of spatial Earth-reference cues might improve working and living conditions by enhancing the diversity of cosmonaut experiences, we currently have little information about the types of visual materials that might enhance the well-being of crewmembers during long space missions. The current research attempts to fill this gap using a spacecraft interior simulation to determine whether esthetically pleasing Earth-reference cues have potential utility in advanced space facilities and other isolated and confined facilities.

# Role of Pictures for Spacecraft Interiors

## Simulating Views Out of Confined Settings

One strategy for utilizing the interior decor of the spacecraft to combat boredom and make long space missions more bearable involves the use of decorative pictures to simulate a view to the outside of the spacecraft. Because esthetically pleasing pictures would periodically catch the viewer's attention, momentarily enlarging the contextual framework of the viewer to include the properties of other settings, they could increase the diversity of cognitive activity. The desire to enlarge this contextual framework has been noted previously under short-term conditions. For example, subjects placed in an isolation chamber were highly motivated to seek changes in the setting. Persky, Zuckerman, Basu, and Thornton (1966) reported that subjects under these conditions kept a television set on continuously except when sleeping.

Using graphical materials to ease the boredom of long space missions is not a new idea. Soviet space habitability researchers have adopted the theoretical perspectives of "technical aesthetics," the Soviet equivalent of industrial design in the West. In their view, technical aesthetics improves the working and living conditions of factory settings by combining features of the natural environment (Gurovskiy et al., 1980) with artwork (Mel'nikov, 1970). An example is found in the "psychological relief rooms" that provide fatigued factory workers with 10-minute simulations of wilderness settings using music and large, back-illuminated, photographic transparencies (Mel'nikov, 1978). Adaptation of this concept to Soviet spacecraft interiors includes the use of postcards and projected slides of landscapes and other images on a "special screen that imitates a window" (Gurovskiy et al., 1980).

The idea that ecologically natural properties of the environment might have restorative qualities is manifested by the desire of city dwellers to visit wilderness areas (Tuan, 1978). Recent research by Ulrich (1984) using hospital recovery data for gallbladder patients has shown that patients with a window view of trees and bushes recovered more quickly than patients who viewed a brick wall. There is some evidence that nature photographs have the potential of lowering physiological arousal that affects a person's well-being (Hess, 1975; Ulrich, 1981).

The current research continues this theme of measuring subjective preferences and physiological arousal but incorporates the context of viewing pictures in a simulated space station interior to determine the most appropriate types for enhancing the esthetic appeal of this technical environment. A high-fidelity mock-up of a section of the wardroom proposed for the habitat module of the International Space Station *Freedom* was constructed in which subjects could view projected slides and pictures under low ambient lighting (3.1 cd/m²). The mock-up comprised a 182-cm² peach-colored wall of high Munsell value equipped with cabinets, a control panel, a computer keyboard, and a flat-screen video monitor simulated by illuminated switches and a 58-cm × 34-cm projection screen. A darker peach value was applied to the lower wall section below the simulated video monitor based on experimental results on how differential color brightness can afford natural body-orientation cues (see Barbour & Coss, 1988). The sides of the mock-up were composed of light-blue fabric walls and curtains similar to other NASA space station mock-ups. Continuous 76-dB background sound provided by two baffled fans simulated the noisy conditions expected in the actual space station interior.

## Picture Topics

The rationale for selecting the wardroom of the habitat module for conducting a large picture survey was based on the proposed dining, conference, and off-duty entertainment functions of this facility. The wardroom would be the ideal location for displaying pictures on the large video monitor proposed for showing video movies. The crews using this facility will comprise mixed nationalities and both genders. With this in mind, the 320 photographic slides used in this study were selected on the basis of their presumed international appeal to both men and women. Ninety-five 16th to 20th century paintings were selected to include a diverse range of artists, techniques, and themes. Also, 225 photographs were obtained from field photography and books and magazines that emphasized high-quality graphical images. The topics sampled were as diverse as the geographic sites, which included scenes of human-built structures from many different cultures. Landscape scenes with and without buildings, animals in natural settings, and people engaged in athletic and recreational activities composed the largest number of photographs.

The picture survey was conducted using 16 separate sets, each of which comprised 20 subjects balanced for gender and 20 photographic slides. Subjects ranged from 18 to 50 years of age and were composed of students, faculty, and staff from the University of California, Davis. Slides of the following types and concomitant ranges were randomly assigned to each survey set: three or four of animals, one or two of sports or recreational themes, two close-up pictures of human artifacts and natural objects, and at least one picture with novel and incongruous elements.

During the experiment, subjects were seated in front of the slide projection screen and provided a brief description of the wardroom mock-up and the objectives of the experiment. Sympathetic nervous system arousal during picture perception was measured using an AIM Biosciences pupillometer to monitor changes in pupil size (see Coss, 1970). This self-report device is worn as a comfortable pair of goggles that occludes one eye but permits comfortable head positioning for visually examining slides. Because variation in slide brightness could elicit pupillary constriction via parasympathetic arousal (Hess, 1972), luminance levels of each slide were measured by spectrophotometry and correlated with each subject's pupillary dilation scores. Subjects did not exhibit significant correlation coefficients.

Four attitudinal questions were developed using a 7-point ordinal scale to address the following subjective topics: (1) Preference; "rate the picture based simply on how well you like it." (2) Interest; "rate the picture based on how interested you are in the topic presented by the picture." (3) Familiarity; "rate the picture based on how familiar you are with the topic presented by the picture." (4) Enhancement; "rate the picture based on its ability to make this setting in here more enjoyable."

Five practice slides were presented to familiarize the subjects with the attitude questions, and 10 or more practice slides were presented to train subjects on how to read the pupillometer. Without removing the pupillometer following this last phase of practice, the subjects then proceeded to report their pupillary scores during the presentation of the 20 experiment slides. The subjects then removed the pupillometer and were requested to subjectively rate the pictures on the 1-7 ordinal scale. Slide presentation order in all experiments was randomized for each of the five dependent variables, and the order of the four attitudinal questions was randomized for each subject.

The average scores for each slide were analyzed by multivariate analyses of variance (MANOVAs) and discriminant analyses (Bray & Maxwell, 1985). Slides were then grouped according to the picture topics discussed above. Several studies indicate that scenes depicting water or moist vegetation are preferred over those that are more arid (see Balling & Falk, 1982; Lyons, 1983). Strong preferences are given to spacious scenes with greater apparent depths of field (see Ulrich, 1977, 1983), especially distant mountain ridges with low hills and sparse trees in the foreground (Buhyoff, Wellman, & Daniel, 1982; Hull & Buhyoff, 1983; Patsfall, Feimer, Buhyoff, & Wellman, 1984).

Analyses of the effects of differences in the apparent depths of field of the various slides (e.g., Ulrich, 1983) will be emphasized here due to the implication that some pictures, especially those of nature, might substitute for windows in the confined technical setting of the International Space Station *Freedom*. Slide differences in apparent depths of field were examined by grouping slides as a function of the following estimated distances between the picture plane and the picture's central topic: (1) 0 to 1 m, (2) 1 to 10 m, (3) 10 m or more. Analysis of variance (ANOVA) was applied to each dependent variable (see Figure 30.1), and the concomitant MANOVA revealed that the groups differed significantly as a function of apparent picture depth (*Multivariate F* = 10.89, *df* = 10, 628, *p* < .0005). Only the first discriminant function was significant (*p* < .0005), and examination of the standardized discriminant coefficients and canonical variate correlations (see Bray & Maxwell, 1985) revealed that interest in the picture's topic, followed successively by preference and interior enhancement, contributed the most to group separation. Physiological arousal was negatively correlated with the first discriminant function, reflecting the general decline in arousal during the visual fixation of the more preferred and interesting slides with the greatest apparent depths of field (compare variables A through E within Figure 30.1). Finally, the statistical assignment of slides to their respective groups was relatively robust in that 63.8% of slides with the least apparent depth and 67.3% of slides with the greatest apparent depth were correctly classified as members of their respective groups.

Since the least preferred but most arousing slides tended to be those with the least apparent depths of field, the distribution of slides on the first discriminant function (see Factor 1 in Figure 30.2) seems to reflect an index of emotional and cognitive "tranquility." This interpretation is further supported by the results of Pearson Product-Moment correlations applied to each group. For slides of intermediate depths of field, physiological arousal was *positively* correlated with slide preference [*r* (99) = .212, *p* < .05, two-tailed test] in significant contrast with the low negative correlation coefficient of arousal and preference for slides of greatest apparent depth (*Z* = 2.29, *p* < .025, two-tailed test).

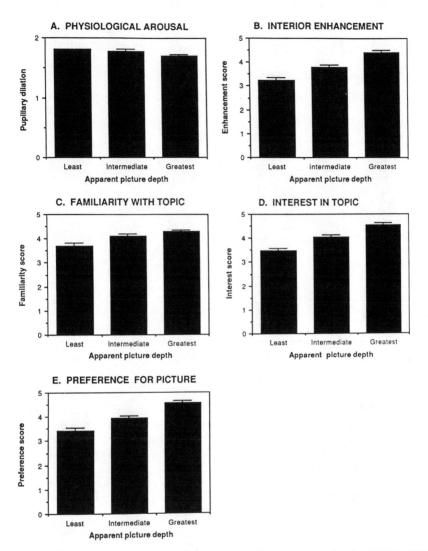

FIGURE 30.1. Comparison of picture groups based on apparent depth of field. [All variables engendered significant ($p < .05$) group differences. Mean and standard error values are shown. Note the inverse trend relationships between physiological arousal evidenced by pupillary dilation (A) and the four attitude measures (B through E) as a function of increasing apparent depths of field.]

## Pictures Perceived Under Low Light or Inverted Conditions

Two follow-up experiments investigated the general applicability of the picture survey findings to other presentation contexts in which lighting or body

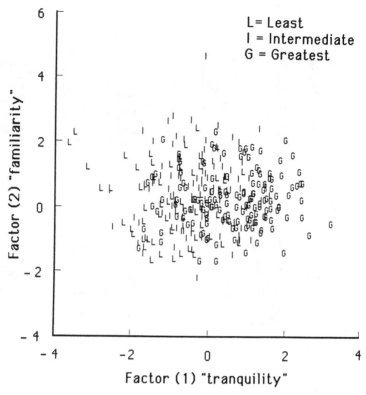

FIGURE 30.2. Discriminant space depicting the distribution of 320 pictures sampled in the general survey as a function of apparent picture depth. [The first discriminant function (Factor 1) was significant ($p < .0005$), whereas the second function (Factor 2) was not significant ($p = .15$). Labeling of "tranquility" and "familiarity" indices was based on interpretation of the canonical variate correlations that revealed that for Factor 1, interest, preference, and interior enhancement variables exhibited nearly equivalent strong positive loadings with physiological arousal loading negatively. For Factor 2, familiarity was the only variable to exhibit a strong positive loading.]

orientation might affect picture perception. Unlike luminous images on the proposed video monitor in the wardroom context, pictures could also be displayed in numerous locations in the space station as printed images that reflect rather than emit light. Since ambient lighting levels for some locations, such as the crew quarters, are likely to be low (10 to 30 lx), certain types of pictures might degrade esthetically when observed under dimly lit conditions. For example, landscape pictures depicting forests with closely space trees were considered particularly vulnerable to low lighting conditions because thick forests viewed in dim light might initiate mild viewer discomfort. In contrast, landscape pictures depicting crimson sunsets were expected to maintain their esthetically pleasing properties despite low ambient lighting because the low light of the evening sky is an important contextual property of the photograph.

Ten highly preferred landscape slides from the general survey were made into 20-cm × 22-cm prints that could be mounted for individual display at eye level on the wall adjacent to the slide projection screen in the space station mock-up. Five prints depicted dense forest vegetation in the background, and 5 prints depicted forests and savannas photographed under sunset and twilight conditions. These pictures were presented randomly to two groups of subjects under two incandescent lighting conditions (1.1 and 9.5 cd/m²) measured as photopic light reflected from the slide projection screen next to the picture. Each group comprised 20 subjects balanced for gender. After a 10-minute period of dark adaptation using practice slides, the subjects were asked to rate the photographic prints on the basis of how well they enhanced the wardroom setting.

A mixed ANOVA revealed that the two lighting conditions had very little effect on the esthetic quality of the prints. Moreover, the prints observed under the two lighting conditions engendered mean ratings that were very similar to those obtained from the projected slides; the prints from both lighting conditions and the projected slides yielded interior enhancement ratings that were also positively intercorrelated ($p < .05$, one-tailed tests). The results of this experiment indicate that ambient lighting does not provide an important constraint on the selection of locations for displaying prints of esthetically pleasing pictures.

Nevertheless, some locations in the station might be inappropriate for displaying pictures because crewmembers moving about in the microgravity environment might see the pictures frequently from oblique or inverted viewing positions. Some types of pictures, notably those with strong orientation cues, might not retain esthetically pleasing properties if displayed in areas where crewmembers frequently rotate their bodies. To examine this potential constraint, the fourth survey experiment was repeated using the same protocol, except that the 20 slides were shown inverted and included 7 slides with ambiguous orientation cues. Subjects were not informed as to why some slides appeared to be clearly inverted until after their ratings were completed.

Data from pupillary dilation and interior enhancement were combined with those of the fourth survey set and treated statistically by mixed ANOVAs. Significant group differences did not emerge for either pupillary dilation or interior enhancement. Right-side-up and upside-down slides produced enhancement ratings that were strongly correlated ($p < .005$, two-tailed test), a result that further implies that pictures can retain their attractive or unattractive qualities irrespective of the percipient's body orientation. In short, these follow-up experiments indicate that, in addition to displaying pictures on the wardroom video monitor, photographic prints can be placed throughout the station with little concern for lighting or viewing angles.

## Role of Pictures for Antarctic Stations

To address the issue of long-term habituation in a confined setting analogous to that of a long space mission, 285 photographic prints derived from the 35-mm slides examined in the space station mock-up were distributed to Australian crews at two coastal Antarctic research stations, Davis and Mawson. The primary focus of this year-long study was to determine whether crewmembers habituated more readily to the same spacious landscape pictures presented in the space station mock-up, which engendered "serene" attitudinal qualities, compared with landscape paintings depicting similar topics and pictures of active humans and wild animals, the latter tending to elevate physiological arousal (Coss & Towers, 1990).

In 1988, 57 all-male crewmembers at Davis and Mawson stations each received packets containing five unique, 20-cm × 22-cm photographic prints to display in their crew quarters and workstations (no pictures were duplicated at each station, but pictures were duplicated between stations). Five picture themes were examined: (1) relatively dry landscape photographs, (2) glittery landscape photographs with contrasting highlights, (3) action-oriented photographs of people, (4) photographs of wild animals in natural settings, and (5) photographs of landscape paintings. Ten attitudinal questions, based on a 1 to 7 ordinal scale, were constructed to evaluate each of the pictures at 4-month intervals throughout the mission year. For comparative purposes, the four questions on picture preference, interior enhancement, topic familiarity, and topic interest developed for the space station mock-up were complemented by additional questions in which crewmembers rated the pictures on (1) their ability to make them feel relaxed, (2) their ability to trigger conversations, (3) their ability to hold their gaze, (4) their ability to act like a window providing a view outside the room, (5) their ability to make them feel good about being in Antarctica, and (6) their ability to make them feel that they would rather be in some place other than Antarctica. The order of questions was randomized for each quarterly evaluation period, and crewmembers were requested to choose pictures randomly for each set of questions. Forty-four crewmembers completed the questionnaires for the four sampling quarters ($n = 23$ and 21 for Davis and Mawson stations, respectively).

Analyses of the questionnaires were accomplished by applying one-factor between (stations) and two-factor within (picture themes and sampling quarters) ANOVAs to the data. In an effort to seek evidence for external validity for the picture-perception survey conducted in the space station mock-up and the Antarctic study, the average preference scores for the five picture themes displayed at Davis and Mawson stations were correlated with the average scores for the same picture themes derived post hoc from photographic slides presented in the mock-up. Although the photographic prints displayed at Davis and Mawson stations generated lower preference scores during the year than those generated during brief visual fixation of project-ed slides in the space station mock-up, the average scores for the five picture themes from the mock-up study were correlated positively at significant levels with both the average first-quarter survey scores (Figure 30.3, A) and last-quarter survey scores from Davis and Mawson stations [r (3) = .992, .935, respectively, $p < .005$, one-tailed tests].

On the average throughout the year, picture themes differed significantly ($p < .05$) for questions dealing with providing a window-like view (Figure 30.3 B), with interest in the topic, with enhancement of the station interior, with topic familiarity, with feeling good about being in Antarctica, and with relaxation. Despite thematic differences, however, crewmembers showed evi-dence of habituation to the pictures throughout the year, notably ($p < .001$) on questions involving picture preference and interest (Figure 30.3 C, D) and also, significantly ($p < .05$) on questions dealing with interior en-hancement and the ability of the pictures to hold gaze, trigger conversa-tions, and make them feel relaxed (Figure 30.3 E). With questions dealing with topic familiarity, simulated window views to the outside, and attitudes about being in Antarctica, the pictures did not exhibit significant declines in attitude scores throughout the year. Further examination of the effects of habituation were examined using linear trend analysis of each picture theme. For example, the picture theme comprising humans in action-oriented scenes was the only theme that did not engender significant habituation for picture preference, but interest in the topics depicted by these pictures and their ability to promote relaxation declined progressively ($p < .05$) during the year (compare Figure 30.3 C through E). In addition to scoring lowest on the relaxation question, pictures of humans did not hold the viewer's gaze very effectively throughout the year.

## Simulated Window-like Views

On the question evaluating their ability to simulate window-like views out-side the station, picture themes showing dry and glittery landscapes scored consistently higher than the picture themes showing humans, animals, and landscape paintings (see Figure 30.3 B), a finding that further reflects their greater apparent depths of fields. These spacious picture themes also provid-ed the highest scores for the other questions in which picture themes were significantly different, especially the questions about station enhancement, feeling good about being in Antarctica, and the ability of the pictures to promote relaxation (Figure 30.3 E). From an overall perspective, comparing the multivariate results of apparent depths of field from the space station mock-up study and window question results from the Antarctic study, land-scape paintings do not appear as spacious as photographs depicting similar scenes, and they fail to engender strong positive attitudes, perhaps the result of their less realistic qualities than photographic images. In short, photo-

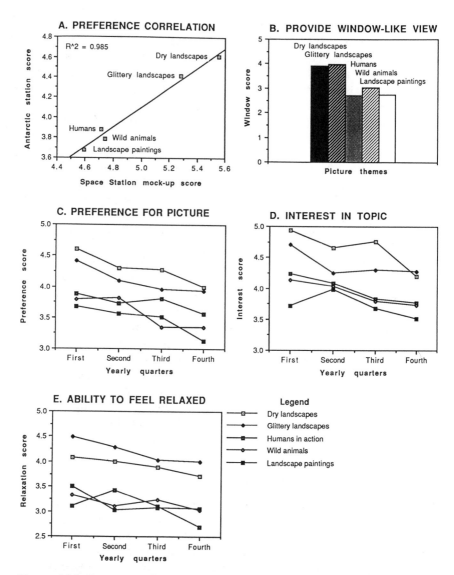

FIGURE 30.3. Responses of crewmembers at Davis and Mawson Antarctic stations. [Average scores are shown. (A) Pearson Product-Moment correlation of preference scores from slides viewed in the space station mock-up and first-quarter preference scores for photographic prints of the same pictures displayed at Davis and Mawson stations. (B) Year-long scores for picture themes acting like windows providing views to the outside. (C) Quarterly changes in preference scores. (D) Quarterly changes in interest in the picture topics. (E) Quarterly changes in the ability of pictures to make crewmembers feel relaxed. Note the consistently strong attitude scores engendered by the dry and glittery landscape themes.]

graphs of wilderness settings that are not occluded by objects in the fore-ground appear to provide the most convincing substitutes for windows in the confined technical setting of Antarctic research stations.

## Discussion

The first phase of the picture-perception experiment comprised a large survey of 35-mm slides presented on a simulated video monitor in a high-fidelity mock-up of the space station wardroom. This survey was aimed at identifying picture topics that are appropriate for enhancing the esthetic appeal of this technical setting in a way that might make long space missions more bearable. One finding was particularly relevant for assessing the utility of pictures in the space station setting: Pictures with the greatest apparent depths of field, irrespective of topic, engendered the strongest esthetic preferences. This finding was supportive of previous studies restricted exclusively to evaluating landscape preferences (e.g., Buhyoff et al., 1982; Patsfall et al., 1984; Ulrich, 1983). Statistical discrimination of slide groups simply on the basis of apparent depth of field suggests that the opportunity to look outside a windowless, confined, technical setting, as manifested by our high-fidelity space station mock-up, is a very desirable feature that can be simulated via spacious landscape photographs but not landscape paintings. In effect, pictures depicting spacious views of nature can provide some substitution for windows in confined technical environments. Moreover, in the second phase of the study, such pictures retained their esthetically pleasing properties when viewed upside down or presented as photographic prints in dim light. Follow-up research at two Australian Antarctic research stations, using photographic prints of the most favorable mock-up slides, provided additional support to the findings that spacious photographs of wilderness can simulate window views in confined technical settings.

With regard to the entire suite of experimental findings, perception of pictures that depict a variety of Earth-reference cues could combat specific forms of experiential deprivation inherent in the confined technical setting of the space station by augmenting the diversity of cognitive activity in ways that are similar to that produced by Earthbound situations. Clearly, work and off-duty activities in the International Space Station *Freedom* will not have the degree of diversity typically experienced by crewmembers before and during mission training on the ground. It is important to consider that, despite Soviet attempts to enhance motivation by providing variation in work and leisure schedules that included frequent contact with family and friends, prolonged deprivation of normal Earthbound activities is a reasonable explanation for the growing homesickness experienced by cosmonaut Yuri Romanenko during the final weeks of his 326-day mission in the *Mir* space station in 1987. Homesickness, however, was not reported by the Soviets during the 1987–1988, 1-year *Mir* mission of Vladimir Titov and

Musa Manarov, indicating that chronic stress may not be inevitable during long space missions and that personality factors may buffer some individuals from experiencing chronic stress. Despite the success of this mission, previous Soviet experience with shorter missions (Bluth, 1981, 1986) indicates that the potential exists for episodes of depression under the much shorter tours of duty planned for the International Space Station *Freedom*. The emergence of depression, however, does reflect underlying neurological changes that in the longer time scale might be functionally analogous to the short-term neurological adjustments to reduced innervation made during the first mission week as a result of the disruption of otolith cues for a gravitational vertical (see Oman et al., 1986).

## Psychobiological Maintenance Aspects of Picture Perception

The group of pictures exhibiting the least apparent depth was the least preferred for enhancing the space station mock-up. As compared with the landscape photographs in the Antarctic study, picture themes with less apparent depth, as inferred from their much lower ability to simulate outside views, yielded similar findings of reduced interior enhancement. On the average, the least spacious pictures presented in the space station mock-up were also the most arousing physiologically, a likely by-product of the more complex cognitive activity associated with the perceptual integration of larger picture components produced by close-up views (Coss & Towers, 1990; Kosslyn, 1987).

Several studies have documented that pupillary dilation occurs with short-term problem solving and other complex information processing tasks (see Beatty, 1982; Beatty & Wagoner, 1978). In contrast with this general finding, physiological arousal was not elevated during the perception of inverted pictures, which present a form of incongruity thought to engender arousal (e.g., Berlyne, 1971). On the other hand, complex cognitive processing may account, in part, for the high arousal and strong positive attitudes engendered by close-up views of people engaged in vigorous athletic activities, such as canoeing and sailboarding. Other examples of pictures that were both esthetically appealing and arousing were more distant views of animals staring at the photographer (Coss & Towers, 1990).

Space station crewmembers experiencing long tours of duty are likely to discard progressively the tendency to maintain a vertical body orientation with respect to the floor and ceiling and explore the station interior using novel viewing angles. Such novel interior views might temporarily delay habituation to the station interior. As the novelty of these viewing angles dissipates during the 4-month missions considered for the International Space Station *Freedom*, pictures that simulate window-like views to the outside, especially those that change frequently, can expand the contextual properties of the setting by fostering the perceptual processing of novel, complex information.

## Arousal and Habituation

With a few notable exceptions in the space station mock-up study, photographs and realistic paintings depicting unobstructed views of mountains in the distance and water in the foreground engendered very little physiological arousal. The low arousal associated with these serene pictures is congruent with previous findings by Hess (1975) using spacious landscapes as control slides for pupillary measurements and landscape perception research by Ulrich (1981) measuring wakefully relaxed brain-wave activity. Since pictures of wilderness tend not to elevate physiological arousal during short-term exposure, it is unlikely that they would augment arousal later as crew-members habituate to fixed exhibits of pictures during long space missions. The results of the Antarctic study support this view. Planned orthogonal comparisons showed that the combined average subjective feeling of relaxation engendered by dry and glittery landscape themes was significantly greater during every sampling quarter ($p < .0005$) than the combined average of the human, animal, and landscape painting themes (see Figure 30.3 E). Although the glittery landscape picture theme characterized by pictures depicting contrasting brightness and, often, moist highlights was consistently the most relaxing theme throughout the year, it did exhibit a significant ($p < .05$) linear decline in its ability to promote relaxation as time progressed.

With respect to the possibility that transient elevation of physiological arousal during brief visual fixation of certain pictures, as shown in the space station mock-up study, might "protect" these pictures from the effects of habituation during long-term exposure, it must be noted that no evidence appeared from the Antarctic study that supports this notion. When viewed briefly in the space station mock-up, the pictures of wild animals selected for thematic comparison in Antarctica were, on average, significantly ($p < .05$) more arousing than pictures of humans in action, especially animals staring at the photographer (see Coss & Towers, 1990). Yet, both themes in Antarctica differed little on most attitude measures, and in particular, pictures of animals scored the lowest at promoting good feelings about being in Antarctica. In short, transient changes in physiological arousal during picture perception in the space station mock-up were not good predictors of long-term changes in subjective attitudes in the Antarctic setting.

## Concluding Remarks

Habituation to pictures selected for display in the proposed International Space Station *Freedom* will not be a problem if pictures are shown for short periods as digitized images on the video monitors proposed for both the wardroom and crew quarters. Because they engendered relatively robust opinions among Antarctic crews during their 1-year mission, landscape pictures would seem to be the most ideal themes for long-term display as photographic prints in fixed exhibits in the International Space Station *Freedom*. Planned orthogonal comparisons of the dry and glittery landscape themes with the other themes further revealed that the Antarctic crews consistently rated these landscape themes as the most effective ($p < .05$) for promoting positive feelings about being in Antarctica throughout the year, albeit these themes also promoted strong feelings ($p < .05$) about wanting to leave Antarctica during the first and last quarters. These latter results indicate, however, that wilderness scenes can promote among the crew feelings of ambivalence about their long Antarctic stay. It is therefore conceivable that, in addition to their potential ability to foster positive attitudes among crewmembers during long space missions, such scenes of nature also have the potential of producing mild feelings of nostalgia. Despite this possibility, our findings from the Antarctic study clearly demonstrate that pictures displayed in public and private areas can contribute to the well-being of inhabitants.

*Acknowledgements.* We thank Dr. Desmond Lugg, Assistant Director of Polar Medicine, Australian Antarctic Division, for the opportunity to conduct picture perception research at Davis and Mawson Antarctic stations and to Drs. John Gill and Tony Tymms for gathering the data during the winter. Christopher G. Barbour, Steven R. Towers, and Dawn Mitchell provided important technical assistance that made these studies possible.

## References

Balling, J. D., & Falk, J. H. (1982). Development of visual preferences for natural environments. *Environment and Behavior, 14*, 5–28.

Barbour, C. G., & Coss, R. G. (1988). Differential color brightness as a body orientation cue. *Human Factors, 30*(6), 713–717.

Beatty, J. (1982). Task-evoked pupillary responses, processing load, and the structure of processing resources. *Psychological Bulletin, 91*, 276–292.

Beatty, J., & Wagoner, B. L. (1978). Pupillometric signs of brain activation vary with level of cognitive processing. *Science, 199*, 1216–1218.

Berlyne, D. E. (1971). *Aesthetics and psychobiology*. New York: Appleton-Century-Crofts.

Bluth, B. J. (1981). Soviet space stress. *Science 81, 2*, 30–35.

Bluth, B. J. (1986). *Soviet space stations as analogs* (2nd ed.) (Final Report NASA Grant NAGW-659). Washington DC: National Aeronautics and Space Administration.

Bray, J. H., & Maxwell, S. E. (1985). *Multivariate analysis of variance*. London: Sage Publications.

Bugayev, V. P., & Denisov, V. G. (1976). *Pilot i samolet: Aviatsionnaya eronmika* [Pilot and plane: Aviation ergonomics]. Moscow: Mashinostroyeniye.

Buhyoff, G. J., Wellman, J. D., & Daniel, T. C. (1982). Predicting scenic quality for mountain pine beetle and western spruce budworm damaged forest vistas. *Forest Science, 28,* 827-838.

Clearwater, Y. A. (1988). Space station habitability research. *Acta Astronautica, 17*(2), 217-222.

Connors, M. M., Harrison, A. A., & Akins, F. R. (1985). *Living aloft: Human requirements for extended spaceflight.* (NASA SP-483) Washington D. C.: National Aeronautics and Space Administration.

Coss, R. G. (1970). The perceptual aspects of eye-spots patterns and their relevance to gaze behaviour. In C. Hutt & S. J. Hutt (Eds.), *Behavioural studies in psychiatry* (pp. 121-147). London: Pergamon Press.

Coss, R. G. & Towers, S. R. (1990). Provocative aspects of pictures of animals in confined settings. *Anthrozoös, 3,* 162-170.

Evans, G. W., Stokols, D., Carrere, S. (1988). *Human adaptation to isolated and confined environments: Preliminary findings of a seven month Antarctic winter-over human factors study* (NASA Contractor Report 177499). Mountain View, CA: NASA-Ames.

Gurovskiy, N. N., Kosmolinskiy, F. P., & Mel'nikov, L. N. (1980) *Proyektirovaniye usloviy zhizni i raboty kosmonavtov.* Moscow: Mashinostroyeniye,

Hauty, G. (1964). Sensory deprivation. In K. E. Schaefer (Ed.), *Bioastronautics* (pp. 200-224). New York: Macmillan.

Heron, W., Doane, B. K., & Scott, T. H. (1956). Visual disturbances after prolonged perceptual isolation. *Canadian Journal of Perception, 10,* 13-18.

Hess, E. H. (1972). Pupillometrics. In N. S. Greenfield & R. A. Sternbach (Eds.), *Handbook of psychophysiology* (pp. 491-531). New York: Holt, Rinehart and Winston.

Hess, E. H. (1975). *The tell-tale eye.* New York: Van Nostrand Reinhold.

Hull, B. R., IV, & Buhyoff, G. J. (1983). Distance and scenic beauty, a nonmonotonic relationship. *Environment and Behavior, 15,* 77-91.

Johnson, C. C. (1974). *Skylab experiment M487: Habitability/crew quarters.* Paper number 74-133 presented at the American Astronautical Society Annual Meeting.

Kidger, N. (1979). The Salyut 6 space station. *Spaceflight, 21,* 178-183.

Konovalov, B. (1982, August 17). New features of Salyut-7 station. *USSR Report No. 17,* 6-8.

Kosslyn, S. M. (1987). Seeing and imagining in the cerebral hemispheres: A computational approach. *Psychological Review, 94,* 148-175.

Lyons, E. (1983). Demographic correlates of landscape preference. *Environment and Behavior, 15,* 487-511.

Mel'nikov, L. N. (1970). Color formulations in small enclosed spaces. In *Problemy sensornoy izolayatsii* [Problems of sensory isolation] pp. 121-125. Moscow: Izd., Instituta Psikhologii.

Mel'nikov, L. N. (1978). Komnaty psikhologicheskoy razgruzki [Psychological relief rooms]. *Mashinostroitel, 1,* 33-34.

Natani, K., & Shurley, J. T. (1974). Sociopsychological aspects of a winter vigil at South Pole Station. In E. K. E. Gunderson (Ed.), *Human adaptability to Antarctic conditions. Antarctic Research Series, Vol. 22* (pp. 89-114). Worcester MA: Heffernan Press.

Oman, C. M., Lichtenberg, B. K., Money, K. E., & McCoy, R. K. (1986). MIT/ Canadian vestibular experiments on the Spacelab-1 mission: 4. Space motion sickness. *Experimental Brain Research, 64*, 316–334.

Patsfall, M. R., Feimer, N. R., Buhyoff, G. J., & Wellman, J. D. (1984). The prediction of scenic beauty from landscape content and composition. *Journal of Environmental Psychology, 4*, 7–26.

Persky, H., Zuckerman, M., Basu, G. K., & Thornton, D. (1966). Psychoendocrine effects of perceptual and social isolation. *Archives of General Psychiatry, 15*, 499–505.

Suedfeld, P. (1980). *Restricted environmental stimulation*. New York: Wiley.

Tuan, Y.-F. (1978). Children and the natural environment. In I. Altman & J. F. Wohlwill (Eds.), *Human behavior and environment, Vol.3* (pp. 5–32). New York: Plenum.

Ulrich, R. S. (1977). Visual landscape preference: A model and application. *Man-Environment Systems, 7*, 279–293.

Ulrich, R. S. (1981). Nature versus urban scenes, some psychophysiological effects. *Environment and Behavior, 13*, 523–556.

Ulrich, R. S. (1983). Aesthetic and affective response to natural environment. In I. Altman & J. F. Wohlwill (Eds.), *Human behavior and environment, Vol. 6* (pp. 85–125). NY: Plenum.

Ulrich, R. S. (1984). View through a window may influence recovery from surgery. *Science, 224*, 420–421.

Weybrew, B. B., & Noddin, E. M. (1979). Psychiatric aspects of adaptation to long submarine missions. *Aviation, Space, and Environmental Medicine, 50*, 575–580.

Zubeck, J. P. (1973). Behavioral and physiological effects of prolonged sensory and perceptual deprivation: A review. In J. E. Rasmussen (Ed.), *Man in isolation and confinement* (pp. 9–84). Chicago: Aldine.

Zubkov, V. (1982). Post-flight interview with Berezevoy and Lebedev. Interview translated from *Sotsialisticheskaya Industriya*, 1982, December 26, p. 4.

# 31

# Windows: Their Importance and Functions in Confining Environments

RICHARD F. HAINES

Windows play a critically important role in making most working and leisure-time environments more habitable. When applied to the design of confining environments at least, the traditional concept is rejected that a window's esthetic characteristics should be considered only *after* all other functional needs (external viewing, illumination, ventilation, heat, and so forth) have been accommodated. Both basic and secondary (e.g., esthetic) characteristics of windows play many important roles in long-term isolated and confined environments. As a number of operational undersea, Earth surface, and space missions already have shown, it is important to have validated human factors design guidelines available with which candidate window designs may be compared and optimized. This chapter discusses selected human factors, psychological, and other design guidelines applicable to windows in confining habitats. The chapter concludes with a brief overview of selected psychological dimensions that impact window design and a brief introduction to an evaluative model (Window Dimensions, or WINDIM) for comparing candidate window designs.

## Window Design Characteristics: A Traditional View

In his *Human Factors Design Handbook*, Woodson (1981, p. 286) suggests that "the aesthetic function (of a window) should be considered only after the other functional needs are completely satisfied. In many cases, the earlier functional needs can be satisfied, while at the same time making the window design quite attractive." This represents the conventional design philosophy. Even if Woodson is referring only to the appearance of the physical structure itself (i.e., dimensions, shape, glazing materials, trim), I believe that such "esthetic" characteristics as these very likely play an often unrecognized yet important role in influencing how a person will react to the view seen through it. A rather obvious illustration is found in floor-to-ceiling windows in tall office buildings. Viewers are able to walk up to the plane of the glazing and look almost vertically downward with little apparent solid structure in front of them. Many people actually are afraid of such windows and will not get near them. Such persons are so conditioned by the design "esthetics" of such windows that they cannot even get near enough to them to be able to appreciate the full view they afford. In some hostile environments, where it is vitally important to be able to see outside in order to properly plan for an outside operation, a window plays a particularly important role, as will be discussed below.

Woodson (1981) points out that the main functions of windows are to provide a view of the external world (from inside an enclosed facility), to support planning for a future operation, to provide natural light for the interior of an occupied facility, to provide ventilation, to provide an auxiliary emergency escape route, to provide a visual communication link between two sides of an otherwise solid wall, and to provide an esthetically desirable focal point for an architectural system. Secondary functions of windows are to provide natural light filtering, to provide a thermal/acoustic barrier, to provide a moisture/dust barrier, and to provide one-way viewing for covert observational requirements.

To Woodson's list may be added other primary benefits of windows: to make it possible to see "all the way through" a building from outside to outside, to see into a building from the outside, and to improve the habitability of a building's interior. Other secondary benefits are to provide means for the eye to focus to apparent optical infinity and, thereby, stress the neurophysiological accommodative mechanism and, in the case of a space station in Earth orbit, to contribute to the physical health of the crew by providing access to controlled amounts of natural solar radiation and to contribute to the mental health of the crew by providing immediate visual and psychological access to the Earth. To the extent that windows admit illumination into a space, lighted rooms will appear less crowded, according to Mandel, Baron, and Fisher (1980) and Schiffenbauer, Brown, Perry, Shulack, and Zanola (1977). Windows also allow for greater flexibility in a given activity site, so that occupants may adjust the interior areas to meet their changing needs.

## The Importance of Windows in Confining Environments

As used here, a confining environment refers to relatively small-volume, built environments (e.g., space station module, undersea habitat, bunker, tunnel, and so on) in which the occupant(s) must remain for extended periods of time. Following are selected comments regarding windows from various occupants of confining environments.

Walter M. Schirra, Jr., wrote concerning the windows on the tiny Mercury capsule:

It might have been a lot easier—and maybe a little safer—to build a spacecraft with no window in it at all. The engineers did claim that they had tried to design one for us but were afraid the tremendous stresses and heat we would encounter in space might crack it. They also pointed out that they had already stuck on a periscope and a couple of small portholes for us to look through. But that just wasn't good enough. We all felt that a pilot ought to have clear visual reference to his surroundings, no matter what kind of a craft he's flying. . . . None of us wanted to die of claustrophobia out there in space, and none of us could see any point in going to all the trouble to get out there in the first place if we were going to be half blind. We were persistent, and we finally got our way. The engineers built us a window. (Carpenter et al., 1962, pp. 90–91)

Astronaut Grissom wrote following his early Mercury capsule flight:

There was a very vivid difference between the blue and the dark. The view through the window became quite spectacular as the horizon came into view. The earth was very bright, the sky was black, and the curvature of the earth was quite prominent. (Zink, 1963, p. 20)

Colonel Glenn also wrote:

Now, for the first time, I could look out the window and see back along the flight path. I could not help exclaiming over the radio about what I saw. "Oh," I said, "that view is tremendous!" It really was. I could see for hundreds of miles in every direction—the sun on white clouds, patches of blue water beneath and great chunks of Florida and the southeastern U.S. (Carpenter et al., 1962, p. 295)

In his review of space station analogues, Stuster (1986) indicated that the favorite leisure-time activity aboard Skylab was viewing the Earth from the wardroom window. The crew were transfixed by the sights beneath them and amazed at the clarity with which features were visible.

The Soviet cosmonauts also have remarked about the importance of windows in their spacecraft. In their monumental review of Soviet space stations, Bluth and Helppie (1986) point out that the Cosmonauts found looking out of their windows to be a favorite pastime and a form of relaxation (cf. Gorkov and Konkov, 1984; Litsov, 1981). Cosmonaut Lebedev wrote in his flight diary during his Salyut 7 mission that, "It's getting increasingly difficult. Only the visual observations have a relaxing effect" (p. I–27). Still later in the same diary were the words, "We just like sitting at portholes. . . . We watch things down on the Earth . . . " (Bluth & Helppie, 1986, p. I–27).

Experiences from America's undersea research efforts and military forces echo the above theme. The periscope is the window of the submarine. Periscope "liberty" is permitted on some boats. Morale has been found to improve after such outside viewing. A crewmember of the undersea research laboratory Project Tektite II stated: "The bubble window in the side of the habitat was very important in maintaining a relationship with the outside environment during daylight hours. At night, when an artificial light was on, it made it possible to view marine life and the sea-floor environment" (Kubokawa, 1987).

## Human Factors Design-Related Issues

A number of human factors design-related functions pertinent to windows for confined habitats are listed in Table 31.1. More detailed discussions of these issues are presented elsewhere (Haines, 1984, 1986, 1987).

## Psychological Design-Related Issues

A preliminary list of psychological design-related issues is presented in Table 31.2 to help guide planners of future confining habitats in which windows are to be included. In general, it may be said that a window is not a static or passive design element but an active contributor to sensory stimulation and psychological and cognitive fulfillment. Every window installation should be conceptualized very early in the design process in order to achieve the best overall compromise in design.

## Selected Psychological Dimensions of Windows

By virtue of its surrounding wall, floor, and ceiling "context variables," its inherent physical appearance, and/or the external view that it affords, every window can be expected to influence different humans in different ways and the same human being in different ways over time. Indeed, every window is unique in some ways. A validated, reliably predictive, design-oriented model is needed with which candidate window design features may be evaluated and compared. A model called WINDIM is briefly introduced here. With *time* as the first dimension of WINDIM, the following four psychological dimensions are considered.

### Visual Inspection/Escape

This dimension is related to concepts such as curiosity, withdrawal, and/or isolation in the sense that one is able to retreat from the immediate social situation within an environment by looking out of a window. In most cultures, it is acceptable to gaze out of a window during an ongoing social exchange without censure. If one stood staring at a blank wall, one would

TABLE 31.1. Human factors window design issues.

| | |
|---|---|
| Window usage | To what use(s) will the window be put during the mission? A comprehensive task analysis is essential in order to design windows to meet the greatest number of planned uses. |
| Field of view | This refers to the instantaneous plane angle subtended through any window. In general, this angle should be as large as possible in the horizontal plane and should be at least 140° arc wide if possible to permit full binocular viewing. |
| Body orientation cues | The eye-to-glass setback distance and geometric orientation of the viewer's head combine to determine the size of the peripheral visual scene. Peripheral cues are important in aiding orientation judgments of dynamic objects in the external scene (Rosenberg, Haines, & Jordan, 1989). They also help one maintain a stable self-orientation within an enclosed environment. |
| Body movement restrictions | This refers to all operational restrictions (imposed by the hardware, layout, or procedures) upon the crew's movements relative to the window. Space should be reserved around all windows so as to accommodate as wide a range of viewing positions as possible as well as to support multiple viewers at each window. |
| Optical transmission | Each window assembly should provide total optical transmission, i.e., the best overall compromise between supporting vision needs and protecting the visual system from radiation-related damage. Personal-privacy requirements also must be considered. |
| Maintenance/repair | The window designer must carefully consider such issues as cleaning, repair, and pane replacement. In hostile environments where the external environment may be life threatening, such design issues are not trivial. |
| Exterior illumination | Each window must be designed with regard to the full range of outside ambient illumination (and solar heat load) falling on it. Such radiation is important for planning activities taking place near the window but may also affect maintenance/repair cycles. |
| Interior illumination | All possible illuminance levels occurring within the habitat must be considered when planning each window. This is often accomplished best through simulation. A design concern is generated when it is darker outside a clear glass window than it is inside. The windowpane becomes a partial mirror with the attendant problems associated with mirrors. |
| Number of viewers | A round window with an area of 1 m$^2$ will have a diameter of only 56.4 cm, which will not permit more than one or two viewers (approximately centered in the window), but a rectangular window of the same area (e.g., 20 cm × 500 cm) will accommodate up to six viewers located side by side. A task analysis will show whether a particular window supports only a subset or all crewmembers. |

TABLE 31.2. Psychological issues related to window design.

| | General issues |
|---|---|
| Need for variety | Every confining habitat needs to present its occupants with as much variety as possible. Register (1984, p. 238) feels that variety is a key ingredient for environmental habitability. |
| Induced psychological tension | Leonard (1969) points out that surfaces can provide first an implied and then an actual restriction to one's movement, eventually inducing tension. A window will act similarly; however, its transparency should allow for far greater latitude of proximity before tension is generated. Past fear of being injured by a broken window may well contribute to tension. |
| Interpersonal contact | "Isolation, confinement, and other spaceflight conditions at once augment people's needs to regulate interpersonal contact and compromise the effectiveness of interpersonal distancing mechanisms" (Harrison, Sommer, Struthers, & Hoyt, 1986, p. 31). Windows may serve as useful mediators of interpersonal distancing in environments where other means are less available. |
| Symbolic meaning | Since a glass window is both solid and transparent, it is reacted to differently than a wall or a door, for example. To some crewmembers, a window may represent a symbol of release or escape from an otherwise intolerable situation. Cultural differences represented among the crew also must be taken into account. |
| | Nonhostile external environment |
| Mission objective reinforcement | Outside window scenes may influence attitudes concerning the validity, desirability, and safety of planned missions outside of the habitat. A window provides the viewer with knowledge of impending conditions that may be faced later, as well as with the general nature of how adequately one will be able to carry out one's duties. |
| Psychological support | A benign external environment can provide continuing support to a crewmember confined for prolonged periods of time. This is particularly true if the internal psychological "climate" is negative, so that the individual gains release by looking out of a window. |
| Privacy/crowding | A window may act as a dynamic mediator for meeting privacy needs within a confining/crowded habitat. This is because one can retreat from the social situation by looking out of a window. |
| | Hostile/dangerous external environment |
| Ventilation/ claustrophobia | In hostile external environments, windows cannot be opened. This will negatively affect the ventilation and personal confinement reactions (e.g., claustrophobia) of the crew. |
| Entrapment | A hostile external environment may act to imprison a person inside a habitat. Windows will provide one means of psychological escape. |
| Unusual personal-space requirements | People who are aggressive, maladjusted, and/or have low self-esteem may have unusual personal-space requirements (Altman, 1975). Windows may help reduce the consequences of such personal characteristics by providing for greater variety of internal space usage. |

invite social criticism. It is postulated here that the longer one is confined within a built environment, the greater will be his or her need for visual escape. If the environment outside of the habitat is considered to be hostile or dangerous, on the other hand, there is the possibility that one might tend to avoid the window's view to reduce the psychological tension associated with the view.

## Situational Awareness

This psychological dimension is made up of spatial, temporal, and energistic features in the environment as they determine one's wholistic attentional/cognitive awareness of what's going on around one. The situation may include past, present, and even expected future events that can be integrated into one's current plans. A good window design tends to increase one's situational awareness in as many domains as possible (e.g., cognitive, imaginative, projective, sensory). To the extent that one's future plans require accurate projections (e.g., carrying out space vehicle trajectory maneuvers), situational awareness is highly correlated with time.

## Novelty

This psychological dimension of WINDIM is related to the degree to which a window provides useful information to the viewer to deal with physical, mental, psychological, and/or physiological problems. It is postulated that a good window design should provide one with practical answers to practical questions. For instance, windows that can be opened permit both light and heat to enter and leave the building, both of which can contribute to pleasure and a sense of well-being and can help one decide what clothing is appropriate when leaving the building. They also permit people to talk to each other through them, to smell the air, and the like. This dimension is also related to the idea of creativity. A well-designed window should contribute directly or indirectly to creative solutions to problems.

## Distraction

WINDIM's fourth and final dimension has to do with the distracting influence(s) of a given window design. It is an abstract concept involving attentional factors that act to reduce one's concentration on a single subject, location, or feature in the environment. This dimension is strongly influenced by what the occupant's objectives are before reaching the window site and the degree to which the window is judged to be important in meeting these objectives. It is postulated that a good window design should yield a low to intermediate level of distraction from ongoing tasks.

## Representation of the WINDIM Model

Variation of one's subjective ratings made along each of these dimensions can be displayed using sets of parallel planes, as shown in Figure 31.1. Each of the four dimensions is shown extending out from a line in four orthogonal directions within the plane. As one moves through an environment, represented by the time line, one sees that each plane represents a single combined "snapshot" of the psychological strength of the four WINDIM dimensions.

Section (a) illustrates the size and shape of a WINDIM plane for a hypothetical "no window" environment. Such an environment should result in lower ratings in all four dimensions so that the total area of the polygon generally should be smaller. If the window is large (cf. section [b]), it is more likely that most, if not all of these dimensions will yield a larger score than a very small window (cf. window section [c]). And, if the viewer could approach the window and move his gaze about in all directions, analogous to the pan/zoom capability of a movie camera, the resulting WINDIM plane might appear as shown in section (d). Space does not permit a full explanation of this model or of the results of a controlled study that has been performed to evaluate it.

The WINDIM model could find application in evaluating various candidate window designs and surrounding visual environments.

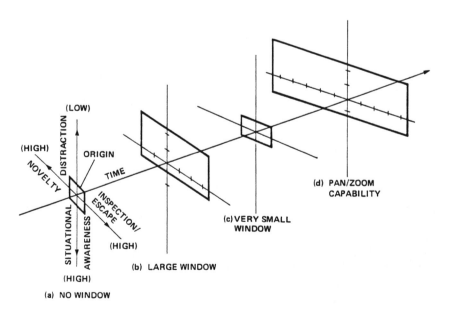

FIGURE 31.1. Schematic diagram of WINDIM dimensions.

# References

Altman, I. (1975). *The environment and social behavior*. Monterey, CA: Brooks/ Cole.

Bluth, B. J., & Helppie, M. (1986). *Soviet space stations as analogs* (2nd ed.). Unpublished NASA grant report, National Aeronautics and Space Administration, Headquarters, Washington DC.

Carpenter, M. S., Cooper, L. G., Glenn, J. H., Jr., Grissom, V. I., Schirra, W. M., Jr., Shepard, A. B., Jr., & Slayton, D. K. (1962). *We seven*. New York: Simon & Schuster.

Gorkov, V., & Konkov, N. (1984, August). *Cosmonaut Berezovoy's memoirs on 211-day space flight*. USSR Report, Space (pp. 51-67).

Haines, R. F. (1984, February–March). *A preliminary human factors planning and design outline of parameters related to space station windows and CCTV monitoring*. Paper presented at the Space Station Human Productivity Conference, National Aeronautics and Space Administration–Ames Research Center, Moffett Field, CA.

Haines, R. F. (1986). Space station proximity operations and window design. In T. Tanner, Y. A. Clearwater, & M. M. Cohen (Eds.), *Proceedings, Space Station Human Factors Research Review* (NASA Conference Publication 2426, Vol. 4, pp. 1-18). Mountain View, CA: National Aeronautics and Space Administration–Ames Research Center.

Haines, R. F. (1987). *Space station proximity operations windows: Human factors design guidelines* (NASA Tech. Memorandum 88233). Moffett Field, CA: National Aeronautics and Space Administration–Ames Research Center.

Harrison, A. A., Sommer, R., Struthers, N., & Hoyt, K., *Implications of privacy needs and interpersonal distancing mechanisms for Space Station design* (NASA Conference Publication 177500, p. 31). Mountain View, CA: National Aeronautics and Space Administration–Ames Research Center.

Kubokawa, C. (1987). Personal communication.

Leonard, M. (1969). Humanizing space. *Progressive Architecture, 50*, 128-133.

Litsov, A. N. (1981, July). *Distinctions referable to sleep, circadian rhythm of physiological functions and parameters of man's performance on the first day after changing from the usual schedules to split periods of alternate sleep and wakefulness*. USSR Report No. 3 (pp. 28-33).

Mandel, D. R., Baron, R. M., & Fisher, J. D. (1980). Room utilization and dimensions of density: Effects of height and view. *Environment and Behavior, 12*, 308-319.

Register, B. M. (1984, September). Making space a nice place to live. *Space World*, U-9-249, 9-16.

Rosenberg, E. L., Haines, R. F., & Jordan, K. (1989). The effects of window shape and reticle presence on performance in a vertical alignment task. *Aviation, Space and Environmental Medicine, 60*, 543-549.

Schiffenbauer, A. I., Brown, J. E., Perry, P. L., Shulack, L. K., & Zanola, A. M. (1977). The relationship between density and crowding: Some architectural modifiers. *Environment and Behavior, 9*, 3-14.

Stuster, J. W. (1986). *Design guidelines for a NASA space station: Habitability recommendations based on a systematic comparative analysis of analogous conditions*. Santa Barbara, CA: Anacapa Sciences.

Woodson, W. E. (1981). *Human factors design handbook*. New York: McGraw-Hill.

Zink, D. L. (1963). Visual experiences of the astronauts and cosmonauts. *Human Factors, 5*, 13–27.

# 32

# Decreasing Stress Through the Introduction of Microenvironments

Paul N. Klaus

Winter-over personnel in the Antarctic have to adjust to many stress factors during their stay. Common reactions in isolated Antarctic environments include depression, irritability, and social tensions (Harrison & Connors, 1984). These stresses require the greatest adaptive effort of the winter populations. Winter-overs are also deprived of certain activities and daily events that may offer stimulation and support in more usual environments. These are serious stresses to which they must adjust. The monotony of the polar landscape and the absence of the usual sources of stimulation and satisfaction that one acquires through interaction with nature are among these significant problems (Mullin, 1960).

The overall objective of the research proposed in this chapter is to determine whether microenvironments could have a positive influence on reducing the stress caused by the sameness of the environment that is so prevalent at the Amundsen–Scott South Pole Station.

At this point it is prudent and necessary to supply a definition and illustrative examples of a microenvironment. A microenvironment is a miniature, living representation of a particular landscape or landscape feature. It can include almost every landscape feature typically encountered. For example, a microenvironment can have mountains, streams, waterfalls, trees, grasses, and even a lake or seashore (Figures 32.1 and 32.2).

Microenvironments are ideal for situations such as those at the South Pole, where living space is at a premium. They can be custom made to practically any size that may be required. A microenvironment is virtually maintenance-free, inexpensive, and constructed of simple materials such as trees, soil, and rocks, which can be broken down into individual components for easy transportation. And, since transportation space is such a

FIGURE 32.1. A seashore microenvironment.

FIGURE 32.2. A miniature forest on a lake.

limited resource in Antarctica, microenvironments would not place a great strain on logistical operations.

In a recent study by Laviana, Mattson, and Rohles (1983), plants were used to "determine if their existence or non-existence as part of the indoor decor affected the perception of environmental quality and affectivity . . . " (p. 738). The results of this study demonstrated that certain selected plants contributed significantly to the perceived quality of the indoor space. The study was lacking due to the fact that the data offered no insight as to why different plants had this effect. However, "it was established that the plants had a significantly positive influence on a subject's feelings toward an evaluation of the interior environment" (Laviana et al., 1983). The plants did not contribute to an "openness" feeling, nor did their presence or consumption of space contribute to a "closed in" feeling. In another study, Laviana conducted a more comprehensive experiment in which he evaluated "the affective and qualitative characteristics of a simulated interior landscaped office" (Laviana, 1985, p. 738). The following were some of the conclusions drawn from the data:

1. The context in which an individual perceives the environment is improved in the presence of plant material.
2. Flowering plants have a positive impact on an individual's perception of odor quality within the interior environment.
3. The occupied space with plants was judged to be more acceptable than an occupied space without plants.

Both of these studies experimented with plants in an interior environment and the effects they have on an individual's perception of that environment. Both attempted to judge the affective quality attributed to environments. The study proposed in this chapter also solicits a response to an individual's perception of an environment, by attempting to determine whether microenvironments could have a positive impact on the human affective state. In addition, this study is based on the findings of studies such as Laviana's. That is to say, plants can have a significant effect on an individual's perception of the surrounding environment, as compared to an environment that is void of any plant material.

The Amundsen–Scott South Pole Station currently has only photographs or paintings of scenic landscapes. These serve to stimulate only the visual senses. Microenvironments, on the other hand, can provide for a more complete sensory experience, such as one might have while walking through a wooded area. They supply visual stimulation, and also, one may touch, smell, hear, and even taste the features of a microenvironment.

Because microenvironments elicit this multisensory experience, it is plausible that if they were introduced into the living spaces of the South Pole Station, they would have a positive influence on the reduction of those stress factors in winter-over personnel that are caused by the sameness of the polar landscape.

The isolation experience in Antarctica is analogous to the isolation experience in other environments such as space. If indeed this research is successful, the practical applications of establishing microenvironments in other exotic environments, such as space station facilities, would be the logical next step.

## References

Harrison, A. A., & Connors, M. M. (1984). Groups in exotic environments. In L. Berkowitz (Ed.), *Advances in experimental social psychology*, (Vol. 18, pp. 49–87). New York: Academic Press.

Laviana, J. E., Mattson, R. H., & Rohles, F. H. (1983). Plants as enhancers of the indoor environment. *Proceedings of the 27th Annual Meeting of the Human Factors Society* (pp. 738–741). Norfolk, VA: Human Factors Society.

Laviana, J. E. (1985). *Assessing the impact of plants in the simulated office environment: A human factors approach*. Doctoral dissertation, Kansas State University, Manhattan Kansas.

Mullin, C. S. (1960). Some psychological aspects of isolated Antarctic living. *American Journal of Psychiatry, 117,* 323–325.

# 33

# Keeping the Peace in Space:
# A Neighborhood Model
# for a Community-Based,
# Conflict-Resolution-Oriented
# Justice System

Donald M. Scott

What he was actually facing was almost like the organization of a new state. And yet, they could not sit down quietly and start out by writing a constitution with a good old-fashioned preamble. No, a particular and troublesome situation faced them, and they must act in the face of it. . . .

— George R. Stewart
*Earth Abides*

We must give serious thought to the prospects of devising procedures for handling these conflicts that are explicitly tailored to Arctic environmental and socioeconomic conditions.

— Interagency Arctic Research Policy Committee
*United States Arctic Research Plan*

Further research is necessary . . . to find ways to reintegrate deviants into the [space-ship's] crew. . . .

— Connors, Harrison, and Akins
*Living Aloft*

The author of a novel about society rebuilding after a plague has destroyed most humans writes of one small community's need to handle a critical conflict without a formal legal system. A committee planning the research agenda for the Arctic discusses the importance of examining appropriate conflict-resolution systems. The authors of a major, pioneering work on human factors in spaceflight express their belief that research in resolving conflicts between "deviants" and crew is necessary. Fiction and fact meet in this age of the beginning of the exploration of space, as speculations become hypotheses to be researched.

Humans have known much isolation and have experience with confined environments; now, driven by the needs of research communities in the polar areas and in space, scientists are seriously examining ways to satisfy all of the human needs of the residents in those communities. One major interest is in successful strategies for the resolution of human conflict.

Since 1977, the Community Board Program of San Francisco has been using a conflict-resolution process with remarkable success. The program, based in the neighborhood known as Visitacion Valley, uses a small, paid staff and a large group of volunteer neighborhood residents. The volunteers are trained to help other residents to resolve long-standing conflicts without recourse to lawyers or courts.

Researchers would profit by examining this program carefully. Their goal should be to determine whether it can be a training model for isolated, confined communities in Antarctica, space, and similar locations. In fact, some preliminary research of the Community Board Program has recently been completed.

## The Community Board Program of San Francisco

In the mid-1970s, an incident occurred that showed the inadequacy of San Francisco's existing justice systems. In an apartment house on the west side of the city, there was a tragic conflict between neighboring tenants. One tenant, an elderly gentleman, did not have a car but wished to keep his parking space clear. The boyfriend of another tenant repeatedly parked in the man's parking space. The elderly man tried to get help from city institutions, but police and other established departments of law are notorious for their inability to resolve such conflicts. The wife of the elderly man was ill with cancer, which added to pressure. Finally, unable to get assistance from anyone and frustrated beyond his limits by the other tenant's boyfriend, the elderly man took a weapon, shot the boyfriend, and shot himself.

Motivated by events like this, a group of concerned individuals met to develop an organization that would resolve such conflicts between neighbors. The group felt that there needed to be an effective alternative justice system in the city. They concluded that this justice system would have to be based in the neighborhoods. The founders decided to use volunteer neighborhood residents to conduct the conflict-resolution program, reasoning that neighbors would have a vested interest in keeping the peace where they live. The neighborhood justice system would deal primarily with the conflicts between neighbors that police disparagingly refer to as "barking dog" cases.

In mid-1977, the program began operation in donated space. Visitacion Valley was chosen as the first neighborhood, in part due to its ethnic mix and in part because of its isolation from urban services. A mountain to the south and a large wilderness park to the northwest physically isolate the area from the city. It is difficult to get quick police response, especially for minor, "barking dog" cases. Social services are lacking.

The Valley is within the city limits of San Francisco but is in fact some-what like an isolated small town. It certainly has much of the feeling of a small town. Near its southern boundary, horses roam the open space of San Bruno Mountain. During Labor Day weekend, the Ringling Brothers Barnum and Bailey Circus train parks in the Bayshore railroad yard and parades the animals to the Cow Palace. On Leland Avenue, the main street, the community conflict-resolution office sits surrounded by an old Italian bakery, a Chinese laundry, a soul music store, the post office, and a store-front library. People often stop on the street to talk with each other. Visita-cion Valley even has a resident beekeeper.

The program in Visitacion Valley was an immediate success. During the late 1970s, other offices were opened in other neighborhoods. A Center for Training and Development was established. Other communities in oth-er areas were trained in the process. Community Boards' founder Ray Schonholz helped to found the National Institute of Peace.

During the domestic budget crunch of the 1980s, Community Board was forced to close some of the neighborhood offices. In spite of that, the Visitacion Valley office is still functioning with vigor.

## Does It Work?

The success of the Community Board Program in Visitacion Valley has been remarkable. Some idea of this success can be presented through the stories of neighbors in conflict:

• An elderly couple that had lived in the neighborhood for years was upset by their new "ethnic" neighbors. The new residents made noise late at night, so the couple suffered from lack of sleep. After some heated discus-sion, it developed that the elderly husband had recently had a heart attack and was terrified by the experience. Hearing this, the new neighbors agreed to make an extra effort to be quiet at night. The disputants left after shaking hands.
• A boy from the neighborhood was caught shoplifting in a South San Francisco store. The security guard asked to bring the case to the commu-nity program since it was the boy's first offense. At the hearing, after acting defiant for a time, the boy admitted that he had shoplifted so that he could keep his savings for a visit to his father in the Philippines. The boy apologized and agreed to make restitution.
• An international hearing involved a wife from San Francisco and a hus-band from Israel. The husband wanted to have his son for the summer, but the wife was fearful that he would try to keep the boy permanently. The case was extended into a second hearing, where a resolution was reached. The Israeli citizen shook the panelists' hands, tears in his eyes, and sug-gested that this community program might consider trying to tackle the Arab–Israeli conflict.

Since it opened its doors, the Visitacion Valley office has handled over 1,200 cases. Of those cases, about two thirds have been resolved or improved by casework. Approximately 400 cases have gone to the hearing stage. Of those hearings, approximately 360 have been completely resolved, and most of the rest have seen improved relations between disputants. In other words, every month since its founding, the Visitacion Valley program has completely resolved three conflicts that no other organization could handle, and it has also helped in the resolution of "unsolvable" disputes each of those months.

## How Does It Operate?

Day-to-day operation of the Community Board Program is currently coordinated by a small, paid staff in the Visitacion Valley office; trained neighborhood volunteers assist in outreach, case development, conflict-resolution-panel work, and other tasks. Only volunteer neighborhood residents may sit on the panels.

Volunteers enter the program primarily in one of two ways: they have themselves been disputants, or they are responding to publicity for the free training program. The training teaches the skills of conflict resolution in the context of the Community Board panel hearing. There are no strings attached to this free training, but most participants donate service to Community Boards as panelists. After some panel experience, volunteers may be given further training in outreach or case development, follow-up, or other work.

The pool of volunteers is critical, because each panel is usually designed to reflect the demography of each conflict. That is, a panel will ideally include members from the age, ethnic background, life-style, and sex of the disputants involved. This is done primarily to reassure the disputants during the pressures of a hearing.

The community conflict-resolution process is simple (Community Boards of San Francisco, 1977):

1. A problem—a conflict—develops between neighbors or between a resident of the neighborhood and someone else.
2. One of the disputants contacts the program office.
3. A case developer phones, and then visits, the parties involved. He or she explains that there is no fee for any Community Board service. All communication is nonjudgmental. (Most conflicts are resolved, or at least reduced, at this stage.)
4. If the conflict is not resolved by this point, and if both parties agree, a hearing is scheduled.
5. At the hearing, trained volunteer neighborhood residents guide the dispu-

tants through a simple but effective procedure designed to enable the disputants to resolve their own conflict. This panel is nonjudgmental and will not assign blame. Most disputants, after some heated but respectful discussion, design their own resolutions during the hearing.

6. After the hearing, community members follow up on the case to verify that the agreement is working.

The hearing is the heart of resolution of deep-rooted conflicts. Throughout the six stages of the hearing, the trained panelists manage the work of conflict resolution that is being done by the disputants.

## Introduction

Panelists welcome the disputants into the hearing room. Each person on the panel gives his or her name and tells where he or she lives in the neighborhood. The panelists take their seats, and the disputants theirs; at this time, the disputants are seated facing the panel. The chairperson reads an opening statement that explains that the program does not seek to make judgments but, rather, to help the disputants resolve their differences. At the conclusion of this statement, the chairperson asks all persons involved in the hearing to agree to three simple rules: that in the first part of the hearing the disputants will speak only to the panel and not to each other; that disputants will not interrupt each other; and that all participants will treat each other with respect. When agreement is expressed, the second stage of the hearing begins.

## Telling the Story

In this stage, each of the disputants tells his or her version of the conflict to the panelists. The disputants speak in turn. Panelists ask questions that are designed to define the issues clearly. Panelists also ask questions that help the disputants to get in touch with their feelings. At the end of this stage, disputants' main concerns are summarized by a panelist.

## Understanding Each Other

At the beginning of this stage, disputants are asked to turn their chairs so that they now face each other rather than the panelists. A panelist will ask a question that encourages one disputant to speak to the other about his or her feelings in one issue area. This section of the hearing can get powerful, as deep feelings about the issues and the perspective of the other disputant are permitted to be expressed. Yet, in most hearings, there will come a moment when one disputant says something like "I guess that next time I could do this in a way that it will not cause a problem for you," and the next stage of the hearing has begun.

## Sharing Responsibility

Building on disputants' acknowledgment of their responsibilities to resolve their own conflict, the panelists seek specific statements of responsibility for the disputants for each main issue. After the turning point has been reached, this stage usually happens quickly, in a growing atmosphere of mutual trust and respect.

## The Agreement

Each disputant is asked for specific solutions to the main issues identified in Stage 2. The solutions, when mutually agreed upon, are written on a standard Community Board form.

## Concluding

The written agreement is read by a panelist. Sometimes, there will be modification of the agreement, particularly if any of the solutions are vague and open to evasion. All panelists and disputants sign the agreement. Closing remarks by the chairperson of the panel are congratulatory and positive.

# Would the Community Board Process Be Effective in Antarctica, Outer Space, and Analogous Environments?

For many reasons, it would be valuable to begin researching possible applications of the Community Board Program to isolated communities such as those in Antarctica and in space.

Anecdotes and preliminary research reveal major conflicts occurring in isolated, confined communities such as those of the polar regions and spacecraft. There is a growing realization of the need to find some method of conflict resolution that will be effective.

The Community Board Program has gathered a depth of experience—12 years—in conflict resolution in one neighborhood, Visitacion Valley. Concurrently, through the work of their Center for Training, Community Boards has gained a breadth of experience by helping many types of communities in many locations to develop programs based on the Community Boards model.

In considering the Community Boards program in Visitacion Valley, some important research and operations questions suggest themselves: Why does the Visitacion Valley program work well? Can the need for peaceful human interaction in isolated, confined research communities be realized through some type of partnership with Community Boards?

## Why Does the Visitacion Valley
## Community Board Office Work so Well?

This is an intriguing question, especially if researchers consider the fact that the Visitacion Valley office was the first in the neighborhoods, acted effectively during the expansion of the program into several neighborhoods, survived the cutbacks of the 1980s, and continues to be a very effective agency for conflict resolution in San Francisco. Researchers would be advised to examine the following variables: the quality of the management in the Visitacion Valley office, as opposed to other Community Board offices; the characteristics and the personal histories of the volunteers in Visitacion Valley; and the median age of volunteers in Visitacion Valley.

The age factor is particularly interesting, since there seem to be a significant number of middle-aged volunteers in the Visitacion Valley neighborhood (as compared to other neighborhoods with active volunteers). Space research is revealing that middle-aged males often handle the effects of spaceflight better than young males (Connors, Harrison, & Akins). Is it possible that middle-aged people, such as those in the Valley neighborhood, handle conflict better than young people?

## Can the Community Board Program
## Help Polar and Space-Based Researchers
## Resolve Conflicts in Their Communities?

Important questions for researchers to examine in this line of research include the following: How analogous is Visitacion Valley, or San Francisco, to polar and space communities? Has the Community Board Center for Training developed variations of the conflict-resolution program for use in other places that might have applicability for polar and space-based uses? If the Community Board methods prove themselves for space and polar use, what is the best method of training astronauts and "ice-o-nauts" to use them?

## Community Boards with a Wider Focus

Examining the applicability of the Community Board method for use in space has in fact already begun. Through the efforts of Wider Focus, an organization based in the San Francisco Bay Area, a meeting was arranged between Community Boards management and the National Aeronautics and Space Administration (NASA)–Hastings School of Law (University of California) project. The NASA–Hastings project has been researching a new legal system for use in space. The project team has hypothesized that a system based on conflict resolution would be desirable. NASA–Hastings coordinator George Sloup indicated great interest in studying the Community Board process.

After the initial meeting, the NASA–Hastings team began a period of observing the neighborhood training and some conflict-resolution hearings. At the end of these observations, the team requested that the Community Board Center for Training prepare a brief paper comparing the Board's conflict-resolution system with other, similar systems; the paper has since been submitted. During this same period, NASA–Hastings researcher Scott March delivered a paper that reported on the Community Board method to the National Commission on Space.

## Conclusion

The effective conflict-resolution method of the Community Board Program in the Visitacion Valley neighborhood of San Francisco could well hold the key to successful conflict resolution – and therefore to more successful missions – in the polar regions and in the isolated, confined environments of space. NASA–Hastings researchers are beginning to seriously study the Community Board system. Wider Focus, as its resources permit, will continue to act as a catalyst in this effort.

Other researchers who are studying the human factors of isolated, confined environments are encouraged to study this remarkable conflict-resolution program. All such researchers would be well advised to keep in mind that the Earth itself, from the perspective of space, is an isolated and confined environment.

## References

Community Boards of San Francisco. (1977). *Community Board member community member manual.* San Francisco: Author, Community Boards of San Francisco.
Connors, M. M., Harrison, A. A., & Akins, F. R. (1985). *Living aloft: Human requirements for extended spaceflight* (NASA SP-483). Washington, DC: National Aeronautics and Space Administration.

## Additional Reading

Interagency Arctic Research Policy Committee. (1987). *United States Arctic research plan.* Washington, DC: Author.
McKay, C. P. (Ed.). (1985). *The case for Mars II: Proceedings of the Second Case for Mars Conference.* San Diego: Univelt.

Stuster, J. W. (1986). *Space station habitability recommendations based on a systematic comparative analysis of analogous conditions* (NASA Contractor Report 3943). Washington, DC: National Aeronautics and Space Administration, Scientific and Technical Information Branch.

# 34

# Antarctica and Outer Space: Emerging Perspectives and Perceptions

HARRY H. ALMOND, JR.

The prospects for the exploitation and use of outer space, particularly that rim closest to the Earth, are very great. But experience has shown that the activities, even the presence, of human beings in any arena lead to pollution, destabilization of fragile environments, and often irreparable damage. Attempts to overcome these harmful impacts from human activities in Antarctica have been framed under a number of treaty regimes. The fundamental goal in these attempts so far has been to ensure that the states active in Antarctica will move cautiously and assume responsibility in maintaining their presence, in seeking to exploit the resources, and in conducting their scientific experiments.

To what extent is the experience in Antarctica transferable to regulating activities in outer space? Are states willing to accept a regime in outer space in which their activities are substantially regulated by institutions and procedures that they share? To what extent are they, or would they be, willing to delegate their "sovereign" decision-making competence to third parties? Can they avoid disturbing the fragile conditions that characterize outer space by simple expedients such as reporting on all activities, assuming for themselves the responsibility of avoiding damage to that environment, and so on? Or must they move toward an institutional base for outer space that has more substantial enforcement powers to assure that these responsibilities are met?

While these questions range deeply into all of the activities among states — into the orbiting of space objects, currently serving communications

This chapter consists exclusively of the opinions and arguments of the author.

as well as military support objectives, into the launching and testing of space objects and the current practice of dumping components of launched space objects to form orbiting debris—this inquiry will stress the deeply felt need among them to impose controls, commensurate with the security of all states, to avoid conflicts in outer space.

## Aggression

Foremost of the goals of states in establishing public order is that of preventing or deterring aggression. Aggression with nuclear weapons is often referred to as invoking a "first strike" (as opposed to "first use," where hostilities are presumed to have started and the use then occurs during hostilities). Aggression under customary international law, and under state practice pursuant to Article 2(4) of the United Nations Charter, is recognized as the impermissible use of force. The standards of impermissibility are those created among the members of the global community and developed in the practice of states in a process of claim. Permissible uses of force are largely those that relate to the exercise of the right of self-defense or that resort to the larger, and more ambiguous, right of self-help.

The problem of aggression is linked with the problem of establishing global order among states with contending and opposing value preferences. The democratic states seek to promote the values most closely concerned with human dignity and to moderate the promotion of the power of the state, particularly over the citizen: The values and this posture represent the true security of the nation, and the security within states provides a guarantee of security among them. The totalitarian states, at times referring to themselves as "communist" and at times as "socialist," seek primarily power, because this value ensures the primacy of the state and the collective order. While there are indications of a desire among the communist states to restructure themselves internally, the shift toward democratic values remains at this time a matter of speculation. Hence, most important, the possibilities of contention continue. Moreover, competition for the scarce resources, the allegiances of peoples, resources, wealth, skills, and technologies, aggravate this contention and, rather than lead to cooperative enterprise, are just as likely to lead to hostile competition. To ensure minimum order and security, states must have common objectives particularly as to fundamental values.

The contention among democratic and totalitarian states over global order spills into the contention with regard to the legitimacy of using force. Community standards that should provide the basis of judgment in these matters are not easily found when some states seek totalitarian goals and others democratic goals for the global order. Nonetheless, state practice provides standards of reasonableness—and that practice suggests that these relate to the legitimacy of the targets to which force is aimed; the proportionality, or amount and duration, of force weighed against the object to be attained; and the balancing of the necessities in using force against the humanitarian elements of avoiding the infliction of unnecessary suffering.

The framework among states is found in the United Nations Charter and in the customary international emerging from the practice of states under the Charter. Article 2(4) provides for undertakings to refrain from the use of force (or threats to use it) among members of the United Nations in their international relations. Article 51, however, provides that their rights, innate rights, of self-defense remain supreme. There is no provision relating to who determines whether these provisions are being fulfilled, so that community standards must be applied through a claim and counterclaim process. Changing circumstances in which force is used have affected this practice, and the impacts of terrorism, the violence identified with drug trafficking, and so on are familiar to us all.

To return to the problem of assimilating state differences and establishing a global order aimed at promoting human dignity, if states were able to share common interests and objectives, they would establish amongst themselves a global order—and that order would apply in general or in arenas, such as Antarctica, outer space, on the high seas, and so on. Accordingly, one of the major foreign policy goals of states is to achieve such an order, while preserving their own values. But there is no evidence that such a shared array of interests and goals has been reached: All attempts commencing with the Concert of Europe at the close of the Napoleonic Wars and extending through the period thereafter have been tentative and insufficient. Conferences at the Hague to this end were concluded in 1899 and 1907 but fell short, unable to provide the needed institutions or for an international tribunal to accommodate differences. Similarly, the League of Nations was moribund almost at its start, because states were not treated equally. The United Nations was created, but with the "realistic" perception that the major states would never reach agreement about global order unless each had a veto over measures that it did not like and unless that veto was limited to the major states (five of them) in the Security Council. Unlimited veto powers reflected differing goals for global order and global social processes.

Accordingly, the controls on the *initiation* of force or a threat of force presupposed in Article 2(4) of the Charter never reached coherence, because the community base had remained insubstantial. Since 1945, the totalitarian states have gradually adopted a practice in which they assert the permissibility of their use of force (such as the Soviet Union in Eastern Europe, Afghanistan, Africa, and elsewhere) and thereby proclaim a community that supports and is supported by the totalitarian values of that nation. While we may find that such assertions are muted by the United Nations, and even that the demands of democratic members in that organization may lead to reducing aggression, we cannot confidently assume that the organization is likely to be a global organization of a community of states in the near future. Instead, the opportunities remain open for future devices to assert the exclusive interests of states, even through aggression. And, as in the past, it is also evident that these assertions will be made in their self-interest by states, particularly those bent on aggression, and not effectively opposed unless states move toward common objectives.

## Community Interests

Efforts to move toward a community of common interests may appear in limited arenas, for limited purposes. It is too early to determine whether this has been the case in Antarctica. The Antarctic Treaty of 1961 sought two objectives with regard to armed conflict: It incorporated the United Nations Charter and its regime; it imposed arms controls on the states that ratified the treaty. These controls depend upon future practice — upon how states behave and how they enforce their controls in their mutual interest. But they are aimed at "peaceful purposes." While this is an ambiguous term because its content is unknown — and obviously depends upon what states confirm in future practice — it symbolizes expectations and a point of reference in judging that future practice. The controls, specifically, prohibit military measures, military bases and fortifications, military maneuvers, and the *testing of any type of weapon*.

To a very large extent, conflicts break out in populated areas and among populations or their armed forces, so that the "common areas" have so far been free of combat. They can for this reason be constituted as a demilitarized zone, and that is the case with Antarctica: Weapons and military activities of all kinds are banned. Limited verification of all activities is available through on-site inspections, afforded on a reciprocal and largely voluntary basis. The ultimate instrument of enforcement, characteristic of all arms-control efforts, enables a state to renounce the treaty if it finds that other states refuse to correct behavior amounting to a substantial, or "material," breach of the treaty provisions. The possibility of providing pressure, short of renunciation, through institutions among the concluding states remains open. Hence, Antarctica offers a proving ground in which, as states become more active in the use or exploitation of the continent, they might also, concurrently, set up the institutions to protect the arena from abuse from all such activities. Should they do so, the effectiveness of such cooperation in that arena would be a decided impetus to adopting a similar institutional base for outer space.

Antarctica lacks a regime, however, that controls the use of force under its own treaty. However, the Antarctic Treaty and the United Nations Charter govern the continent, so that the two instruments both apply to state relations and activities that occur there. Thus, aggression in Antarctica, even if not proscribed by the provisions of the Antarctic Treaty, are proscribed by the Charter.

It is not clear that this is a matter that can be overcome with finality. The Latin-American Nuclear Free Zone (Treaty of Tlatelolco) attempts to do this by having the contracting states declare their undertaking not to use nuclear weapons. Such a promise, however, is tenuous because of the conditions expressed or implied that go with it. Moreover, that treaty is also subject to renunciation, and it is probable that if hostilities broke out and if the weapons were available, even if transferred into the arena from outside or brought in by third-party allies, there might be occasions where the military command would call for the use of such weapons. In short, treaties symbolize expectations, and the effectiveness of prohibitions of this kind must be tested by the strength of the social order under which the treaty operates. We cannot test the effectiveness of such prohibitions by the language of treaties.

If hostilities break out, we shift from law that is applied to deter or prevent aggression (i.e., the impermissible use of military or armed force) and from the treaty controls that establish the arms-control regime to the law of war. That law has similar standards of reasonableness to those of aggression. The principle of military necessity embodies as complementary principles the necessity that legitimates belligerent claims in warfare, balanced out against their obligation (and need) to limit the damage of warfare. They must refrain from the uses of force that might lead to unnecessary suffering, or uses that are disproportionate to the military objectives to be attained, or the uses against nonmilitary targets including the noncombatants, or the excess use of force in any form.

These standards relating to the use of force are imposed by the global community. However, the failure of the global community to act as a community is evident in the hostile incidents and wars that have occurred since the Second World War. Most of these wars were terminated without war crimes tribunals and without attempts to correct the damages that were created. Compensation and reparations were not imposed in many of the situations, and the belligerents refrained from diplomatic actions including apologies for their conduct. Moreover, the nature of the hostilities has changed. Some states, notwithstanding their ratification of the Kellogg-Briand Pact proscribing the use of war as an instrument of national policy, have used hostilities for this purpose. And the Geneva Conventions of 1949 finally adopted as the triggering mechanisms the "armed conflict," purposely intended to avoid the restrictive element associated with the use of the term "war."

Accordingly, the law of war, unlike the law relating to the use of force, adopts a principle of conservancy and seeks to minimize the deprivations to values (i.e., conserve the values) that are created by results of hostilities. Moreover, these standards of reasonableness apply to all states—i.e., whether or not they are responsible for initiating the warfare, or hostilities, or whether or not they are representing, for example, the Security Council under directives from that organ in behalf of the United Nations.

Under this broader perspective, we discern states and other entities as participants in forming public order, but we fail to perceive them as being the public order itself. Instead, we perceive public order as continuously being shaped by the practice of states. We refer to this process as one that is shaping law and public order and doing so through the claims and counter-claims among states. This broader perspective about the process is transfer-able from Antarctica to outer space, transcending differences or limitations of the treaties of both regimes.

Our focus, however, is on the dynamic element — the element of continu-ous and rapid change among states. Moreover, that focus must be upon the characteristic feature of such an element — to wit, upon the decision- and policy-making process among states. It compels us to look into how states pursue this process internally — how they manage their own affairs, what values they prize and seek to promote and protect, and in particular, how they perceive power and its place in the public order.

Without clarification of the internal, or domestic, decision-making pro-cesses among states, it is impossible to be clear about their external pro-cesses, in which they are presumed to be sharing the development of a global order. Unless we are willing to follow these activities and perspectives, clari-fy them and the goals of states, build upon the past trends in their practices, the strategies adopted, and above all, the conditioning factors that make up those past trends, we are not in a position to speak or think clearly about how states will behave in the future, regardless of the arena.

For these reasons, the dynamic element of policy, associated with the decision flow among or within nation-states, must be clarified as to those decisions that states identify as law — as the decisions that regularize their behavior and underly the expected patterns of behavior. Here are the indices for a system of *emerging* law — the only law useful in an emerging social process such as those in the globe at large, as well as in Antarctica and outer space is law emerging from an accommodation among perspectives.

We perceive law as having an authoritative element — in which it is per-ceived to come from an accepted authoritative source or process. We per-ceive it as having control — control over future decisions and policies to meet certain policy goals embodied in that law or to ensure that activities are conducted pursuant to a community-shared notion of reasonableness. And we perceive in law its policy, or content — the subject matter of law that emerges as the law is promoted and strengthened. With treaty regimes such as those for outer space or Antarctica and with the expectation of arms-control measures included in both regimes, it is important to be aware that policy, or the content of the treaties, is shaped by practice under the treaty. In fact, that practice may even gradually reshape the treaty itself, as indeed has been the case with the Anti-Ballistic Missile (or ABM) Treaty, where the practice of the United States and the Soviet Union, notwithstanding official statements, lays bare a treaty regime that will recognize the full development and testing of space-based systems using physical principles other than those adopted when the treaty was concluded.

Hence the process of claim and counterclaim: States with contending public orders have differing perspectives and attitudes about the legitimacy of their actions and the objectives of public order. They bring these matters, in the form of claims, into their communications, into how they interact in their practice, and so on and in the resolution of the claims process, they ultimately reach the levels of tolerance—or intolerance—about behavior that is identified as the law. Moreover, because law and legal order are dependent upon a social order and because such an order is now emerging in both Antarctica and outer space, much of this claims process—and the decisions reached—can be broken down into those decisions that are *constitutive*, or designed to shape the order and its allocations of authority and competence within that order, and those that are simply *decisional*, in which states invoke law that they believe is law in being. States are thus invoking their law to legitimate their decisions, as well as to shore up the legal order expected to be shared amongst themselves. The treaties, though "sacred documents," are not so sacred as to be frozen for all time: They are way stations on the path to a more substantial legal order, to be replaced as necessary.

## Conclusions

A few conclusions can therefore be reached as to translating the experience of Antarctica to outer space—and in view of the dynamics of outer space—back to Antarctica. The Outer Space Treaty of 1967 differs somewhat in the weapons-control regime: It prohibits weapons of mass destruction including nuclear weapons, and outer space is thus made a partially demilitarized zone, not fully demilitarized as in Antarctica. The verification, hence the compliance, process is very tenuous so that states can carry on activities free of community supervision. Testing of weapons can take place—limitations are made on nuclear explosive devices (through the Limited Test Ban Treaty) in outer space, but testing is not prohibited, as in the Antarctica regime, as to all weapons.

The transferable element is that of the decision- and policy-making process. If states, terrestrially, can strengthen this process so that their community is brought into being, they can do so in outer space, and conversely. However, outer space is closely linked to terrestrial space: From the strategic viewpoint, outer space is vital to states. The principle of technological mastery—partially operative in Antarctica—is fully controlling in outer space: space cannot be effectively used for military or peaceful or aggressive activities without such mastery.

States that gain mastery over space and Antarctica will be enabled to do so through superior technological capabilities. Past trends indicate that such capabilities may become instruments for enhancing national power, so that states will be tempted, at least, to invoke their technologies as instruments of power. If this tendency is not checked, we are likely to find that states return to their traditional, if not innate, activities identified with competition over power, with the possibility that they might turn to hostilities. Perhaps the most substantial check is and will continue to be that of the nuclear weapons held exclusively for deterrence but with the unchanging awareness that should they be used in Antarctica or outer space, as well as elsewhere on Earth, they would endanger the environment of the Earth in general.

For both areas—Antarctica and outer space—there are potential threats arising from unregulated exploitation or use. For both, the exploitation of food resources—a higher current likelihood in the waters surrounding Antarctica—or of resources for energy, the more extensive use of orbiting objects, the failure to clear away space debris or space waste, the probability that some states may turn to nuclear power to propel their space vehicles or to improve their maneuverability, the dangers of collision and incidents arising from collisions, and, finally, the ever-present possibility of armed conflict leave open only for speculation the kind of behavior states will tolerate for the future.

A few recommendations can be made from this preliminary overview. *First*, states can encourage either among their own officials or acting with others a concerted and substantial inquiry into the institutions, procedures, and processes that states must adopt to protect the two arenas and their environments. From this inquiry they may find that past experience is applicable. But such experience may be limited to practice under a particular public order: The environmental impact statements and environmental regulations and practice in the United States are not likely to be applicable without alteration among states.

*Second*, states might consider more effective controls—and therefore far more effective compliance processes in the regulatory arrangements—over weapons deployed in both arenas. Here again, caution is advised. Nuclear and mass destruction (chemical; biological; radiation, X-ray) weapons could readily be introduced. Current controls are still promissory in nature and are not a sufficient means to prohibit their use or to prohibit warfare, but the existing control process can be a step in states' acquiring the pattern of control on a shared basis. This may help them to replace resorting to the weapons (because they then have a stake in the control process) or at least to create an obstacle to their use. However, even here it must be recalled that the nuclear weapons provide both the balancing mechanisms and, through the intolerable destruction inherent in such weapons, the assurance of control.

*Third*, and most important, states must not forego major efforts to shift towards goals that will advance and optimize the human dignity of the individuals who compose the global community. Totalitarian values are not values that can be promoted as values of human dignity, and the promotion of totalitarian regimes or their values supporting such regimes are a major source of human unrest and instability. Hence, the social order least likely to lead to instability, conflict, tensions, and the outbreak of hostilities is democratic, in the sense just mentioned, and must be promoted. Movement toward social orders whose objective is primarily that of promoting human dignity in itself would indicate that global public order may be both conceivable and attainable. Moreover, engaging in the effort to achieve such goals should have a moderating impact, making controls over conflicts more accessible and reducing the tendencies to resort to hostilities as a strategy or instrument of policy.

*Fourth*, attitudes toward competition need separate assessment. In the United States, early recognition that competition — like greed — is an element of human nature and must be harnessed to serve social purpose or goals led to the patent laws as well as to the regulatory systems of the antitrust laws. Each of these was designed not to eliminate the human nature involved but to ensure that checks would prevent the more powerful contenders from gaining and then maintaining control. Such attitudes among states are far more complex, and the inquiry into them must establish, at the level of global law, the appropriate processes.

*Finally*, the matter of human habitation in outer space is a matter of very large concern. The Outer Space Treaty of 1967 forbids the claims of states to outer space that would lead to sovereign controls or jurisdiction and provides that outer space shall be the "province of mankind." Such limiting provisions run counter to human experience, though they can provide the general, or broader, guidelines for state behavior. Human habitation will require areas that are exclusively reserved to the habitants, and unless peoples and states modify their current behavior patterns, it is unlikely that the states will seek to fund, and promote, habitable areas to be shared with others. The possibilities of modifying such behavior, however, should be fully and continuously explored. Habitation may assist in reducing the will of states toward force in space because of the likelihood of harm to such habitation whenever force is used in that arena.

In conclusion, the treaty instruments currently before us — the arms-control agreements, the agreements relating to outer space and Antarctica, the United Nations Charter, and others — are vehicles to form relationships for particular purposes. But such instruments are only as effective as states are willing to make them. Moreover, while such instruments are treated as "law," experience shows that what they provide may differ from what we expect from law. Under conditions of this kind, we must be aware that the treaty as a strategy or policy instrument is limited and may need to be replaced, or will be replaced, by the subsequent practice of states. In short, the treaty has not displaced the customary international law, nor its processes, but has only provided a written statement imposed as part of that legal process, offering precision but not necessarily permanence. The transfer of experience among states is a transfer that may or may not be assisted by conveying that transfer through treaties.

This was expressed by the economic summit in Toronto, 1988 (cited by Rozanne L. Ridgway before the House Foreign Affairs Committee, June 29, 1988, in *Current Policy 1090*, Department of State):

In several important respects changes have taken place in relations between Western countries and the Soviet Union since we last met. For our part this evolution has come about because the industrialized democracies have been strong and united. In the Soviet Union greater freedom and openness will offer confidence. Each of us will respond positively to any such developments.

Ms. Ridgway noted in citing this:

If the Soviet Union moves in those directions [proposed by Gorbachev] it will be a better place for Soviet people to live in. It may be a more responsible partner in world affairs. But we cannot know whether, or how far, the Soviet Union will, in fact, move in those directions. And we cannot make our policy depend on the answer to those questions. Instead, we need a policy that gives the Soviets a clear, consistent view of the interests we will be pursuing in our dealings with them as they pursue theirs with us.

# 35

# Justice in the Antarctic, Space, and the Military

F. Kenneth Schwetje

Hardly a day went by during the summer of 1987 without some reference in a major newspaper to the workings of the military justice system. Let's review some of those big stories:

- A number of U.S. marines were accused of espionage in the Soviet Union. Daily reports in the media detailed the apprehension, restraint, and investigation of these servicemen. The American public had an opportunity to watch a military criminal prosecution develop. A marine faced a general court-martial as a result of these allegations.
- At the highest levels in the Department of Defense, decisions had been made about the captain of the USS *Stark* and some of his subordinate officers. As a result of the investigation into the attack on the *Stark*, speculation ran high that some judicial action would be taken against those in command. The officers have been allowed to resign their commissions rather than face trial.
- At the pinnacle of publicity in 1987, we found two naval officers, Rear Admiral John Poindexter and Lieutenant Colonel Oliver North. From the beginning of what is commonly called the "Iran–Contra Affair," suggestions have come from various sources that Poindexter and North be court-martialed. The daughter of the President made a public statement that they should be tried for treason because they lied to her father. A former Justice of the Supreme Court recommended that the admiral and colonel

The view and conclusions expressed in this chapter are those of the author and do not necessarily reflect the official policy or position of the Department of Defense, the United States Air Force, the Joint Staff, or the United States Government.

be brought before a court-martial and then granted immunity so that they could testify before Congress without the necessity for congressional immunity. All of these suggestions demonstrated naivete as to the nature of justice in the military.

The old cliche has it that military justice is to justice as military music is to music. Well, a lot of people like military music and think it has a proper place in our cultural life. This comparison of music and justice really only reflects a prejudice against everything "military." The book by the same name (Sherrill, 1969) became popular when the military was at its recent peak of unpopularity—during the Viet Nam conflict. I would not pretend that everything about the military justice system has always been perfect, nor ever will be. My career has coincided, more or less, with the end of our involvement in Southeast Asia and, in its aftermath, renewed appreciation of the contributions made to the peace and security of America by the sacrifice of this relatively small portion of the population. It is with this heightened awareness of military justice and greater public acceptance of things military that I approach the topic of this chapter.

The purpose of the chapter is to discuss some of the attributes of the military justice system that would have significant value in a legal regime utilized by long-term space voyagers and for permanently manned space stations or extraterrestrial colonies, whether civilian or military. The theme of the conference *The Human Experience in Antarctica: Applications to Life in Space* was to explore the human experience in Antarctica and determine what, if any, lessons learned there will improve our chances for success in the exploration of space.

The legal regime that applies to our future space explorers will certainly have its roots in some existing system here on Earth; yet, we must recognize, as we did during the conference, that the space environment will produce unique situations not encountered on Earth. The legal regime in space must make allowances for the novel psychological, physiological, and sociological phenomena encountered by spacefarers.

In determining what legal regime might best suit space exploration, we must keep certain salient facts in mind:

1. All spacefaring nations are parties to multilateral treaties that limit or direct the final form of what might be adopted.
2. Unlike our forefathers, who had years or even centuries to develop an adequate system of law, we have immediate need of a fairly comprehensive legal regime. This requires us to anticipate what we wish to control, how we wish to control it, and how we will respond to those unearthly needs we should expect.
3. The exploration of space will grow as an international endeavor. Witness the combined efforts of the United States, Japan, Canada, and some European nations to participate in the U.S. space station project. Most Americans believe we have a wonderful system of law, and we do. Each of

our international partners may have made similar value judgments about the way it governs its citizens. Can we afford to design a form of jurisprudence that applies to some on a space station but not others, depending on nationality? If the answer is no, how can we resolve some of the conflicts inherent in different systems of law?

4. How far can we go in fashioning new rules to provide for "space–specific" crimes and defenses? What sort of procedural changes will be required given the nature of planned space activities?

## Jurisdiction

Jurisdiction is the right and power of a court to adjudicate a matter before it. The law requires that there be jurisdiction over the subject matter of the lawsuit and the person against whom it is brought. Under well-accepted principles of international law, such power can be extended beyond the territorial boundaries of a given state. This is known as "extraterritorial jurisdiction." To reach this state of affairs, we begin with the proposition or presumption that jurisdiction is territorial. Then international law develops the extraterritorial aspect along one of two lines: first, the territorial theory, that the court has jurisdiction because an act occurred in an "extension" of its territory, or second, that there is a substantial and genuine connection between the subject matter and the territorial base (Brownlie, 1979). Customary international law permits states wide discretion in their exercise of extraterritorial jurisdiction so long as there is a genuine link between the persons, things, or events over which jurisdiction is claimed. International law recognizes a number of theories or principles on which a state may exercise jurisdiction.

## Space Law and Jurisdiction

No particular treaty governs criminal jurisdiction in space, but certain principles are contained in the current body of space law to permit fashioning a system that could be acceptable to most spacefaring nations.

The cornerstone of international space law is the 1967 Outer Space Treaty. Article II of that treaty reads: "Outer space, including the moon and other celestial bodies, is not subject to national appropriation by claim of sovereignty, by means of use or occupation, or any other means." The treaty thus precludes the assertion of strictly territorial jurisdiction but does not preclude other kinds (Bruton, 1984). The one specific type of jurisdiction is stated in Article VIII of the same treaty, in part as follows:

A State Party to the Treaty on whose registry an object launched into outer space is carried shall retain jurisdiction and control over such object, and over any personnel thereof, while in outer space or on a celestial body. . . .

This and other provisions of subsequent space treaties make it clear that the parties to the treaties have not only the right but also an international obligation to maintain order during their space activities.

While the Outer Space Treaty may establish a framework for the exercise of jurisdiction, it does not resolve all of the questions. These issues will be settled as they arise through the evolution of state practice and through international cooperation in forging additional rules (Bruton, 1984). Continuing cooperation is best exemplified by the negotiations between the United States and its potential space station partners to draft a legal annex for the space station agreement. Our experience with the Antarctic Treaty's criminal jurisdiction regime may be instructive in this effort.

Like the Outer Space Treaty, the Antarctic Treaty restricts territorial sovereignty as a basis of jurisdiction; but unlike the space treaty, it does not internationalize the continent. In Article IV of the Antarctic Treaty, claims of sovereignty are suspended while the treaty is in force.

Article VIII of the Antarctic Treaty establishes jurisdiction over persons, e.g., over observers carrying out inspections, scientists, and their staff. The second clause of that Article provides that the "Contracting Parties concerned in any case of dispute with regard to the exercise of jurisdiction in Antarctica shall immediately consult together with a view to reaching a mutually acceptable solution."

Apparently, this provision would be used to resolve jurisdictional conflicts involving persons other than those enumerated in clause 2. The Antarctic Treaty avoids criminal jurisdiction issues rather than resolving them (Bruton, 1984). As with other sections of this treaty, the provision contemplates that these issues will be resolved mutually by the countries concerned. Because this arrangement lends itself well to negotiated jurisdictional arrangements, the space station negotiation may well provide a similar model for outer space.

## U. S. Legislation

Within the international legal framework for the exercise of criminal jurisdiction, a state's own domestic legislation must extend the reach of its criminal laws to the Antarctic or space. As a rule, the United States does not apply its criminal laws beyond its territorial boundaries. Exceptions proscribe conduct abroad having substantial domestic effects (Blakesley, 1979). Many federal laws have been applied to criminal behavior abroad, but a list of examples would add little to the current discussion. Rather, I would prefer to focus on three federal laws that could have significance: The Uniform Code of Military Justice (UCMJ), the Special Maritime and Territorial Jurisdiction of the United States (18 U.S.C. 7), and a recent amendment to the National Aeronautics and Space (NAS) Act of 1958.

In the early days of manned space activities, there was not a great need for extended U.S. criminal jurisdiction in space. Until the shuttles began to orbit the Earth, nearly all astronauts were military officers attached to the National Aeronautics and Space Administration (NASA). The territorial applicability of the UCMJ is set out simply in Article 5, which reads in its entirety: "This chapter applies in all places." All members of the armed forces, military academy cadets, reserves on active duty, military retirees, military prisoners, prisoners of war, and a limited class of civilians are subject to it. Subsection (12) of Article 2(a) subjects to the code persons under any "treaty or agreement to which the United States is a party . . . within an area . . . reserved or acquired for use by the United States which is under control of the Secretary concerned and which is outside the United States. . . . " An argument could be made that under the proper international agreement the entire UCMJ could apply to civilians (Adams, 1983), as in the other enumerated circumstances. As our space activities have increased, the need to fill the gap or void in criminal jurisdiction over the growing number of nonmilitary personnel in space has become apparent.

In 1981, Title 18 of the U.S. Code, the Federal Criminal Code, was amended to extend the special maritime and territorial jurisdiction of the United States to space vehicles on the registry of the United States. The previous amendment to this section occurred in 1952, after a federal court dismissed a case for lack of jurisdiction. In that case, *United States v. Cordova* (1950), the defendant repeatedly assaulted other passengers and the crew of an airliner over the high seas. No particular legal theory was held to be sufficient for the court to retain jurisdiction over these offenses, so Cordova went unpunished for his crimes. Not willing to have this embarrassing situation repeated, Congress extended the jurisdiction of the code to aircraft over the high seas. In 1984, this section was further amended to extend the jurisdiction of U. S. federal courts to "[any] place outside the jurisdiction of any nation with respect to an offense by or against a national of the United States."

The primary purpose of this amendment was to fill any lacuna in our ability to prosecute terrorists. No doubt, however, this amendment could be used equally well to prosecute crimes in space or the Antarctic.

I see problems with the use of the U.S. Code, as extended by section 7, to prosecute criminal activity in space. First, only the conduct specifically proscribed in the code (generally common-law felonies) can be prosecuted. Not every crime that could be anticipated is contained in those enumerated. Some system will eventually develop to punish those minor offenses normally handled by civilian police courts or justices of the peace and by nonjudicial punishment in the military.

Second, I note that the special maritime and territorial jurisdictions of the United States have been strictly construed by the courts. The 1981 amendment covers offenses committed on "any vehicle designed for flight or navigation in space. . . . " The legislative history of the act indicates that a *space vehicle* is intended to comprehend the meaning of the term as defined in subsections 103(2) and 308(f) of the NAS Act of 1958. While the definitions are broad enough to encompass almost all objects *launched* into space, including a space station, the amendment would probably be restricted to its literal terms. A question arises in my mind as to whether a crime committed away from a lunar station would be covered by the definition of space vehicle. We could have the following situation: At a Moon colony, a German national murders a Greek national while both are outside the confines of the lunar habitat. To complicate the hypothetical, only lunar material was used to manufacture the habitat. A literal reading of subsections (6) and (7) would leave us with no jurisdiction to prosecute the German, even if he was part of a U.S. scientific team.

Another problem is that registration by the United States is a condition of jurisdiction. It is doubtful that colonies on the Moon or elsewhere will be "registered" as space objects. Space colonists have a right to public order, which will be difficult to maintain if fine legal distinctions allow persons to commit offenses and go unpunished.

The third space-related legislation is the amendments to the NAS Act. Under the authority contained in subsections 203(c) and 304(a) of the act, the administrator is authorized to issue regulations governing the operation of NASA and establishing requirements, restrictions, and safeguards for national security. The NASA administrator has issued regulations with respect to the space transportation system. These regulations authorize the shuttle commander to enforce order and discipline over all personnel aboard. Failure to comply with the commander's orders subjects a person to criminal penalties.

These regulations are specifically limited to the "space transportation system," not a space station or other space object. A violation has never been prosecuted, so the question remains open as to whether or not they are overly broad or vague, conditions that would make them unconstitutional. The use of these regulations or of the special maritime and territorial jurisdiction provision of the U.S. Code contemplates a prosecution long after the event, using the normal federal criminal procedures and rules, in a courtroom on Earth. None of this may be possible or practical during extended space voyages or space colonization.

The use of U.S. domestic legislation may be unacceptable to foreign partners during joint space endeavors. For some time now, negotiations have been conducted among the United States and representatives of the space agencies of Japan, Canada, and Europe the European Space Agency (O'Brien, 1987). The issues during these negotiations closely resemble the conflict-of-laws situation we find in the Antarctic. No nation particularly wants its nationals to be subject to foreign laws and most certainly is not amenable to prosecution in foreign courts. A number of oppositions have developed on how these matters can be resolved. One view is that the primary jurisdiction to prosecute an offense would lie in the state of the accused's nationality. Another position focuses on who has the physical custody of an accused. A third view is to ignore any preconceived plan and resolve each case as it occurs.

Whatever the outcome of these negotiations, two conclusions are obvious. First, we must make provisions for the differences in the laws of the partners. It would be unfair to expect every crewmember of a space station to be aware of the entire criminal code of all of the partners in the meantime. In conjunction with this, whenever a national of one partner is to be prosecuted by another partner, certain basic rights must be guaranteed, such as a speedy trial, the right to counsel, and the right to be confronted by the witnesses for the prosecution. Absent from these guaranteed rights will be a trial by jury. This right is unique to the Anglo–American system of jurisprudence. In the majority of other countries, a jury of one's peers is rare in a criminal trial. The United States is a party to a number of Status of Forces Agreements (SOFA) governing the stationing of our military forces in other countries. The typical SOFA requires only that our service members get a fair trial in compliance with the rights guaranteed by the host country's nationals; generally this does not include the right to a jury trial.

Second, the United States must have a comprehensive legal system available to implement. As I have pointed out, the current laws applicable to criminal activities in space are inadequate. In determining what might best serve our needs in space, we should not be short sighted. A legal regime that requires trials on Earth may be highly impractical. For this reason and others described below, I would advocate that a modified version of the UCMJ be utilized.

## Uniform Code of Space Justice

As mentioned above, the existing language of the UCMJ might be used to extend the applicability of that code to civilians serving with the armed forces in space or the Antarctic. Certain problems arise if this procedure were to be followed. Paragraphs (11) and (12) of Article 2 embrace "persons serving with, employed by, or accompanying the armed services outside the United States" and "persons within an area leased by or otherwise reserved or acquired for use of the United States which is under the control of the Secretary concerned and which is outside the United States." The use of either of these could lead to factual (Bilder, 1966) or constitutional challenges. Civilians in the Antarctic have a more tenuous relationship with the military than those involved in cases challenging court–martial jurisdiction over the class of civilians enumerated in Article 2(11); consequently, their argument of nonapplicability would be strong (Bilder, 1966).

My proposal is to draft a new code closely akin to the UCMJ that would be applicable to all U.S. personnel in space or on celestial bodies and to foreign nationals present in areas under U.S. jurisdiction as provided for in the Outer Space Treaty unless their own nationals assert jurisdiction over a criminal act or omission. This system would instantly fill the gaps described above for civilians in space. The "parallel" codes would proscribe similar conduct for both military members and civilians. Legislatively, this could be done by adding another clause to Article 2, establishing jurisdiction over spacefarers with exceptions for "purely military" offenses, or by enacting an entire code for space deleting the "military" articles. If similar procedural rules are designated for both groups under either option, the difficulties of conducting criminal trials, authorizing searches, and enforcing minor disciplinary rules will be alleviated.

The U.S. military justice system developed over two centuries to meet the same needs we expect will be present in space. Activities of armies, navies, or spacefarers are often far from the usual fora of resolution. Major offenses cannot wait to be resolved until the expedition or force returns to its homeland. Extended operations will require some procedure to punish minor infractions of discipline such as sleeping at a workstation.

A number of articles have been written on how disputes will be resolved in space (March, 1983; Stennon, 1985). The conclusion reached by most authors on the subject is that a comprehensive code of substantive and procedural law is a logical starting point for the legal regime. There are a number of obvious constitutional issues that will arise if U.S. criminal law is used in space. It may be unrealistic to assume that the same Constitution that has served the United States so well for over 200 years can continue to perform the same functions for a society in space (Stennon, 1985). Many of these concerns have been addressed and adequately answered under the military practice.

Let us assume that a Uniform Code of Space Justice was promulgated, with the commander of the space ship, space station, or lunar colony occupying a position and power equivalent to a military commander. Certain command functions would be delegable (March, 1984). Subordinate crewmembers would enjoy some status similar to the military rank structure. Neither the commander nor any subordinate need be a commissioned officer of a military service.

## Jurisdiction Over the Offense

A 1987 Supreme Court decision, *Solorio v. United States*, (1987) changed a quarter century of military law. Since 1969, a court-martial was without jurisdiction over a service member unless there was "service connection" (*O'Callahan v. Parker*, 1969). *Solorio* dispensed with this judicially created requirement. The only test to be met is the status of the accused as a person subject to the code. Assuming that the line of reasoning developed in *Solorio* would also be applied to space operations, the "court-spatial" would have jurisdiction over any person committing an offense. We could still expect a few challenges based on status—such as the accused is not one of those persons subject to the space code—just as there are occasional challenges to court-martial jurisdiction for lack of jurisdiction due to improper enlistments.

## Arrest or Apprehension

Many civilian jurisdictions require an arrest warrant except in exigent circumstances. Under the UCMJ, all officers and those delegated the authority (military police) may apprehend. Apprehension is different from "arrest," which is defined in Article 8 of the UCMJ. This lack of a requirement for a warrant issued by a magistrate provides the flexibility necessary in the special circumstances of military or space operations.

## Pretrial Investigation

In the civilian federal practice, a preliminary hearing is held to determine if there is probable cause for detention, to set bail, and to determine if the case should be sent to a grand jury. There is a right to counsel at this critical stage (*Coleman v. Alabama*, 1970).

The next step in most federal prosecutions is an indictment by a grand jury. The Fifth Amendment states that "no person shall be held to answer for a capital, or otherwise infamous crime, unless a presentment or indictment of a grand jury, except in cases arising in the land or naval forces. . . . "; however, such an adversarial proceeding would further complicate the logistics of exercising criminal jurisdiction in space (Stennon, 1985).

In the military system, a single investigating officer conducts a hearing analogous to a grand jury. Unlike the grand jury, which may be held in secret and will exclude the defendant, an Article 32 investigation is public, includes the accused and his counsel, and is required only in cases referred to General Courts-Martial. The majority of cases in the military are tried at Special Courts-Martial. Special Courts-Martial may adjudge 6 months' maximum confinement as punishment for any offense or number of offenses, as well as lesser punishments. Constitutionally, an indictment would not be necessary for cases tried before a court with such limited powers of punishment. For a variety of reasons, the grand jury system will not be workable in outer space. I would suggest a simpler, more efficient method such as that embodied in Article 32 of the UCMJ be considered.

## Courts-Spatial

The Sixth Amendment guarantees a public and speedy trial. Most federal prosecutions are held in a public courthouse with a traditional jury composed of 12 unbiased peers of the accused. Rather than describe the participants and procedures of the civilian practice, known to most from jury duty, the media, movies, and television, I will describe what I believe can be a model for trials in space.

The military uses a small "jury" in its trials. For special courts, only three members compose a quorum, five for a general court-martial. The verdict need not be unanimous; in most cases, a two-thirds majority will suffice for conviction or adjudging a sentence. In trial by special court-martial, the prosecution and defense counsel do not have to be attorneys. Although military judges must be attorneys, this was not always the case; the senior presiding officer acted as the "judge" in courts-martial years ago. Many states still permit nonlawyers to be judges.

The military uses a modified version of the Federal Rules of Evidence (FRE), the Military Rules of Evidence (or MRE). The modifications to the FRE were required by the unusual needs of trial by court-martial. A similar set of rules, Space Rules of Evidence (or SRE), could be easily tailored to fit the needs of courts–spatial. The military modifications are designed to aid the conduct of trials often hampered by geographical locations, combat conditions, and the nonavailability of witnesses; in limited circumstances, videotaped testimony can be used (*United States v. Crockett*, 1986).

There are dangers in using videotapes or direct television broadcasts of testimony. However, we are moving into the 21st century; our legal system must utilize state-of-the-art technology, or it will be left behind as technology moves to the outer edges of the solar system. For years, courts resisted the use of videotapes. Now they are fairly common in civil trials and admitted in limited circumstances in criminal trials. Changes in the law are produced by necessity. If we need special rules of evidence for courts-spatial, we can have them.

## Space Specific Crimes and Defenses

I would like to conclude this chapter with a few thoughts about what might eventually be the state of substantive law in space. Primarily, I have been addressing procedure up to now—how will we try offenders? and How does our municipal or domestic law fit into the international regimes for space and the Antarctic?

What we have learned from the experience of human exploration of Antarctica and space is that the old rules do not always fit. Our laws are a collection of Earth-oriented norms. From time to time, humorous articles appear in the media describing some seemingly strange law. Closer examination usually reveals a good reason led to what is now viewed as an anomaly in the law.

A few years ago, we did not have statutes that adequately proscribed the theft of computer software; there was no reason for a law before there was a need. Conferences such as *The Human Experience in Antarctica* are a valuable experience for us all to pool our knowledge and experience. Attorneys recognize the types of legal issues that might arise in the social context of life in space. Much of this is an extrapolation of work done in Antarctica. Some of the potential major legal issues are discussed in closing.

## Property Ownership and Privacy

Most of our law concerning theft, search and seizure, robbery, invasion of privacy, peeping toms, and a host of others incorporates a notion of individual right to property and privacy that cannot survive in the cramped environment of a space ship or moon habitat.

## Survival Homicide

This involves the concept of knowingly taking the life of another human to ensure the survival of at least one or more under circumstances in which the normal benefits of earthly society cannot be applied (Robinson, 1980).

## Sexual Relations

Prolonged absence from members of the opposite sex may create unusual frustration and tension in space explorers. The presence of no or few women in the Antarctic has led to some minor problems, a topic that was discussed by a panel at the conference. Such an unnatural condition may excuse or mitigate a criminal act.

A new twist arises in space — the difficulties with conception and birth of humans in space may require a law that there be total abstention from sex. Gravity plays an important part in how babies are born and how their bones and muscles develop and in their aerobic capacity. Lest we create a race of humans unable to survive on the planet Earth, conception in space will be banned unless sufficient gravity can be ensured.

## Psychological Irritability

This may become a major defense to offenses committed in space. Our legal system is based on what a "reasonable man" would do under a given circumstance. This standard will surely need adjustment for spacefarers in close quarters, for long durations, performing tedious and routine tasks.

## References

Adams, P. F. (1983). A proposal for a commissioned corps of space travelers. *Akron Law Review.*

Bilder, R. B. (1966). Control of criminal conduct in Antarctica. *Virginia Law Review, 52,* 231, 248.

Blakesley, C. L. (1979). United States jurisdiction over extraterritorial crime. *Journal of Criminal Law and Criminology, 73,* 1109, 1123, 1126–1127.

Brownlie, I. (1979). *Principles of public international law*. New York: Oxford University Press.

Bruton, T. (1984). Jurisdiction in outer space. *Proceedings of the XXIVth conference of the IABA* (p. 137).

*Coleman v. Alabama*, 399 U.S. 1 (1970).

March, S. F. (1983, Fall). Dispute resolution in space. *Hastings International and Comparative Law Review 7*, 211.

March, S. F. (1984). Authority of the space station commander: The need for delegation. *Glendale Law Review, 21*, 73.

O'Brien, J. E. (1987). The U.S. international space station. *Journal of Space Law, 15*, 35.

*O'Callahan v. Parker*, 396 U. S. 258 (U.S. Ct. App. 3d Cir. 1969).

Robinson, G. S. (1980). Astronauts and a unique jurisprudence: A treaty for spacekind. *Hastings International and Comparative Law Review, 7*, 483, 492.

Sherrill, R. (1969). *Military justice is to justice as military music is to music*. New York: Harper & Row.

*Solario v. United States*, 483 US 435 (U.S. Supreme Ct. 1987).

Stennon, B. A. (1985). Problems in exercising criminal jurisdiction on space vehicles in the future. *Journal of Astrolaw, 1*, 29.

*United States v. Cordova*, 89 F. Supp. 298. (U.S. District Court, C. D. New York, 1950).

*United States v. Crockett*, 21 MJ423, (U.S. Ct Mil. App. 1986).

# Conclusion: Recommendations for Future Research

ALBERT A. HARRISON, YVONNE A. CLEARWATER, AND CHRISTOPHER P. MCKAY

An early 1980s review noted that research on men and women in isolation and confinement had peaked and declined and that in some areas, such as group dynamics, it had been reduced to "a trickle" (Harrison & Connors, 1984, p. 76). Although we may not have resumed the relatively rapid pace of the 1960s, the chapters in this volume provide clear evidence of renewed interest and progress. At the time of writing, the National Science Foundation (NSF) is sponsoring behavioral research in Antarctica, and there are active human factors research groups at two National Aeronautics and Space Administration (NASA) centers, Ames Research Center and Lyndon B. Johnson Space Center. In September 1989, NASA began a major human factors planning effort.

How can we accelerate our learning about men and women in isolation and confinement? How can we combine the interests of mission planners and managers, operational personnel, and behavioral researchers? Recent literature coupled with presentations and discussions at the Sunnyvale Conference led us to develop a set of recommendations for agencies that sponsor groups in Antarctic, spaceflight, and underseas environments and for re-

The views and recommendations expressed in this section are those of the authors and do not necessarily reflect the policies or views of the National Aeronautics and Space Administration, the National Science Foundation, or any other governmental agency. A preliminary version of these recommendations appeared in A. A. Harrison, Y. A. Clearwater, and C. P. McKay, 1989, "The Human Experience in Antarctica: Applications to Life in Space," *Behavioral Science, 34*, pp. 253–271. Adapted and used with permission.

searchers who are interested in studying such groups (Harrison, Clearwater, & McKay, 1989).

## Recommendations for Agencies

Agency support for behavioral research is justified on two bases. First, basic research is a central mission of organizations such as NSF and NASA, and behavioral research is consistent with this mission. Second, since behavioral research has implications for safety, performance, and quality of life, it is also justifiable on pragmatic and humanistic grounds.

1. *Funding for behavioral research should be a regular part of agency budgets.* Careful, well-thought-out proposals require substantial "front time" on the researcher's part, front time that is difficult to justify if behavioral research may or may not be in vogue at the time that the proposal is completed. Moreover, high-quality, programmatic behavioral research usually requires a commitment of more than 1 year. To motivate talented researchers, funding should be a regular part of agency budgets and not fluctuate wildly as a function of short-term considerations such as the salience of current operational problems.

2. *Funding levels should be sufficiently high to support sustained, high-quality research efforts.* Very low levels of funding create two problems. First, researchers' selections of topics should be guided by scientific merit and practical value, and their choice of procedures by scientific appropriateness and rigor. When budget is the controlling factor, choices are made on the basis of convenience and expediency. Research that ignores the important questions or involves inadequate methodology serves nobody. It is inherently worthless, and the bad impressions that it creates erect hurdles for other researchers who are capable of superior work. Second, when only token funding is available, competition for funds reaches undesirable levels: Investigators spend more time attacking each other than attacking the problem.

3. *Provide access to research subjects.* Researchers need access to human research subjects. Agencies can provide this by releasing lists of names and addresses of personnel and providing travel to operational sites. Agencies can also promote positive attitudes among those who work under the agencies' sponsorship. They can make it known that since behavioral research is in the interests of both the agency and science, the spirit of scientific cooperation should extend to behavioral as well as physical and natural scientists.

4. *Encourage realistic time lines.* Another recurring difficulty is unrealistic or unworkable time lines. There seems to be a tendency to postpone behavioral research until engineering or other problems are solved. This can result in rushed, if not "crisis," research, with predictable effects on

quality. Another reason that it is important to initiate research early is that results have important implications for habitat design, personnel selection, and other issues that need to be resolved well in advance of the mission.

5. *Develop clear research priorities.* Organizations that have vested interests in behavioral research in Antarctic, outer space, and comparable settings should develop and publicize research priorities. Whereas any good research is better than none, coordinated research in pursuit of a limited set of goals is likely to pay bigger dividends than an equivalent number of uncoordinated projects. Both scientific criteria and practical concerns can help shape priorities.

6. *Show extreme care in the peer review process.* Peer review provides the best mechanism known for assuring scientific quality. Since there are relatively few researchers who are interested in isolation and confinement, proposals are often reviewed by scientists who are in appropriate substantive areas (for example, communication or stress management) but who have no real familiarity with unusual environments. Some reviewers do not even begin to imagine the practical considerations that have shaped the proposal. Reviewers have to understand *both* the basic substantive area and the peculiarities of conducting research in unusual settings.

7. *Rank research proposals relative to others within the same disciplinary area.* Scholars from different fields may show differing degrees of stringency or leniency when evaluating one another's proposals. For this reason, agencies should consider rating proposals against other proposals within the field, rather than against proposals across all fields.

8. *Provide researchers with briefings.* Prospective researchers may have vague or erroneous ideas concerning contemporary Antarctic or spaceflight settings. Researchers should not expect a free ride on the shuttle or a vacation in Antarctica before writing a proposal. However, materials regarding current selection and training procedures, detailed and honest descriptions of the spacecraft or polar camp, and the like would be of inestimable benefit. Researchers should be provided with at least the same access to training bases, equipment, habitats, and briefing materials as is accorded reputable journalists.

9. *Establish continuing dialogues with behavioral researchers.* There have been many changes in isolated and confined environments (ICEs) since the 1960s, and there have been many changes in the behavioral and social sciences. This has led to a knowledge lag, with each "side's" perceptions of the other's interests and problems running years behind. Unattended, the knowledge gap is likely to widen. Maximum benefit requires mutual understanding of current operational conditions and behavioral research theories and methods. Special conferences and symposia should be supplements to rather than substitutes for continuing dialogues.

10. *Explore mechanisms for interagency cooperation.* The United States'
NASA and NSF are only two of many agencies that share interests in
advancing science and productivity at remote work sites. Collaboration
among such agencies can produce a faster rate of gain than can be
achieved by any one agency alone. In the United States, the Department
of Defense, each branch of the military service, the Department of
Transportation, the Federal Aviation Administration, the Department of
Energy, and the National Park Service have the potential to work syner-
gistically to unravel the problems of life in isolation and confinement.
International cooperation, involving agencies such as the European
Space Agency and the Scientific Committee on Antarctic Research,
opens entirely new vistas.

A possible showcase for NASA/NSF cooperation would be the development of an Antarctic base as a testing and training ground for future spaceflights ( Bluth, 1987; Harrison, 1988; McKay, 1985; Palinkas, 1987,1988).
As Harrison (1988) notes:

Behavioral research in Antarctica could be of particular benefit to the Mars mission.
The time line is a good one: unlike the Space Station, the Mars mission is not slated
too soon for a carefully planned, large scale research program to bear fruit, and
unlike interstellar migration, it is not so far away as to seem meaningless. Also, the
degree of correspondence between Antarctica and Mars is particularly close. Unlike
the Space Station, the Mars mission involves a surface base, and Antarctic geography more closely approximates that of Mars than that of the Moon. . . . In both
locations, scientific personnel are prominent and have similar research strategies and
goals. For example, the first Mars astronauts will erect a home base and then
establish satellite camps to conduct research in geoscience, atmospheric science, and
life science.
    Antarctica provides the opportunity for testing structures, supplies, and equip-
ment as well as people, a fact that has not gone unnoticed by U.S. aerospace and
architectural firms. Of interest to both polar and space enthusiasts would be small,
compact, transportable research stations. Another area of mutual interest is the
design of equipment that will perform reliably under trying conditions, and training
programs for those who will operate and repair the equipment. There is also the
opportunity to study supplies. This involves not only the usual needs assessments,
but also surveys of consumer acceptance and mechanisms for inventory control.
    In the realm of operations, Antarctic bases could serve as useful assessment cen-
ters, that is, locations for comprehensive personnel selection procedures involving
interviews, psychological testing, and performance testing by a variety of evaluators.
. . . Antarctic training sites would preserve many of the features associated with
Mars bases, but would be less costly to operate than training sites in space. Antarctica could be the second or intermediate step in a three step selection and training
process which would begin in simulators at home and end aboard the Space Station.
. . . The sheer distance from home should make the training involving and realistic,
and whereas the trainee in the US or Russia knows that he or she can always
terminate the experience by walking out through the door, it is not so easy to quit
during an austral winter . . . (pp. 17–18).

## Recommendations for Researchers

Increasing research in isolation and confinement is not the sole responsibility of sponsoring agencies. Potential researchers have to justify agency support by offering high-quality, relevant research projects that are consistent with agency requirements.

1. *Exude competence.* As Marc Levesque and William Douglas pointed out, astronauts, polar scientists, and submariners are bright, highly competent individuals. These attitudes, coupled with the high expense of conducting research in isolated and confined settings, dictate that only intelligent, knowledgeable, and dedicated behavioral researchers can hope to succeed. Potential researchers need full command of the background literature on isolation and confinement, as well as in their disciplinary specialties.

2. *Pay special attention to ethics.* Although always important, ethical concerns gain even greater salience in isolated and confined settings. Ethical concerns include (1) obtaining informed consent; (2) not imposing unwarranted noxious conditions; and (3) guaranteeing the anonymity of individual subjects. As captives of the situation, subjects may not feel free to decline participation. The time required for participation may make it difficult for subjects to complete their own research. Because relatively few subjects are involved, it may be difficult to conceal individual subjects' identities. Above all, sensitive questions regarding such issues as personal popularity may threaten to disrupt relations within the crew. All such problems must be examined before the research is initiated.

3. *Join the group.* In a sense, groups of astronauts, polar expeditioners, and submariners form exclusive "clubs." We know that members of exclusive groups are likely to show high regard for one another while being somewhat disparaging of "outsiders." As a result of practical considerations or indifference, psychologists may attempt to conduct research from afar. As Marc Levesque noted, views of behavioral researchers as people who maintain an air of superiority and an unwillingness to share environmental hardships tend to discourage cooperation. Behavioral researchers should seek to actually join the groups in situ; if this is impossible (as in the case of spaceflight), they should take other steps to establish themselves as members of the overall team.

4. *Do not penalize participants.* Operational personnel do not always find behavioral research to be in their best interests (Harrison, 1986). Mission managers may be put in an uncomfortable position if the results somehow reflect poorly on their judgment or leadership skills. Also, recommendations might be forthcoming that reduce managerial discretion. Then there is the threat that results could challenge participants' images as tough and resourceful people or draw attention to controversial activities. An emphasis on the negative side of human behavior could lead to bad publicity and the withdrawal of public support.

There are several strategies for reducing apprehensions associated with participation in behavioral research. These include frank reassessments of goals and procedures on the part of researchers and educational programs aimed at participants. But the key is to involve both operational personnel and behavioral scientists in the research planning process. Whereas experienced Antarcticans, astronauts, and submariners may have firsthand knowledge of practical matters and a good grasp of practical behavioral issues, they typically lack the training required to conduct behavioral research. Trained behavioral scientists, on the other hand, usually have little or no understanding of the realities of life in isolation and confinement. Joint participation of researchers and operational personnel in the planning process should foster rapport and understanding, promote the identification and prioritization of research topics, and encourage the development of workable and effective research procedures.

5. *Show methodological ingenuity.* Serious logistical problems are among those that must be overcome to do field research in ICEs. Limitations on the number of people who can be accommodated within the habitat may make it difficult for the researcher to participate personally. In some cases, researchers may be able to find volunteer assistants within the crew. Other techniques include remote surveillance; debriefings by means of interviews and questionnaires; and unobtrusive measures such as the study of diaries, logs, and other records. All of these approaches have technical drawbacks (for example, faulty memories may undermine the value of postmission debriefings, and activity may take place outside of the surveillance equipment's range), and some of them (for example, unremitting remote surveillance) may be objectionable to the crew. Procedures must be found that are at once rigorous, workable, and acceptable to the potential research participants.

6. *Attend to theory.* Theories serve several useful functions (McCain & Segal, 1973; Shaw & Costanzo, 1970). First, theories impose order and meaningfulness on observations that might otherwise seem chaotic. Second, theories tell what should be expected under conditions that have not yet occurred and, thereby, aid the process of prediction. Third, theories take us into the realm of understanding, since a good theory provides a plausible accounting or explanation. Finally, theories serve to stimulate and guide future research. For such reasons, it is useful to build a theoretical component into behavioral research, and ICE research is no exception.

7. *Address problems of information dissemination and utilization.* The findings of ICE research are often unpublished or located in obscure outlets or archives. As a result, many new researchers have found themselves "reinventing the wheel" before going on to make their own contributions. Recent articles appearing in the *American Psychologist, Aviation, Space, and Environmental Medicine, Behavioral Science,* and other major outlets have improved the situation since the early 1980s. Nonethe-

less, in the interests of both accessibility and credibility, it is important to "mainstream" research reports (Harrison & Connors, 1984; Helmreich, 1983). Other possibilities would include the establishment of a quarterly journal dedicated to isolation and confinement research or the appointment of an associate editor to review this kind of material for an already established journal.

8. *Cultivate newcomers.* The psychology of isolation and confinement, like any other specialty, appeals to only a limited number of professionals. Add to this meager funding, restricted access to subjects, a less than overwhelming level of action within the field, and indifference on the part of some journal editors, and an already small pool of talent is reduced further. Given that many of today's leading scholars have been producing for 20 or 30 years and given the need for researchers who qualify medically for life under rigorous conditions, it is important to attract young, qualified researchers.

## References

Bluth, B. J. (1987). *Space station/Antarctic analogs* (NASA Grant Reports 2-255 and BAGW-659). Washington, DC: National Aeronautics and Space Administration.

Harrison, A. A. (1986). On resistance to the involvement of personality, social, and organizational psychologists in the U.S. space program. *Journal of Social Behavior and Personality, 1*(3), 315–324.

Harrison, A. A. (1988, August) *Antarctica: Prototype for outer space.* Paper presented at the XXIV International Congress of Psychology, Sydney.

Harrison, A. A., & Connors, M. M. (1984). Groups in exotic environments. In L. Berkowitz (Ed.), *Advances in experimental social psychology*, (Vol. 18, pp. 49–87). New York: Academic Press.

Harrison, A. A., Clearwater, Y. A., & McKay, C. P. (1989). The human experience in Antarctica: Applications to life in space. *Behavioral Science, 34*, 253–271.

Helmreich, R. L. (1983). Applying psychology to outer space: Unfulfilled promises revisited. *American Psychologist, 38*, 445–450.

McCain, G., & Segal, G. (1973). *The game of science* (2nd ed.). Monterey, CA: Brooks/Cole.

McKay, C. P. (1985). Antarctica: Lessons for a Mars exploration program. In C. P. McKay (Ed.), *The case for Mars II* (pp. 79–88) (American Astronautical Society, Science and Technology Series, 62). San Diego: Univelt.

Palinkas, L. A. (1987). *Antarctica as a model for the human exploration of Mars* (Report No. 88-16). Bethesda, MD: Naval Medical Research and Development Command, Naval Health Research Center.

Palinkas, L. A. (1988). *The human element in space: Lessons from Antarctica* (Report No. 88-8). Bethesda, MD: Naval Medical Research and Development Command, Naval Health Research Center.

Shaw, M., & Costanzo, P. (1970). *Theories of social psychology.* New York: McGraw-Hill.

# Index